LEARI

PHYSICAL EDUCATION IN THE SECONDARY SCHOOL

What skills are required of secondary student physical education teachers?

What are the key areas that these student teachers need to understand?

How can current challenges be addressed by these student teachers?

Learning to Teach Physical Education in the Secondary School combines underpinning theory and knowledge with suggestions for practical application to support student physical education teachers in learning to teach.

Based on research evidence, theory and knowledge relating to teaching and learning and written specifically with the student teacher in mind, the authors examine physical education in context. The book offers tasks and case studies designed to support student teachers in their school-based experiences and encourages reflection on practice and development. Masters level tasks and suggestions for further reading have been included throughout to support researching and writing about topics in more depth.

This fully updated third edition has been thoroughly revised to take into account changes in policy and practice within both initial teacher education and the National Curriculum for Physical Education. The book also contains a brand new chapter on the role of reflective teaching in developing expertise and improving the quality of pupil learning. Other key topics covered include:

- lesson planning, organisation and management;
- observation in physical education;
- developing and maintaining an effective learning environment;
- inclusive physical education;
- assessment;
- developing wider community links;
- using ICT to support teaching and learning in physical education.

Learning to Teach Physical Education in the Secondary School is an invaluable resource for student physical education teachers.

Susan Capel is Professor and Head of the School of Sport and Education at Brunel University, UK.

Margaret Whitehead works as a Physical Education Consultant.

LEARNING TO TEACH SUBJECTS IN THE SECONDARY SCHOOL SERIES

Series Editors: Susan Capel, Marilyn Leask and Tony Turner

Designed for all student teachers learning to teach in secondary schools, and particularly those on school-based initial teacher education courses, the books in this series complement *Learning to Teach in the Secondary School* and its companion, *Starting to Teach in the Secondary School*. Each book in the series applies underpinning theory and addresses practical issues to support student teachers in school and in the higher education institution in learning how to teach a particular subject.

LEARNING TO TEACH PHYSICAL EDUCATION IN THE SECONDARY SCHOOL

A companion to school experience

3rd Edition

Edited by

Susan Capel and Margaret Whitehead

Routledge
Taylor & Francis Group

LONDON AND NEW YORK

This third edition published 2010
by Routledge
2 Park Square, Milton Park, Abingdon, Oxon, OX14 4RN

Simultaneously published in the USA and Canada
by Routledge
270 Madison Avenue, New York, NY 10016

Routledge is an imprint of the Taylor & Francis Group, an informa business

Typeset in Times and Helvetica by FiSH Books, Enfield
Printed and bound in Great Britain by TJ International Ltd, Padstow, Cornwall

British Library Cataloguing in Publication Data
A catalogue record for this book is available from the British Library

Library of Congress Cataloging-in-Publication Data
Learning to teach physical education in the secondary school: a companion to school experience /
    edited by Susan Capel and Margaret Whitehead. — 3rd ed.
        p. cm.
    1. Physical education and training—Study and teaching (Secondary)—Great Britain. 2. Physical
    education teachers—Training of—Great Britain. I. Capel, Susan Anne, 1953- II. Whitehead,
    Margaret, 1940-
    GV365.5.G7L43 2010
    613.7'071'241—dc22   2010004303

ISBN10: 0-415-56165-5 (hbk)
ISBN10: 0-415-56164-7 (pbk)
ISBN10: 0-203-84852-7 (ebk)

ISBN13: 978-0-415-56165-5 (hbk)
ISBN13: 978-0-415-56164-8 (pbk)
ISBN13: 978-0-203-84852-4 (ebk)

CONTENTS

1 STARTING OUT AS A PE TEACHER   1

SUSAN CAPEL

■ why did you become a PE teacher? ■ an overview of teaching
■ how are you going to develop into an effective PE teacher?

2 AIMS OF PE   13

MARGARET WHITEHEAD

■ definitions and broad purposes ■ aims, objectives and intended learning
outcomes (ILOs) ■ aims of education, a school and a subject ■ aims of PE

3 PLANNING IN PE   24

CATHY GOWER

■ influences on planning in PE ■ a general framework for planning schemes of
work ■ planning units of work ■ planning lessons ■ assessing and evaluating
your lessons

4 OBSERVATION OF PUPILS IN PE   46

ELIZABETH MARSDEN

■ why are observation skills important for the PE teacher? ■ what aspects
of the lesson should be observed? ■ How can I best carry out observation?

ILLUSTRATIONS

TABLES

FIGURES

TASKS

CONTRIBUTORS

Richard Blair is lecturer in physical education and coaching at Brunel University.

Mark Bowler is senior lecturer in physical education at the University of Bedfordshire.

Peter Breckon is senior lecturer, subject leader for physical education and course leader for the BSc secondary physical education degree at Brunel University.

Susan Capel is professor and Head of the School of Sport and Education at Brunel University.

Anne Chappell is lecturer in education and physical education and secondary PGCert physical education course leader at Brunel University.

Suzanne Everley is senior lecturer in ITT physical education and secondary PGCE physical education coordinator at the University of Chichester.

Gill Golder is senior lecturer at University College Plymouth St Mark and St John, where she is the programme leader for the BEd secondary physical education degree as well as operations manager for the Local Delivery Agenda and line lead for the Sport and Active Leisure Diploma.

Cathy Gower is lecturer in physical education and Deputy Head (Teaching and Learning) in the School of Sport and Education, Brunel University.

Tim Hewett is senior lecturer in adventure education at the University of Bedfordshire.

Will Katene is lecturer in education and course leader for the PGCE physical education at the University of Exeter.

Julia Lawrence is principal lecturer in physical education at Leeds Metropolitan University.

Elizabeth Marsden is a senior lecturer and researcher in physical education at the University of the West of Scotland.

Angela Newton is principal lecturer and leader of the BA physical education QTS course at the University of Bedfordshire.

Karen Pack is Assistant Deputy Headteacher and Director of Specialism at The Coopers' Company and Coborn School.

Gary Stidder is senior lecturer and the PGCE route leader for physical education at the University of Brighton, Chelsea School.

Philip Vickerman is Professor of Inclusive Education and Learning at Liverpool John Moore's University.

Margaret Whitehead is a physical education consultant.

Andy Wild is principal lecturer in ITT physical education and Head of Continuous Professional Development at the University of Chichester.

Jes Woodhouse is an education consultant concerned primarily with the initial and continuing professional development of teachers in relation to physical education.

Paula Zwozdiak-Myers is lecturer in education and Secondary PGCert course leader at Brunel University.

INTRODUCTION TO THE SERIES

The third edition of *Learning to Teach Physical Education in the Secondary School* is one of a series of books entitled *Learning to Teach (subject name) in the Secondary School: A Companion to School Experience* covering most subjects in the secondary school curriculum. The subject books support and complement the generic book *Learning to Teach in the Secondary School: A Companion to School Experience* (Capel, Leask and Turner, 5th edition, 2009) which deals with aspects of teaching and learning applicable to all subjects. This series is designed for student teachers on different types of initial teacher education programmes, but is proving equally useful to tutors and mentors in their work with student teachers.

The information in the subject books does not repeat that in *Learning to Teach*, but extends it to address the needs of student teachers learning to teach a specific subject. In each of the subject books, therefore, reference is made to the generic *Learning to Teach* text, where appropriate. It is recommended that you have both books so that you can cross-reference when needed.

The positive feedback on *Learning to Teach*, particularly the way it has supported the learning of student teachers in their development into effective, reflective teachers, has encouraged us to retain the main features of that book in the subject series. Thus, the subject books are designed so that elements of appropriate theory introduce each topic or issue, and recent research into teaching and learning is integral to the presentation. In both the generic and subject books tasks are provided to help you to identify key features of the topic or issue and apply them to your own practice. In addition, the requirement for material to be available to support student teachers' work at Master's level in PGCE courses in England has been met in the latest editions by the inclusion of advice about working at this level and by a selection of tasks labelled 'M'. The generic book referred to above also has a companion Reader (*Readings for Learning to Teach in the Secondary School*) containing articles and research papers in education suitable for 'M' level study.

Although the basic structure of all the subject books is similar, each book is designed to address the unique nature of the subject. The third edition of *Learning to Teach Physical Education in the Secondary School* retains the strengths of the second edition but has been revised to reflect changes and developments in: the standards for gaining qualified teacher status; governmental policy (e.g. the 2007 National Curriculum for Physical Education (NCPE) and the Every Child Matters agenda); health and safety legislation and requirements; information and communications technology resources;

and ways of working with others, which is now a key aspect of physical education teachers' work. The practical application of guidance in the book has been reinforced and material has been included to support the requirement for Master's level study.

We as editors have been pleased with the reception given to the earlier editions of this book as well as to the *Learning to Teach* series as a whole. Many subject books have moved into their third editions and others are in preparation. We hope that whatever initial teacher education programme you are following and wherever you may be situated you find the third edition of *Learning to Teach Physical Education* supports your development towards becoming an effective, reflective teacher of physical education. You should also find the companion practical book, *A Practical Guide to Teaching Physical Education in the Secondary School*, of value. Above all, we hope you enjoy teaching physical education.

When you move to being a newly qualified teacher we recommend the more advanced book *Starting to Teach in the Secondary School: A Companion for the Newly Qualified Teacher* 2nd edition (Capel, Heilbron, Leask and Turner, 2004), which supports newly qualified teachers in their first post and covers aspects of teaching which are likely to be of concern in the first year of teaching.

Susan Capel, Marilyn Leask and Tony Turner
March 2010

INTRODUCTION

LEARNING TO TEACH

All top sports people and dancers spend hours learning and practising basic skills in order to be able to perform these effectively. Once learned, skills can be refined, adapted and combined in various ways appropriate for a performer's personality and a specific situation, in order to create a unique performance. Developing excellence in performance is informed by scientific understanding, including biomechanical, kinesiological, physiological, psychological and sociological. There is therefore art and science underpinning excellence in performance.

Likewise, there is an art and a science to teaching. There are basic teaching skills in which teachers require competence. Effective teaching also requires the development of professional judgement in order to be able to adapt the teaching skills to meet the demands of the specific situation, to take account of, for example, the needs and abilities of pupils, the space, the environment in which the lesson is being delivered. Teachers also require broader knowledge and understanding, for example, it is important that the aims of PE inform planning of schemes of work, units of work and lessons. It is also important to have knowledge and understanding of the wider world of education. However, there is no one right way to teach. Different teaching strategies are appropriate for different learning situations. Further, as we know, teachers have different personalities and characteristics. They therefore refine and adapt basic teaching skills and combine them in different ways to create their own unique teaching style. The process of development as a teacher is exciting and the ability to blend art and science should lead to a rewarding experience as a teacher.

In PE, physical skills are sometimes described on a continuum from open skills (those performed under variable conditions) to closed skills (those performed under consistent conditions). For open skills, for example, a dribble in hockey or basketball, it is important to have competence in the basic skill, but just as important to be able to use the skill appropriately in a game situation. For closed skills, for example, performing a forward roll or throwing a discus, it is most important to refine the technique and the ability to perform the skill under the pressure of competition. Some skills, for example, a putt in golf, fall along the continuum.

Different methods of practice are needed in order to learn and perform effectively skills at different points on the continuum. For an open skill practice is needed in the basic techniques of the skill, but practice is also needed in how to adapt the skill to respond to different situations which arise. On the other hand, for a closed skill it is most appropriate to practise to perfect the techniques of the skill.

Using the analogy of open and closed physical skills, teaching skills can be considered open skills. You need to practise and become competent in basic teaching skills, but you also need to be able to use the right skill in the right way at the right time. On your initial teacher education (ITE) course you are likely to have a variety of opportunities and experiences to develop competence in basic teaching skills, starting in very controlled practice situations and moving on to teaching full classes. You are unlikely to become a fully effective teacher during your ITE course. Refinement and the ability to adapt teaching skills as appropriate to the situation are continued into your work as a newly qualified teacher and beyond, as part of your continuing professional development (CPD) as you continue to develop your ability to reflect and your professional judgement.

There is a lot to learn to develop into an effective teacher. There are bound to be ups and downs. We cannot prepare you for a specific teaching situation, but we can help you to understand the complexities of teaching. We aim to help you to develop:

■ competence in basic teaching skills (the craft of teaching), to enable you to cope in most teaching situations;
■ the ability to apply these basic teaching skills to meet the needs of specific situations;
■ knowledge and understanding of the wider context of PE;
■ your professional judgement;
■ your ability to reflect critically on what you are doing and on your values, attitudes and beliefs and begin to develop your own philosophy of teaching PE.

In so doing, you should be able to develop, adapt and refine your teaching skills to meet the needs of specific situations, respond to the changing environment of education and inform your continued professional development as a teacher. You should also be able to look more critically and reflectively at aspects of teaching and to begin to articulate your own philosophy of teaching PE. This helps you to meet the requirements of working at Master's level – on your ITE course, where appropriate, and/or in CPD.

ABOUT THIS BOOK

This book contains 18 chapters which can be divided into five sections:

■ Section 1 (Chapters 1 and 2) provides an introduction and background information about teaching and the aims of PE.
■ Section 2 (Chapters 3 to 8) introduces some of the basic teaching skills in which you need to develop competence during your ITE course.
■ Section 3 (Chapters 9 to 12) addresses aspects/areas of teaching/teaching situations in which you will be expected to apply the basic skills.
■ Section 4 (Chapters 13 to 16) locates your work as a PE teacher in the wider educational context.
■ Section 5 (Chapters 17 and 18) looks ahead to your continued development as a teacher.

In this book we look at general principles which can be applied to areas of activity/activities included in a PE curriculum. We do not consider content knowledge in detail although, throughout the book, there are references to activities included in PE curricula. You need to refer to other sources for content knowledge. There are many books which focus on specific activities included in PE curricula. In addition, you need to draw on material you covered in your first degree course, including the disciplines of biomechanics, kinesiology, physiology, psychology and sociology. Your understanding of these disciplines should underpin your work as a PE teacher, for example, the use of biomechanical principles in identifying learning/teaching points for a skill, of aspects of physiology in encouraging pupils to adopt healthy, active lifestyles, or areas of psychology in understanding the effects of competition or reasons for attrition from sport in considering an extra-curricular programme.

In this book, each chapter is laid out as follows:

■ *introduction* to the content of the chapter;
■ *objectives*, presented as what you should know, understand or be able to do having read the chapter and carried out the tasks in the chapter;
■ the *content*, based on research and evidence to emphasise that teaching is best developed by being based on evidence and critical reflection. The content is interwoven with *tasks* to aid your knowledge, understanding and ability to do;
■ *summary and key points* of the main points of the chapter;
■ *further reading*, selected to enable you to find out more about the content of each chapter.

We try to emphasise links between theory and practice by including examples from relevant practical situations throughout each chapter and interweaving theory with tasks designed to help you identify key features of the behaviour or issue. A number of different inquiry methods are used to generate information, for example, reflecting on the reading, an observation, or an activity you are asked to carry out, asking questions, gathering information, observing lessons or discussion with your tutor or another student teacher. Some of the tasks involve you in activities that impinge on other people, for example, observing a PE teacher teach or asking for information. If a task requires you to do this, *you must first of all seek permission of the person concerned*. Remember that you are a guest in school(s), you cannot walk into any teacher's lesson to observe. In addition, some information may be personal or sensitive, and you need to consider issues of confidentiality and professional behaviour in your inquiries and reporting. In order to support you in your Master's level work, some of the tasks are at Master's level (these are marked by a symbol in the margin). These challenge you both to look more critically and reflectively at aspects of teaching and to begin to articulate your own philosophy of teaching PE.

The main text is supported by:

■ an appendix which looks at learning outside the classroom; and
■ material on the website associated with the book (www.routledge.com/textbooks/ 9780415561648).

The website contains:

■ a PowerPoint of material in each chapter;

- additional documents associated with particular chapters;
- observation sheets;
- a sample apparatus plan for gymnastics;
- two chapters from previous editions of this text, which give you insights into the National Curriculum for Physical Education (NCPE) in England as it has developed since 1992. These are: Murdoch, E. (1997) The background to, and developments from, the National Curriculum for PE, in S. Capel (ed.) *Learning to Teach Physical Education in the Secondary School: A Companion to School Experience*, London: Routledge, pp. 252–70; and Murdoch, E. (2004) NCPE 2000 – where are we so far?, in S. Capel (ed.) *Learning to Teach Physical Education in the Secondary School: A Companion to School Experience* (2nd edn), London: Routledge, pp. 280–300);
- web links to other important sites.

The text is also supported by other books in the series, to which we refer in a number of chapters, including:

- Capel, S., Breckon, P. and O'Neill, J. (2006) *A Practical Guide to Teaching Physical Education in the Secondary School*, London: Routledge (we particularly ask that you complete tasks in that book as they support the content of many of the chapters in this text), and two generic texts:
- Capel, S., Leask, M. and Turner, T. (eds) (2009) *Learning to Teach in the Secondary School: A Companion to School Experience* (5th edn), London: Routledge. You can also access material on the website associated with the generic *Learning to Teach* text (http://www.routledge.com/textbooks/9780415478724), which contains material on the Every Child Matters Agenda in England and on Safeguarding Children. This website also contains a chapter from the *Starting to Teach* text: 'Using research and evidence to inform your teaching', which provides advice for you in undertaking the kind of action research project which could lead to Master's level accreditation;
- Capel, S., Heilbronn, R., Leask, M. and Turner, T. (2004) *Starting to Teach in the Secondary School: A Companion for the Newly Qualified Teacher* (2nd edn), London: Routledge. This text is written for teachers in their early years of teaching.

ABOUT YOU

We recognise that you, as a student PE teacher, have a wide range of needs in your development as a teacher. We therefore do not feel that there is one best way for you to use this book. The book is designed so that you can dip in and out rather than read it from cover to cover, however, we encourage you to use the book in ways appropriate to you.

We also recognise that you are studying in different places and on different types of ITE course. We have tried to address as many of your potential needs as possible, irrespective of where you are studying and what type of ITE course you are on. Although it is expected that most student teachers using this book are on ITE courses in which there is a partnership between a higher education institution (HEI) and schools, we recognise that some of you may be on courses which are entirely school-based or not in partnership with an HEI. The book should be equally useful to you. Where we refer to work in your HEI, you should refer to the relevant person or centre in your school.

Although ITE is generally referred to generically, where we do refer to specific requirements, we make reference to requirements in England. If you are not learning to teach in England you should refer to the requirements of your own ITE course at this point. Where we have needed to link the theory to specific situations in schools or specific requirements of teachers in implementing the curriculum, we have linked it to the NCPE in England (Qualifications and Curriculum Authority (QCA), 2007). We recognise that some of you are not on ITE courses which are preparing you to teach in state schools in England, therefore we suggest that you do two things whenever information and tasks specific to the NCPE are used in the book:

1   substitute for the information and task given, the curriculum and requirements which apply to your situation;
2   reflect on the differences between the curriculum and requirements which apply to your situation and those of the NCPE.

In doing either/both of the above, not only are the information and tasks relevant to your own situation but, also, you can attain a greater understanding by comparing your own experience with another student teacher, other requirements for ITE or another curriculum.

YOUR PROFESSIONAL DEVELOPMENT PORTFOLIO

We strongly recommend that you keep a professional development portfolio (PDP). As you read through the book and complete the tasks, we ask you to record information in your PDP. You can use this information for a number of purposes, for example, to refer back to when completing other tasks in this book, to help you with assignments on your course, to help you reflect on your development and to provide evidence of your development, your strengths and areas for further development. The material in your PDP is also useful to you as you move from ITE into your teaching career, as it can inform future decisions about your CPD. In England, you can use your PDP in completing your career entry and development profile (CEDP). You should refer to Chapter 18 in this book and the introduction to Capel, Leask and Turner (2009) *Learning to Teach in the Secondary School* for guidance about keeping and using your PDP.

TERMINOLOGY USED IN THE BOOK

We have tried to mix, and balance, the use of *gender terms* in order to avoid clumsy he/she terminology.

We call school children *pupils* to avoid confusion with students; the latter referring to people in further and higher education. We use *student teachers* for people in higher education who are on ITE courses. We refer to *ITE* as we would argue that your course (and this book) provides not merely training (as in initial teacher training) but also education of intending teachers. By this we mean that learning to teach is a journey of personal and professional development in which your skills of classroom management develop alongside an emerging understanding of the learning and teaching process. This process begins on the first day of your course and continues throughout your career.

The important staff in your life are those in your school and HEI with a responsibility for supporting your development as a teacher; we have called all these people *tutors*. Your ITE course will have its own way of referring to staff.

Your ITE course may use terminology different to that used in this book. For example, where the word *evaluation* is used in this book, on some courses the word appraisal is used. In this book, the term aim is used to describe the intended outcomes of schemes of work, objectives is used to describe the intended outcomes of units of work and intended learning outcomes (ILOs) is used for the outcomes of individual lessons. Both objectives and ILOs describe pupil responses, i.e. what pupils should know, understand and be able to do by the end of the unit of work or lesson; objectives for units of work being longer term than those for lessons. However, different terms may be used on your course, e.g. ILOs for both units of work and lessons – in which case, use the terminology used by your course. You should check the terminology used on your course.

We hope that you find this book useful in supporting your development as a teacher, in helping you to maximise pupils' learning. If so, tell others; if not, tell us.

We wish you well at the start of what we hope will be an enjoyable, exciting and rewarding career.

Susan Capel
Margaret Whitehead
April 2010

STARTING OUT AS A PE TEACHER

Susan Capel

INTRODUCTION

As a student PE teacher you are embarking on the long, but exciting, process of becoming an effective teacher; of translating your knowledge and love of PE into the ability to encourage pupils' learning and progress towards becoming physically educated. You need to understand both the wider role of the teacher and your specific role as a PE teacher, as well as what you are aiming to achieve in your lessons. There are numerous teaching skills you need to develop, along with the ability to use the right teaching skill in the right way at the right time to improve pupil learning. An understanding of how teaching skills interact with each other in a lesson is also valuable. To develop into an effective teacher you also need to be aware of the range of factors that impact on your teaching, including understanding yourself, your values, attitudes and beliefs and be able to reflect on how these influence what you are doing and therefore on how they impact on pupils' learning.

Your development into an effective teacher is challenging and not always smooth. At times you may be anxious or concerned about your development or your teaching performance, may lack confidence to try something out or may feel frustrated or despondent at not being able to cope with a situation or not knowing how to respond. Early in your development you may not have the teaching skills or experience to cope effectively with a specific situation. Part of the challenge of learning to teach is becoming able to adapt what you do to suit the unique needs of any situation. When you can adapt your teaching skills to the context and situation to achieve specific intended learning outcomes (ILOs) you are rewarded for your hard work, as you are well on the way to a satisfying career as an effective teacher. This ability enables you to change your focus from yourself to your pupils' learning.

OBJECTIVES

At the end of this chapter you should be able to:

■   recognise the variety of reasons why people choose to become PE teachers;
■   recognise factors which influence what, why and how you teach;

■ have an overview of the teaching skills required to develop into an effective teacher who focuses on pupils and their learning, and begin to see how these skills interact in the teaching situation;

■ have an overview of the steps you need to take to be an effective teacher.

Check the requirements for your course to see which relate to this chapter.

WHY DID YOU BECOME A PE TEACHER?

Task 1.1 asks you to consider why people become PE teachers. Complete this task before continuing.

Task 1.1 **Why do people want to become PE teachers?**

List your reasons for wanting to become a PE teacher. Compare your reasons with those given by other student teachers and by experienced PE teachers you know. Are there any reasons common to all those to whom you spoke? Are there any different reasons? Why do you think this is so? Put your list in your professional development portfolio (PDP).

You have been at school for 11 years or more and in all probability wanted to become a PE teacher because you enjoyed PE, were able and successful, wanted to pass on your knowledge, understanding and love of PE and wanted to work with young people. If you found also that these were the major reasons given by other people for becoming a PE teacher, your findings support results of research (for example, Evans and Williams, 1989; Mawer, 1995). Similar reasons for becoming a PE teacher suggest some agreement/consensus/homogeneity in values, attitudes and beliefs about PE and about PE teaching.

Your positive experiences of PE and your ability and success in physical activities and sport give you positive perceptions of PE teachers, their role, what they do and how they teach the subject. As you are likely to spend considerable time, professionally and socially, with other PE professionals, it is easy to forget that there are many pupils in schools and, indeed, people in society at large, who do not share your values, attitudes and beliefs about PE and hence about participation in physical activity and sport. You can, no doubt, think of friends who had less positive experiences of PE at school, who have more negative perceptions about PE lessons and PE teachers. Unfortunately, these negative perceptions seem to be all too common. The sad outcome of this situation is that these individuals may well opt out of all physical activity once they leave school. An effective PE teacher is one who can help all pupils (including those who do not readily enjoy and/or who are not as able and successful at physical activities) to enjoy participation and to value their experiences and, hence, to be physically educated (see Chapter 2). Your goal is to develop into such a teacher with the benefits this brings to young people and the satisfaction it affords to you.

AN OVERVIEW OF TEACHING

First and foremost you are a teacher of pupils; a member of a profession with a responsibility to help pupils to learn by developing knowledge, practical skill and understanding to achieve broader goals of education (see Chapter 14). Second, you are a teacher of PE, with a specific responsibility for teaching the knowledge, practical skill and understanding specific to PE. You therefore have two roles, a wider role as a teacher (see Unit 8.2 in Capel, Leask and Turner, 2009) as well as a subject-specific role as a PE teacher.

In Task 1.2 you are asked to consider the role of PE teachers.

Task 1.2 **What is the role of PE teachers?**

List what you believe to be the role of PE teachers. You may want to create two lists for this task; one list which identifies how the role of all teachers applies to PE teachers and one which identifies the role undertaken specifically by PE teachers. Compare your list with that of another student teacher, then discuss it with your tutor so that you understand what you are working towards, therefore the knowledge, teaching skills and understanding required to enable you to get there. Put this information in your PDP and refer back to it at different times in your initial teacher education (ITE) course.

This text concentrates on helping you to develop your skills for teaching PE, but also indicates, in Chapter 14, ways you can fulfil your wider responsibilities as a teacher.

You cannot address at once all the teaching skills required to develop into an effective teacher. On your ITE course, and in books such as this, teaching skills are addressed separately. If your tutors on your ITE course, or we in this book, tried to address teaching skills in combination, we are likely to give you too many things to think about and concentrate on at any one time, overwhelming you with information or even confusing you, rather than helping you to develop as a teacher. However, an approach in which you look at teaching skills separately as presented in this book only provides you with a partial picture of teaching which gradually builds up over time. You only recognise the complete picture when you suddenly realise that you see it. It is helpful, therefore, at this stage, to have an overview of teaching so that you know at what you are aiming and how the teaching skills in which you are developing competence fit together.

This overview should help you to think about what you are doing, its effectiveness in terms of pupils achieving ILOs and on which teaching skills you need to concentrate in order to develop your teaching further. This is a similar exercise to planning lessons and units of work. You know what you want to achieve by the end of a lesson (your ILOs) and by the end of a unit of work (objectives) therefore can plan how to achieve these (see Chapters 2 and 3).

We now look at the role of teachers, specifically focusing on part of that role, that is teaching lessons, and the teaching skills required to promote pupil learning.

What is required for effective teaching of PE?

Teaching is a complex, multifaceted activity. First and foremost it is an interaction between *what* is being taught (the content), *why* and *how* it is being taught (the process).

What is taught in PE is guided by the aims of the curriculum used in the placement school in which you are working. In England, these should be based on the government guidelines set out by the Qualifications and Curriculum Authority (QCA, 2007a). It is the case that in some countries there may be no government or national aims or guidelines on the content to be taught. In England the aims of PE are broadly expressed and, thus, so are the activities that constitute the content. The National Curriculum for Physical Education (NCPE), currently NCPE 2007 (QCA, 2007a), sets out specific guidelines on how to select content. The rationale for selection is based on a range of Key Concepts, Key Processes, a Range and Content directive which teachers should draw on when teaching the Key Concepts and Key Processes and the provision of certain Curriculum Opportunities that should be provided (see Chapter 13). Notwithstanding these guidelines and similar ones in earlier PE National Curricula the choice of activities does not always match up to the guidelines. For example, despite efforts in the NCPE to focus on breadth of experience in pupil's learning, the curriculum in many schools in England is biased towards games (see, for example, Penney and Evans, 1994). This and other issues in selecting content in PE are worthy of reflection. It is useful, therefore, for you to consider why games are dominant – is it due, for example, to the desire of schools to produce good school teams, the preference of the teacher, because the curriculum has always been biased towards games, or a combination of factors? Is this to the benefit of pupil learning in PE? Do *all* pupils enjoy games – in year 7, in year 9, in year 11? How many pupils choose to continue to participate in games out of school or when they leave school? Would pupils prefer to participate in other activities, e.g. non-competitive or individual activities? Would this encourage them to participate more in physical activity outside and post-school?

Task 1.3 is designed to help you familiarise yourself with the aims and content of the PE curriculum in your placement school.

Task 1.3 **Activities included in the PE curriculum**

Familiarise yourself with the aims and content of the PE curriculum used in your placement school. Find out what activities are included in the curriculum in your placement school. Compare these with the aims, content and activities identified by another student teacher working in another school. What are the similarities and differences and why? Are there other aims that should be addressed? Are there other activities, which are frequently taught in schools, which are not on your list? Keep these lists in your PDP for future reference.

Obviously, every teacher needs good knowledge and understanding of the subject content (Chapter 4 looks at effective observation being, at least in part, related to the depth of knowledge about the activity you are teaching). You are likely to have considerable content knowledge of one or more activities included in PE curricula. You need to identify which activities are your strengths and those activities in which you need to gain further experience in order to be able to use them effectively to promote pupil learning.

In your ITE course there is limited time available to learn about every activity you may be asked to teach. It is therefore likely that there are a number of activities in which you have to take the initiative to improve your knowledge and understanding. This book is not designed to cover the activities included in a PE curriculum. You therefore need to consider ways in which you can gain the required knowledge and understanding of these activities. There are many ways in which you can do this, some of which are identified in Chapter 18. We advise you to start work on this aspect of your teaching as soon as you can. Alternatively, where you have good knowledge in one/some areas, you need to be clear where you gained that knowledge and how (e.g. from the PE curriculum, from sports clubs/teams) and consider whether the content and teaching methods are appropriate for the groups you are teaching.

It is also important to recognise, however, that there are other aspects of knowledge that you need to develop on your ITE course. Together these constitute the knowledge *of* teaching. If you concentrate solely on developing your subject content knowledge, that is of the activities you are to teach, you are unlikely to develop into a fully effective teacher. Chapter 18 covers broader subject content knowledge in more detail, considering the knowledge bases identified by Shulman (1987). Task 1.4 is designed to help you address areas for the development of subject content knowledge.

Task 1.4 **Addressing areas for development in your subject content knowledge**

Using the list of activities included in the curriculum in your placement school (compiled for Task 1.3), identify whether each is a strength or an area for development in terms of your knowledge and understanding. Identify ways in which you can address your areas for development (e.g. observation in schools; sharing knowledge and understanding with other student teachers on your course; gaining governing body awards; peer teaching; teaching PE lessons; watching matches; officiating at school activities; reading; watching video recordings). Do not try to address all areas for development at once, but consider how you can spread this over your ITE course and even into your first year of teaching. Retain this information in your PDP for reference as you proceed through your course.

Why you are teaching PE and *why* you are teaching particular schemes of work, units of work and lessons also need consideration. These are each of a different order and are briefly looked at one at a time.

- Why you are teaching PE has been covered in the sections above. For example your love of physical activity and your interest in helping pupils to have similar positive experiences;
- Why you are teaching particular schemes and units of work is driven, in England, by the overall government and school policies;
- Why you are teaching a lesson, and why you are teaching it in a particular way, depends on characteristics both of the pupils and of yourself and on aspects of the teaching situation such as the venue. What your ILOs are form the chief reason why

you are teaching the way you do (see Chapter 10 on teaching strategies). Significant also are the age, ability, experience and motivation of the pupils, as well as practicalities such as the lesson length, the size of the working space and, if you are outside, the weather conditions. Why you are teaching in a particular way depends also on your teaching style (See Chapter 10). In addition, as you become more experienced your teaching also evidences your personal values, attitudes and beliefs about the subject.

How the content of the PE curriculum is taught is left to the professional judgement of the individual school, department and teacher (see also Unit 1.1 in Capel, Leask and Turner, 2009). How you teach relates to the aims of the school and PE curriculum, the characteristics of the pupils you are teaching, as well as your own objectives for a unit of work and ILOs for any particular lesson (see Chapters 2 and 3). In Chapter 10 aims, objectives and ILOs are considered in relation to teaching strategies. Thus, you need to think critically about how you are teaching a particular activity to ensure that you achieve your aims, objectives and ILOs.

What you see happening in a lesson is only the tip of the iceberg as far as the teacher is concerned (see Figure 1.1.1 (p. 13) in Capel, Leask and Turner, 2009). Planning and evaluating are also integral aspects of teaching. Prior to teaching a lesson, long-term aims for the scheme of work and medium-term objectives for the unit of work have been established, followed by general planning of the unit of work and detailed planning and preparation of the lesson, including short-term ILOs for the lesson. After the lesson the effectiveness or otherwise of parts of the lesson and the whole lesson should be evaluated to inform planning and preparation of the next lesson. Planning and evaluation are addressed in Chapter 3.

The tip of the iceberg, i.e. what happens while interacting with the pupils in the lesson, is of course very important. How far pupils are successful in achieving the ILOs relates to how you conduct the lesson. Included in this is how you respond to pupils in the ongoing teaching situation. You need to be flexible and to adapt the plan, if necessary; that is if the pupils do not respond as you had expected, in relation to a particular task. How the lesson is conducted includes not only the teaching skills used but also the qualities displayed by the teacher, such as empathy, perception, sensitivity and responsiveness. All these aspects are relevant in evaluating the lesson. Task 1.5 asks you to observe what happens in a PE lesson.

Task 1.5 **What happens in a PE lesson?**

Observe a lesson taught by an experienced PE teacher and note the types of activities in which the teacher is involved, their sequence and the time spent on each one. You should aim to get an overview of what happens rather than great detail. You may want to organise your observation into what happens:

■ before the teaching starts (for example, takes the register whilst pupils are changing, collects, reads excuse notes and talks to any pupils not doing the lesson, collects valuables, hurries along anyone slow to change, locks the changing room after the last pupil has left, etc.);
■ during the teaching part of the lesson;
■ after the teaching has finished.

Chapter 6 covers organisation and management of lessons. There are some obser-vation sheets on this book's website (see www.routledge.com/textbooks/9780415561648).

Remember that the lesson starts as soon as pupils arrive at the changing rooms and finishes when they move to their next lesson or to a break in the day. Put in your PDP for future reference.

Teaching skills and teacher behaviours you may well have observed in the teaching inter-action, once the pupils are in the working space, include observation, giving instructions, using PE-specific language, questioning, reminding, demonstrating, accommodating pupils of different ability, reprimanding. In addition, you may well have seen the teacher managing pupils, time and space and responding to situations in which safety needed attention. You are likely to have seen the teacher giving praise and feedback, which is intended not only to improve performance but also to promote motivation and pupil self-esteem. You may also have observed the teacher using ICT and possibly carrying out assessment procedures. You will also have seen evidence of teacher planning and teacher preparation and clearance of the working space.

Rink (1993) and Siedentop and Tannehill (2000) (see further reading) both provide an overview of teaching PE in which they categorise what a teacher does in a lesson broadly as below, i.e.:

■ *instructional activities* (activities associated with imparting subject content to pupils);
■ *organising and managing activities* (activities associated with organising the learn-ing environment and managing the lesson to maintain appropriate behaviour in order for learning to occur); and
■ *other activities* (activities to develop and maintain an effective learning environ-ment, such as the use of praise).

It would be useful for you to examine what you identified the teacher does (from Task 1.5) and group these teacher behaviours into these three categories. All the skills listed above are drawn on in one or more of these categories and all are covered in this book. For example, Chapter 5 looks at communication, while Chapter 6 focuses on organisa-tion and management and considers the time pupils spend actively engaged in learning (academic learning time) and how this is affected by activities that are not directly related to pupil learning. Chapter 7 discusses maintaining an effective learning environment.

Some teaching skills are specific to particular categories while others are important in all categories of teacher behaviour, for example, observation (see Chapter 4) and management of issues concerned with safety (Chapter 9).

A starting point for identifying teaching skills in which you need to develop compe-tence by the end of your ITE course, and indeed the key reference throughout your course, are the skills required of newly qualified teachers (NQTs), as set out in a govern-ment publication towards which you are working or by your higher education institution (HEI). Even where skills required are centrally determined, HEIs generally also produce their own set of skills based on those in the relevant document. In Task 1.6 you are asked to consider the skills you need to pass your ITE course.

Task 1.6 **Teaching skills**

Look at the skills identified in your ITE programme or other official documents that you need to develop to pass your ITE course and identify those on which you should work in order to become competent. Discuss with your tutor which teaching skills you should work on immediately and which you should leave until later. As part of the regular reviews you undertake with your tutor during your ITE course consider which teaching skills you should work on at that particular time. Keep these in your PDP as they are a record of your development as a teacher.

Being competent in basic teaching skills is not enough for your lessons to be effective. In order to develop into an effective teacher you need to be able to refine and adapt these teaching skills and combine them so that they are used in a way appropriate to the specific situation. You need to consider how the skills interact in a lesson. Your appreciation of this interaction develops as you become more experienced. It is well to remember that *what* you teach and *how* you teach are interdependent and that ILOs will not be achieved unless you take time to consider both of these aspects of teaching fully (see Chapter 10). Very important to your teaching is your critical reflection, after each lesson, on how far your teaching was effective in achieving the ILOs and your willingness to try different approaches should these be needed. Further, you need to move your focus from yourself and your teaching, to focus on pupils and their learning.

There are a number of reasons why you do not always achieve your ILOs. Sometimes this is due to lack of appropriate planning. We have seen some student teachers plan the content of their lessons thoroughly, but leave the organisation and management of the tasks, the equipment or the pupils to chance. In contrast, we have seen some student teachers plan how they are going to control a class without considering the appropriateness, quality and progression of content. If a student teacher has not planned how to organise and manage the lesson, the pupils may not be clear about what they are to do and what is expected of them, therefore the teacher has to spend considerable time organising and managing and cannot deliver the lesson in the way intended. On the other hand, if the student teacher concentrates on organising and managing the class, pupils are likely to achieve little and what they do achieve is likely to be of low quality. The lesson plan in Chapter 3 directs your attention to both of these.

You must be aware that pupils 'test out' student (and new) teachers and try to negotiate an acceptable standard of performance, effort or behaviour. We have all seen situations where pupils try to negotiate a longer game if they do a practice effectively or where pupils promise to work hard if they can work with friends. Discuss with another student teacher other ways in which pupils may try to negotiate boundaries so that you are aware of them as you start to teach a new class.

Make sure that you only accept performance, effort or behaviour of an acceptable standard right from the beginning, otherwise you may find it hard to get pupils to accept this later. Pupils may make less effort to complete a task appropriately in future if you accept initially a performance, effort or behaviour below that of which they are capable. You may, for example, set a task in gymnastics which requires pupils to develop a sequence comprising five movements, with at least one each of three different types of movements – rolls, jumps and balances. Pupils are given the opportunity to develop and practice an appropriate sequence then show this to the class. How you respond to the way pupils complete the task is important. If, for example, a pupil uses the three required movements to complete a sequence but makes no effort to link them together or to perform them in an effective way and you accept this, you send a message to the class that they can complete the task in any way they want.

There are other reasons why pupils may not perform or make an effort or behave to the standard expected. The task may be, for example, too easy or too difficult or not interesting, therefore pupils are not motivated to do the task. You may not have presented the task clearly or you respond differently to the same performance, effort or behaviour on different occasions. Pupils may, therefore, be bored, unclear or confused about what is required of them, therefore they may modify the task to make it easier or more difficult, try not to accomplish the task or, on occasion, refuse to do the task altogether. Can you think of any other reasons why pupils may not perform or make an effort or behave to the standard expected?

HOW ARE YOU GOING TO DEVELOP INTO AN EFFECTIVE PE TEACHER?

Many changes occur as you develop your teaching skills and teaching strategies. Changes have been identified by a number of authors as stages or phases of development (see Unit 1.2 in Capel, Leask and Turner (2009) for consideration of phases of development as a teacher). Maynard and Furlong (1993) and Perrott (1982) identified stages in development of student teachers and Siedentop and Tannehill (2000) identified these specifically for student PE teachers. Guillaume and Rudney (1993) found that in developing as teachers, student teachers not only think about different things, but also think about the same things differently.

If there are different stages in your development as teachers, it follows that you may need different learning opportunities and experiences at different stages. Learning opportunities and experiences include observing experienced teachers teach; role play; small group micro-teaching situations with peers or groups of pupils; team teaching with your tutor, either teaching a small group for part or the whole of a lesson or the whole group for part of the lesson; teaching a full class. These are not sequential. Each can be used at any time on your ITE course in order to achieve a particular purpose. These learning opportunities and experiences allow you to practise and become competent in basic teaching skills, possibly for use for a specific purpose, and to spend time using your developing teaching skills in a variety of situations. These allow you to refine them so that you can adapt them as appropriate to the situation to enable you to use the right teaching skill in the right way at the right time to promote pupil learning. It is important also that as you become more confident in your teaching skills you reflect critically on what you want to achieve and on what you want the pupils to achieve – your aims, objectives and ILOs, therefore what teaching strategies and learning activities enable the pupils to achieve these (see Chapter 10).

Getting started

In order to make the most of the learning opportunities and experiences in school you need to understand the context in which you are working. Gathering essential background information to inform your work in school is an essential part of this. On preliminary visits prior to each school experience you need to collect information about the school and PE department. This information comes from many sources. You observe the PE environment, including the facilities, displays and equipment. You ask questions. You talk to tutors about policies and procedures of the school and PE department and observe them in practice. You read school and department documents such as schemes and units of work, policy statements, prospectuses. A document such as the school prospectus can provide valuable information about the whole school and its pupils. Whole school and PE policy statements covering such issues as assessment, equal opportunities and extra-curricular activities are important in providing the context for your work in the department. Other documents give you essential guidance on how to conduct yourself (for example, the school dress code) and how to relate to pupils within the department. Your tutor will, no doubt, give you guidance about what information to collect and mechanisms to help you. To supplement guidance from your tutor, if needed, on this book's website (see www.routledge.com/textbooks/9780415561648) there are examples of questions designed to help you gather information about the school, the PE department, the PE facilities and resources, by focusing your observations, the questions you ask and identifying some key documents to look at.

This book's website (see www.routledge.com/textbooks/9780415561648) also includes examples of observation schedules to help you to observe different teaching skills in action. In addition to using these to observe the teaching skills identified, you can use them to help you devise your own observation schedule for a specific purpose. Chapter 17 addresses observation and other information-gathering techniques to help you make the most of your learning opportunities and experiences in schools.

Metzler (1990) indicated that tutoring should be a teaching process in itself. Your tutor should help you to make the most of the learning opportunities and experiences on your ITE course in order to study, observe and practise teaching skills in situations appropriate to your stage of development. You and your tutor may undertake different roles as you undertake different learning opportunities and experiences in school, therefore you need to determine how best to work with your tutor at different stages in your development, e.g. direction, guidance, negotiation, freedom.

Task 1.7 is designed to help you to work with your tutor.

Task 1.7 **Working with your tutor**

Discuss with your tutor your immediate development needs and what learning activities you both feel might be best to help you address those needs. Take part in the learning activity and then evaluate with your tutor how effective that activity was in addressing your development need. Keep these in your PDP and refer to them to help you to learn from them and continue to develop.

As well as undertaking a range of activities to help you develop as a teacher, it is important that you develop your ability to reflect critically. You need, for example, to think critically about what you are teaching, why and how. This is covered in Chapter 17.

SUMMARY AND KEY POINTS

Your past experiences of PE have influenced your decision to become a PE teacher and have moulded your values, attitudes and beliefs about PE and about PE teaching. In order to become an effective PE teacher, you need to be aware of how your values, attitudes and beliefs influence you and to understand that not all pupils you teach, nor all parents, nor all other teachers, share your values, attitudes and beliefs. You need competence in basic teaching skills before you can refine and adapt these skills to be able to use them in the right way at the right time. It is only then that you can combine them effectively to enhance pupils' learning and achieve the ILOs of a lesson and objectives of units of work and work towards achieving the aims of the schemes of work and PE curriculum in which you are working. In order to do this, you need also to understand the complex interactions between teaching skills, physical activities and pupils' learning, including how specific teaching strategies help to achieve specific ILOs. Teaching skills tend to be introduced on your course, and written about in books such as this, in isolation from one another. This chapter has attempted to provide a picture of how they fit together and interact so that you know at what you are aiming. One way it has done this is by approaching the whole enterprise of teaching by addressing the questions concerning the what, why and how of teaching. Chapters 3–8 address particular teaching skills while Chapters 9–12 focus on applications of these basic teaching skills. After you have read those chapters we suggest that you return to this chapter to help you reflect on how teaching skills fit together and interact.

As you start out as a student PE teacher you are likely to find that teaching is more complex than you thought. Your previous experience, your enthusiasm and your wish to pass on your knowledge, understanding and love of PE are not enough. Your ITE course is designed to give you different learning opportunities and experiences to help you develop as a PE teacher. We hope that this book helps to support your development as a teacher and that you enjoy the challenge.

Check which requirements for your course you have addressed through this chapter.

FURTHER READING

Armour, K. and Jones, R. (1998) *Physical Education Teachers' Lives and Careers. PE, Sport and Educational Status.* **London: Falmer Press.**

> The complex links between physical education, education and sport, as experienced by PE teachers, are explored in this book. It includes consideration of how their personal involvement in sport has influenced their establishment of personal philosophies and professional practices in PE. This should help you to think through your own careers.

Mawer, M. (1995) *The Effective Teaching of Physical Education*, **London: Longmans.**

> Chapter 1 in this book considers why people become PE teachers, their socialisation into the PE profession and stages in their development as teachers. Chapter 2 focuses on being a student PE teacher and early lessons taken by student PE teachers.

Rink, J. E. (1993) *Teaching Physical Education for Learning,* **2nd edn, St. Louis, MO: Times Mirror/Mosby College Publishing.**

> Chapter 1 provides an overview of the teaching process, including content and skills of organisation and management used in a lesson.

Siedentop, D. and Tannehill, D. (2000) *Developing Teaching Skills in Physical Education,* 4th edn, Mountain View, CA: Mayfield Publishing Co.

Chapter 1 addresses a number of issues concerned with learning to teach PE effectively, including stages of development of student PE teachers. Chapter 5 introduces three primary systems: the managerial task system; the instructional task system; and the student (pupil) social system; and how they interact.

AIMS OF PE

Margaret Whitehead

INTRODUCTION

Chapter 1 provided you with a broad overview of the role of the PE teacher and of the skills, knowledge and understanding needed to fulfil this role successfully and with confidence. Among the topics discussed were issues concerning the aims of PE and how your teaching can promote the achievement of these aspirations. This chapter looks specifically at the aims of PE. It is important to be clear about aims as these are the foundation for planning schemes of work, units of work and individual lessons. Detailed guidance on planning is covered in Chapter 3. Aims influence both the content and the teaching method you select in your work with pupils. You will probably want to return to Chapters 1 and 2 regularly throughout your initial teacher education (ITE) course to remind you of what you are aiming to achieve in PE.

OBJECTIVES

At the end of this chapter you should be able to:

■ understand the terms aims, objectives and intended learning outcomes (ILOs);

■ appreciate the relationship between overall educational aims and the aims of PE;

■ differentiate between aims of and justifications for PE;

■ appreciate that aims of PE are of two types: those unique to the subject and those that are broader educational aims shared with other curriculum subjects;

■ understand that aims, objectives and ILOs influence your design and delivery of lessons.

Check the requirements for your course to see which relate to this chapter.

DEFINITIONS AND BROAD PURPOSES

You will hear the words *aims*, *objectives* and *ILOs* frequently in your ITE course and beyond. These terms are different statements of intent and serve a number of purposes:

■   they identify what you intend the pupils will achieve;

■   they guide how you will teach, informing your scheme/unit/lesson planning;

■   they provide a benchmark against which to assess pupil learning, thus informing you whether your planning and teaching achieved the desired ILOs.

Aims therefore give your work direction in purpose, guidance in planning and focus in assessment. These functions can be understood as essential, if looked at broadly in terms of a journey you are to make. In planning and carrying out a journey you need to know where you are going, how you are going to get there and how you recognise that you have arrived. All are important in teaching.

AIMS, OBJECTIVES AND INTENDED LEARNING OUTCOMES (ILOS)

Aims and objectives

Aims and objectives are the basis for educational planning. *Aims* provide *overall purpose and direction* and therefore relate to more general intentions. A school has long-term aims or purposes. You should be able to find these in your placement school documentation. There are aims for the curriculum as a whole, for example, those identified by the government in England within the Every Child Matters (Department for Education and Skills (DfES), 2003) policy. In addition there are aims set out for each subject such as in the Importance Statement in the National Curriculum for Physical Education (NCPE) 2007 (Qualifications and Curriculum Authority (QCA), 2007a). Aims and objectives become more focused and precise the shorter term and closer to the point of delivery they become. Therefore, aims become more specific from education, to school, to curriculum, to subject. Aims of education specify what should be achieved over a period of time, for example, for the time pupils are required to be at school. They offer general guidance about the purposes of, and outcomes from, education, rather than defining any specific achievements, whereas the aims of a subject such as PE, although still long-term aspirations, are more specific.

    The *aims* or purposes of a subject form the starting point for devising *schemes* of work. Typically schemes of work span a whole year or phase of education. Units of work refer to a shorter period of time such as half a term or a term. While schemes characteristically have aims, *units have objectives*. Objectives are more specific purposes and intentions. Thus, objectives are building blocks or stepping stones which, when put together, result in the achievement of an aim(s).

Intended learning outcomes (ILOs)

As indicated above, longer term schemes of work have aims and these generate the objectives of constituent units of work. However, neither aims nor objectives can be used directly to help you plan a particular lesson. They need to be broken down into 'operational' segments, each with a more specific focus. These become ILOs for individual lessons. Aims and objectives are the intended end products of, respectively, the scheme of work or unit of work, whereas ILOs identify what pupils should achieve in a specific lesson. For example, an aim of a PE scheme of work might be to initiate pupils into playing a competitive game. An objective of a unit of work derived from this aim could be for pupils to be able to play a 5 v 5 game in, e.g. hockey. An ILO of a lesson within this unit could be that pupils understand and can demonstrate the roles of attack and defence in a 5 v 5 situation in hockey. ILOs describe what pupils should be able to do, know or understand at the end of a lesson. They are usually included at the start of a lesson plan and are introduced by a statement such as 'by the end of the lesson pupils will be able to ....'. They are fundamental aspects of a lesson plan as they challenge the teacher to devise specific learning activities in the interests of their achievement. In addition, ILOs focus the pupils' and teacher's attention during the lesson in that they are likely to generate individual tasks, initiate key teaching points and be the focus of pupil assessment. Furthermore they are the ground against which you evaluate the success of a lesson.

AIMS OF EDUCATION, A SCHOOL AND A SUBJECT

Unit 7.1 in Capel, Leask and Turner (2009) considers aims of education in some detail. It is suggested that you refer to that unit now for background information. It would be useful at this point to read the aims of the whole school/curriculum in your placement school. Any school aims are likely to reflect the current broad philosophy underlying a country's overall education philosophy. In England and Wales, for example, the National Curriculum requires a broad and balanced curriculum in schools. The key aims of the National Curriculum (QCA, 2007a) are for all young people to become:

■   successful learners who enjoy learning, make progress and achieve;
■   confident individuals who are able to live safe, healthy and fulfilling lives;
■   responsible citizens who make a positive contribution to society.

(QCA, 2007a)

Chapter 14 considers the role of PE in achieving these broad aims. At this stage, however, it is important for you to realise that you are one of a team of people in school all working to common educational aims or aspirations. Each subject should make a contribution to achieving these aims and each teacher should ensure that all planning and delivery of teaching in their subject is firmly grounded in these aims. Both the material covered in lessons and methods of engaging pupils in their learning can make valuable contributions to achieving these aspirations.

AIMS OF PE

PE has taken a number of forms since its inclusion in the school curriculum in the late nineteenth century. Early forms of PE were called drill and physical training (see Davis *et al.*, 2000). The term PE was introduced in 1945 when the then Department of Education took over responsibility for the subject from the Ministry of Health. Since its introduction into schools the subject has worked to achieve a variety of aims. For many years those teaching PE were free to select the specific aims towards which they worked. Early aims included promoting health, improving discipline and developing loyalty and teamwork. A list of aims gathered from surveying teachers' priorities is given in Figure 2.1.

Now carry out Task 2.1, which encourages you to reflect on the list in Figure 2.1.

Task 2.1 **Prioritising aims of PE**

Study the list in Figure 2.1 and identify the four aims that you feel are the most important to achieve in PE. Compare this list with that created by another student teacher, discussing and defending your different priorities. Record this debate and put the notes in your professional development portfolio (PDP).

- develop physical skills;
- develop self-esteem and self-confidence;
- introduce every pupil to a wide range of activities;
- ensure pupils continue with physical activity after leaving school;
- develop creativity and inventiveness;
- produce world class athletes;
- provide activity to keep youngsters off the street and away from crime;
- teach pupils the role of physical activity in stress prevention;
- promote joint flexibility and muscle strength;
- teach respect for the environment;
- teach pupils to handle competition;
- develop social and moral skills;
- prepare pupils to be knowledgeable spectators;
- teach pupils the place of sport/dance in UK (English/Welsh/Scottish/Northern Irish) culture;
- open up possibilities for employment post-school;
- promote health – freedom from illness – especially cardiovascular health;
- promote physical growth and development;
- develop perseverance;
- promote emotional development;
- provide enjoyment;
- win inter-school matches and tournaments;
- ensure pupils are alert to safety at all times;
- provide an area of potential success for the less academic;
- ensure every pupil has sufficient time to become proficient at a particular sport;
- develop water confidence to promote personal survival;
- develop aesthetic sensitivity;
- enable pupils to express themselves through movement;
- promote cognitive development;
- develop good posture and approach a mesomorph build, neither overweight nor underweight.

■ **Figure 2.1** Aims of PE to which teachers have aspired

Nowadays, however, in England, the National Curriculum spells out what each subject should aspire to achieve. This is set out in an Importance Statement. Teachers are expected to design work and teaching approaches to realise the aims inherent in the Importance Statement for their subject and to assess pupils in respect of achieving these aims.

The Importance Statement in the NCPE 2007 (QCA, 2007a) can be found in Chapter 13. Aims for PE arising from the Statement are that pupils should:

■ enjoy and succeed in many kinds of physical activity;
■ develop a wide range of skills and abilities to use tactics, strategies and compositional ideas;
■ think about what they are doing, analyse situations and make decisions;
■ reflect on their own and others' performances and find ways to improve them;
■ develop confidence to take part in different physical activities;
■ learn about the value of healthy active lifestyles;
■ be able to make informed choices about lifelong physical activity;
■ develop personally and socially;
■ be able to work on their own and in groups and teams;
■ be able to take on different roles and responsibilities;
■ learn how to be effective in competitive, creative and challenging situations.

See Chapter 13 for further details of the NCPE concerning the Concepts and Processes developed from the Importance Statement that should guide the work of PE teachers.

Recommendations in the NCPE become more specific in referring to Key Stages of learning. For example, in relation to Key Stages 3 and 4 (that is for work with pupils from 11 to 16 years) the guidelines spell out more specific aims and purposes of PE. These are for pupils to:

■ become skilful and intelligent performers;
■ acquire and develop skills, performing with increasing physical competence and confidence, in a range of physical activities and contexts;
■ learn how to select and apply skills, tactics and compositional ideas to suit activities that need different approaches and ways of thinking;
■ develop their ideas in a creative way;
■ set targets for themselves and compete against others, individually and as team members;
■ understand what it takes to persevere, succeed and acknowledge others' success;
■ respond to a variety of challenges in a range of physical contexts and environments;
■ take the initiative, lead activity and focus on improving aspects of their own performance;
■ discover their own aptitudes and preferences for different activities;
■ make informed decisions about the importance of exercise in their lives;
■ develop positive attitudes to participation in physical activity
  http://www.standards.dfes.gov.uk/schemes2/Secondary_PE/?view=get (2009).

There are three important points to be made about the aims listed above. These relate to the range of aims that are aspired to, the difference between aims and justifications and the inclusion of two distinct types of aims – those unique to the subject and those shared with other curriculum subjects.

The range of aims for PE

The range of aims presented in the NCPE at Key Stages 3 and 4 can seem very daunting. However, it has always been the case that numerous aspirations have been identified by

PE teachers, as can be seen from Figure 2.1. Attempts have been made to rank or prioritise aims but little consensus has been reached. In this context, to help you see the way forward and avoid being overwhelmed by too many aims it is useful to approach the issue from a slightly different perspective. This can help the multitude of aims to fall into place. The question at the heart of the issue is 'What would you hope would be the end result of PE in school?' Put simply the answer could be that you would want all your pupils to be *physically educated*. Task 2.2 asks you to discuss what being physically educated might mean.

Task 2.2 **Defining what is meant by being physically educated**

Discuss with another student teacher how you would describe a physically educated person. In other words what knowledge, understanding, skills and attitudes would you expect to find in a physically educated person? Write a brief description and then consider how the aims of the NCPE (in England) or the aims of PE in your country or school are designed to help pupils achieve this goal. Keep this description in your PDP, possibly reviewing it periodically throughout your course.

It is likely that your description includes reference to physical skill and to enthusiasm to participate in physical activity. It might also include the ability to work with others in an activity context and to have some grasp of the importance of physical activity to health.

An alternative overall aim for PE has been suggested as the development and nurturing of physical literacy. A brief definition of physical literacy reads: 'As appropriate to each individual's endowment, physical literacy can be described as a disposition, evidenced through the motivation, confidence, physical competence, knowledge and understanding to maintain physical activity throughout the lifecourse' (Whitehead, 2010). There has been growing interest in, and acceptance of, this concept not least because establishing physical literacy promotes participation in physical activity by every individual throughout the lifecourse. Working to achieve physical literacy in PE not only aims to produce a physically competent individual but, importantly, to motivate all to continue with activity, at an appropriate level, into adulthood and old age. Task 2.3 challenges you to consider how the aims of the NCPE (in England) or the aims of PE in your country or school might help pupils to become physically literate.

Task 2.3 **Relating PE aims to physical literacy**

Discuss with another student teacher how far the aims of the NCPE (in England) or the aims of PE in your country or school might foster the development of physical literacy. Compare these notes with the notes from Task 2.2 and debate how far physical literacy is achievable in today's schools. Put these notes in your PDP.

For further information about physical literacy see the website www.physical-literacy.org.uk. Consideration of the relative merits of aspiring to physically educate or to foster physical literacy is a key task at the end of this chapter.

Physical literacy is not the only relatively new concept being discussed by physical educationists. For example, some advocate a focus on *sport education* rather than PE. (See Chapter 14 for discussion of this approach to teaching.) The article on this issue by Kinchin *et al.* (2001) is thought provoking and challenging. Task 2.4 suggests that you read this article and compare your views on the ideas it presents with those of another student teacher.

Task 2.4 **Sport education**

Read the article on this issue by Kinchin *et al.* (2001). Discuss your perceptions of this approach with another student teacher. Identify opportunities and potential problems in following a sport education approach in PE. Put your notes in your PDP.

Physical literacy and sport education each arise from taking a particular perspective on PE, its priorities, potential, and its role in education. Other writers have put forward different views and their philosophies are well worth reading. Carry out Task 2.5 to appreciate some other perspectives on PE.

Task 2.5 **Considering other philosophies of PE**

Read Chapter 1 in Macfadyen and Bailey (2002) 'Thinking about Physical Education in the Secondary School' and record areas in which you agree or otherwise with the views of the writers. Discuss your views with another student teacher. Put your notes in your PDP.

Over time you develop your own views on the aim or aims at the heart of PE. In other words you arrive at your own philosophy of PE. As you discuss this with colleagues you will be expected to justify your opinions. The next section looks at issues surrounding values and justification of PE.

Aims, values and justifications

Statements about the aims of PE are often confused with values of, and justifications for, the subject. This is partly because they often contain very similar material. However, there is a subtle difference between these concepts which needs to be appreciated.

There are always three potential questions:

■ First, why are you engaging pupils in a task or activity?
■ Second, what is the value of the task/activity?
■ Third, can you justify why you are of the opinion the task/activity is of value?

Aims, objectives and ILOs provide the answer to the first question. For example if asked 'Why have you designed this unit to enable pupils to progress from 2 v 2 to 5 v 5 situations in a competitive team situation?' The answer here could be to achieve the objective of developing teamwork.

The second question in this case might be 'What is the value of developing teamwork?' The answer here could be to enable pupils either, sometime in the future, to play the full game, or to promote social development.

A follow-up question could be 'Can you explain why learning to play a full game/promoting social development is valuable?' That is, what is your justification for attention being given in education to achieving this goal(s)?

In the first case the answer could be that participating in a full game gives pupils confidence to continue to be involved in a competitive activity after they leave school, thus providing a worthwhile use of leisure time which can also promote health. In the second case the answer could be that social skills are essential to effective collaboration throughout life, particularly in the workplace.

It is useful at this stage to read Chapter 1 in Capel, Breckon and O'Neill (2006) and carry out Activities 1.1a and 1.1b. Activity 13.3 is also useful. Task 2.6 challenges you to identify, articulate and debate the value of and justification for some of the aims and purposes of the NCPE.

Task 2.6 **Justifying aims**

Working with another student teacher, each select a different aim from the NCPE Key Stage 3 and 4 aims listed above and each prepare an argument to identify and justify its value in an educational context. Now engage in a debate, with each student teacher in turn 'playing devil's advocate' in relation to the justification for the aim supported by the other. Keep these notes of your deliberations and put them in your PDP.

It is very important that as a PE teacher you can identify the value of achieving the aims of the subject, that is, to be able to justify its inclusion in the curriculum, and can engage in a debate as to the educational worth of the values claimed. There can be little dispute over a reference to an aim in respect of your answering the question 'Why are you engaging pupils in this type of work?', however anyone could challenge you about the value of an aim. For example, while most people could not argue with you when you identify that the ILO of a particular lesson is to enable pupils to create a gymnastics sequence, some people might ask what is the value of pupils achieving this outcome. In this situation you would need not only to cite, for example, the fostering of creativity as valuable, but also justify your belief in the value of developing creativity in young people.

Two distinct types of aims

An analysis of the numerous aims and aspirations of PE set out above reveals that they are of two types. One type is concerned with aims that are unique to PE, aims that no other subject area could achieve. The other type identifies broader educational aims that are shared with other curriculum subjects. Task 2.7 asks you to recognise these two different types of aims.

Task 2.7 **Recognising two types of aims**

Using the list of aims from the Key Stage 3 and 4 documentation (QCA, 2009) identify those that are unique to the subject and those that are shared with other
curriculum subjects. Carry out the same exercise with the aims listed for PE in your
placement school. Discuss your lists with your tutor and put these notes in your
PDP.

There is wide debate about how far PE can achieve both the broader aims of education
as well as the subject-specific aims. As outlined in Chapter 10, it is suggested that while
content tends to focus more on PE-specific aims, the way that teaching is conducted, that
is your teaching approaches, can be instrumental in achieving broader aims. It is recommended that early in your development as a PE teacher the principal aims, objectives and
ILOs for you to focus on should be those that are unique to PE (for example, for pupils
to develop a range of physical skills and succeed in many kinds of physical activity). At
this stage, ILOs for lessons that are concerned with the material of the subject provide a
focus for your early planning, enable you to check that you understand the material you
are teaching and form the criteria against which you judge the success of your lessons
and against which your teaching is judged by others.

It is, however, important to remember that PE can and should, indeed is required
to, in England, contribute to the broader aims of education and as soon as you have
mastered the achievement of the subject-specific aims you should start to address some
of the broader educational aims shared with other curriculum subjects (see Chapter 14
'Wider role of a PE teacher'). While broader educational aims may not be your first
priority in learning to become a PE teacher, there is no doubt that you have a responsibility as a teacher to address overarching educational aims such as Personal Learning and
Thinking Skills as described in Chapter 14. Indeed it is the potential of PE to realise some
of these broader goals that has contributed to PE being retained in the curriculum.
However we are open to the challenge to prove that we can, in fact, deliver these wider
aims, and this must be a serious concern for the profession. There are two important
points to be made here – one reassuring and the other challenging.

It is very good to know, through the work of the QCA in England, that there is
growing evidence that PE can make a significant contribution to broader aims of education, such as developing self-esteem, improving attitudes to learning and behaviour
throughout the school day. You are recommended to visit the QCA website to access this
information (www.qca.org.uk/pess).

However, the challenge with respect to this achievement is that, while we undoubtedly
can be successful here, this only occurs if we tailor our planning and teaching appropriately.
Physical educationalists are sometimes guilty of claiming a great deal for the subject, but
have little evidence that these aspirations have been achieved. Work planned to achieve
subject-specific aims such as skill improvement does *not* automatically deliver broader
aims. The significant variable here is *how* we teach and *how* we engage pupils in their learning. If we claim, for example, to promote self-esteem, foster creativity or develop social
skills, our planning and teaching must be designed with this in mind. For example, a PE
lesson does not promote self-esteem unless tasks that are set are within the grasp of pupils,
and the teacher is positive and encouraging. Again work in dance does not automatically

develop creativity nor does participation in football necessarily improve social skills. For dance to develop creativity pupils must have the necessary movement and choreographic skills and knowledge, and be given time and opportunities in the lesson to experiment and use their imagination. For involvement in football to promote social skills it is essential for teams to plan, compete and evaluate together, with the teacher encouraging exploration and discussion, with everyone in the group included in these debates. See Chapter 10 for further discussion of teaching approaches to achieve aims, objectives and ILOs.

SUMMARY AND KEY POINTS

The aims of education and schooling and more specifically the aims of curriculum subjects, including PE, used in the placement schools in which you work provide guidance about what you are aiming to achieve. In this chapter you have been introduced to the range of aims of PE and alerted to the two different types of aims: those that are unique to PE and those that are broader and are shared with other curriculum subjects. The difference between aims and justifications has been discussed and the importance of your being able to articulate the value of work in PE has been outlined.

The aims of the PE curriculum used in your placement schools should guide your decisions about objectives for units of work, ILOs for lessons, as well as the selection of appropriate content and teaching approaches. Early in your development as a PE teacher the principal ILOs for you to include in your lessons should be those that are unique to PE. At this stage, aims identifying the mastery of physical skills and the effective participation in physical activities provide the focus for your planning, teaching and assessment. As you master the challenge of planning units of work and lessons focused on achieving subject-specific ILOs and as you gain experience and confidence, you can start to address some of the broader aims of the PE curriculum. As explained above, achieving these broader aims depends to a considerable degree on how you teach, that is how you engage pupils in their learning. We suggest that you return to this chapter at different points in your ITE course and consider its content in detail towards the end of your course, when you have mastered the basic teaching skills and can reflect on the aims of PE and what it means to physically educate pupils.

Check the requirements for your course to see which relate to this chapter.

Task 2.8 asks you to critically examine the concept of physical literacy and to write a short piece setting out the benefits or otherwise of adopting the concept of the rationale behind all work in PE

Task 2.8 **Physical literacy and PE**

With reference to the website www.physical-literacy.org.uk and *Physical Literacy Throughout the Lifecourse* (Whitehead, 2010), consider the value or otherwise of adopting this concept as the rationale behind all work in PE throughout the years of schooling, possibly constructing a SWOT grid. This is a square divided into four equal squares, headed Strengths, Weaknesses, Opportunities, Threats (See this book's website for an outline grid; www.routledge.com/textbooks/ 9780415561648). Write a paper of 2,000–3,000 words and discuss this with your tutor. Keep the piece in your PDP.

FURTHER READING

Bailey, R., Armour, K., Kirk, D., Jess, M., Pickup, I. and Sandford, R. (British Educational Research Association (BERA) Physical Education and Sport Pedagogy Special Interest Group) (2008) The educational benefits claimed for physical education and school sport: an academic review, *Research Papers in Education*, 24 (1) March: 1–27.

> This detailed paper looks at the research into the benefits of PE, specifically physical, affective, social and cognitive. The article below is a shorter version on the same theme.

Bailey, R. (2006) Physical education and sport in schools: a review of benefits and outcomes, *Journal of School Health*, 76, 8: 397–401.

> This article explores the scientific evidence that has been gathered on the contributions and benefits of PE and sport in schools for both children and for educational systems.

Capel, S., Breckon, P. and O'Neill, J. (2006) *A Practical Guide to Teaching Physical Education in the Secondary School*, Abingdon, Oxon: Routledge.

> This book contains a useful chapter on aims of PE and some simple observation instruments.

Capel, S. and Piotrowski, S. (eds) (2000) *Issues in Physical Education*, London: RoutledgeFalmer.

> A wide-ranging text which includes a debate on issues surrounding aims of PE. Chapter 1 looks at 'Aims as an issue in PE' and covers topics such as extrinsic versus intrinsic aims and the use of PE as a means to achieve broad aims or as an end in itself.

Whitehead, M.E. (ed.) (2010) *Physical Literacy Throughout the Lifecourse*, London: Routledge.

> This book sets out the background and application of the concept. Further information and papers can be found on the website: www.physical-literacy.org.uk.

3 PLANNING IN PE

Cathy Gower

INTRODUCTION

Effective planning is at the heart of effective learning and teaching. This chapter examines planning in the long- (schemes of work) (pp. 26–27), medium- (units of work) (pp. 27–32) and short-term (lesson plans) (pp. 32–44). In your school experiences you are not normally required to plan for the long-term (i.e. to design schemes of work). Rather, you are expected to plan units of work and lessons within these units which fit into existing schemes of the department. However, when you start teaching you will be expected to be involved in long-term planning. In order to do this you need to understand the construction of schemes of work. Therefore, this chapter is designed to help you to understand the planning processes; it encourages you to consider the whole planning cycle and then aims to enable you to plan units of work and lessons on school experience.

Your planning is based on the curriculum framework in use in schools in which you are learning to teach. In England, this is the National Curriculum (NC) and the National Curriculum for Physical Education (NCPE). These are used in this chapter as illustrations of a particular model of planning. If you are working within a different curriculum framework, replace the NCPE terminology with appropriate terminology/key points from that framework. The model also emphasises the crucial relationship between planning and assessment, in which information gathered from assessment of pupils' learning is evaluated critically to inform future planning, within the current lesson, in future lessons and for units of work.

This chapter focuses on the mechanics of planning. However, it is important that you think critically at all stages of the planning cycle if you are to provide a valuable learning experience for pupils and enable longer term aims to be achieved. Thus, it is important that you understand and critically evaluate the range of factors which influence planning. Some school-based factors which influence planning are included. However, as you develop your ability to plan, it is important that you consider the broader range of personal factors that influence all aspects of planning, such as your values, beliefs and attitudes about PE; to this end, we have included some texts in the further reading at the end of the chapter.

OBJECTIVES

At the end of this chapter you should be able to:

■ understand the relationship between long-, medium- and short-term planning;

■ plan units of work and lessons and understand how schemes of work are constructed;

■ apply a model of planning that enables you to plan effectively for pupils' PE experiences;

■ appreciate that planning is driven by pupils' learning needs;

■ use assessment outcomes to inform the next phase of planning;

■ understand the importance of thinking critically at all stages in the planning process.

Check the requirements for your course to see which relate to this chapter.

INFLUENCES ON PLANNING IN PE

One of the most significant influences on planning in PE is the statutory framework in the particular context in which you are learning to teach. If you are learning to teach in England, this is the NC, first introduced in 1988 and the NCPE, first introduced in 1992, with the most current version being NCPE 2007 (Qualifications and Curriculum Authority (QCA), 2007a) (available at http://curriculum.qca.org.uk/index.aspx). NCPE 2007 is explained in Chapter 15. Since 1992 changes to curriculum requirements in the NCPE have been significant. It is useful to be informed of the debate about, and developments in, the NC since 1988 and the NCPE since 1992 so that you understand the influences of the curriculum framework (see, for example, Murdoch, 1997; 2004 (both of these are available on this book's website: www.routledge.com/textbooks/9780415561648); Penney and Evans, 2000).

In addition to the curriculum framework, there are a number of other possible factors which determine the schemes of work in any one school. These include: teachers' background and experience, including their perceived strengths and weaknesses; history and traditions in relation to what is offered in the curriculum and in extra-curricular activities, which are, in turn, linked to the perceived strengths of staff; and facilities. On a purely practical level in relation to facilities for example, the Office for Standards in Education (Ofsted, 2002a) indicates that, in most schools, the availability of facilities and resources is a significant influence on how the curriculum is planned and delivered. If a school has limited indoor facilities, for example, the activities offered are often dominated by outdoor games, with limited opportunity for activities such as gymnastics and dance. Very few schools have ready access to a swimming pool without the inconvenience of travel and thus swimming is often not included as a part of the planned curriculum experience.

When faced with planning PE learning and teaching experiences for the first time, it is natural to rely on your own previous experiences and the advice and guidance of those you view as more experienced. Whilst it is important to take account of both of these, you should avoid passively planning to match what and how you were taught at school or implementing ideas absorbed from other sources without critiquing their origins and how they relate to your aims, objectives and intended learning outcomes (ILOs). Effective planning requires you to be proactive and both critically aware and evaluative in order to physically educate your pupils, thus moving their learning forward. Pupils' learning and your teaching evolve as a result of critical thought and, as a teacher, you are central to the process of promoting change and development in pupils' learning.

A GENERAL FRAMEWORK FOR PLANNING SCHEMES OF WORK

Although you are unlikely to be involved with writing schemes of work on school experience it is important to understand the broader picture they represent so that you can see where the units of work and lessons you do plan fit in. Schemes of work are long-term curriculum planning documents, which are used to outline expectations for learning across a period of time, for example, a year or a Key Stage (KS). Schemes of work need to take into account the particular circumstances of the school in order to provide a range of opportunities with breadth and balance of experience to enable the requirements of the curriculum framework in which you are working to be met. In England, they should identify which particular activities are being used as the contexts for learning for the five key processes, as well as aspects of learning and teaching which meet the broader aims of the National Curriculum. These broader aims are covered in Chapter 14. Careful attention should be paid to how progression and continuity are planned for across years and within and between KSs. Progression has been defined as: 'The sequence built into children's learning through curriculum policies and schemes of work so that later learning builds on knowledge, skills, understandings and attitudes learned previously' (Department of Education and Science (DES), 1990: 1). Continuity has been defined as: 'The nature of the curriculum experienced by children as they transfer from one setting to another' (DES, 1990: 13). Thus, to achieve progression and continuity, increasing demands and expectation are placed on pupils. These can be broken down into four aspects:

■ a gradual increase in the complexity of the sequence of movement;
■ an improvement in the demonstrated performance qualities;
■ greater independence in the learning context; and
■ a gradual challenge to the level of cognitive skills required.

These can be tracked through assessment of pupils; through the eight level descriptions in the NCPE document (QCA, 2007a). For example, a scheme of work for KS3 needs to be pitched to cover level descriptions 3 to 7, with, for example, expectations that year 7 pupils are working generally between levels 3 and 5, with expected attainment pitched at level 4 (see Chapter 15).

However, there may be some restrictions to be taken into account when planning and designing a scheme of work, including timetabling, the available facilities, staffing and grouping strategies (see above).

Schemes of work include a range of background information, including:

■ Year or KS;
■ Focus of scheme of work;

- Time/number of sessions;
- Aims;
- Activities – to cover the requirements of the NCPE or other curriculum framework into which it fits;
- Resources;
- Outcomes.

Task 3.1 enables you to look in detail at some schemes of work.

Task 3.1 **Schemes of work**

Obtain a copy of the schemes of work for one KS in your placement school. Compare these with those obtained by another student teacher in another school. Discuss with your tutor the coverage of the requirements of the NCPE for this KS.

Store the information in your professional development portfolio (PDP) to refer to when you are developing a unit of work from one scheme of work or, later, when you start your teaching career and you are writing your own schemes of work.

PLANNING UNITS OF WORK

Understanding the mechanics of effective long-term curriculum planning should help you to understand the relationship of long-term planning with medium- and short-term planning of units of work and lessons. Well-planned schemes of work form the basis for planning units of work for particular groups of pupils and individuals; they should be written to meet the needs of a particular group of pupils. Units of work are medium-term plans which should be planned for and, hence, outline expected learning for particular groups of pupils within a year group over a specified period of time. In order to achieve any degree of depth in learning, the Department for Children, Schools and Families (DCSF) (2009) recommend that units of work should be between eight to eighteen hours in duration according to the pupils' stage of development.

Initially, the thought of having to plan a whole unit of work may seem a little daunting. However, if you work to a structure and plan step by step, you should find that it is not as difficult as it might at first seem.

A simple formula for planning might go in this order:

- Who am I teaching? (information about pupils)
- What are the objectives I want the pupils to achieve in the range of curriculum requirements (e.g. in the five key processes)? (These are developed from the aims of the scheme of work into which the unit of work fits)
- What am I teaching? (activity and material)
- How can I teach it? (learning activities, teaching strategies and organisation)

As with schemes of work, before you can begin to plan a unit of work for a specific group you need to record some important basic information, including information about the class you are going to teach – the KS and year group, to ensure appropriate provision (see Figure 3.1).

The needs of the pupils you are teaching are most important in your planning and they must have first consideration; the activity or material you are teaching comes second. Unless planning for the next phase of learning is based on the outcomes of previous assessments of the group, it is difficult to ensure challenge and development through continuity and progression in learning. Assessment information allows you to pitch the learning experiences appropriately and to take account of both whole group and individual learning needs. Thus, you need to record prior learning on the unit of work plan. Information on prior learning should be gathered from a range of sources. If you are teaching the group for the first time you may need to consult existing assessment outcomes from previous units of work to construct an appropriate unit of work. This might be annual reports on the pupils or might be informal records kept by the teacher in their register or teacher planner. Either way, at the very heart of effective planning is taking into account the prior learning and experience of the group with whom you are working to inform planning.

Once you have the information about the pupils and know what the activity is, then you can begin planning by setting your objectives. Throughout each individual unit of work it is important that you plan objectives related to the total requirements of the curriculum framework and do not focus on one (often on developing motor skills). Thus, in England, the objectives should cover all five key processes. By planning the objectives of the unit of work first, you have a good idea what the outcome should be at the end of the unit and think about what you want to achieve through the length of the unit of work. This forms the basis for development over the unit of work. Thus, you start by planning the end first.

The specificity of the objectives in a unit of work and ILOs in lessons (see below) is crucial as they provide criteria for assessing learning. Thus, your use of language in being able to specify expectations for learning is very important in planning in the medium and short term (and later also in the long term). Words such as control, accuracy or fluency (as in the NCPE attainment target (QCA, 2007a)), do not necessarily provide a clear enough set of criteria to help move learning forward. It is important, therefore, that the outcomes include a *verb* and specification of *context* and *quality* to outline expected attainment of the objective, which in turn relate to the specific curriculum requirements. Thus, effective use of language is a skill which you need to develop, and this needs to be based on good subject knowledge (for further information about developing language see Chapter 5).

The *verb* relates directly to the targeted key process, e.g. pupils will be able to: travel (in Developing Skills in Physical Activity); devise (in Making and Applying Decisions); describe (in Evaluating and Improving); select (in Choices About Healthy, Active Lifestyles); motivate (in Developing Physical and Mental Capacities). Verbs themselves might be able to be broken down further, e.g. travel could be jump, hop, skip. The ability to relate verbs to specific key processes should help to identify outcomes for all key processes, rather than focusing on one key process (there is often a focus on developing skills in physical activity, sometimes at the expense of other key processes). This would help to overcome a concern of Ofsted (2002b: 4) that: 'Pupils' skills of observation and evaluation remain relatively weak because pupils are not always given opportunities to develop these aspects.'

When specifying the *context* for learning, the unique context of each activity and the transferability of learning across different activities should both be recognised. Sometimes the objective is specific to an activity, e.g. pupils will be able to: 'respond to different basic rhythmic patterns showing an awareness of beat and pulse', takes account of the uniqueness of the dance context in developing specific aspects of movement to a specific stimulus. On the other hand, sometimes the objective could be applied in a range of activities/contexts, promoting connectivity across different activity contexts, e.g. pupils will be able to: 'devise short phrases of movement which show variation in moments of stillness and fluent movement into and out of held positions'. This could apply to dance, synchronised swimming, gymnastics, for example, and therefore could be used to promote this aspect of performance in all three contexts.

Finally, specific aspects of *quality* in a pupil's response are identified. The meaning of words like control, accuracy and precision need to be clear. Does, for example, control in one context, e.g. gymnastics, equate with control in another, e.g. swimming? Vague use of language can result in a lack of consistency in the assessment of pupil learning, as what one teacher perceives as accuracy may be different to another teacher's perception. A more specific identification of aspects of quality expected from pupils in different activity contexts is needed. For example, pupils will be able to: 'shift the centre of gravity in order to best maintain balance when static or when moving', represents a specific criterion for assessing the ability to demonstrate the expected control in movement at level 4 of the attainment target without limiting the outcome to a specific activity context.

Figure 3.1 is an example of objectives for a unit of work for a year 7 group within the NCPE, using gymnastics as its context for learning and mapping in different aspects of range and content. The objectives are selected from the aims identified for a particular scheme of work, specifically to 'tailor' the unit for a particular group of pupils. Thus, in order to identify objectives for a specific unit of work you would need to refer to the aims of the scheme of work within which you are planning your unit of work.

A unit of work plan also includes information about:

■ the duration of the unit of work;
■ facilities and resources needed to assist in teaching the unit, e.g. use of the sports hall or the need for video/music resources;
■ the specific aspects of language you expect pupils to have acquired by the end of the unit of work;
■ the broader aspects of learning to be addressed as referenced to the NCPE (QCA, 2007a).

These are shown on Figure 3.2.
Now complete Task 3.2.

Task 3.2 **Understanding a unit of work plan**

Complete a unit of work plan, using either the template in Figure 3.2 or one provided by your HEI, for a particular group of pupils you are going to teach in the near future (otherwise for a hypothetical group of pupils). Take account of the information identified above which you need to consider in your planning. Discuss your unit of work plan with your tutor and amend if appropriate. As you teach this unit of work, evaluate it carefully and record in your PDP how you might plan such a unit differently in future.

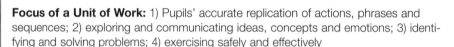

Focus of a Unit of Work: 1) Pupils' accurate replication of actions, phrases and sequences; 2) exploring and communicating ideas, concepts and emotions; 3) identifying and solving problems; 4) exercising safely and effectively

Learning Context: Gymnastics

Duration of Unit of Work: 12 hours

Objectives (grouped under the five key processes in the NCPE in England):
By the end of this unit of work pupils will be able to:

Developing Skills in Physical Activity:
- Demonstrate a range of different body shapes during flight, balance and travel showing clarity of body shape
- Repeat simple footwork patterns in order to take off and land effectively before and after flight
- Shift the centre of gravity in order to best maintain balance when static and when moving
- Perform simple movement patterns and phrases which show effective transitions between different types of movement

Making and Applying Decisions:
- Select the most appropriate body shape in order to control the degree of rotation during flight
- Devise short phrases of movement which show variation in moments of stillness and fluent movement into and out of held positions
- Create short phrases, motifs or sequences of movement which show appropriately selected variations in body shape and use of whole or part body actions according to the context and apply this understanding when refining patterns of movement
- Devise simple phrases, motifs or sequences showing variation in speed, size, level and direction of movements

Evaluating and Improving:
- Describe an observed response or own response to a set task and identify key features within it using a set of specified criteria
- Identify strengths and areas for improvement in the response and communicate these constructively using key words

Choices about Healthy, Active Lifestyles and Developing Physical and Mental Capacities
- Choose and use a range of conditioning exercises to develop muscular strength and flexibility
- Demonstrate the self-motivation and application to complete the processes of designing and performing a sequence of movement which shows flexibility and muscular strength
- Adopt appropriate posture and understand its importance for maintaining a healthy back

■ **Figure 3.1** Examples of aspects of key processes that could feature as objectives in a unit of work for KS3 pupils

UNIT OF WORK

TARGETED ASPECTS OF RANGE AND CONTENT:	SELECTED ACTIVITY/ACTIVITIES:
KEY STAGE AND YEAR GROUP:	DURATION:
RESOURCES:	LANGUAGE FOR LEARNING:
PRIOR LEARNING:	NC BIG PICTURE LINKS:

INTENDED LEARNING OUTCOMES	LEARNING ACTIVITIES	TEACHING AND LEARNING STYLES AND STRATEGIES
DEVELOPING SKILLS IN PHYSICAL ACTIVITY (SPA)		
MAKING AND APPLYING DECISIONS (MAD)		
DEVELOPING PHYSICAL AND MENTAL CAPACITY (PMC)		
EVALUATING AND IMPROVING (EI)		
MAKING INFORMED CHOICES ABOUT HEALTHY AND ACTIVE LIFESTYLES (CHAL)		

■ **Figure 3.2** Template for a unit of work plan (based on the requirements for the NCPE)

PLANNING LESSONS

Units of work are devised to meet the identified needs of a group of pupils using the departmental schemes of work, and in turn they are the basis for lesson planning, the next stage in the planning cycle. The unit of work plan should be seen as an outline, or framework, for supporting lesson planning, rather than pre-determining the outcomes and content of each lesson. The detailed planning occurs each week in the lesson plan. Lesson plans focus on the short-term learning needs of pupils. In order to impact on the quality of pupil learning in PE you need to use assessment outcomes to think critically about the quality of learning in one lesson to inform planning of the next. This requires that, if genuine progress is to be made, you assess pupils' learning on an ongoing basis to inform the planning of your next lesson. This may result in adaptations to the unit of work and individual lessons as the unit progresses.

Having an initial overview of where pupils are in terms of their learning, where you want them to be at the end of a unit of work and how they are going to get there is an important starting point for planning a sequence of lessons in a unit of work. It is important that you do not devise a unit of work outline which identifies content and ILOs in a lesson-by-lesson format and then follow this each week with your different groups, moving on to the next lesson specified in a unit of work regardless of what has or has not been learnt or whether the ILOs of the previous lesson were achieved. Such an approach means that you are tempted to follow your plan irrespective of pupil response. Rather, as the sequence of lessons progresses, you use your unit of work to map whether you are on target to meet your initial expectations for the group or whether you need to adjust these expectations as a result of the ongoing response of the group. At times you have to deviate from your original unit of work plan.

An outline of a lesson plan is included in Figure 3.3. Although this model is used in this chapter, it is just one way of writing lesson plans. Your HEI may provide a different format, in which case you should use that. Whichever format you use, it is quite likely that you will be required to think through and plan using a series of headings similar to those in the plan used in this chapter.

Each lesson plan is written for a specific group of pupils with a particular focus for learning, taken from the unit of work. Thus, the lesson plan requires you first to complete background information about:

- the year group/KS of pupils;
- the content/activity;
- the number of the lesson in the sequence of lessons in the unit;
- the time available for the lesson;
- the working area;
- the number of pupils in the lesson; and
- the equipment required.

Practical considerations such as ensuring that the facilities and equipment you are planning for are available are very important at the planning stage. This includes taking account of, for example, the number of pupils in the group and the number of mats available to use in a particular lesson.

Once you have planned these important considerations you can then decide how you are going to achieve the focus for learning in the particular lesson and build your plan around it. At this stage it is important to take into account the action points you have

LESSON PLAN

DATE	YEAR GROUP/ KS	RANGE AND CONTENT/ ACTIVITY	LESSON IN UNIT	TIME	WORKING AREA	NO. GIRLS/BOYS	EQUIPMENT REQUIRED

ACTION POINTS FROM ASSESSMENT OF WHOLE CLASS LEARNING LAST LESSON
ACTION POINTS FROM ASSESSMENT OF SAMPLE OF PUPILS' LEARNING LAST LESSON

NCPE KEY PROCESSES	KEY WORDS FOR THIS WEEK'S ILOS – REFER TO LAST WEEK'S ASSESSMENT DATA AND USE THESE TO INFORM YOUR ILOS IN THE SECTION BELOW AND YOUR LPS INSIDE THIS PLAN	NAME OF PUPIL	DIFFERENTIATION REQUIRED FOR THIS LESSON – REFER TO LAST WEEK'S ASSESSMENT DATA AND USE TO INFORM DIFFERENTIATED LEARNING ACTIVITIES COLUMN INSIDE PLAN

SPECIFIC AND ASSESSABLE INTENDED LEARNING OUTOMES – CROSS REFERENCE THESE TO YOUR UNIT ILOS, NUMBER AND ANNOTATE AGAINST YOUR SELECTED NCPE KEY PROCESSES FOR THIS LESSON AND WRITE AS 'VERB, CONTEXT, QUALITY'

By the end of this lesson pupils will be able to:

NUMBER	PROCESS

Figure 3.3 Template for a lesson plan

Time	ILOs	Whole Class Learning Activities	Differentiated Learning Activities for Individuals and/or Ability Groups	Learning Points – ensure these address processes identified in the lesson ILOs	Organisation of Pupils, Equipment, Resources and Space	Teaching Styles and Strategies

■ **Figure 3.3** Template for a lesson plan (continued)

ASSESSMENT OF WHOLE CLASS LEARNING

ILO NO. AND KEY PROCESS																
KEY WORDS FROM THIS LESSON'S ILOS AND LPS																
ASSESSMENT OF WHOLE CLASS LEARNING USING ABOVE KEY WORDS FROM THIS LESSON'S ILOS AND LPS																

ABILITY GROUP	WT	ACH	WB	WT	ACH	WB	WT	ACH	WB	WT	ACH	WB	WT	ACH	WB
APPROX % OF PUPILS															
KEY WORDS FOR NEXT LESSON'S ILOS															

ASSESSMENT OF LEARNING AGAINST ILOS FOR IDENTIFIED SAMPLE OF PUPILS

PUPIL NAME	ILO 1	ILO 2	ILO 3	ILO 4	ILO 5	ASSESSMENT OF PUPIL LEARNING USING IDENTIFIED KEY WORDS FOR THIS LESSON	ACTION POINTS FOR LEARNING IN NEXT LESSON. USE TO INFORM NEXT LESSON'S DIFFERENTIATION

EVALUATION OF YOUR OWN LEARNING

WT = working towards; ACH = achieving; WB = working beyond

■ **Figure 3.3** Template for a lesson plan (continued)

identified from assessment of whole class learning and from assessment of a sample of pupils' learning in the last lesson, or from other sources if this is the first time you have taught the class. This ensures that you plan one lesson based on the outcomes of, and learning from, the previous lesson – using the crucial link between planning and assessment of, and for, learning (see assessment in Chapter 8).

Just as objectives are identified for units of work, ILOs need to be specified for all lessons. The selected ILOs for a lesson should relate back to the objectives for the unit of work. Ideally, an effectively planned unit of work helps you to establish the focus and level for these. ILOs for lessons should be pitched to meet the needs of the majority of pupils within the group, identified from prior assessment outcomes. Thus, your specific ILOs for the lesson build specifically from the previous lesson. As with objectives for units of work, these outcomes are clearly specified using *verb*, *context* and *quality* (see above), should represent learning across the NCPE key processes and also provide pupils with opportunities to demonstrate broader aspects of learning from the NC (see Chapter 14).

Below is an example of how an ILO for *making and applying decisions* in a lesson using the verb, context, quality framework relates directly to the exemplar unit of work provided in Figure 3.1 above.

■ *Unit objective: devise short phrases of movement which show variation in moments of stillness and fluent movement into and out of held positions.*
■ *Related lesson ILO: compose a short individual phrase of movement into and out of an inverted balance using rolling actions demonstrating that the end of one movement becomes the beginning of the next.*

Now complete Task 3.3

Task 3.3 **Devising lesson ILOs**

Observe a PE lesson taught by an experienced PE teacher. Write down what you think the ILOs of the lesson are. Afterwards, discuss with the teacher:

■ the planned ILOs and those which you identified to see if you are in agreement;
■ whether you think the ILOs (both yours and the teachers, if they were different) were achieved in the lesson; and
■ how the lesson ILOs relate to the overall unit of work objectives.

Store this in your PDP to reflect on when you write your own ILOs.

Be careful that your lesson plans do not include a predominance of ILOs and, hence, activities for developing skills in physical activity but few relating to any of the other key processes in the NCPE. There should be ILOs and activities for all key processes over the course of a unit of work. ILOs for all key processes not only help you to think more broadly than developing skills; if you do not plan for the key aspects in your ILOs and activities, they are unlikely to be included in a lesson and, therefore, key aspects of learning are omitted. Sometimes assumptions are made, for example, that pupils are able to evaluate and improve effectively. Thus, it is unlikely that ILOs for evaluating and improving the work of a peer are achieved if there are no learning activities to ensure that pupils are, for example, taught to stand in the right place to observe, use a set of criteria to observe against, analyse response using these criteria, use appropriate technical language to feedback and to be constructive in their feedback by identifying strengths as well as areas for development. Pupils need to learn how to evaluate and improve; this does not just happen. You, therefore, need to plan how pupils are going to learn this. However, even ILOs and activities for developing skills can be superficial if careful attention is not given to them. ILOs and activities should specify what you want to see in the response and how you expect it to be demonstrated, but also should prompt you, and subsequently the learner, to consider why a skill is performed in such a way and possibly when and where it is most appropriate to use such a skill. For example, you should articulate why the side-on body position opens up the body to release the arm as a lever to vary the level of weight and power behind a throw and not just state that you want to see a side-on body position to throw an implement. By doing this you are also enabling pupils to develop transferable knowledge, skills and understanding to help them make connections across activities.

In planning a lesson, by setting ILOs first, you have begun planning what you hope to achieve at the end of the lesson first (as with setting unit of work objectives first – see above). This is vital in keeping you on course and ensuring that you and your pupils can see a purpose to each task. Having decided on your ILOs, next you need to look at how you can begin to achieve them. Where do you start? What would be the most appropriate way? What do you want to achieve initially? These are questions which you need to ask yourself at this stage. The second stage of planning is, therefore, to go to the beginning and plan the specific content of the lesson. However, you may also want to plan this backwards. For example, if you have an ILO for pupils to compose a short individual phrase of movement into and out of an inverted balance using rolling actions demonstrating that the end of one movement becomes the beginning of the next, the first question might be what shorter sequences might they put together to be able to build up to the longer sequence? The next question might be what learning activities will help pupils learn the individual skills (balance, roll, travel), a range of ways of linking these and the creativity to develop an individual sequence. Likewise, if you have an ILO for pupils to be able to outwit an opponent in a game of 5 v 5 hockey, a question you may ask is: what smaller side game experience would be helpful for them to experience first? e.g. outwitting an opponent in a 2 v 2 situation. The next question might be what skill(s) do they need to master to work effectively in the 2 v 2 situation? e.g. being able to send and receive from both right and left. A final question might be how can I use the introductory warm-up activity to prepare the pupils for the skills I am to work on? Many PE lessons are broken down into three parts: introduction and warm-up; main part; conclusion.

Although the first teaching part of the lesson is the introduction and warm-up, the lesson actually begins at the moment the bell goes. It is important, therefore, that you plan for what happens before you begin teaching. The beginning and end of lessons, especially in PE, can eat into a large amount of lesson time. You must organise and manage the pupils getting changed and into the teaching space as quickly as possible so that you can begin your lesson promptly. If the lesson is 35 minutes long, you could finish up with only 15–20 minutes of teaching, so it is essential that as little time as possible is wasted. You need to plan the time in the changing room and when pupils first enter the working space in order to maximise learning opportunities. You can save a lot of time in the first part of the lesson by planning to use tasks which serve as a warm-up but also involve the practice and development of the topic. The introduction and warm-up can be shortened or extended according to the total length of time available (Chapter 6 covers organisation and management in more detail).

Introduction and warm-up

This part of the lesson might start with a brief verbal introduction. Perhaps you could remind pupils of work covered in the previous lesson, explain the ILOs and/or the topic or theme for this lesson or just set up the first task and identify key words pupils will be using during the lesson to support learning. You need to tune-in the pupils to the topic or theme of the lesson. With this in mind, select material for this early part of the lesson which has a bearing on what is to follow; perhaps the warm-up can embed movement patterns which pupils will use later on in the lesson within a particular activity. This not only emphasises what is being covered but it also helps you to give pupils the right sort of preparation and practice. In any case, keep your talk to a minimum at this stage in order that pupils can be involved immediately in activity, especially if it is a cold day. The initial warm-up task needs to be of an aerobic nature to increase the heart and lung rate and begin to warm the pupils.

Main part

This part of the lesson is probably the most important because it is the development of the topic or theme and should help to promote pupil understanding. It forms the major part of the lesson, both in time and work covered. It is generally the part of the lesson in which pupils are introduced to new skills, revise and practice old skills or are given the opportunity to practice and improve a whole activity. However, the structure can take a number of forms, depending on the focus of the lesson. The lesson may, for example, focus on making and applying decisions or evaluating and improving activities. It may include the practice of a particular skill(s) associated with an activity or may be practising the whole activity (e.g. a whole game in order to understand the links between technical and tactical response). It may be piecing together a dance, with pupils developing and practising their dance to show at the end of the lesson (for which time must be given). It may, for example, follow a whole-part-whole approach whereby the whole activity is tried, and then it is broken down into parts before the whole activity is tried again. As well as the focus of the lesson, the actual structure depends on the length of time of the lesson (see also time below). For example, if you have a very short gymnastics lesson, you might only be able to complete a floor work session as there is not time to get apparatus out. Alternatively though, in another short lesson, perhaps the following one, you might spend all the time doing apparatus work. In a longer lesson both floor work and apparatus work may be covered.

Conclusion

This is a very small part of the lesson in terms of time, perhaps only a few minutes, but an extremely important part for a number of reasons and needs to be built into the lesson plan. You must allow for this part of the lesson in your overall plan. You must allow time to recap on what has been covered and what learning has taken place, returning, for example, to the key words that pupils have learned to consolidate their learning and give time for a calm, orderly and purposeful conclusion. Also, make sure that you finish your lesson on time, so that pupils are not late for their next lesson.

Most of your lesson time should be given to learning activities in the main part of the three-part structure. You need to plan the time to be given to each learning activity/part of the lesson. The 'teaching time' of the lesson (that is the amount of time you actually have on the field or in the gymnasium) determines the overall structure, and the length of time given to each part.

The main body of the lesson plan in Figure 3.3 has been set out in seven columns, under the headings of:

■ time;
■ ILO to be achieved in this part of the lesson;
■ whole class learning activities to achieve the ILO;
■ differentiated learning activities to achieve the ILO;
■ learning points (some HEIs use the term teaching points instead of learning points);
■ organisation of pupils, space, equipment and resources;
■ learning and teaching strategies.

This seven-column plan is a useful method of helping you to think through in detail your planning and preparation. It focuses on each aspect of the lesson so that you can prepare yourself carefully with regard to the ILOs. It focuses you on pupils' learning but also ensures that you plan carefully the content/material you plan to teach, the relevant learning points, as well as learning and teaching strategies and the various organisational points of space, equipment and pupil groupings in order to achieve the ILOs. By reading across the seven columns of the lesson plan, you can see a logical link between all these aspects of the lesson.

Writing down a time allocation at the side of each activity/part of your lesson plan may help you to keep within certain time limits, but you must allow for some deviation and be prepared, if necessary, to change the time allocated to each activity/part as you go through the lesson according to your observations of pupils' responses. Think about the following suggestions which also help to save time, but ensure that you still achieve quality in your teaching. Can you:

■ Simplify the game (for example, smaller numbers, fewer rules, less complex to set up)?
■ Shorten the sequence (for example, fewer moves or skills required)?
■ Show half a class at a time instead of many groups (and focus the observation)?
■ Cut down on your instructions (keep explanations concise) (see also Chapter 5)?
■ Keep up the pace of your teaching (be brisk and avoid any time-wasting) (see also Chapter 7)?

Now complete Task 3.4

Task 3.4 **Managing lesson time**

Observe a lesson taught by an experienced PE teacher. Make a note of the amount of time given to each learning activity. Then plan a lesson for an activity and group of your choice, allowing for 40 minutes of teaching time. Apportion the time as you think most appropriate. If you get an opportunity, try out the plan with a class and evaluate it in terms of time allocation. Store the plan and evaluation in your PDP to refer to, as appropriate, in future planning.

Learning activities should be selected to enable specific ILOs to be achieved. These should be pitched to meet the learning needs of the majority of pupils within the group. If the ILOs reflect learning across the NCPE key processes and broader aspects of learning, the learning activities should do so as well. Therefore, you should build into your lesson planning a process of cross mapping the selected ILOs to the learning activities. For example, below is a lesson ILO for evaluating and improving and the development of communication as a key skill:

■ *Observe a pair motif and provide feedback on how changes in level and pathway are utilised using key words, identifying strengths in response first followed by areas for development.*

This requires pupils to engage in at least one learning activity in which they have the opportunity to observe and analyse performance. To achieve this learning activity, therefore, pupils need to be provided with specified key words that form criteria with which to analyse the response and to understand how to structure feedback, working on their communication skills. This might involve the pupils working in threes, a pair performing the motif while one pupil observes using key words written on to a worksheet or a whiteboard.

You should also consider how you are going to differentiate the learning activities to meet the needs of different groups of pupils, including those pupils who are achieving at levels above or below the majority of the group. You can differentiate in many different ways, for example:

■ increasing or decreasing the complexity of the sequence of movement they are performing;
■ adapting or changing the working space, equipment or resources in some way;
■ altering the way in which you are grouping the pupils;
■ adjusting your use of language to the needs of the pupils by, for example, changing the nature of your questioning techniques or supporting spoken language with visual stimuli.

Approaches to differentiation can be by task set (different tasks are set), by the outcome (pupils undertake the same task but different levels of outcome are expected), by assessment (pupils undertake the same tasks but are assessed differently), by approach (some pupils respond better to, for example, a didactic approach whilst you are trying to develop the independence of others).

After you have identified and carefully selected your lesson ILOs and activities and planned the time for each one, you should be planning the detail of making these work. This includes how you are going to organise and manage the pupils, space, equipment and resources to make maximum use of the time available, and taking account of safety factors right from your first point of contact with the pupils. Planning of organisation and management should focus on the whole lesson, but particular attention should be paid to planning transition phases – how pupils move from one task into another. (Organisation and management is covered in Chapter 6 and safety in Chapter 9.) You also need to plan the learning and teaching strategies. You should also cross-reference with your ILOs and learning activities to ensure that they enable the ILOs to be achieved (selecting appropriate teaching strategies is covered in Chapter 10).

Once you have planned a progressive sequence of learning activities and appropriate teaching strategies and how these are to be organised to support pupil attainment against your ILOs, you need to consider and plan a set of specific criteria to help you assess whether the ILOs have been met during and after the lesson. Learning points (for each of the key processes) enable you to observe, analyse and provide feedback formatively during the lesson as well as summatively against the achievement of the ILOs. Many student teachers find it easiest to identify learning points for how a skill should be performed, but not always why, where and when. They find it more difficult to identify learning points for making and applying decisions and evaluating and improving. Thus, particular attention must be given to planning learning points for those key processes.

Tasks 3.5, 3.6 and 3.7 are designed to help you make sense of the various aspects of lesson planning by working through these in relation to one of your own lessons.

ASSESSING AND EVALUATING YOUR LESSONS

You have identified in your ILOs, learning activities and learning points, criteria for assessment for and of learning (see Chapter 8). You can plan opportunities during the lesson to enable you to utilise the criteria, for example, in a small sided game take time to stand back and observe and analyse the response. The outcome enables you to adapt the next part of the lesson according to pupils' response and progress in the lesson. This requires you to be flexible and to deviate from your lesson plan if needed.

Likewise, you can use the criteria for assessment to evaluate the lesson after you have taught it. Before you can begin to think about planning the next lesson, you need to use information from lesson assessment to evaluate the effectiveness of the lesson in terms of both what pupils learnt and the quality of pupils' learning. Assessment of the quality of learning is broken down into assessment of whole group and individual pupil learning. You can analyse the quality of response across the whole group, estimating how many pupils have achieved the ILOs, how many are still working towards them, and how many are working beyond them. If a low percentage of pupils achieve the expected attainment in one ILO, that tells you that you need to revisit this for the whole group in your ILOs next week. If a high percentage of pupils achieved the expected ILO, you can move the group on to a more challenging aspect of learning. However, you have to consider not only whether the ILOs of the lesson were achieved, but also whether the expected attainment was pitched appropriately in the first place, i.e. whether they were, in fact, realistic and appropriate. The lesson plan outline also encourages you to select a sample of pupils (e.g. a range of ability or gender) within the group to assess against the ILOs. This should help you to plan differentiated tasks for the next phase of learning, within the lesson or in the next lesson. These tasks should be pitched to meet the needs of individuals or the groups that these individuals are representing as part of your whole class planning and to adjust your teaching strategies to meet the needs of the group. This is essential if pupils are to make progress.

Assessment of pupil learning should also prompt you to evaluate the effectiveness of your teaching and what you as the teacher learnt from teaching the lesson. Evaluation of teaching must be informed by assessment of pupil learning if it is to be at all meaningful and impact upon the quality of response by both the learner and the teacher. Knowledge and understanding of learners' responses should help to adapt and change many aspects of your teaching. Therefore, planning structures should prompt you to assess pupil learning and use this information to reflect critically on how to

Task 3.5 **Lesson planning**

Take one of your lesson plans and use this monitoring sheet to check that you are taking account of the following considerations in planning your lessons.

Discuss with your tutor and identify areas of strength and areas for development in your planning. Store this in your PDP and complete on future occasions to help you understand how your planning is developing.

Activity and group .... Lesson in unit .... Date	
Aspect of Planning	**Comment**
ILOs are both specific and assessable. They are written in terms of what pupils will **learn** rather than what you will **do** or what you will teach and include **verb**, **context** and **quality**	
ILOs relate to the unit of work objectives and do not just include developing skills in physical activity but map across all NCPE key processes	
Key words are identified from the ILOs for this lesson and they have been informed by assessment outcomes from the previous lesson	
Action points are included for a sample of pupils	
Learning activities are differentiated – for individuals and/or groups	
Learning points are 'bullet pointed' and relate to what you expect to observe. These should also represent all the NCPE key processes identified in the ILOs	
Full consideration has been given to organisation and management of pupils, space, equipment and resources, including transitions, taking account of safety factors	
Comments and targets for future lesson planning	

Task 3.6 **Structuring lessons**

Write out two *different* but *consecutive* lesson plans for short lessons of gymnastics (maximum teaching time 25 minutes), one of which must include apparatus work (some suggested plans for the lay-out of apparatus are included on this book's website: (www.routledge.com/textbooks/9780415561648). Discuss the plans with your tutor and evaluate the feasibility of each one. Include the plan and evaluations in your PDP for reference in future planning.

Task 3.7 **Planning progressions**

Select one particular ILO for a lesson you are planning to teach and think out three stages of practice (progressions) which would help a beginner pupil to build up to the outcome. Try these practices out yourself and ask another student teacher to observe. Decide between you whether the progressions are logical, but also how you could adapt the practices to make them easier or harder for pupils of varying abilities. Try these out in a teaching situation. Record your progressions and adaptations in your PDP and refer to them to inform planning of other progressions.

improve pupil learning and also your approaches to teaching. In any evaluation all the questions are focused around one important factor and that is 'what did the pupils achieve?'

The different aspects of a lesson evaluation can be summarised in three questions:

1   *What* did the pupils achieve/learn or not achieve/learn?
2   *Why* did they achieve/learn or not achieve/learn. In other words why did this learning take place/not take place? What aspects of my planning/teaching were effective/less effective, e.g. was it too difficult, was there not enough time etc.?
3   *How* should I plan/teach in the next lesson to accommodate these findings? What do I continue to do next time or what do I need to do differently to promote learning, e.g. differentiate more/better, provide more specific feedback etc.?

The lesson plan in this chapter requires you to assess whole class and individual pupil's learning before evaluating your own teaching. If you structure your evaluation under the three headings:

■   assessment of whole class learning;
■   assessment of learning for identified sample of pupils;
■   evaluation of your learning,

you can begin to be quite critical in your analysis of the lesson of what the pupils achieved and how this matched up with the ILOs, but also the effectiveness of the lesson.

In addition to evaluating whether the ILOs were achieved, there are many aspects of your lessons on which you can focus in evaluation. At the beginning of your school experiences these might focus, for example, on your organisation and management, on your voice, on whether you planned the right amount of material for the length of the lesson or how you responded to pupil behaviour. As you gain experience, the focus of the evaluation should change. You cannot consider too many foci in one lesson, therefore you may want to focus some evaluations on selected aspects of the lesson. The aspects on which you focus may be the result of, for example, previous observations or evaluations. You must also consider how you can address any issues or areas for development in the evaluation and try to put this into practice in future lessons. This is prompted on the lesson plan by identifying action points for the next lesson.

You will find it helpful to evaluate the lesson and write down comments about it as soon as possible after you have taught it. This makes it easier to clarify your thoughts whilst they are still fresh in your mind and allows you to reflect on what happened in that particular lesson (especially if you have to teach a similar lesson to a different class on another day).

The information you gather when completing assessment of pupils' learning and evaluations of their learning and your teaching can feed into assessment of pupils over a unit of work. This system should allow you to plan for the next unit of work. This reflects the cyclical nature of planning – teaching – assessing and evaluating. Task 3.8 is designed to help you with evaluating lessons.

Task 3.8 **Evaluating lessons**

Following one of your lessons (possibly the one used in Task 3.5) use this monitoring sheet to evaluate the lesson.

Discuss with your tutor and identify areas of strength and areas for development in your evaluation. Store in your PDP to refer to when working on developing your ability to evaluate lessons.

Aspect of evaluation	Comment
What did the pupils achieve/learn or not achieve/learn?	
Why did they achieve/learn or not achieve/learn?	
What do I continue to do next time or what do I need to do differently to promote learning?	
Comments and targets for future lesson planning	

SUMMARY AND KEY POINTS

Planning is at the heart of what it means to be a professional. It is crucial that you recognise that taking ownership of this process, valuing it and understanding how it impacts on pupils' experiences in school can help to drive forward pupils' learning and your own teaching. This chapter has provided a model for planning in PE which takes you through the processes of long-, medium- and short-term planning in PE. The chapter worked through practical examples of planning units of work and lesson plans. Closely aligned with the need to plan effectively is the need to assess against ILOs. The chapter highlighted how information gathered about how ILOs have been met can be used to plan the next phase of learning and to evaluate the effectiveness of your approaches to teaching. The model illustrates how this cyclical process can be organised. However, at the heart of this chapter is a prompt for you to think critically about your planning and not to repeat practice you experience or copy current practice without questioning it.

Check which requirements for your course you have addressed through this chapter.

FURTHER READING

Capel, S., Breckon, P. and O'Neill, J. (2006) *A Practical Guide to Teaching Physical Education in the Secondary School*, **London: Routledge.**

This book contains four chapters which cover planning (Chapter 5: Long-term planning of the physical education curriculum; Chapter 6: Medium- and short-term planning on physical education; and two chapters on planning for broader dimensions of pupils' learning: Chapter 7 focuses on citizenship, social, moral, spiritual, cultural and personal development; and Chapter 8 focuses on key skills and the use of information and communications technology). It would be useful to complete activities 5.3, 5.5, 5.7, 6.3, 6.4, 6.9, 6.10.

Cohen, L., Manion, L. and Morrison, K. (2004) *A Guide to Teaching Practice*, **5th edn, London: Routledge.**

This book focuses on important basic skills you need to develop for learning to teach. It includes a section on planning.

Kerry, T. (2004) *Learning Objectives, Task Setting and Differentiation*, **Cheltenham: Nelson Thornes.**

This book should help you to design effective learning objectives, then to focus on setting tasks and differentiation in relation to these identified objectives.

OBSERVATION OF PUPILS IN PE

Elizabeth Marsden

INTRODUCTION

'Observe the children. Analyse their movement. Make a decision whether to change the task, provide a cue, offer a challenge or provide feedback. Seems easy.' Graham (2008) reported hearing this from student PE teachers before their first school experience. But he, along with all effective PE teachers, knows the fallacy of that belief: observation is certainly *not* easy. Observation is more than just looking; it involves preparation and good movement knowledge; focus and attention to individuals, small groups and whole classes; recording and reporting strategies and a willingness to use this information to inform future teaching. It is a skill that improves with time and practice once you have a grasp of why you are observing, what you are observing and how you are observing. In order to promote learning, you must strive to become a perceptive observer of human movement. This chapter gives you guidelines, strategies and challenges to help you to develop your observation skills, both within the National Curriculum for Physical Education (NCPE) (Department for Education and Skills (DfES), QCA, 2007a) and in respect of teaching classroom-based work in General Certificate of Secondary Education (GCSE) and General Certificate of Education Advanced (A) Level.

OBJECTIVES

At the end of this chapter you should be able to:

- understand why you are observing;
- identify aspects of teaching in which good observation is essential;
- be aware of the knowledge base you need in order to observe, analyse and reflect on human movement successfully;
- choose an observation strategy appropriate for a specific focus;
- use observation as part of classroom-based action research.

In short, you should understand why you observe, what you are observing and how you can observe. Check the requirements for your course to see which relate to this chapter.

WHY ARE OBSERVATION SKILLS IMPORTANT FOR THE PE TEACHER?

Observation skills are needed to support class management, to ensure pupil safety at all times and to monitor whole class and individual pupil's work, thus being able to provide feedback to promote their learning. In addition, observation enables you to gather information as to the effectiveness of your teaching and to learn from watching experienced teachers at work. Developing your observation skills also helps you to support pupils in their development of observation and to provide information that needs to be recorded for the completion of pupil records and reports.

Class management and safety in the working environment

Organisation and management are fundamental skills you need as a PE teacher. It is essential that at all times you are alert to pupil activity in respect of on task and off task behaviour and to all aspects of safety. Organisation and management and managing pupil behaviour is covered in Chapter 6, while the focus of Chapter 9 is safety. Perceptive observation enables you to pick up potential areas of concern before they become significant problems. This is particularly important in respect of safety. As a teacher, you are responsible for the well-being of your class at all times. This means that you are not only concerned with their learning but also their physical and emotional safety. This is especially challenging for you as your teaching environment is large and possibly changing, for example in outdoor lessons, in inclement weather, in situations where pupils are moving in many directions and at varying speeds and in your use of potentially dangerous apparatus and equipment. These facts alone should motivate you to become a keen observer. Figure 4.1 depicts a situation you should avoid at all costs!

"NEW FANGLED COURSES! OBSERVATION TRAINING? RUBBISH!.."

■ **Figure 4.1** Chaos rules OK?

Monitoring learning and providing feedback

As learning is the focus of your attention, an ability to see whether learning is taking place or not is obviously critical. If you are unable to observe and analyse what is actually happening in the lesson, you cannot know whether the intended learning outcomes (ILOs) are being achieved by one pupil, a small group, the whole class or no one at all; nor can you assess whether the lesson is too challenging or too simple, or be able to offer any advice for improving movement or motor skills. You need to be able to tell whether the class is just being kept 'busy, happy and good' (Placek, 1983) rather than applying themselves to the set task. Experienced teachers are constantly reading non-verbal messages that pupils are intentionally or non-intentionally communicating. Teachers take in this information and make on-the-spot adjustments to their lessons.

Observation is a very challenging skill as it is difficult to try to remember everything you are observing if you are also teaching at the same time. Many PE teachers find the use of stick-it pads invaluable. As they see something, they make a note on the paper and then stick it on the wall. Each note can then be retrieved at the end of the lesson. The use of a camcorder is often most helpful at the beginning of a teacher's career as, unlike other subjects, there are no pupil workbooks to collect after the lesson so that you can see if the pupils understood and achieved the correct ILOs. Once a movement has been completed, it disappears from view. If you do decide to use a camcorder then you need to check the policy on its use in the school.

Observation to provide feedback on own teaching

A very important contribution that observation makes to your teaching is to give you feedback on the appropriateness of your planning and the effectiveness of your delivery in the lesson. Observing the class can give you information about your organisational planning, your selection of material and your management of pupil behaviour.

For example, you have planned to organise the space in a particular way and to use certain apparatus or equipment. If you see pupils are struggling you need to ask yourself why. Have they enough space in which to work? Is the equipment the wrong size or not working properly? Do pupils know how to use it or are they afraid of it? Is there enough equipment? Can all the pupils hear you? Are they too hot or too cold? Observation should give you answers. All of these situations are potentially frustrating and may lead to off task and possibly disruptive behaviour.

Looking at the material you have planned you may need to ask yourself if pupils are having difficulties because the task set is too easy or too difficult, because they have not understood the task or because they are uncertain about the way in which they are to be involved in their own learning, for example peer assessment or problem solving. With respect to behaviour management your observation can pick up whether appropriate rules and routines have been established and standards of behaviour have been clearly set out and are being adhered to (see Chapter 6 for discussion of rules and routines).

By 'reading' the class in these ways you can pick up how effective your teaching is and, of course, what you can do in the lesson to improve the situation. However, critically important is that you record the observations in your lesson evaluation (see Chapters 3 and 8). Constructive self-criticism is the platform from which improvement takes place. Observation provides you with the information for this development. In the short term the improvement might be in planning the next lesson, ensuring that the same problems or difficulties do not arise again. Your lesson evaluation is one way that observation generates written information.

Observation to learn from experienced teachers

One way of becoming more aware of the nature and constituents of teaching is to observe experienced teachers at work (see also Chapter 17). It is useful both to observe different teachers and to observe the teaching of different aspects of PE. Of course, in all cases you need to ask permission of the teacher you hope to observe. It is quite likely that this teacher may ask you what aspect of his/her teaching you are particularly interested in observing. For example, you may want to observe organisation, management of pupil behaviour, task setting or responding to pupils' progress or problems. In all cases, it is useful to ask to have a copy of the lesson plan, both to see how the teacher achieves the ILOs and how the plan needs to be modified in the light of pupils' response. There are a number of observation instruments that you can use to observe teaching. These are discussed in Chapter 17 and examples can be found in Activity 4.3c in Capel, Breckon and O'Neill (2006) and on this book's website (www.routledge.com/textbooks/9780415561648). It is useful to discuss your observations with the teacher after the lesson (remember to thank the teacher for allowing you to watch the lesson). Task 4.1 encourages you to observe how experienced teachers manage lessons.

Task 4.1 **Observing experienced teachers**

Observe three experienced teachers and for each lesson record one or two of the following aspects of the teacher's work. Prepare for this observation by familiarising yourself with the teacher's ILOs and then note how the teacher:

■ constantly checks for the safety of the environment;
■ organises space/groups/equipment/apparatus;
■ checks that pupils have achieved success before moving on to new tasks;
■ encourages individuals to improve their movement vocabulary and motor skills;
■ maintains a happy, purposeful and confident atmosphere throughout the lesson.

This task can be undertaken observing other aspects of teaching. Discuss your observations with the teacher and put these notes in your professional development profile (PDP). When you feel ready ask the teacher to conduct the same observation on your teaching.

Supporting pupils in observing and evaluating in PE

Once you have mastered observation the next step is to help pupils acquire this skill. In England there is a requirement in the PE curriculum that pupils learn to analyse movement, and are able to identify strengths and weakness and to plan ahead how to improve performances. This ability, the assessment aspect of which is covered in Chapter 8, depends on pupils developing good observation skills. Pupils need to be able to use observation to analyse the performances of others and also, via use of video recording, their own movement. (See Chapter 12 on the use of information and communications technology (ICT) in PE.) Teachers very often introduce observation skills as part of demonstrations when they ask the class to look particularly at one specific aspect of the performance being shown. A direct development of this is to ask pupils to carry our peer observation and watch each other. It needs to be remembered that, unlike you, the pupils do not have a thorough grasp of the material being taught and therefore need guidance as to what to look for. Initially, with pupils in pairs, you can 'orchestrate' the observation. For example, you can ask each observer to look at how far their partner attains a symmetrical position in jumping from a box in gymnastics. In the breast stroke observers can be asked to see if the fingers are close together. Following observation each pupil gives feedback to partners. This guidance can be developed using wall posters or work cards setting out criteria against which observers can check partner's performance. Specific guidance from the Elastic Boxes or Carr's skill analysis can be used here (see below). Guidance about positions from which to observe are also likely to be needed (see below on positioning for observation. This applies equally to pupils observing as to your own observation). It needs to be remembered that your role as the teacher in these instances is to support pupil observation rather than directly comment on movement performances. Task 4.2 asks you to introduce an observation exercise with pupils who are new to this challenge.

Task 4.2 **Introducing peer observation to a class**

Select a class that have had no experience in peer observation. Select a skill that is to be worked on in the lesson and create a wall poster of four key points to be observed. With pupils working in pairs, taking it in turns to be active or to observe, ask the pupils to observe and give feedback on single points from the poster, one key point at a time, orchestrated by you. Support the pupils in this task by reinforcing perceptive observation and guiding those who have not grasped the nature of their role.

For the next lesson, with the same skill being worked on, again create a wall poster, but this time ask observers to decide which key point their partner needs to work on.

Reflect on the class's developing ability to observe and put these notes in your PDP. Refer to these notes when you carry out a similar exercise with another class.

Observation to provide information for recording and reporting on pupil progress

While your lesson evaluation records how far the class as a whole achieved your ILOs, your observations are also important for you to chart the progress of individual pupils. You are expected to know how your pupils are progressing and at what level they are working. Formal assessment procedures (see also Chapter 8) that are implemented at the end of a unit or scheme of work are planned by the PE department as a whole and may involve the analysis of video recordings or other teachers coming into your lessons to observe. However, on a lesson to lesson basis you need to record pupil performance. Again there may be a department wide pro forma for this, however the data you record is the outcome of your in-lesson observations of pupils. It is important that you keep these records up to date, not least because you will refer to them in talking to parents and in writing pupil reports. Be certain that you know how *all* the pupils are progressing. It may be helpful to decide, in a particular lesson, to observe, for example, six pupils about whom you are not certain of their standard.

WHAT ASPECTS OF THE LESSON SHOULD BE OBSERVED?

Before reading this section complete Task 4.3.

Task 4.3 **Considering what there is to observe in a PE lesson**

Reflecting on what has been discussed in the chapter so far, make a list of all those aspects of a lesson it is important for you to observe. Compare your list with the areas set out below.

Keep your list in your PDP.

What you observe arises directly from the previous section on *why* you observe. Areas to be observed might fall into three categories: learning, organisation and safety and pupil behaviour.

Foremost in your mind, as you monitor the class, is how far pupils are progressing in their *learning*, that is, whether they are achieving the ILOs. Observation tells you if the class have understood the task set, if the task is too difficult, if the task is too easy, if the class are bored with a task, if the most able or the least able need additional support. As a result of this observation you decide on your next feedback to, or instruction for, the class. Remember that ILOs are not only concerned with motor skill development, some may be concerned with adhering to the rules of a game or adopting certain tactics. Others may be to do with creating a sequence or a composition – for which you observe if all aspects of the task are being covered and the transitions are well managed. In addition, your ILOs may include those from among wider educational objectives (see Chapter 14). For example, you may need to observe pupils' ability to work with others, their communication skills or their ability to be independent or creative. If you have set pupils the challenge to observe and help a partner, you need to observe if they are doing this accurately. What you observe is therefore diverse. To be most effective, exactly what you are going to observe (e.g. progress towards and achievement of a specific ILO) needs to be planned.

Observation of learning is critical as it provides you with the information you need to give feedback to the class, a group or an individual and it tells you what your next step needs to be in your teaching. For example, it tells you if you need to modify your ILOs or if you have to find a different way to achieve these for which you have not planned. Remember that these guidelines are as relevant in classroom teaching as they are in practical activities.

Underpinning this observation of pupil learning is an alert monitoring of all aspects of *organisation and safety*. You are particularly concerned with the safe use of space and the safe use of apparatus or equipment. The detail of what you need to be looking at here is covered in Chapters 6 and 9, respectively.

Pupil behaviour is the final area to which you need to be alert. As you monitor learning and safety you also pick up instances of 'off task', inappropriate behaviour and this must be dealt with expeditiously and appropriately. For specific information on observation of pupil behaviour see Chapter 6.

In the early stages of developing your observation skills it is essential that you plan exactly what you are to observe in a lesson. In many lesson plan pro formas there is a column for key observation or teaching points. It is useful to complete this carefully and to focus your attention on these key aspects of pupil response (see Chapter 3 on planning).

HOW CAN I BEST CARRY OUT OBSERVATION?

This section looks at teacher positioning to facilitate observation, the knowledge and understanding needed to observe effectively, using movement principles as a tool in observation, using skill analysis as a tool for observation, and using Carr's five step analysis.

Observation and positioning

Effective observation usually requires you to take time out of dialogue with pupils to stand back and survey the class activity. This time, apparently 'doing nothing' is absolutely critical to good observation. Do not rush this stage in the process. Systematically observing the pupils' execution of a skill and focusing, initially, on improving only a small part of that skill, avoids your being overwhelmed by too much visual information. It can also be useful to begin by focusing your observation on individual pupils and then on small groups. Whole class observation is challenging but is helped if you observe specific ILOs rather than try to pick up everything that is taking place. For example, in teaching a swimming stroke, rather than observe the whole movement pattern, focus just on the use of the arms and the hands. In a game of hockey, instead of surveying how all players are fulfilling their role, concentrate on how far the forwards are aware of each other and working together.

In order to gather information through observation your positioning in the working space is critical. This aspect of class management is covered in Chapter 6. However, it is useful to rehearse some key points here. From the moment that pupils enter the working space your positioning is important. It is good to begin with a welcoming stance and a readiness to respond to the mood of the class. Careful observation enables you to identify the mood of the class. Throughout the lesson, your observation strategy is likely to change, for example moving between scanning the whole class to focusing in on an individual or small group. Scanning is necessary for safety, for creating a teacher 'presence' and for a general idea of how the whole group are coping with the set tasks. In order to scan well, you need to have a good vantage point so that you can see most of the class at once. Keeping your back to the wall is the most common method used by PE teachers because standing in the centre of the space allows at least half of the class to become invisible. Staying at only one wall throughout the lesson results in the whole of the back of the class being only partially visible, if at all. So make sure you are constantly moving

'I TOLD YOU GYM WAS FUN! SHE NEVER SEES US AT THE BACK!!'

■ **Figure 4.2** Having a great time. Wish you were here!

on the outside perimeter so that the 'back' of the space eventually becomes the 'front'. This advice about positioning is as relevant in the classroom as in the practical working space. Figure 4.2 shows what can happen if you leave the same pupils at the back of the class for too long!

In order to focus in on an individual or small group, you need to choose a position where you can see the movement clearly. If the skill being performed is fast, a more distant vantage point is required than if the movement is slow. Knudson and Morrison (2002) suggest the best view is achieved from between 5 and 10 metres and at right angles to the plane of motion. In order to get an holistic view of any movement, it is a good idea to ask the pupil to repeat the movement and for you to take up a variety of positions to enable you to view the skill from a number of angles: e.g. side, front, back.

Another situation when positioning is important, both for you and the class, is when you or a pupil(s) is providing a demonstration. It is essential both that the demonstration is clearly visible to all and that observers are in the optimum position to see the critical aspects of the movement. This is an important area and is covered in detail in Chapter 5.

Knowledge and understanding needed for effective observation

In your early experiences of teaching it is likely that you found it easier to observe skills in activities with which you were familiar. You have more experience of seeing and performing these skills and are familiar with the technical language used in respect of their execution. It is also likely that you were not so confident in observing a skill in an activity with which you were less familiar. This is a salutary lesson revealing that it is critical that you are knowledgeable about the material you are to teach. The fundamental knowledge you need can be addressed from a number of perspectives. A straightforward way to approach this challenge is to appreciate that you need a grasp, first, of the basic constituents of movement, second, of the nature of skills you are teaching and, third, of the form and procedures of the activities that you are teaching.

The constituents of movement are often referred to as the principles of movement and these are spelled out in the section below. The broad principles of skill analysis are also set out below. However, the detail of specific skills can be found in the textbooks concerning different activities, as can details of the up-to-date rules, regulations, procedures and tactics of these activities. This book is not designed to give you this information, however it is an essential element in enabling you to be an effective teacher and study of this information should be a priority for you.

Another aspect of knowledge it is useful to have is a basic understanding of how motor skill develops generally, from the young child through to the adult (Gallahue and Cleland, 2003; Haywood and Getchell, 2009). This is particularly helpful if you are teaching pupils with special educational needs as their development may be delayed and your expectations must take this into account. There are usually teachers who are experienced in working with these pupils who can advise you. Alternatively the pupil may have contact with a physiotherapist who could give you information and guidance.

Using movement principles as a tool in observation

In order to monitor learning you need to have acquired, and be able to apply, knowledge and understanding about the constituents of movement and of the make up of movement skills. Gallahue and Donnelly (2003) refer to movement principles or concepts as a special *language* of movement. This language enables teachers both to observe and describe movement in a wider and fuller way. These two researchers have based their developmental PE programme on the following movement principles:

> Developmental physical education incorporates a movement framework by focussing on important movement concepts (i.e. how the body *can* move) as well as skill concepts (i.e. how the body *should* move). This helps children become more skilful movers, knowledgeable movers and expressive movers.
>
> (Gallahue and Donnelly, 2003: 386)

Movement principles were first described by Rudolf Laban (Davies, 2001) as consisting of four elements: body awareness (what the body can do); spatial awareness (where the body can move); effort or dynamic awareness (how the body can move) and relationship awareness (with whom or with what the body can move). The movement principles provide a very simple and clear framework for the PE teacher to observe, analyse, evaluate and record movement. It can also be used to plan balanced PE lessons for all pupils including those with a disability (Sherborne, 2001; Hill, 2006; Marsden and Egerton, 2007).

Figure 4.3 shows a simple framework of the movement principles. Using one 'box' at a time, any movement, motor skill or pattern of movements can be analysed by circling the appropriate movement vocabulary indicated. The vocabulary in each box is not definitive and you can add more yourself as necessary. For example, if you are observing swimming, you may want to add in 'diving' or 'tumble turn' into the Body Box under Body Actions. In this way, the framework is 'elastic' and can expand as your observation skills increase.

ELASTIC BOXES	
BODY	**SPACE**
Actions: stepping, jumping, rolling, sliding, vaulting, twisting, turning, balancing, freezing **Parts of body:** can lead, can support, can relate, can move symmetrically or asymmetrically **Body shape:** round (ball), twisted (screw), thin (pin), wide (wall)	**Levels:** high, medium, low **Directions:** left-right, up-down, forward-backwards **Air and floor patterns:** angular, straight, curved, twisted
EFFORT/DYNAMICS	**RELATIONSHIPS**
Time: slow, medium speed, fast **Weight:** strong, moderate, light **Space:** direct, some curving, flexible **Flow:** free, some restraint, bound	**People:** alone, partner, small group, large group, whole class **Apparatus:** floor/gravity, small apparatus (benches, mats), large apparatus (box, climbing frame, horse) **Equipment:** small (balls, hoops etc.), Large (goals, weights etc)

■ **Figure 4.3** Elastic boxes: a framework for observing movement

Using the elastic boxes framework as an observation tool opens your eyes to your pupils' movement vocabulary and movement mastery. It is a tool to help you see if, and how, pupils have mastered the constituents of movement. It also enables you to see in what aspect of movement each pupil is less confident and so needs both encouragement and guidance. You can see where they lack experience and thus you are able to address this in your future planning. For example, a rapidly growing adolescent male may not have mastered control of his limbs during the growth spurt. This could result in movements which take up vast amounts of space, tend to be strong, flexible and fast with an over-emphasis on limb actions and no awareness of the trunk. He may appear clumsy and somewhat uncontrolled for those working in close proximity. By planning the next PE lesson to include awareness of the trunk, the clumsy teenager may increase his body awareness sufficiently to feel the connection his trunk is making with his upper and lower body sections and so begin to regain control over his whole body movements. Similarly, by manipulating the effort/dynamics elements to light, direct and sustained movements in the next planned lesson, you are giving him the opportunity to experience movements that are not natural to him and so his movement vocabulary is increased. Task 4.4 challenges you to use the elastic boxes as a tool for observation. There is no right or wrong when using this tool, however, the structure gives you a framework within which to observe pupil learning.

Task 4.4 **Using the elastic boxes as an observational tool**

■ Observe an individual pupil in a dance or gymnastics lesson. Describe the individual's spatial awareness and their effort/dynamics awareness. How would you cater for the needs of this individual in your next lesson?

■ Observe a group of pupils in a games or athletics lesson. Analyse and record their body awareness and relationship awareness. What teaching points would you give to improve their skills and would you change any of the equipment used?

Discuss your observations with your tutor and put your notes in your PDP. Return to this task later in your course and reflect on ways in which you have become a better observer.

Using skill analysis as an observation tool

In your own learning with teachers and coaches it is likely that you have experienced teaching based on the observation of whole skills. These practitioners have approached the task of improving skill by comparing their understanding of the correct or optimum way to execute a skill with the performance of their pupils. Observing a pupil's movement requires you to have a clear mental picture of the stages of a skill development. To do this, research a pictorial representation of the skill from a text such as Haywood and Getchell (2009) or video clip or website. Many observation texts are written wholly for the improvement of skill performance. There have been long debates about the best method of observing motor skills in order to offer teaching points and feedback to further improve the skill. While there are a number of approaches to this observation, as a general guide, the following procedure based on Carr's 5 steps (1997) has proved successful in systematically observing and analysing skill performance.

Carr's five-step analysis

The main emphasis in this skill analysis is on improving the mechanical aspects of a specific skill. In order to clarify Carr's explanation, the overarm throw for distance is used as an example. Before beginning your observation analysis, make sure you are positioned well (see above) and are prepared to move that position as necessary. Also, ensure that the performer is fully warmed-up and performing in a natural environment. The performer's and other participants' safety should also be paramount.

Step 1: watch the whole skill through from an appropriate vantage point. With the overarm throw, for example, check that you can see the run up, the wide base with feet planted in the direction of the throw, the taking back of the throwing hand, the transference of power from the feet, through the hips, into the shoulders, the whipping through of the throwing arm, the balance of the non-throwing arm, the position of release of the ball (45 degrees from the shoulder if thrown for best distance) and the follow through. You need to have a clear mental image of each of these stages. Repeat the observation several times, if possible. Note the three most important aspects of the skill facts about this observation. Concentrate only on three aspects or you will become overwhelmed by the task initially.

Step 2: watch the Preparation; the Action; the Recovery of the skill and note key features. In the case of the overarm throw, the Preparation is that part of the skill where the performer is getting into the best possible position from which to throw for distance, i.e. a fast run up and planting a wide base with the throwing arm as far back as possible whilst opening the shoulders so that the body is in a sideways-on position, weight over the back foot. The Action is that part of the skill where the main action of the skill is executed, i.e. the actual transference of weight through the body starting from the back foot, through the hips into the shoulders, the whipping through of the arm and the release of the ball at the optimum angle. Finally, the Recovery of a skill is that section of the skill where the body takes action to regain balance and stability. In the case of the overarm throw for distance, it usually involves the continuation of weight transference in a forward direction where the trailing leg comes forward to 'catch' the momentum and to stop the body falling forwards. The upper body usually bends forwards also to absorb the force from the throwing arm.

Step 3: use your previous knowledge to assess the mechanical efficiency, starting with the stability of the base and continuing on through the stages of the skill as described for the overarm throw for distance. If it is helpful, watch a video/DVD of a 'perfect' execution of the skill you have chosen to observe so that you are really clear about each stage.

Step 4: select two main errors in the execution of the skill.

Step 5: concentrating on each error in turn, give one teaching point per error to the pupil and allow the pupil time to practise. Remember to use praise when appropriate.

This 5-step analysis is described above in respect of a single pupil. However, it is also applicable to observing groups or the whole class. Task 4.5 asks you to use the technique with a single pupil, a group and then a class.

Task 4.5 **Observation of motor skills**

■ Observe one pupil who is performing a motor skill, with which you are familiar, and that incorporates Preparation, Action and Recovery phases, with minimal success. Using Carr's method above, make a careful observational skill analysis. In which phase do you detect key errors? Decide on two teaching points to help to correct the error and give this guidance to the pupil, one teaching point at a time.

■ Take time to become familiar with a skill that is new to you that incorporates the three movement phases. Observe a small group of pupils who are learning this motor skill. Using Carr's method above, make a careful observational skill analysis. Looking particularly at the Preparation, Action and Recovery phases, can you detect an error common to all or most of the group? Decide on two teaching points to help to correct the error and give this guidance to the group, one teaching point at a time.

■ Observe a class of pupils, taught by another teacher, who are being introduced to a skill, with which you are familiar, for the first time. Using Carr's method above, make a careful observational skill analysis, looking particularly at the Preparation, Action and Recovery phases. Can you detect an error common to all or most of the class? Decide on two teaching points to help to correct the error.

Discuss this task with your tutor and put the notes into those sections of your PDP that address the teaching of the activities you observed.

To further your observation skills, it is a very valuable exercise to videotape a pupil or class and replay the execution of the skill many times until you begin to distinguish more and more critical features. Your observation skills, like any other, improve as you practice. A helpful resource to assist in such practice is 'Observing and Analysing Learners' Movement' which is a CD-ROM presenting a selection of motor skills for analysis (www.observinglearnersmoving.co.uk). This interactive resource offers frame by frame and slow-motion observation of the skills, as well as the facility to view skills from different angles.

Knowledge of the rules and regulations of any activity you teach is essential for you to present work with authority. For example, you need to know procedures in athletics about what counts for a jump/throw or a no-jump/throw, rules in swimming about the way turns have to be executed and what constitutes an acceptable bowling action in cricket. You need to be confident of the current rules in any competitive game you teach. An up-to-date rules book in your pocket can be an asset and avoid confrontations between players! In addition, in some activities, such as cross-country running and orienteering, there are safety rules to be followed and again you must be aware of these (see Chapter 9 on safety and afPE, 2009).

Observation as part of action research

Later on in your career you may be involved in a process known as Action Research (see Chapter 17), in which you investigate, in detail, a specific aspect of pupil learning or your teaching. Action Research is carried out in the teaching situation and depends significantly on observation skills. See Figure 4.4 for a representation of the observation cycle. This cycle is, in fact, the foundation for all teaching observation. In everyday lessons, starting from the top of the cycle, you plan your lesson to achieve your ILOs. Moving in a clockwise direction you then teach the lesson. As you teach you observe, evaluating and assessing pupil response and your own teaching as discussed earlier in this chapter. As appropriate, you record your observations and then reflect on how far the ILOs were achieved and what aspects of your teaching were more and less effective. As a result of this reflection you reassess ILOs and teaching as you plan the next lesson. The cycle then starts again. In an Action Research setting you set yourself a challenge such as to investigate the best method to accommodate a wide variety of abilities in a lesson or to improve your own use of a particular skill such as non-verbal communication. Prior to starting this research you read widely to become fully informed of theories and previous research in your area of interest. Building from this reading and from the practicalities of the class(es) you are teaching you plan the strategies you are going to use. It is often the case that in this situation an observer attends your lesson and records key information from the lesson. In most cases you create an observation instrument for this observer to complete. This recorded data forms a significant element in your reflection and contributes to how you develop your teaching in the next lesson (see Chapter 17 for more information about Action Research).

Task 4.6 asks you to discuss this suggestion with your tutor.

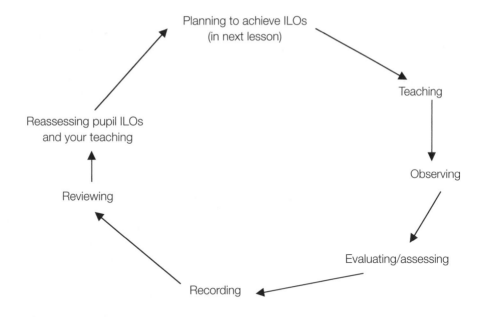

■ **Figure 4.4** Observation cycle

Task 4.6 **Relevance of the observation cycle in all PE lessons**

Discuss the cycle with your tutor, considering how it relates to your everyday lesson observation. Put the notes from the discussion in your PDP.

SUMMARY AND KEY POINTS

Observing human movement is a complex skill which requires years of practice. At first, the task seems overwhelming as large amounts of visual stimuli cannot easily be processed and movement is such a transitory phenomenon. However, it is one of the most important skills you possess as a PE teacher, as shown by the observation cycle. Without observation skills, you never know whether your pupils have achieved the ILOs or how to plan the next step in your teaching. Observation demands a knowledge base of movement principles and motor skill performance. The process of observing movement is made easier by mastering the optimum teacher positioning and knowing when to scan the whole class and when to focus in on individuals. Being able to see and adjust the environment and the tasks, and being able to respond to whatever mood the class may be displaying are also essential. Some tools to assist you in observing are the pictorial representations of the elastic boxes and Carr's motor skills breakdown process.

Where you use observation as part of Action Research you can decide exactly what you are looking for during a lesson and can construct your own schedule and method of recording. Eventually, you realise that you are observing movement without conscious attention and it has become, indeed, a skill for life.

Check which requirements for your course you have addressed through this chapter. Now complete Tasks 4.7, 4.8 and 4.9, putting your work in your PDP as evidence of Master's level study.

Task 4.7 **Influences on observation**

Write a 2,000 word essay critically considering the assertion that 'The knowledge and expectations of the observer strongly influence what is observed' (Knudson and Morrison, 2002: 96).

Task 4.8 **Bringing objectivity into observing**

Discuss the following issue with another student teacher. When observing movement, PE teachers face constraints due to their own values, beliefs, abilities and experiences. If so, what allowances do teachers need to make in order to observe lessons objectively?

Task 4.9 **A research project involving observation**

Propose a small research project involving observations of small groups from one of your classes relating to developing pupil communication skills. How would you ensure reliability and validity in your study?

FURTHER READING

Haywood, K.M. and Getchell, N. (2009) *Life Span Motor Development*, 5th edn, Champaign, IL: Human Kinetics.

These authors have been in the field of motor development for many years yet they consistently search for more enlightenment based on new research. They explore new ways of studying human movement, growth and development.

Knudson, D.V. and Morrison, C.S. (2002) *Qualitative Analysis of Human Movement*, 2nd edn, Champaign, IL: Human Kinetics.

This is a very useful text for an in-depth study of observational theory. The authors base their arguments on social science research and pedagogy and present some challenging thinking.

Observing and Analysing Learners' Movement. CD-ROM.

This is a very useful resource for the student of observation. It includes over 90 video clips of children performing a range of motor patterns (i.e. shot put, forward roll, javelin throw, hockey dribble, hurdle, pair balance etc). Children at different stages of development are included and the motor patterns are shown from a variety of camera angles. (See www.observinglearnersmoving.co.uk)

COMMUNICATION IN PE

Paula Zwozdiak-Myers

INTRODUCTION

This chapter is concerned with effective communication in PE. Clearly, communication is crucial in all teaching. Without communication, teaching cannot take place and poor communication leads to confused/garbled and incomplete messages which result in inadequate learning.

Each subject makes specific communication demands. The PE teacher has to contend with a variety of contexts (classroom, gymnasium, sports hall, swimming pool, playing field), and must also recognise the intrinsically practical nature of the subject. Although good use of spoken language is essential, over-talking is unforgivable because it can deny the pupil valuable activity time. Explanations and instructions should be succinct. You have almost certainly had the experience of listening to a teacher drone on when what you wanted to do was to get going on a physical activity. Pupil talk can also be used effectively in PE lessons to deepen and extend learning but, again, talk must not dominate in practical sessions where your objective is to get the class moving.

PE like all subjects has its own technical vocabulary and part of the pleasure of being an expert in a discipline is knowing subject-specific words and phrases and using them with other experts. Most pupils, however, are not experts and your teaching language must not confuse them. Of course, if you have General Certificate of Secondary Education (GCSE) or General Certificate of Education (GCE), A or AS level classes pupils will expect to hear subject-specific language, but with a year 7 group, you must use a way of speaking appropriate to their level of understanding. If you are going to include a technical term, it must be carefully explained or have an obvious meaning in context.

OBJECTIVES

At the end of this chapter you should be able to:

■ understand the central role of communication in all teaching;
■ have a good idea of the quality and flexibility of your voice;
■ understand the role of teacher language in the teaching and learning of PE;

- understand the key role of questioning in PE lessons;
- understand the importance of teacher feedback to promote learning;
- understand the role of pupil language in PE lessons;
- have an increased awareness of modes of communication through which to convey messages;
- explore the use of demonstration to communicate effectively to promote pupil learning.

Check the requirements for your course to see which relate to this chapter.

THE PE TEACHER'S VOICE

As a PE teacher you need a good voice which can be adapted to a variety of settings, some of which are difficult and demanding. It is sensible to get to know what your voice sounds like by recording yourself talking on a dictaphone or tape recorder. Task 5.1 asks you to listen to your own voice.

Task 5.1 **Evaluating your voice**

Record yourself reading a piece of text in a natural voice or having an ordinary conversation with a friend. If you have not heard yourself on tape before, prepare for a shock. You may sound quite different from what you expect. Remember though that you hear your voice coming 'back' from your mouth whereas most people hear it coming 'forward'.

Listen to your voice positively and discover your strengths. Is the tone pleasant? Do you vary the pitch to give interest? Do you sound like a friendly individual?

Vary the recording context to include different spaces where you teach. How do you sound in the classroom? gym? sports hall? swimming pool? outside?

Note down what you perceive as the strengths and weaknesses in your voice, share these thoughts with your tutor and put these notes in your professional development portfolio (PDP).

When you have become accustomed to the sound of you speaking and have grown to like what you hear, think about ways in which you could vary your voice. You can experiment with the following elements of paralanguage:

- pitch;
- speed;
- pause;
- stress;
- volume;
- enunciation.

Now complete Task 5.2.

Task 5.2 **Voice variation**

It is worthwhile practising voice variation. Use a tape recorder to explore pitch and speed variation. Read a passage from a book and use pause for effect. Add stress to highlight certain words or phrases. You will probably feel silly doing this but the practice is invaluable. It has been said that somebody who can tell a story well will make a good teacher. This may be an exaggerated claim, but certainly an expressive and flexible voice is a tremendous asset in teaching.

You should also use real lessons for voice practice. A radio microphone would be ideal but you could ask your tutor to concentrate on your use of voice during some lessons and to provide you with feedback. You want positive comment as well as suggestions for improvement.

Put your tutor comments in your PDP. It is useful to repeat this task later in your course, at which time you can refer back to these notes.

All of these variations have an effect on the pupils you teach. A high voice generates more excitement; a deep voice is calming and is useful when disciplining a class. Your normal voice can vary considerably in pitch without discomfort. A lower voice is usually better indoors whereas a higher tone will carry better outside.

Speed can give pace to a lesson, whereas a slow delivery has the opposite effect. If you are teaching gymnastics with a large class using apparatus in a small space, you may choose to speak slowly to create a safe, careful environment. A speedy delivery might be needed with a small group in a sports hall if you want to generate enthusiasm and evoke an energetic response.

Pause can be an effective strategy for teachers. Very often, instead of allowing a brief silence, a teacher uses a filler like 'er' or 'um'. One filler, much loved by PE teachers, is 'right', said with purpose and emphasis. There is nothing wrong with that but over-use of the same filler can be damaging. Pupils may concentrate on how many times you say 'right' and could ignore any important teaching points you make! Pause is also valuable as a gentle form of discipline. If you are talking to the class and a pupil is not listening, a pause in your delivery linked to a pointed look can bring the offender onside.

Stress is a useful tool because it is a way of highlighting important information. Stress must be used sparingly though. It is tiring to listen to somebody who is continually stressing words. Instructions about safety and key elements in a skill can be stressed so they stand out from the normal more relaxed delivery. This 'baseline' voice should be audible, pleasant to listen to and unforced.

It is obviously vital that what a teacher says is audible and audibility is sometimes linked to volume. PE teachers have to cope with large spaces and classes outside where wind and traffic noise compete. A simplistic deduction suggests that you should shout or roar to be heard by your pupils. It is certainly helpful to have volume available if needed, but audibility is based on a number of factors. If you have a lot to say to your class, then they should be close to you not dispersed. You should always position yourself so all the pupils are in front of you. It is very hard to hear somebody whose back is to you. In general, if you are behind somebody, audibility is reduced by 75 per cent.

Sometimes, even when pupils are gathered round, you have to gain silence by a loud 'quiet, please'. Once you have silence, the golden rule is not to shout into it.

Moderate your voice and speak naturally to the class. You do not want to become the sort of PE teacher who *always* speaks loudly even in social settings.

Enunciation is important for PE teachers. You should speak precisely so pupils can hear easily the words you speak. In ordinary conversation, careful enunciation is not normally necessary but when you are talking to a dispersed group of pupils in a large space, care is essential. In addition, some of your class may learn English as an Additional Language (EAL) or have Special Educational Needs (SEN) such as mild hearing loss, so you must ensure that no words are lost otherwise your message may be confused or incomprehensible. (For more information on supporting pupils learning English as an additional language see Department for Education and Skills (DfES), 2002a and the Physical Education initial teacher training and education (PEITTE) website http://www.peitte.net/.)

If you do have to talk to a scattered class, you must first ensure that they are quiet and attentive. You then use good projection to make yourself heard by the pupils furthest from you. Projection involves careful enunciation and a concentration on reaching the remotest pupils by pushing the voice out with conviction. This sounds somewhat painful, but good projection becomes a habit and then it is easy to make even a whisper carry a long way.

It is important to recognise that how you use your voice reinforces the meaning behind the message you want to convey. Pupils often take more notice of how something is said rather than on what is said. If you praise a pupil but deliver the praise in a flat unenthusiastic way, the pupil will not be convinced you mean it. Equally, if you discipline someone, your voice should indicate firmness or displeasure at some unacceptable behaviour. To use your voice effectively, each element of paralanguage or non-verbal communication needs to be woven together sensitively like a finely tuned instrument (see Unit 3.1 in Capel, Leask and Turner, 2009; Robertson 1996).

THE TECHNICAL LANGUAGE OF PE

As with all disciplines, PE has its own specialist language. This language is invaluable because it helps experts in PE to communicate succinctly with each other. Part of the development of any discipline is this accumulation of subject-specific terminology.

PE teachers are familiar with the words and phrases of their subject, but their pupils may not have met the vocabulary before or may have only a hazy idea of what the various terms mean. These should be introduced gradually and explained or, better, exemplified in practical situations. If the class see a lay-up shot performed and labelled, they will have learnt the phrase and the meaning in the most effective way. Of course, many pupils need to have the learning reinforced by questions or repetitions. Carry out Task 5.3 to analyse technical vocabulary in an aspect of PE.

Task 5.3 **Technical language**

Select one activity which you are teaching (for example, cricket or gymnastics) and make a list of technical terms associated with that activity. Do not forget that you are an 'expert'. What seems to have an obvious meaning to you, may well be much less obvious to a pupil in year 7 (for example, a straight drive or a headstand). When you have completed your list, which in both the activities cited would be very long,

---

consider how you might explain some of the key terms to pupils. With a verbal description? By a demonstration? By use of a diagram? A chart? A video excerpt? Try this out in one of your lessons teaching this activity.

Reflect on the effect of your particular awareness of language in a lesson and put these notes in your PDP.

SPECIFIC FORMS OF LANGUAGE USE IN THE TEACHING OF PE

This section reminds you that your use of voice will be influenced both by where you are teaching and what you are teaching. It also looks at questioning and feedback as specific forms of language use in PE

PE covers a range of activities taught in a variety of contexts and each particular blend of activity and context should have an effect on your use of language. One of the simplest polarities is indoors/outdoors. If you are teaching a games lesson outside on a cold winter's morning, your instructions and explanations must be concise, in order for pupils to start moving as soon as possible, to keep warm throughout the lesson. It might even be advantageous to consider how much of your verbal input could be given in the changing rooms beforehand.

Some activities taught in PE (for example, swimming) are very skills-based and also potentially dangerous. The swimming pool is also a difficult setting acoustically. Language is likely to be command-style in tone and wording, associated with a strong motivational element – praise linked to skill acquisition.

Dance, on the other hand, is about creative movement, and the risk factor in a well-organised class is small. This does not mean that as a teacher you have a licence for verbosity but rather your language is likely to be more metaphorical and expressive, based on stimulating description and open questions to encourage diverse pupil responses to tasks given.

Questioning is a universal feature of teacher language in all disciplines. It also helps pupils to learn the subject-specific terminology of PE, develop their listening and thinking skills, and monitor their knowledge and understanding of key concepts, skills and processes. Research has shown (Brown and Edmondson, 1984) that teachers spend about 30 per cent of their time asking questions and ask about 400 questions a day. A majority of these will be checks on knowledge recall. For example:

■ How many players are there in a volleyball team?
■ What do we call a tennis shot made before the ball bounces?

In a PE lesson, the response to such a question could be linked to a pupil movement or demonstration. For example:

■ Which part of the foot do you use to pass the ball?
■ At what point do you release the discus?

All the questions quoted above are closed; there is only one correct answer, which the pupils should already have been taught. It is inappropriate to ask pupils closed questions on topics they have not covered.

There are other questions you can ask which demand more thought of the pupils. These are generally open questions. It is not sensible to make all the questions you ask searching ones because if you do the pace of lessons will move slowly as pupils need time to prepare and deliver their responses. However, in one-to-one contexts and as pupils progress in PE, you should encourage them to think and become reflective learners. You might use evaluative questions such as:

■ What do you think is more effective in football, the cross cut back to the forwards or the pass lofted forward to them?

or questions which call for understanding such as:

■ Why do you pass with the side of the foot not the toe?
■ What is the point of the follow through?

Task 5.4 requires you to analyse your lesson talk and questioning in lessons you teach.

Task 5.4 **Analysing your lesson talk and questioning**

Ask your tutor or another student teacher to observe one of your lessons and check on the amount of time you talk in lessons by using a stop watch. This might seem a fairly crude measure, but it gives you an idea of how much you talk and whether you may want to try and reduce the verbal input. Of course, some talk is to static pupils (for example, giving instructions) while some is to active ones (for example, giving feedback to pupils while working on a task). You might like to differentiate these.

On another occasion ask an observer to write down all the questions you ask. This is not easy and some are likely to be missed. That does not matter because the record obtained should still give you a flavour of your questioning approach. Check how many questions you ask and what type of questions they are. Who answers them? You? Nobody? A range of pupils? Just one or two pupils? After each lesson discuss the findings with your observer. Identify what aspects of your teacher talk you need to work on. Put these notes in your PDP and repeat this exercise later in your course.

The effective use of questioning is a complex process. Table 5.1 illustrates how different types of questioning might be used to support the development of pupils' higher order thinking skills in relation to Bloom's (1956) taxonomy of educational objectives.

Black and Wiliam (2002) provide further insights on the use of Bloom's taxonomy in relation to questioning and Wragg and Brown (2001) classify the content of questions related to learning a particular subject as one of three types: empirical questions, conceptual questions and value questions. You might like to refer to this literature for more information.

The capacity to ask questions effectively is a skill you can develop during your course and into your teaching career. It is important that you ask clear, relevant questions

■ **Table 5.1** Linking Bloom's (1956) taxonomy to the development of higher order thinking skills

Cognitive objective	What pupils need to do	Use of questioning to develop higher order thinking skills
Knowledge	Define, Recall, Describe, Label, Identify, Match	To help pupils link aspects of existing knowledge or relevant information to the task ahead
Comprehension	Explain, Translate, Illustrate, Summarise, Extend	To help pupils to process their existing knowledge
Application	Apply to a new context, Demonstrate, Predict, Employ, Solve, Use	To help pupils use their knowledge to solve a new problem or apply it to a new situation
Analysis	Analyse, Infer, Relate, Support, Break down, Differentiate, Explore	To help pupils use the process of inquiry to break down what they know and reassemble it
Synthesis	Design, Create, Compose, Reorganise, Combine	To help pupils combine and select from available knowledge in order to respond to unfamiliar situations
Evaluation	Assess, Evaluate, Appraise, Defend, Justify	To help pupils compare and contrast knowledge gained from different perspectives as they construct and reflect upon their own viewpoints

Source: adapted from DfES, 2004a, Unit 7: Questioning: 13-14

and use pause appropriately so that pupils have time to think about their answer before they respond. Muijs and Reynolds (2005) suggest that 3 seconds or slightly longer is a reasonable time for any such pause, although up to 15 seconds might be required for open-ended, higher level questions. You can use closed or open-ended questions or combine the two into a series of questions depending upon the nature of the task at hand and context. Devising a series of questions is an effective technique for extending pupils' knowledge and understanding about a particular task or topic you might have introduced earlier.

If pupils encounter problems answering your questions you should find alternative ways to ask the same question. Muijs and Reynolds (2005) identified three types of prompts which can be used for this purpose:

■ verbal prompts – cues, reminders, tips, references to previous lessons or giving part of a sentence for the pupil to complete;
■ gestural prompts – pointing to an object or modelling a behaviour;
■ physical prompts – guiding a pupil through movement skills.

These prompts, used alone or in combination, can be useful devices in getting pupils both to understand and answer questions. The latter two types of non-verbal prompts are important elements of questioning and must relate directly to the words that you use. By incorporating a range of prompts and different stimuli into your teaching, the questions you ask can be more easily understood by pupils who are visual, auditory and/or proprioceptive/kinaesthetic learners.

The protocol of answering questions needs to be defined and enforced. Some teachers ask named pupils and redirect unanswered questions to other named pupils. Another technique is to ask a pupil who puts a hand up. The problem with using this strategy is that some pupils never put their hand up, possibly through fear that a wrong response could result in criticism or ridicule from you or from their peers, whereas others do so without knowing the answer because they wish to be seen as keen or knowledgeable.

Pupils also ask you questions. Sometimes a brief response suffices. In some instances, you can relay the question to the class and get them to think about possible answers. On occasion, the question will be a challenge to your authority and you will have to use techniques like humour or deflection.

Questioning that is used during lesson episodes to review guided practice and as a plenary activity to mark the closure of a lesson provides opportunities for interaction between you and your pupils that should be sensitively orchestrated to create a positive, non-threatening, working environment. The questioning techniques you adopt should be varied to accommodate the different learning/teaching strategies you are using and the learning needs of all your pupils.

Bailey (2002) provides further insights on 'questioning as a teaching strategy in PE' and, Spackman (2002) discusses the importance of questioning in PE in relation to 'assessment for learning'. Task 5.5 is a Master's task to complete near the end of you course.

Task 5.5 **Reflecting on your use of questioning**

Write a 2,000 word essay closely examining the cognitive processes pupils would need to carry out in order to realise the objectives identified in Table 5.1. Select one of the classes you teach and carefully consider how you:

■ currently use questioning;
■ could use questioning;

to develop your pupils' higher order thinking skills. Consider the implications of this analysis in relation to the future development of your teaching. Put this essay into your PDP as evidence of Master's level work.

TEACHER FEEDBACK

Teacher feedback is an essential component of the teaching process as it is a key element in learning. Feedback is fundamental to learning in that it directs pupils' attention to specific intended learning outcome (ILOs) and informs them of their progress, where they have mastered an aspect of a movement/skill/composition/game and where they need to focus their attention to improve. The feedback must therefore highlight this aspect of learning *and no other*. For example, if you are working to develop choreographic skills, but all your feedback is focused on individual movement performance, it is unlikely that the ILO will be achieved. On the other hand, if you want to achieve a polished performance of a sequence, feedback focused on choreography is distracting. (See Chapter 10 for a detailed discussion on matching feedback to ILOs.)

You give feedback in a number of situations in lessons. For example, you may call a class to gather round you, you may ask pupils to stand where they are and listen, or you may give feedback while the class is working. Further, you may give feedback to a group or to an individual. However, whenever feedback is given, when, how and to whom you give the feedback, it must be clear and accurate. This means that you must have a sound knowledge and understanding of what is to be mastered. Clear knowledge of the material enables you to observe effectively, use appropriate terminology as well as give productive feedback. This is important because if the teacher gives incorrect information this can inhibit rather than promote learning.

Certain types of feedback have been found to be more effective than others, depending on the characteristics of the skill and the learner. Mawer's (1995: 183–91) work on feedback is of value as it includes considerable discussion about types of feedback. He proposes that general feedback such as 'good' can do little to reinforce learning as pupils do not know what aspect of the task is being referred to. He advocates the use of positive feedback that also identifies which aspect of the work is being performed well – for example, 'Good work, Peter, you remembered to keep your back rounded as you moved into your forward roll'. As a teacher of PE you should avoid negative critical comments as this can be humiliating to pupils whose efforts are on show for all to see. Where a pupil is having difficulty, encouraging constructive and informative feedback should be used – for example, 'Well tried Clare, you need to remember to keep your fingers together as you practise your breaststroke arm action'. From a more general perspective it is always better to draw attention verbally or in a demonstration to what *is* to be done, rather than what *is not* to be done and what *is* correct or appropriate rather than what *is not* correct or appropriate. A pupil who is not wholly attentive may miss preliminary comments and believe the wrong example is the one to emulate.

Feedback which includes advice on how to improve is most effective if you are able to stay with the pupil to see if they can act on the advice given and improve. You can then give wholly positive feedback to the individual pupil. This is excellent for motivation. With a large class, however, it is difficult to give constructive feedback to each pupil and you may want to use pupils to provide feedback to each other. This approach is incorporated into the Reciprocal Teaching Style (Mosston and Ashworth, 2002). If you try this approach, which has a great deal to offer, remember that pupils may be unfamiliar with the role of commenting directly on a partner's work. Pupils need to be introduced to peer feedback in a step-by-step approach, as it demands observational, verbal and social skills. It is not unknown for Reciprocal Teaching to have the opposite effect to that intended. For example, pupils inexperienced in giving feedback can be negative, critical and dismissive.

Mosston and Ashworth (2002) identify four forms of feedback which are not dissimilar to those discussed by Mawer. These are Value statements, Corrective statements, Neutral statements and Ambiguous statements. They discuss the strengths and weaknesses of these forms of feedback. For example, Corrective statements are seen as essential elements in promoting learning, whereas Ambiguous statements are viewed as confusing and unhelpful to the learner. Cole and Chan (1994) also look at how and when to use different types of feedback. They suggest that the less confident pupil needs more feedback which is supportive and gives guidance. By contrast the confident pupil needs less feedback and that given could challenge the individual to employ methods of self-evaluation.

Research undertaken by the Assessment Reform Group (ARG) (1999) identified feedback as a key element in their work to promote assessment for learning. The underlying message behind this research is that all assessment, including feedback to pupils, should be formative. That is, it should be designed to point the way to achieving or enhancing the learning of each pupil. This is a challenging notion but is surely valid. Simply to tell a pupil what they *have* or *have not* achieved is hardly likely to promote further learning. (See Chapter 8 for further discussion on assessment for learning.)

The most valuable feedback is given to an individual, is encouraging, specific, informative, constructive and should lead the pupil on to further learning. Feedback given to a whole class is not without value, but is less effective in the learning process as it is, of necessity, non-specific and seldom directly relevant to every pupil.

Task 5.6 is a Master's level task and should be completed near the end of your course.

Task 5.6 **Main purposes for using different types of feedback**

The main purposes of using different types of feedback, as identified in Unit 12: Assessment for learning (DfES, 2004b: 12), are to:

- acknowledge what pupils have learned and encourage them to reflect on and extend their learning still further;
- recognise that pupils need time to reflect on their learning;
- encourage pupils to pose further questions to clarify or further develop their own or each other's thinking;
- encourage pupils to make next steps.

Critically evaluate how these purposes are translated in your own teaching. Identify aspects of feedback you would like to further develop and plan appropriate opportunities which enable you to realise these goals.

Put these reflections in your PDP as evidence of Master's level work.

WRITTEN LANGUAGE IN PE TEACHING

Because PE is seen as a practical subject involving a great deal of movement from teachers and pupils, talk might be viewed as the exclusive medium of teaching. This would be a pity because there are many instances where the written word is appropriate, useful and can support the development of pupils' reading skills. It is important to use written language which is appropriate and can be accessed and understood by all those for whom it is intended.

If there is a whiteboard or an overhead projector (OHP) in the gymnasium or sports hall, you can write up the key terminology, teaching points or the elements of a practice for pupils. Transparencies can be prepared beforehand and filed for individual or department reference. If you are writing in the lesson, it needs to be clear (see below). Diagrams can also be drawn or displayed. A flexible jointed 'figurine' can be used on an OHP or visualiser to illustrate body positions.

Of course, with examination classes, there is more emphasis on writing. You have to develop an acceptable board writing style – clear, neat, even and of a size which can be read by a pupil at the back of the class or one with poor eye sight. Avoid misspellings. If you are not sure how to spell a word, check it before the lesson. Your pupils should also be encouraged to write accurately and legibly.

Many PE teachers use work cards and these can be valuable resources. It is important that they are well presented, user friendly and preferably laminated to last. You should check your spellings and grammar. Written materials, including handouts, can also be valuable in wet weather lessons, or with pupils who are not participating in lessons or who are off school for an extended period. Again, get into the habit of filing all your written materials and resources for easy access and future use.

Another writing task for you as a PE teacher is the production of notices and posters. Again, the clarity, correctness and presentation quality are very important as these modes of communication send out non-verbal messages to pupils, colleagues and visitors to the school (like Office for Standards in Education (Ofsted) inspectors). You will want to ensure these are the messages you want to convey.

Wall displays and posters on the notice boards in a PE department should be vibrant, colourful, topical and updated regularly. Pupils identify with numerous sporting 'heroes' and 'heroines' across a range of physical activities. Visual images which reflect their diverse interests can be an inspiration and act as a stimulus to promote healthy active lifestyles and the personal pursuit of physical challenges.

Information and communications technology (ICT) can be invaluable and greatly enhance the production of written and graphical materials. See Chapter 14 for more information on the use of ICT in PE teaching. Task 5.7 asks you to pay particular attention to your writing to convey information.

Task 5.7 **Using written language**

In one of your next indoor lessons, see if you can use a whiteboard or OHP to illustrate and reinforce/support your teaching. You might want to list the sections of the lesson, provide appropriate terminology that may be new, stress the teaching points or display some pupil ideas.

Ask your tutor or another student teacher to observe and comment on how the strategy worked. Were you at ease with the writing role? Was your writing clear? Did the pupils react well? Did any look at what was written later to check? Did it take up too much physical activity time? How could you improve your use of the board or OHP in future? Put these comments in your PDP and use them to improve your technique next time you use such resources.

PUPIL TALK IN PE LESSONS

Pupils inevitably talk in all lessons. It is part of the socialising process. They talk subversively when the teacher is not watching, but it is clearly better to direct the need to talk into a constructive channel. Silence, of course, is important too. Pupils should watch a demonstration in silence and they should not talk when the teacher is giving instructions or explanations. You should not start talking until all pupils are silent and attentive.

Some activities taught in PE make pupil-to-pupil talk very difficult. Pupils in the swimming pool tend not to talk to each other because the setting is not conducive. They might squeal when they enter the cold water or shout with the pleasure of the experience. A strenuous game of football or hockey can also make pupil conversation difficult. Language tends to be used to call for the ball or to indicate the proximity of an unseen opponent. Indeed, if you find there is a lot of pupil talk going on that is not related to the activity, you might need to condition the game in some way to enhance pupils concentration and increase their participation level.

Pupil talk, however, is a very valuable aspect of PE. Talk can be used in a variety of ways to assist learning, deepen understanding, identify misconceptions and provide opportunities for pupils to express their opinion.

One obvious way for pupils to learn is by asking the teacher questions; but they are generally reluctant to do that. Asking questions can make pupils seem 'stupid' and could be interpreted as 'creepy' behaviour by their peer group. Answering questions can help learning, especially if the pupil is encouraged by being given time to think and if initial answers are followed by further probing. Such a process is best done at an individual or small group level but can be time-consuming. It is to be encouraged and all pupils should benefit from such focused attention from time to time, but the reality of PE and of teaching in large spaces where vigilance is essential means that it cannot happen more than once or twice a lesson.

Discussion is the most available form of pupil talk to encourage learning. A number of activities can benefit from pupil discussion – the construction of a group sequence in gymnastics; a problem-solving exercise in outdoor education; the planning of a trio dance as the development of a motif. All of these inevitably demand pupil interaction with ideas being voiced; perhaps tried practically; then refined and developed with the help of further discussion. The problem for you as a PE teacher in such situations is to control the balance between pupil talk and physical activity and to ensure that the talk is task-directed and not merely social.

The composition of a group is important. Friends may work well together and discuss productively; they may, however, be tempted to chat as friends do. A mixed ability group may operate effectively, but there is the danger of the able being held back or the less able being ignored. There is no formula guaranteed to achieve results. You must monitor the progress of groups and mix and match accordingly. Remember though that if you define a number of groups over a period of time there will probably be a marked reluctance to change that system. This may be appropriate in some situations, for example, if using Sport Education (see Siedentop, 1994) as a means of teaching a particular game. It may not be appropriate in other situations. If you want flexibility tell the pupils that you intend to vary groupings and establish the principle by making regular changes.

Another important factor in achieving a good discussion environment is the clarity and nature of the tasks set. Imprecisely defined tasks lead to woolly and unfocused discussion. That does not mean that all tasks need to be closed. PE has a number of areas which require open-ended tasks, especially with older and more experienced pupils, for example, a group sequence in gymnastics or discussing issues in the sociological aspect of GCE A level. However, open-ended tasks can still be couched in precise accessible language, for example, in a dance lesson a teacher could say, '*This music is called "The*

Market Place". Listen to it carefully and then discuss in your group what could be going on in this market. Use your ideas to create a short dance work based upon your interpretations of the mood and rhythm of the music.'

Task 5.8 asks you to pay particular attention to pupil talk in a lesson.

Task 5.8 **Group talk**

Plan to include a group task in one of your next lessons. Your specific observation task is to check on the discussion pattern of individual groups. Is there a dominant pupil? Is there a non-contributor? Is talk task-focused? Is there enough physical activity? Should you think of re-jigging the groups next time to improve the quality of discussion? How can you improve the quality of the discussion in the groups in future? Discuss this with your tutor and try to put any changes identified into practice. Put these notes in your PDP.

In PE, talk has a valuable role in testing hypotheses, suggesting tactics, exploring the consequences of physical initiatives. The imagination is an important element in successful physical activity and, although skills learning is fundamental, pupils should be encouraged to use their imagination, to make suggestions and, where possible, to test ideas in practice.

Reciprocal learning can be used to good effect in PE lessons. In this situation pupils work in pairs with one acting as the teacher and the other as the learner. The 'teacher' needs to be clearly briefed about what aspect of a skill is to be worked on. It is general practice to give the key teaching points and the best ways to do this may be on a wall poster or a work card. Inevitably, this process involves pupil talk, with the 'teacher' giving instructions, providing feedback and praising effort and competent performance. Interaction between you and the pair of pupils is with the pupil acting as 'teacher' to reinforce this role. See Chapter 10 for more information about teaching strategies.

When pupils are engaged in group tasks and are talking constructively about what they will do, the teacher has a monitoring role. It is important to give the groups some initial time to get their ideas going. If you intervene too quickly in a group, you may hinder rather than help. Your role is to assess when a group has stalled or broken down and to support by question or advice.

AN EXAMPLE OF COMMUNICATION AND ITS LINK TO OBSERVATION: DEMONSTRATION TO PROMOTE PUPIL LEARNING IN PE

An often quoted cliché 'a picture speaks a thousand words' suggests that, as sighted people, we gain much information through our eyes. In practical subjects such as PE, demonstration can be an invaluable teaching aid. There are many reasons why demonstrations are used – for example, to explain, to encourage, to reinforce and to evaluate. The following exemplars give possible reasons for deciding to use demonstration as a teaching aid to promote pupil learning:

■ to *set a task*. A demonstration can be more effective than a lengthy verbal explanation and is a more economical use of your time. A good strategy to use is – set up the activity with one group while the rest of the class is working, then stop the class to show the demonstration;

■ to *teach a new skill/activity*. Here demonstration can focus on specific teaching and movement observation points such as, where to place hands in relation to the head for a headstand in gymnastics or the point at which you lose contact with the ball for a push pass in hockey;

■ to *emphasise a particular aspect/help pupils' understanding*. For example, use of demonstration to show a change of speed, direction, flexibility or strength;

■ to *improve quality/set standards*. Use of demonstration can focus pupils' observations so that you can show what is expected and educate them to look more closely at each element that builds into the competent performance of a skill. For example, body tension used to perform a vault in gymnastics, the fluency of transitions in dancing from one movement phrase to another or the placement and use of fingers when dribbling the ball in basketball;

■ to *show variety*, especially to show *creativity*. Demonstrations allow pupils to observe the different responses pupils make to given tasks in, for example, gymnastics, dance and manoeuvres used in games to create space;

■ to *reward improved/well done work*. Use of a demonstration can be particularly important when you call on a pupil or group of pupils who may not be outstanding but always work to the best of their respective abilities and deserve recognition;

■ to *stimulate/motivate*. Demonstration can show pupils' flair and individuality, to motivate all pupils and to challenge the more able to set personal targets – for example, to work toward achieving a slice serve in tennis or master the Fosbury Flop technique in the high jump;

■ to *show completed work*. At the end of a unit of work demonstrations provide opportunities to show and reward the individual pupil, pairs, small groups and half-class groups. Knowing that they could be called upon to demonstrate often stimulates and encourages pupils to work at refining the quality of their physical movements.

There are many factors you need to consider when setting up a demonstration.

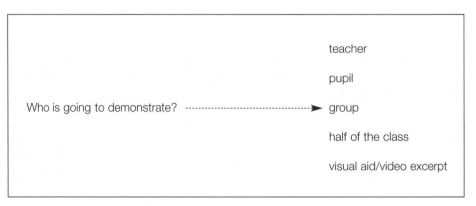

■ **Figure 5.1** Who is going to demonstrate?

You have to decide *who* is going to demonstrate and *why* (see Figure 5.1). Generally it is more motivating for the class if a pupil demonstrates, but it may be more appropriate for the teacher to demonstrate particularly if there is not a pupil who is sufficiently skilled, or if a new or difficult skill is being shown. Consider which pupil(s) you could ask to demonstrate and be mindful not to use the same ones each time. Do not always ask the most able pupil as this may demoralise others. It is important that sometimes you select a mid-ability level pupil to demonstrate. A group can show their expertise, or to save time half the class may demonstrate. Visual aids such as posters of good gymnastic movement, work cards for games tactics and video excerpts of swimming techniques can also be effective tools in showing good form and movement to a class.

Before you engage pupils in demonstrating to the class consider the following:

■　Have you asked the pupils if they mind demonstrating in front of a class?

■　Do the pupils know what is expected of them? Have you briefed them, have they practised the demonstration, do they feel confident in demonstrating?

■　What role is the pupil to take in the demonstration? You need to know your pupils and recognise their strengths – for example, if they are taking on the role of the feeder in a practice.

■　Is the environment and situation safe?

■　If pupils make an error give them the opportunity to try again and do not allow other pupils or yourself to laugh at the mistakes.

■　Always remember to praise the demonstrators and to thank them afterwards.

How can pupils get the most out of a demonstration?

In the exemplars of reasons identified for using demonstration above, the word 'show' recurs which indicates that an important component part of demonstration is *observation* (see also Chapter 4 on observing pupils in PE). The pupils who are 'looking at' the demonstration need both to *see* and *understand*. It is important to educate pupils to *observe* intelligently by using such techniques as:

■　directing their attention to specific aspects of the demonstration;

■　asking them well-structured questions about the demonstration;

■　focusing their attention on the quality of the work being shown;

■　helping them to perceive similarities and differences in the work being performed.

Figure 5.2 illustrates important factors that you need to be aware of when pupils *observe a demonstration*. The first priority is safety (Chapter 9 addresses safety issues in PE). You must also consider the best position for the pupils to view the demonstration. A number of considerations should be taken into account – for example, whether the demonstrator is right or left-handed, the position of the sun if outdoors (you should be facing/looking into the sun, with the sun behind the pupils so that they can see the demonstration), or whether there are any distractions (pupils should not be facing any distractions, therefore should have their backs to another group or to a classroom). You also need to consider the speed of the demonstration (beginning slowly) and that some pupils may need to see the demonstration more than once.

Before you set up the demonstration consider the environmental conditions, particularly as these will affect the pupils' ability to *hear the explanation of the demonstration*

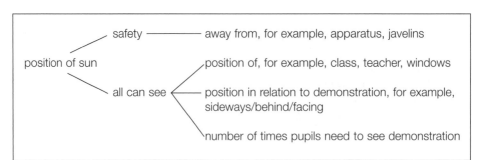

■ **Figure 5.2** Observing a demonstration

(see Figure 5.3). Is it very windy? if so bring the group in close to you so that they can hear the accompanying explanation. As the demonstration is performed state the most important teaching points in clear, concise language. Always remember to follow the demonstration up with a question/answer session and positive, constructive feedback on the pupils' performance.

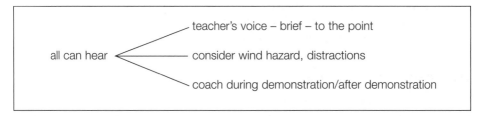

■ **Figure 5.3** Hearing the explanation of a demonstration

You must *focus the pupils' attention* on a specific aspect of the demonstration (see Figure 5.4) to ensure that they know what they are looking for. Once identified, all pupils should listen to verbal explanations and observe the demonstration carefully. Following this up with a question/answer session ensures that pupils have been concentrating and understand the teaching points being made. This is vitally important for improving pupils' evaluative skills.

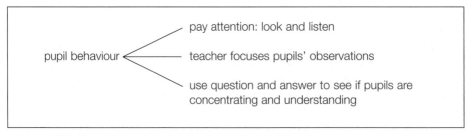

■ **Figure 5.4** Focusing pupils' attention in a demonstration

Now carry out Task 5.9 to monitor your management of demonstrations.

Task 5.9 **Observation of a demonstration**

Devise an observation sheet that focuses on the use of demonstration. Use the information above to identify important aspects of demonstration that you want to include and/or further develop. Ask your tutor to use this observation sheet to monitor your use of demonstration in a lesson. Discuss the outcome of this observation exercise with your tutor after the lesson. Put these observations into your PDP. In future lessons endeavour to put into practice what you learn from this experience. Also, try to incorporate the feedback received into future observation sheets to further support use of demonstration in your observation of teaching and learning.

It is important for you as the teacher to be knowledgeable and to be able to demonstrate well, because pupils imitate good practice in order to become more proficient. Sometimes this process is called 'modelling'. Also remember that 'practice' makes 'permanent', so demonstrations do need to be 'perfect'! Now carry out Task 5.10 to clarify your rationale for using a demonstration.

Task 5.10 **Clarifying your use of demonstration**

Design a lesson that incorporates demonstration. Use the following questions to clarify key factors that you need to consider when setting up a demonstration:

- *What* is the nature of the demonstration?
- *How* will this promote pupil learning?
- *When* during the lesson could this be introduced most effectively?
- *Where* in the teaching space will the demonstration take place?
- *Who* is going to demonstrate?
- *Why* am I using this demonstration?

Discuss your responses to each question with a tutor or another student teacher. Use these questions to clarify your use of demonstration in future PE lessons. Put these notes in your PDP for later reference.

Cautionary endnote – what not to demonstrate and when not to use demonstration!

It is strongly recommended that you avoid demonstrating *what not to do*. Occasionally pupils misunderstand and think what they see is what they should do! And there are times when it is not appropriate to use demonstration – for example, at the beginning of a lesson when the class needs to be active quickly and on a very cold day when standing still to watch a demonstration is not appropriate.

SUMMARY AND KEY POINTS

This chapter has explored language skills in relation to communication in PE lessons. It has stressed the importance of audibility and the appropriate use of your voice in different situations and contexts. The importance of your grasp of, and accurate use of, technical language has been stressed. The use of questioning has been considered in some detail with the challenge for you to use different types of questions to challenge pupils in a variety of ways. Feedback has been highlighted as a key aspect of communication that has a significant effect on pupil learning. The need to ensure that all written work sets pupils a good example and is of a high standard has been discussed and the role of pupil talk has been introduced as an issue to be considered. By developing these aspects of language skills you are well on the way to becoming an effective communicator.

The chapter has also explored demonstration as one exemplar of communication in practice. You should now appreciate how effective, purposeful demonstration can be used to set tasks quickly and to help pupils better understand the task. The value of demonstrations in the learning process has also been outlined.

As was recognised in the introduction to the chapter, communication is at the heart of teaching. The teacher is, above all, a communicator. Language is one of the most significant tools of the teacher's trade. Communication is the vehicle through which knowledge is passed from the teacher to the pupils. Without effective communication, ILOs will not be achieved. Desired learning will not take place. Many other aspects of teaching rely on effective communication, such as feedback, organisation and class management. To bring together all the important aspects of communication complete Task 5.11 below.

Check which requirements for your course you have addressed through this chapter.

Task 5.11 **The place of communication in teaching**

Write a 2,000 word essay on the following topic: 'Critically consider the claim that communication is the most significant of the teacher's tools in the promotion of learning.'

Put your essay in your PDP as evidence of Master's level work.

FURTHER READING

Godefroy, H. and Barrat, S. (1993) *Confident Speaking*, **London: Judy Piatkus.**
This book gives some helpful practical tips about how to use your voice and language effectively.

McGuire, B., Parker, L. and Cooper, W. (2001) Physical education and language: do actions speak louder than words?, *European Journal of Physical Education,* **6, 2: 101–16.**
This paper discusses findings from a research study that investigated the nature and extent to which PE lessons can provide effective language experiences and contribute to pupils' oracy development.

Muijs, D. and Reynolds, D. (2005) *Effective Teaching: Evidence and Practice,* **2nd edn, London: Paul Chapman (Sage).**
Chapter 2 discusses the important relationship between pupils' learning and interactive teaching. Components of effective questioning techniques are highlighted and examined in relation to class discussion.

Robertson, J. (1996) *Effective Classroom Control: Understanding Teacher–Student Relationships,* **3rd edn, London: Hodder and Stoughton.**
Chapter 4 discusses how gestures and speech, vocal behaviour and meaning, and eye contact and speech can be used to convey enthusiasm to sustain pupils' attention. The bibliography is a rich resource for classroom management and control.

Wragg, E. and Brown, G. (2001) *Questioning in the Secondary School,* **London: RoutledgeFalmer.**
This book combines practical resources with relevant research which enables you to examine how you use questions, how you might develop your use of questioning and how pupils can be encouraged to question and provide answers.

Young, R. (1992) *Critical Theory and Classroom Talk,* **Clevedon: Multilingual Matters Ltd.**
This book provides some insights into how teaching language and teaching voice can affect pupil response to subject and teacher.

Endnote

The author would like to acknowledge the significant input of Roger Strangwick to earlier editions of this chapter.

LESSON ORGANISATION AND MANAGEMENT

Julia Lawrence and Margaret Whitehead

INTRODUCTION

According to Wilson and Cameron (1996: 190) 'a successful instructional environment is one where pupils are on task and settled', allowing them to concentrate on their learning. Thus the organisation and management of pupils during a lesson is a key factor to ensure that effective learning takes place. In respect of PE this would be reflected in pupils being actively engaged 'on task'. That is, they are involved in motor and other activities related to the subject matter in such a way as to produce a high degree of success, with intended learning outcomes (ILOs) of the lesson more likely to be met.

Research (e.g. Richardson and Fallona, 2001; Wilson and Cameron, 1996) suggests the development of organisation and management skills occurs over a long period of time. Thus the development of these aspects of your teaching is likely to be ongoing and worthy of focused reflection throughout your teaching career. However, potentially, they may be one of your main concerns when you first start teaching lessons on school experience. The aim of this chapter is to give you some guidance of when and where organisation and management skills can be applied effectively within the teaching environment to enhance pupil learning.

OBJECTIVES

At the end of the chapter you should be able to:

- organise people, the space, the equipment and time, before, during and after lessons;
- establish effective rules and routines;
- understand how to increase the time pupils spend on task in lessons;
- manage pupils' behaviour and maintain discipline and control.

Check the requirements for your course to see which relate to this chapter.

ORGANISATION AND MANAGEMENT OF THE LEARNING ENVIRONMENT

The organisation of the learning environment is an important aspect of the planning and delivery of teaching. Organisation is not only about planning how to achieve ILOs but also about being prepared for the unexpected that can take place before, during and after the lesson. A well-organised teacher is better able to respond to situations during lessons than one who has not fully prepared. Your organisation should focus on people (your pupils and yourself), the space, the equipment and the best use of time. Three key organisational points can be identified, being: before the lesson starts, during the lesson and once the lesson has finished. Table 6.1 shows a summary of some of the key areas requiring consideration in your organisation.

■ **Table 6.1** Some organisational tasks that need to be completed before, during and after a lesson

Before the lesson	During the lesson	After the lesson
■ Plan the lesson – people, space, equipment and time	■ Oversee entry into the lesson	■ Evaluate the lesson
■ Mark homework	■ Monitor changing, collect valuables, take the register	■ Plan the next lesson (see Chapter 3)
■ Check the space	■ Organise space	
■ Check the resources	■ Organise equipment	
■ Check equipment	■ Establish teaching tasks/activities	
■ Set work for pupils not doing the lesson	■ Give instructions	
	■ Organise groups	
	■ Move from one activity/task to another	
	■ Oversee exit from the lesson	

Organisation before the lesson

The planning and organisation of a lesson prior to the arrival of a class is very important. You may find it useful to discuss your lesson organisation with your tutor in order to identify potential stress points and receive guidance on how you might prepare for and respond to problems that may arise. The more confident you are with the material and how you are going to organise and teach the lesson, the more able you are to deal with any situations that may arise during the lesson.

Within your planning you should identify your work areas and familiarise yourself with any potential hazards (issues concerned with safety are covered in Chapter 9). It is always worth confirming with other staff the areas you are going to use. Do not assume that just because you have planned to use the field that someone else might not want to use it too. You should also check when examinations or other events, e.g. a school play, are being held and whether this changes the space that is available for use. Knowledge of wet weather provision is also important. While most lessons tend to carry on regardless of the weather, be aware that in some cases you may need to double up groups indoors if the weather is very poor. Pupils quickly pick up if you have failed to plan effectively, and this may result in disruptive behaviour. It is always worth planning for both an indoor and outdoor lesson if there is some doubt about the venue.

Any space in which you work has a variety of aspects that can be used in your teaching, for example, walls, lines, markings, grids and apparatus. Best use of these needs to be considered in planning and organisation. (You should have collected such information on your preliminary visits to the school – see Chapter 1.) Schools have appointed groundskeepers, many based on site, who may be able to provide additional markings if given the appropriate amount of notice. You should plan to use the working space as appropriate for a specific lesson – for example, using grids for practices or setting up equipment for a circuit. If you are in a confined space using apparatus/equipment your organisation has to be planned carefully to ensure that:

■   the environment is safe at all times;
■   the apparatus is not too close to walls;
■   you are aware where misplaced balls/shuttles may go;
■   it accommodates large groups for activity (e.g. badminton);
■   equipment/apparatus is stored and accessible;
■   you are using the space most effectively for the activity and the pupils.

It is essential that you spend time planning transitions within your lessons. For example, do you need to collect in equipment in order to set up for the next activity or can the working area be used in different ways? Can the next activity be set up while the previous task is being carried out? Can you involve pupils in setting up their own practice areas? Within your planning, consideration should be given to the nature of the class being taught, including the number of pupils in the class, their motivation, their gender and how well they cooperate together. You also need to consider how much equipment/apparatus is available for a particular activity (e.g. rugby, athletics or hockey) as this determines how you can organise tasks/practices/games.

Your planning therefore links numbers of pupils with resources and equipment that are needed and available for the lesson. Thought needs to be given in your planning to the collection of equipment at the start of the lesson and/or getting out equipment during the lesson, its location and use during the lesson, and the methods employed to put it away at the end of the lesson. Further consideration also needs to be given to the placement of equipment and where those not participating are positioned. By organising resources and equipment prior to the lesson, you give your class a sense of readiness and organisation that should filter through to the lesson itself.

The following is a checklist for you, the PE teacher, for organising the lesson *before* it starts. You should have:

■   *Planned and prepared the lesson.* It is essential to plan each lesson well before it is taught, in this way you have a clear understanding of what you want to achieve in each lesson you teach (see Chapter 3).
■   *Checked the working space.* Is it available and safe for use? At the beginning of the day it is important to check your working space so that you have a smooth start to your lesson. It may, for example, have been used for evening classes and equipment (e.g. badminton posts/nets) may not have been put away.

■ *Checked and counted all equipment.* Is it readily available and in good order? You may delegate this task to pupils, but it is important to ensure the equipment is ready (e.g. basketballs are inflated for your lesson). Consider setting aside time in which this is done every week.

■ *Have prepared team lists, bibs, visual aids, work cards and spare whistles.* As part of your preparation it may be advantageous to prepare team lists for when you move to the game section of your lesson, visual aids to give pupils more ideas, work cards to help pupils complete a task and spare whistles so that pupils can take on the role and responsibility of umpiring/refereeing in your lessons. This makes for smooth transitions and little wasted time.

■ *Set work for pupils not participating practically in the lesson through injury, illness or for other reasons.* It is useful to check your school policies and procedures regarding these non-participants. Ideally these pupils play a constructive role in the lesson rather than 'sitting out'. For example, they may be able to give useful feedback to pupils who are active, or umpire or score. On some occasions these pupils may be asked to make notes on aspects of the lesson. Lessons outdoors may be a problem if the weather is very cold and it may be appropriate for pupils who are 'off practical' to do some theory work indoors on the specific activity being taught (see also using ICT to include non-participants in PE in Chapter 12). Tasks set for these pupils can address some of the broader aims of PE as set out in Chapter 14.

■ *Marked homework.* It is important that you meet deadlines and return homework with appropriate feedback for pupils. This is also very important for pupil motivation (see Chapter 7).

Task 6.1 is designed to alert you to the ways in which teachers prepare for lessons.

Task 6.1 **Teacher preparation before a lesson**

Shadow an experienced PE teacher in your placement school for a morning and record the way each lesson is prepared for in advance of the pupils arriving. Record these observations in your professional development portfolio (PDP). Check back to the list above as you begin to take more responsibility for lessons.

Organisation and management during the lesson

Organisation and management during a lesson begins when the pupils arrive in the changing room to start the lesson and concludes when they leave the PE area. During this time you are expected to respond to many situations, both planned and unplanned. One way to improve organisation and management during this period is to establish routines with which both you and your pupils are familiar. Primarily pupils need to know what is expected of them in terms of behaviour, effort and task completion. Establishing routines, therefore, plays a vital role in the success of lessons. By providing pupils with terms of reference, in the form of rules and routines, pupils have a framework on which to base behaviour. The use of appropriate sanctions to reinforce inappropriate behaviour must also be identified. If you need to issue sanctions make sure that they are consistent, appropriate and enforceable. In most schools, home–school contracts now exist, providing teachers, parents and pupils with information on what each can expect from the other. Do not be surprised to see codes of conduct displayed in the school environment, again providing terms of reference for both staff and pupils. The management of pupil behaviour is referred to in more detail towards the end of this chapter. Tasks 6.2 and 6.3 require you to look at some of the rules and routines that may be useful for you to employ.

Task 6.2 **Rules and PE**

Read the school and PE department rules for your placement school, then discuss these with your tutor. Ask if there are any additional rules for specific activities you are teaching. Put your findings in your PDP. Add to these notes as you implement these rules in your lessons.

Task 6.3 **Routines in PE lessons**

Routines in PE are valuable and important. Examples of aspects of PE lessons for which routines are advantageous are: entering the changing rooms, changing, taking the register, entering the working space, giving instructions, collecting equipment, starting work, gaining attention, finishing a task, moving into different groups, moving from one task/activity to another, putting equipment away, leaving the working area/space, leaving the changing rooms.

Can you think of any more? If so, add them to this list.

Observe two different members of the PE department in your placement school teaching lessons, looking specifically at the way they enforce the rules and what routines they have for those tasks and behaviours which occur frequently. How are the routines different? How are they the same? Can you suggest why this might be? How can you apply these in your lessons? Put your observations in your PDP.

Rules, routines and procedures are very often specific to particular activity settings, for example swimming, athletics and outdoor and adventurous activities (OAA). Table 6.2 sets out some examples of activity-specific rules, routines and procedures and Task 6.4 asks you to add further examples.

■ **Table 6.2** Some examples of rules, routines and procedures

Activity	Rule/routine/procedure
Gymnastics:	No large apparatus to be used until the teacher has checked it for safety. No running at times when apparatus is being put out or dismantled.
Swimming:	No one to enter the pool without permission. No running on poolside. No screaming in pool.

■ **Table 6.2** continued

Activity	Rule/routine/procedure
Hockey:	One short sharp whistle: stand still, face the teacher and listen.
Javelin:	Always walk when carrying a javelin. Have the sharp end pointing down. Never throw unless given permission by the teacher.

Task 6.4 **Rules and routines for specific activities**

Table 6.2 identifies some rules, routines and procedures for specific activities. Add to this list rules, routines and procedures for three activities you are teaching on school placement.

Activity 1

Activity 2

Activity 3

Discuss these suggestions with your tutor and put these notes in your PDP.

General organisational situations: the changing rooms

The success of a lesson invariably stems from how pupils first arrive at, and prepare for, the lesson. It is here that much time can be wasted if you are not properly organised. It is essential that you are there when the pupils arrive to let them into the changing room. Different schools have different policies regarding what to do on arrival. Task 6.1 has alerted you to the strategies employed within your placement school.

Being present in the changing rooms while pupils are changing allows you to set the tone of the lesson, helps to prevent inappropriate behaviour and encourages pupils to change as quickly as possible. In some cases it also provides the opportunity to take the class register, thereby reducing the need to have this as a separate activity. Being present in the changing rooms can also give you the opportunity to outline the focus of the lesson, to set up the first task the pupils are to undertake or to organise some of the key aspects of the lesson – for example, what size groups pupils are going to work in during the first part of the lesson or which pupils are responsible for taking out the equipment. It is important, however, to remember that you should not go into the opposite sex changing rooms. If you are teaching a mixed class, you have to adopt a different approach. Check with your tutor the procedure adopted in your placement school.

Be aware of when and how notes to be excused from the lesson are dealt with and how such pupils are integrated into the lesson. Consider what happens to those pupils who arrive late or without the appropriate kit. Again your department should have procedures to be undertaken in these situations.

Below is a checklist of procedures that you might wish to use in the changing room:

■ Establish pupils' entry into the changing room. This should be orderly and quiet. Schools/teachers have their own routines (see Tasks 6.2 and 6.3 above).

■ Establish routines for attending to such tasks as collecting pupils' valuables, excuse notes and giving out kit to pupils who have forgotten theirs. Routines prevent time being wasted at the beginning of a lesson.

■ Take the register. This can be done while pupils change without wasting too much time. However, there may be times when it is better to take the register in the working space before the lesson starts, e.g. for a mixed gender class.

■ Establish routines for organising taking out equipment. There are many different methods for doing this (see below).

■ Set a task from the work in the previous lesson so that pupils start working quickly. For example, in hockey, you can ask pupils to 'remember the practice of beating your opponent that we covered in last week's lesson; practise this when you get to the pitch'. Pupils can therefore start as soon as they are ready.

■ Check all pupils are out of the changing room and lock the door. Most changing rooms are locked for security. It is your responsibility to check all pupils are changed and have left the changing room.

Organising and managing people: pupils and yourself

PUPILS

As has already been identified, you begin the organisation of pupils in the changing rooms at the start of the lesson. However, during the lesson itself, you organise pupils for, for example, an activity and/or to change the activity, to collect or put away equipment or put pupils into groups or teams. There are many reasons for specific groupings of pupils – for example:

■ mixed ability: where pupils of a wide range of abilities work together. This type of grouping is a good context for fostering leadership and cooperative skills;

■ similar ability: for specific activities such as swimming;

■ contrasting ability: here you may consider utilising the strengths of more able pupils to support other pupils' performance, effort or behaviour in positive ways;

■ social friendship: this is useful with older pupils as it can promote motivation.

It is your responsibility to devise methods of putting pupils into groups and to check all pupils have a group, as quiet, shy pupils may not tell you if they have not found a group with which to work. Your method of grouping pupils should take as little time as possible. Generally try and avoid the pupils picking groups, which can result in a lot of wasted time and poor self-esteem for some pupils.

Although it is more efficient to maintain grouping throughout a lesson there can be situations, such as needing to differentiate between pupils, in which changing group structure is important. This change constitutes a significant transition and needs to be planned by you before the lesson. If you do change the grouping in a lesson you need to plan how this can be carried out swiftly. Where possible, try to build from current groups into the next grouping, for example, develop groups from 1s to 2s or 3s; 2s to 4s or 6s; or 3s to 6s, so that there are smooth transitions and continuity in the lesson. This is particularly important outside on cold days. Some methods you may use for grouping pupils are:

■ Calculate the number of pupils participating from the register taken in the changing room, or count heads as the pupils are warming up, so you know the number in the class and can think of any adaptations you may need to make to your planned groups during the lesson.

■ In 2s of similar height and build for a warm-up task.

■ Pupils jogging, teacher calls a number, for example 2, 3, 5 or 7. Pupils quickly get into groups. Eventually the stated number go into first practice/apparatus/team group.

■ If you know the class you may devise appropriate groupings/leaders/team lists before the lesson.

■ Into 2s, number yourselves 1 and 2, number 2 get a ball. Have balls in a designated area central to the working area.

■ Develop above practice to 4s with one ball. Join with another 2 and put one ball away as quickly as possible (the teacher may number pupils 1 and 4 and state a number, for example, 3, who puts the spare ball away).

■ Mixed ability – 28 pupils into teams of 7 – find a partner (into 2s), join with another 2 to make a 4 – in your 4s number off 1 to 4, all 1s together, all 2s together, all 3s together, etc. to form teams of 7.

Wherever possible, organisation between activities should be kept to a minimum (see Figure 6.1, which shows progression in groupings in volleyball as well as use of workspace). The same principles for developing grouping can be used in other activities.

YOURSELF

Most teachers work in a classroom with seating and the teacher needs to plan the most effective seating for the task in hand. As a PE teacher, however, you more often work in spaces without pupils in set places/seats. Good teacher positioning and movement is vital in establishing and maintaining learning, discipline and safety in your lessons (see also teacher positioning in Chapters 4 and 9). You need to position yourself so that your voice is audible, with the appropriate volume for the specific environment – for example, a swimming pool, hockey pitch on a windy day or a sports hall with poor acoustics. You must always be aware of the whole class and avoid having your back to the group, standing in the middle of a group of pupils or having pupils behind you. Good positioning enables you to observe effectively so that you can monitor, for example, pupils' progress or behaviour and give them feedback either as individuals, groups or as a whole class (see Chapter 4 for observation of pupils in PE). The same principles hold for a classroom setting when you are teaching theoretical aspects of PE. Try not to stay in one place throughout these lessons. Move among the pupils and monitor their work and give feedback as you pass pupils.

In a practical setting your positioning changes constantly depending on your working space and the purpose of a task (e.g. setting up a practice or demonstrating). You need to be aware of your positioning in relation to the class and also of the class in relation to you, other groups, the sun and any other important factors. For example, if it is sunny, you should be positioned so you are looking into the sun so that the pupils can see you. The following are some examples of the many different situations you experience when teaching PE in which effective positioning is important in your lesson organisation and management:

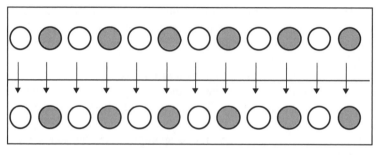

1 v 1 warm up activity – volleying to partner over net down centre of space

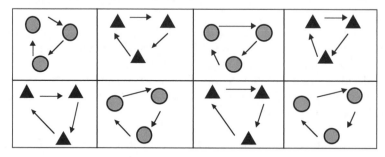

Into 3s – divide space equally. Set a practice for continuous volley, dig etc.

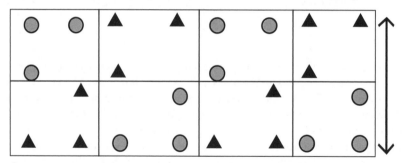

3 v 3 – set up a conditioned game – serve, receive, set, spike etc.

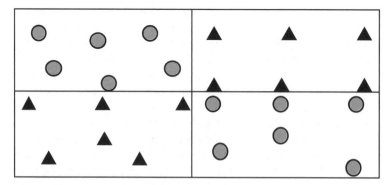

6 v 6 – join with another 3 and set conditions of play

■ **Figure 6.1** Progressions in groupings and use of working space in volleyball (adapted from National Coaching Foundation, 1994)

■ When getting the equipment/apparatus out, establish set routines and give the class clear instructions, then make the pupils responsible, stand back where you can see everyone and watch, only helping when and where necessary.

■ Setting up a demonstration (see Chapter 5).

■ When setting a class task you need to be able to see everyone and to ensure that all the class can see and hear you. This is much easier to do in a smaller indoor space than in an outdoor space. In your outdoor lessons, define the working area for pupils – for example, refer to the use of lines on the court or pitch, so that you do not lose contact with your class.

■ Monitoring your class. This is best done from the perimeters – for example, from the corners of an indoor space, from the back of a tennis or badminton court. From your observations you are able to assess whether the whole class understands the task. If most of the pupils are doing one thing incorrectly or the task is too easy or too difficult, you need to stop the whole class and give further guidance or clarify instructions.

■ Helping individuals/small groups. Here you may be supporting a pupil in gymnastics or dividing your attention between several small 4 v 4 football games. At all times you must be able to see the rest of your class as you work with a particular pupil(s). This is achieved best by monitoring from the perimeter and looking in towards the class.

■ When setting a class competition ensure that you are in a position, before you begin the competition, where your peripheral vision enables you to see all the pupils as well as who wins.

■ Be near to a misbehaving pupil(s). It is important to circulate and be close to a potential trouble zone. Knowing your pupils and their names helps you control potential disruption (see Chapter 7). Take steps to learn pupils' names so that you can establish contact from wherever you may be in the working space (see Chapter 7 and particularly Task 7.4 for further information on learning pupils' names).

■ It is important to be aware of any pupils with special educational needs (SEN) and the nature of their specific needs – for example, poor hearing or eyesight – so you can position them advantageously in your lessons (see Chapter 11).

In Task 6.5 your tutor or another student teacher observes you and notes down how effective your positioning was in a number of different lessons.

Task 6.5 **Teacher positioning**

Ask your tutor or another student teacher to observe and record how effectively you position yourself when teaching three different activities – for example, gymnastics, swimming and outdoor games. Keep these records. At the end of these observations you should be able to draw up a list of ways in which teaching position influences pupil learning and behaviour. You also appreciate how different activities in PE require different teaching positions. Try to use this knowledge to improve your positioning in your next lessons. Put the information in your PDP.

Organising and managing the space

As a PE teacher you work in a number of spaces (e.g. gymnasium, sports field, swimming pool, classroom). During your initial teacher education (ITE) course you gain knowledge regarding the health and safety requirements of each area and the need to conduct appropriate risk assessment (see Chapter 9) and this aspect of your work must never be forgotten. Much organisation of space occurs before the lesson starts (this has been covered earlier in this chapter) and should be reflected in your planning. However, it is also important that you are able to organise and manage the workspace efficiently and effectively to maximise safety, pupil involvement and activity.

There are a number of ways to identify your workspace. Line markings in a sports hall or field/court area are useful, as is the use of cones, although consideration needs to be given here to risk management and safety in respect of the type of cones used. Where possible, cones should be set out prior to the practice to be conducted. This might be while the pupils are involved in a warm-up, or by using those not participating. It is also possible to allow pupils to set up their own work areas once they have received a practical demonstration.

Some examples of how to use the available space are given in Figure 6.2. While focusing on netball, the same principles for using working space can be applied to other activities. Task 6.6 then asks you to focus specifically on space management in a PE class.

Task 6.6 **Organisation of your working space**

Design an indoor circuit for a class of 30 pupils for an activity and year group of your choosing, the use of which is planned to achieve specified ILOs. In your planning consider safety, activity levels of the pupils and methods of recording pupils' results. After completing this task, teach the lesson. In your evaluation identify how far the space organisation enabled you to achieve the ILOs. Note areas requiring further development and use this information to design further circuits. Put this information in your PDP.

Organisation and management of equipment

Use of equipment is central to most work in PE and is an important area of organisation. You need to decide what equipment is needed for pupils to achieve the ILOs and ensure that this is available. As identified in the introduction, pupils learn most effectively when engaged on a task. Therefore to achieve maximum activity and learning, you should, wherever possible and appropriate, provide each pupil with an individual piece of equipment (e.g. when working on individual skills in football or basketball). This increases the number of opportunities for practice and should promote skill development. Also, when pupils are working with others, group sizes should be kept as small as the amount of equipment allows so that they are actively engaged in the activity. The use of small group practices reduces the time spent waiting, thereby increasing the amount of actual activity time per pupil. Equally, the use of small-sided games allows for increased opportunities for pupils to apply the skills they have learnt during practices in larger game situations. All these strategies ensure that pupils are actively involved, increasing the opportunities for learning and reducing the opportunities for inappropriate behaviour.

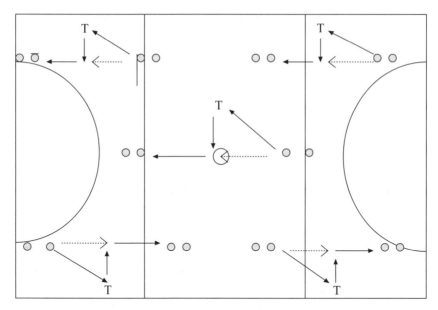

Organisation on netball court: five groups of 5 players

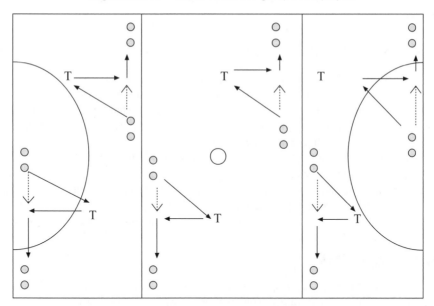

Organisation on netball court: six groups of 5 players

■ **Figure 6.2** Organisation of your working space in netball (adapted from Crouch, 1984: 123)

Your lesson should develop logically so that you are not putting equipment away and getting it out again. Some general aspects to consider are where the equipment is stored and the best or most appropriate methods for getting it out and putting it away. Some methods you may use are:

■   first pupils ready take equipment out – remember that equipment should always be counted;

■   pupils line up outside store room individually or in groups and collect equipment when told;

■   certain groups always take equipment out, others always bring it in;

■   as groupings change, any spare equipment must be put away for safety reasons. Have containers near to the working area. Decide how/who is to put equipment in these containers;

■   at the end of a lesson make sure you count the equipment again, organise its collection and/or involving pupils in these tasks.

These are general principles for organising equipment but you should appreciate that you need specific rules and routines for organising equipment for each activity (see Task 6.4). In gymnastics, for example, line up in 2s by the mat trolley, the first mat to go to the furthest part of the gym. Pupils should be made responsible for caring for the equipment and at all times safety procedures must be adhered to.

The same principles apply when you are taking a classroom lesson as there are books and other resources to be managed. Organisation is just as important in this setting and poorly planned management of resources can mar the effectiveness of a lesson. For example, if text books are not available or samples of bones are missing, certain ILOs will not be achieved.

Organisation after the lesson

Once the lesson has finished, you need to evaluate it as soon as possible. This might initially be verbally with the member of staff observing you, but should also be written so that you can return to this self-assessment and reflect on what you have learnt. Your evaluation should focus on pupils' learning as well as the specific personal goals you wanted to achieve (for example the teaching standards on which you were focusing/being observed). However, it is also important to reflect on whether your organisation and management could be improved, particularly in order to create more time for learning. This evaluation informs the planning of your next lesson. Chapter 3 discusses both planning and evaluation in more depth. Activity 9.1 in Capel, Breckon and O'Neill (2006) is a useful exercise to do at this point to review the areas covered in this chapter so far.

MANAGING TIME

Throughout the chapter so far frequent mention has been made about how well-planned and efficient organisation can use time to best effect, promote learning and guard against pupils moving off task. In fact time management is a key element of teaching. This refers both to managing pupils' time and to managing how you spend your time (see also Unit 1.3 in Capel, Leask and Turner, 2009).

Ideally, in PE, pupils are active most of the time, however, because of the nature of the subject there are always parts of the allocated lesson time during which pupils are not active. For example pupils are not active when:

■   they change before and after the lesson;

■   the register is taken;

■ they listen to instructions, watch demonstrations and receive teaching points;

■ they wait for their turn on a piece of apparatus;

■ they observe a partner's work;

■ they read task cards or study criteria to guide performance;

■ they consider how to solve a problem;

■ they plan together in group settings.

There are, of course, times in the lesson when pupils are, quite legitimately, not physically active, but are nevertheless engaged 'on task'. Examples are identified in the third and last bullet points above. However, care should be taken to ensure that as far as possible pupils are active for most of the time. Indeed the art of effective time management is to ensure only the minimum time is spent on the non-active aspects of the lesson (including organisation). Where overlong periods of time are given to any of the non-active parts pupils' attention is likely to wander, they may become disruptive with resultant behaviour problems. Time taken to deal with these problems is not time well spent! All the guidance given in the chapter so far should help you to use time to best effect.

Lessons can vary from 35 minutes to 70 minutes or longer. In some schools transportation to off-site facilities may also have to be accounted for as part of the overall length of the lesson. This time may be used productively to prepare pupils so that they are ready to start the lesson as soon as they arrive at the facility (e.g. you may recap on previous learning and/or cover some new learning which can then be put into practice). The tempo of the lesson should ensure logical, smooth transitions, avoiding overdwelling on a particular task. When you are inexperienced it is sometimes difficult to judge how much time to spend on a task. This depends ultimately on the pupils' responses to your material and you, as the teacher, must be aware of pupils who work at different rates. It is important that you monitor pupils' responses to check if they are working satisfactorily or if they are uncertain what to do, perhaps because the explanation was not clear or the challenge set is too hard. This is sometimes known as 'reading' the class. Having 'read' the pupils' response you need to respond appropriately. This may be to do nothing, to explain the task again, to modify the task or to give specific feedback to all or some pupils. During the lesson you also need to manage pupils' movement, noise levels and behaviour.

The allocation of time in your lesson should allow time for, for example:

■ Pupils to complete tasks and receive feedback from the teacher.

■ Pupils to use the apparatus and have time to put it away. It is pointless to get apparatus out in a gymnastics lesson if pupils do not then have enough time to put the apparatus away safely, without hurrying.

■ Pupils to have a game if they have practised skills/small sided games. Pupils need time to experience how well they can apply their earlier learning to a game situation. This may also inform you of pupils' understanding of tasks set.

■ Pupils to complete a circuit and to collect scores.

■ You to give feedback about the lesson. It is important to highlight the learning you hoped to achieve (e.g. with a question and answer session) to conclude your lesson.

■ You and the pupils to finish the lesson smoothly.

■ The pupils to shower and dress after the lesson.

■ You to ensure pupils are not late for their next lesson!

Task 6.7 is designed to make you aware of how pupils spent their time in lessons.

Task 6.7 **Monitoring pupils' use of time**

Observe a lesson taught by another student teacher and watch one pupil through-out the lesson. Record when this pupil is active or not, and whether this is productive or non-productive activity. After the lesson discuss your observations with the student teacher and debate ways that active time can be increased. Ask the student teacher to conduct the same exercise on one of your lessons. Using the outcomes of the discussion work to improve use of pupil time in future lessons. Put both records in your PDP and use this to increase pupil time engaged in productive activity in future lessons.

ACADEMIC LEARNING TIME IN PE (ALT-PE)

Given the importance of active learning time, it is not surprising that considerable research attention has been directed to this aspect of teaching. One such research initiative is known as Academic Learning Time in PE (ALT-PE, Siedentop *et al.*, 1982). This research divided activity time in lessons into:

- That time in which pupils are engaged in motor and other activities related to the subject matter in such a way as to produce a high degree of success and for ILOs of a lesson to be met. This has been called time 'on task' (or 'functional' time) (Metzler, 1989). It is often seen as a determinant of effective teaching in PE.
- Other time in which pupils are engaged in motor tasks but which is not time on task – for example, the task is too hard or too easy or pupils do not apply themselves to learning (e.g. they may hit a shuttle over the net in a badminton lesson but not work to achieve a specific ILO such as the use of a particular stroke or specific tactic).

Siedentop and Tannehill (2000) reported results of research which showed that these two account for, on average, 25–30 per cent of total lesson time. However, time on task may account for only 10–20 per cent of total lesson time (Metzler, 1989). Siedentop also identified differences in the amount of time on task in lessons in which different activities are being taught. Least time on task was found in lessons in gymnastics and team games, with time on task rising in lessons in individual activities to highest time on task in dance and fitness activities. More recently research conducted in Greece (Derri *et al.*, 2007) highlighted that whilst focusing on ALT in PE improved skill retention, success was dependent upon the effective use of managerial and organisational strategies if learning is to be enhanced.

Task 6.8 is a refinement of Task 6.7 and involves an observer noting specifically what the pupils are doing during one of your lessons.

Task 6.8 **Time pupils spend on different tasks**

Ask your tutor or another student teacher to observe one of your lessons and record the amount of time in which pupils are:

1   Actively engaged in motor tasks (e.g. practising a skill, playing a game).
2   Actively engaged in non-motor learning tasks (e.g. choreographing a dance with a partner or watching a video of a particular skill being learned, activities to achieve broader goals of PE).
3   Supporting others in learning motor activities (e.g. holding equipment, support-ing a partner).
4   Moving from one task to another.
5   Waiting.
6   Receiving information.
7   Engaged in other organisational tasks.
8   Engaged in other tasks or activities and not working towards achieving lesson ILOs.

(The ALT-PE observation schedule (Siedentop et al., 1982) is available on this book's website, www.routledge.com/textbooks/9780415561648).

How much time is spent on each of these eight types of tasks (a) individually and (b) on 1 to 3, and on 4 to 8, respectively? What is the relative percentage of time pupils spend working directly to achieve lesson ILOs (1–3) and on other tasks (4–8) in the lesson? Do you think this is acceptable? Discuss these with the observer. As appropriate, work to change the time allocation in your lessons. Repeat this task later in your ITE course to check if the time spent on different tasks has changed. Put these observations and notes in your PDP.

Task 6.8 should have highlighted the interactions between different aspects of a lesson – for example, the more time you spend organising, the less time pupils can spend on task. Hence, increases in time on task in your lessons cannot be achieved without effective organisation. Task 6.8 should also alert you to managerial and behavioural issues within your classroom, both of which influence the time pupils spend on task. Task 6.9 is an exercise to compare time on task in different lessons.

Task 6.9 **Gathering information about time on task in different lessons**

Ask your tutor or another student teacher to complete the ALT-PE observation sched-ule (Siedentop et al., 1982; available on this book's website, www.routledge.com/textbooks/9780415561648) while observing two lessons you are teaching in different activities, to see if there are any differences in time on task between lessons in different activities.

After each lesson reflect on the results and discuss these with the observer, to inform your evaluation of the lesson(s) and to identify what you can do to increase time on task. Ask the observer to undertake the same observations after you have had time to try and increase pupils' time on task in the lesson. After all the observations compare the time on task in lessons in different activities. Put this information in your PDP.

The importance of time management in PE is paramount as without effective use of time ILOs are unlikely to be achieved. Further, pupils can become disengaged and behaviour problems arise. The next section looks briefly at behaviour management.

MANAGING PUPILS' BEHAVIOUR

Teachers are expected to be good classroom managers. Administrators often consider teachers who exert strong control to be their best teachers, while parents and the community expect students to be taught self-control. Likewise students expect teachers to exert control and establish a positive learning environment.

(Cruickshank *et al.*, 1995: 393)

Whilst much has already been said about organisation and management and their impact on pupils' behaviour, it is necessary to take a more focused view of managing pupil behaviour in lessons. Unit 3.3 in Capel, Leask and Turner (2009) gives an overview of managing classroom behaviour (it takes a positive approach to classroom management, focusing on behaviour for learning). Your colleagues, school management, parents and society expect you to manage pupils effectively. However, the means by which this is achieved differs according to the behaviour management policies employed within the schools in which you work. Through hearing of the difficulties encountered from other student teachers in other schools, you are likely to be concerned about management skills in your early work in school. So that you have a clear context within which to work, it is wise to familiarise yourself with your placement school's policies on behaviour management. Working from within these expectations and patterns of sanctions enables you to adopt procedures that are common across the school. Pupils may well try you out when you first work with them, but if you are clear what is expected, they soon appreciate that you are in control and not 'a soft touch'. Parry (2007) has created a DVD designed to support you, providing a picture of what you are trying to achieve.

The task of establishing discipline and control is particularly challenging in PE, both because safety is a key issue and because in relatively unrestricted spaces (such as a games field or sports hall) there is considerable opportunity for misbehaviour. One way to approach behaviour management is to start from a positive standpoint. Thus the focus is on rewarding acceptable behaviours. Rather than looking to avoid problems, a useful goal is to set yourself the objective of keeping pupils on task. Pupils who are on task are both less likely to misbehave and more likely to master the ILOs. Keeping pupils on task demands a range of teaching skills, many of which have been referred to above, or in other chapters. According to Davison (2001) the behaviour of a class can be affected directly by the teaching skills you employ as a teacher. He identifies three main reasons for misbehaviour:

■ boredom;
▤ inability of the pupils to complete the task set;
■ too much effort required.

Consideration therefore needs to be given to such factors during the planning stage of your lesson. Throughout this chapter reference has been made to the need for organisation and management to be integral to the planning process. It is often the case that pupils look forward to PE as a lesson they enjoy and it might follow that we should have few problems with disinterested pupils. However, pupils' interest in a lesson depends, in part, on the tasks you have planned for them. If the work set is too simple or too demanding pupils' effort is likely to wane. Alternatively, if your organisational planning has not been carefully thought through, and there are prolonged awkward episodes during which no productive work is going on, pupils' attention wanders.

Apart from careful planning the key to effective management of behaviour is alert observation and an immediate response, if and when you see signs of pupils straying from the set task and beginning to misbehave. Teacher positioning in order to keep all the class in your sight has been outlined in this chapter and following these guidelines is very important. Figure 6.3 usefully maps out the pattern of observation and response (the numbers which follow refer to the numbers on the figure).

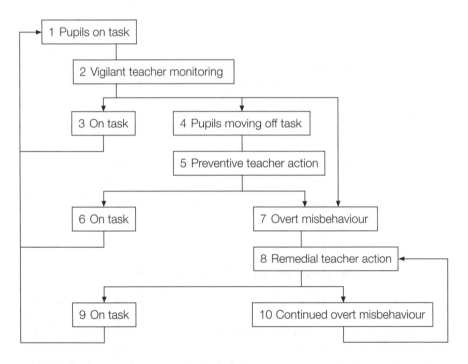

■ **Figure 6.3** A paradigm for managerial behaviour (adapted from Morrison and McIntyre, 1973)

In (1) all pupils appear to be on task. You are moving round the working space monitoring what is going on (2). While all pupils are on task (3) you proceed to provide teaching points to enhance pupils' learning and encouragement. However, should you see some pupils moving off task (4) you need to respond rapidly with preventive teacher action (5). This response could simply involve your moving close to the off task pupils or it could be a private or public reminder to the pupil(s) of the task in which they should be engaged. Alternatively, you could ask the off task pupils a question or take time to help them with their movement. However, if monitoring (2) reveals that a good many of the pupils are straying off task, a different response may be needed. Perhaps the task is proving too easy or too hard; maybe the class are ready for a change or need feedback from you as to how well they are progressing. Here the preventive action (5) is to stop the whole class and redirect the work. Hopefully on task behaviour (6) follows. If you do not pick up whole-class problems it is very likely that passive off task behaviour may turn into overt misbehaviour (7) by some pupils. Again rapid response is essential to avoid problems spreading to the whole class. It is useful to remember that there is some truth in the saying that misbehaving pupils are often telling you what others are too polite to say. So there are possibly, but not necessarily, two problems here: one the individual pupil and the other the nature of the whole-class task. It is probably the case that you have to take preventive action (5) with the whole class as above, but first you must enact a specific remedial action (8). This could be similar to that you effected when noticing latent misbehaviour of an individual, but it is likely to require firmer action. As far as possible avoid public confrontations and always identify the behaviour, not the pupil, as displaying unacceptable elements/characteristics/attributes. Never resort to physical intervention. You may need to remove the pupil at once or require a private word with her or him after the lesson. An alternative is to issue a threat that a particular course of action will be taken if on task behaviour is not resumed (9). This threat should be in line with school policy on punishment, but whatever the threat, it must be carried out if overt misbehaviour persists (10). Whenever and whatever your response is throughout this whole cycle it is important that you stay calm. Adopt a stable symmetrical stance, an authoritative posture and a measured tone of voice. Give every impression that you expect to be obeyed.

As you become more familiar with teaching you become able to anticipate times when opportunities for inappropriate behaviour arise, and plan accordingly. As your confidence grows such incidences decrease. Activity 9.4 in Capel, Breckon and O'Neill (2006) focuses on inappropriate behaviour. Task 6.10 asks you to read about and then use the ALT-PE principles in your teaching.

Task 6.10 **Application of ALT-PE principles**

Derri *et al.* (2007) conducted a small-scale study looking at the relationship between ALT and motor skill development. Their findings indicated that whilst an improvement in skill performance and retention was evident, of greater significance was the limited amount of ALT within the lessons observed. Conclusions around the effective use of organisation and management skills were identified as potential reasons for this. Such findings highlight the need for teachers to reflect upon the strategies they employ when teaching.

Having read this article, conduct a small-scale study on your own teaching, focusing upon the enhancement of ALT. Identify the strategies you employ and reflect upon any changes you make to you own practice. When reviewing your findings spend some time reflecting upon how your changes in practice impacted upon the pupil experience. Put these notes in your PDP and use your findings to improve pupil time on task.

SUMMARY AND KEY POINTS

Although all teachers have to organise and manage their lessons, organisation and management in PE lessons need specific consideration as pupils are working in large spaces, using a variety of equipment, with limited time. Although all teachers need to be able to give clear, precise instructions and explanations, PE teachers need to consider how they can give these to pupils who are not sitting in neat rows, behind desks, but moving around in a large space, often at considerable distances from the teacher. As a PE teacher, organising and managing lessons effectively is especially important because of the safety implications of activities and the large space in which you work.

In an effective lesson as little time as possible should be spent on organisation and management. Although effective lesson organisation and management are clearly important and may even be key to the success of a lesson, they are not everything and alone they are not enough. They can create time for learning to take place and an environment suitable for effective learning, but you need to use that time effectively for learning to occur. Effective lessons are those in which the time pupils are on task is maximised. The teacher has planned thoroughly what and how they are going to teach and how they are going to organise and manage the lessons (anticipating, and having planned especially carefully to prevent problems which may occur in the lesson, but having thought through how to respond to problems should they occur). You must be careful not to focus too much on effective organisation and management (especially in the early stages of your school experiences), but to see these as providing time and opportunity for effective teaching and learning to occur.

The way you organise and manage your class is an individual preference. Such skills are based around the establishment of clear rules and expectations, of both yourself and those you teach. Marland (1993: 8) states that: 'To be organized and firm is to have cleared the decks for variety of activity and friendliness, but to be slightly confused and wavering is to produce a muddle that leads only to a frayed temper, cross words, less pupil enjoyment and less learning.'

The aim of this chapter has been to provide an overview of ways in which you can develop your organisation and management skills. For many student teachers, the development of such skills is seen as a high priority. However, such skills develop over time and with experience. Even the most experienced teacher is still learning new ways of dealing with the ever-changing face of the classroom. Take time to reflect on your teaching and identify situations when a different approach may have been more appropriate. Be consistent in both your preparation and planning. Enter each lesson confident about your material. Most of all be clear about your expectations. Once pupils are aware of these, positive relationships can be established leading to enhancement of learning.

Check which requirements for your course you have addressed through this chapter.

FURTHER READING

Capel, S. and Lawrence, J. (2006) Creating an effective learning environment which promotes 'behaviour for learning', in S. Capel, P. Breckon and J. O'Neill (eds), *A Practical Guide to Teaching Physical Education in the Secondary School*, London: Routledge.

This practical guide provides supporting observation tasks which encourage reflection against personal practice. Chapter 9 within this practical book provides further development of some of the concepts explored in Chapter 6 of LTPESS. Of particular interest may be the section which focuses on the management of the classroom climate, as well as activities which encourage you to reflect on other more experienced teachers' practice.

Elton Report (1989) *Enquiry into Discipline in Schools London***, London: Her Majesty's Stationery Office.**

Possibly one of the most comprehensive reviews of discipline in schools over recent years. Using data collated from across professional bodies associated with the education of pupils, it provides an overview of a range of differing pupil behaviours, as well as strategies that may be used to overcome such behaviours.

Mawer, M. (1995) *The Effective Teaching of Physical Education***, London: Longman.**

Chapters 6 and 7 in this book focus on aspects of organisation and management. Chapter 6 focuses specifically on how effective learning environments can be created, particularly focusing on interaction with new classes. Chapter 7 focuses more on the maintenance of learning environments, looking at behaviour management strategies.

Parry, P. (2007) *The Interactive Guide to Behaviour Management for Trainee and Newly Qualified Teachers***, Swansea: Inclusive Behaviour Publications.**

This interactive CD-ROM provides a range of practical examples of behaviour management and lesson organisation strategies to support teachers within the classroom.

Siedentop, D. and Tannehill, D. (2000) *Developing Teaching Skills in Physical Education***, 4th edn, Mountain View, CA: Mayfield Publishing Co.**

Chapters 4 and 5 focus on preventive classroom management, discipline techniques and strategies in PE lessons.

Endnote

The authors would like to acknowledge the significant input of Susan Capel to this chapter in the first two editions of this book.

DEVELOPING AND MAINTAINING AN EFFECTIVE LEARNING ENVIRONMENT

Peter Breckon, Susan Capel, Margaret Whitehead and Paula Zwozdiak-Myers

INTRODUCTION

In this chapter you are introduced to aspects of your work as a teacher designed to create and maintain an effective learning environment to support other aspects of your teaching. Questions addressed include, what messages are you sending to pupils? Do you convey messages that PE and learning are fun? That pupils can achieve the intended learning outcomes (ILOs) of the lesson? That you care about pupils and their learning? That you value your pupils as people? Do you send any hidden messages to pupils? Do your verbal and non-verbal communications send the same message? Are you enthusiastic? Do you convey this to pupils? Are your interactions mostly positive or negative? Are they consistent? Do you motivate pupils?

Developing and maintaining a positive, supportive learning environment does not happen by chance, you need to plan for it for *all* pupils. The National Curriculum for Physical Education (NCPE) (Qualifications and Curriculum Authority (QCA), 2007a) Statutory Inclusion Statement identifies four expectations related to setting suitable learning challenges; responding to pupils' diverse needs; overcoming potential barriers to learning; and devising assessment approaches appropriate to individual pupils and groups of pupils. Inclusion is addressed in detail in Chapter 11. Before continuing, complete Task 7.1.

Task 7.1 **What messages are PE teachers sending?**

Read the situations below and identify what unintended messages you think the teacher is sending. Discuss your perceptions with another student teacher.

■ A teacher arrives at a lesson dressed in a tracksuit that he wore to train for rugby the night before.

■ It is a cold, wet day in the middle of January, the playing fields are waterlogged and cannot be used. The teacher sends the pupils on a cross-country run and returns to the changing room for a cup of coffee.

■ It is a cold, but dry day, the teacher decides to take the class outside for a netball lesson. She does not allow the pupils to wear tracksuit trousers or gloves, but she wears a tracksuit and a thick ski-jacket.

■ A class of 30 pupils have a 60-minute trampoline lesson using two beds. Pupils have one timed minute on the bed and then rotate on and off. At the end of the lesson each pupil has been physically active for a maximum time of four minutes.

■ In a high jump lesson the pupils are taking turns to jump over the bar. The height of the bar is increased at the end of every round. Pupils who did not successfully clear the previous height are not allowed to jump at the new height, therefore sit at the side of the pit and watch as the lesson continues.

■ The bell goes for the start of lessons after the lunch break. The teacher has been coaching the gymnastics team at lunchtime in preparation for an important competition. He has not had any lunch, therefore goes to the staffroom for some lunch whilst the pupils get changed and wait for him to start the lesson.

Record your findings in your professional development portfolio (PDP), to return to at the end of the chapter.

Scenarios such as this have occurred in PE lessons. Such situations do not help to create a learning environment that encourages pupils' learning, but rather lead to the creation of a negative climate in the lesson. They also have implications for safety (see Chapter 9).

A positive lesson climate provides the most effective learning environment. There are many factors which contribute to establishing a positive lesson climate, including self-presentation of the teacher and the presentation of the working space, the purposefulness of the lesson, the interpersonal relationships between teacher and pupils and between pupils, the motivation of pupils and the self-esteem of pupils. In this chapter these aspects of your teaching are considered. In developing these aspects of your teaching you use some of the skills identified in other chapters in this book, particularly those in Chapter 6 on lesson organisation and management. You should therefore refer to other chapters, where appropriate.

OBJECTIVES

At the end of this chapter you should be able to:

■ understand the importance of creating a positive lesson climate and an effective learning environment;

■ appreciate some aspects of self-presentation that are important to PE teachers;

■ appreciate how the appearance of the working space contributes to the lesson climate;

■ understand the importance of purposefulness in a lesson;

■ understand some of the personal and interpersonal factors that influence lesson climate, including characteristics of the teacher, interpersonal relationships, motivation and self-esteem.

Check the requirements for your course to see which relate to this chapter.

DEVELOPING A POSITIVE CLIMATE IN YOUR LESSONS

A lesson with an effective learning environment has a positive climate. What is the climate of a lesson? What do we mean by a positive climate? Why is this important? When we talk about the lesson climate we are referring to the prevailing mood of the lesson. Pupils and their learning are placed at the centre of the lesson planning and delivery. The lesson has a relaxed but purposeful atmosphere in which the pupils have a clear understanding of the ILOs. Pupils are expected to learn and to be on task (see Chapter 6), supported by a caring, enthusiastic teacher. The teacher uses a positive teaching style, identifying and providing feedback on appropriate work, the positive reinforcement motivating pupils to learn and enhancing their self-esteem (see also Chapter 10 and Units 3.2 and 4.2 in Capel, Leask and Turner, 2009). Thus, much of the interaction in the class is positive, creating effective interpersonal relationships. A climate is not positive if it has all of the above, but no learning is taking place. You have, no doubt, experienced lessons in which there was a good atmosphere and pupils were 'busy, happy and good' (Placek, 1983) but no learning was taking place. Task 7.2 is designed to help you consider the positive and negative aspects of your communication with pupils.

Task 7.2 **Positive and negative verbal communication**

Audiotape one of your lessons. You may want to attach a microphone to yourself to ensure you record all your verbal communications. *What* you say to pupils, *why* you say it, *how* and *when* you say it, have a direct influence on the climate you create within your lesson and on the learning of your pupils (see Chapter 5 for more guidance on how you use your voice).

Play the tape after the lesson and as you listen to the tape answer the following questions. Was your communication mostly positive or mostly negative? Was there any pattern to positive and negative communication, for example, was communication positive when you provided feedback: about work but not about behaviour; to able pupils but not to less able pupils; to boys but not to girls? How did your pupils respond to the communication? Did you provide feedback to most pupils? Discuss with your tutor the pattern of your verbal communication, your pupils' response and the implications of this. Identify how you can increase the amount of positive communication, if appropriate. Put your findings in your PDP. Try to put this into practice in your next lessons.

Your self-presentation: what impression do you create to your pupils?

Task 7.3 asks you about an effective PE teacher.

Task 7.3 **An effective PE teacher**

Write down twelve to fifteen adjectives or phrases that you might use to describe an effective PE teacher, for example, 'patient', 'well organised'. Underline all those that refer to how you might *present yourself* as a PE teacher. Compare your list with that of another student teacher doing the same task.

Keep this information in your PDP to refer back to in Task 7.5.

Teacher self-presentation is related to the personality of each individual. However, it would be surprising if your list of adjectives or phrases to describe an effective PE teacher differed radically from that of another student teacher doing the same task. Such is the particular nature of the subject of PE that to be a successful teacher you need to exhibit key characteristics. These enable you to gain the respect of pupils, motivate them to work and to promote learning on the part of each individual pupil.

As an enthusiastic and committed teacher you plan and prepare each lesson thoroughly, identifying appropriate and achievable ILOs for pupils and differentiating learning tasks to accommodate the needs of each individual pupil, arrive early for the lesson, provide a quick pace to the lesson and do not allow minor interruptions to interfere with the lesson. You have a positive approach and teaching style, smile a lot, praise pupils for effort or performance, give specific, positive feedback whenever possible and encourage pupils to achieve obtainable, appropriate and challenging ILOs, therefore developing a positive lesson climate. Further, you dress and act as though you are enthusiastic about, and participate in, physical activity yourself. It is also an advantage to be a positive role model in your skilful execution of movement skills, and it is certainly the case that teacher demonstrations can help to inspire and enthuse pupils. There are three fundamental aspects of effective teacher self-presentation. These are discussed below.

First, a PE teacher needs to be *confident, authoritative* and clearly *in control of the situation.* These self-presentational attributes are necessary because you frequently work in a large space, at some distance from many of the pupils and in an environment that may contain safety hazards (see also Chapter 9). To retain your authority you must convey clearly an assured and business-like self-presentation. Elements that contribute to the teacher's authority have been identified by Kyriacou (2009: 103) as 'Subject knowledge; interest in and enthusiasm for the subject; and, the ability to set up effective learning experiences.' Appropriate and smart clothing are also essential (see also Chapter 5). You are in part an organiser and a safety manager and your presentation must reinforce these roles.

Second, a PE teacher needs to be *energetic* and *enthusiastic*. While all teachers have to engage and interest pupils, you have to motivate pupils to expend considerable effort to gain most from the lesson. A lethargic teacher is hardly likely to have a dynamic and determined class. In everything you do, you need to be alert, lively and encouraging. Do you convey to your pupils your enthusiasm for your subject content, and for them and their learning, improved performances and expenditure of effort? How do you accomplish this?

Although it is difficult to define precisely how enthusiasm is shown, as this is unique to each of you, it is important that as an enthusiastic and committed physical educationalist you convey your enthusiasm to the pupils, therefore enthuse and motivate them to participate. However, it is worth remembering that enthusiastic teachers vary their voice, gestures, expressions; move around the teaching space; and maintain a quick pace to the lesson that involves high levels of interaction with pupils (see Chapter 5).

Third, a PE teacher's self-presentation needs to convey more than an authoritarian, able sports person. The movement skills that are often the focus of the lesson are performed by the pupils for all to see, and so there is a danger of self-consciousness, as the pupil's very selves, their bodies, are the subjects of observation and evaluation. The work in PE is therefore of a very personal nature and you need self-presentational skills that demonstrate a dimension of *understanding* and *sensitivity*. Furthermore, you need to convey to the pupils that you are approachable, sympathetic and caring. You should show both verbally and non-verbally, that concern for pupils and their respective efforts are at the heart of the lesson. If, for example, you learn pupils' names quickly, you send a message to pupils that you care about them as individuals and for their learning. However, it is not easy to learn pupils' names in PE lessons, as they are not sitting at desks. As a new teacher in the school you need to make a special effort to learn pupils' names. Many schools produce lists of photos of all pupils in a class. It can be very impressive to learn the names of the pupils before you meet them! You can learn names by talking to pupils at the beginning of the lesson when taking the register and at the end of the lesson. Teachers often use techniques such as asking pupils to say their names when they talk to them; set a goal of using pupils' names in, say, 50 per cent of interactions with them or set targets of learning, say, six names each lesson. However, it is difficult to hear what is being said in, for example, a swimming pool or when pupils are scattered in a large area, therefore you need to find techniques appropriate for the situation. Whatever technique you use it is important that as a student teacher you learn pupils' names. Task 7.4 asks you to try techniques to learn pupils' names.

> ## Task 7.4 **Learning pupils' names**
>
> As soon as you can, get a register of all pupils in your classes. Ask experienced PE teachers what techniques they use to learn names. Make a particular effort to learn the names of pupils as soon as you can. If one technique is not working, try another one until you have found a technique that works for you. Record in your PDP why a specific technique worked or not.

Caring is revealed both in the interaction between teachers and pupils and between pupils. A *caring pedagogy* (Noddings, 1992, cited in Siedentop and Tannehill, 2000) embraces pupils' personal and social growth and achievement to try to 'create a synergy between the learning goals and social goals of physical education' (Siedentop and Tannehill, 2000: 106). Thus, teachers care that pupils learn and improve. It is based on the belief that if pupils feel respected and accepted by the teacher and their peers they are more likely to apply themselves to their learning. A caring pedagogy includes:

- Pupils who are supportive, responsible, accountable, cooperative, trusting, empowered, identify with the class, and committed to fairness and caring.
- Learning communities which have boundaries, persist over time, share common goals, value cooperative practices, identify with community symbols and rituals, and are committed to fairness and caring.
- Strategies for sustaining fairness and caring, such as collaboratively developed class procedures and discipline codes, class meetings to solve problems and develop class norms, challenging learning activities emphasising respect, opportunities to know one another, and willingness to deal with values in the curriculum.
- Investment in the development of pupils and sustaining conditions within which pupils protect the rights and interests of classmates.
- Teacher practices such as helping, valuing pupils, treating pupils respectfully, being tolerant, encouraging and supporting which are viewed by pupils as caring.
- Caring teachers who plan challenging and significant activities and help pupils achieve important outcomes.
- A caring teacher with skills and knowledge that relate to diversity issues in pedagogy and in the content being taught.

(adapted from Siedentop and Tannehill, 2000: 115)

Unit 3.1 in Capel, Leask and Turner (2009) addresses how to convey attributes of confidence, enthusiasm and involved sensitivity and Unit 1.2 addresses the school's expectations of the student teacher, which relates closely to self-presentation. This unit also includes consideration of professionalism. It is certainly the case that your self-presentation should at all times demonstrate your professionalism and genuine concern for each individual pupil. Task 7.5 focuses on self-presentation.

Task 7.5 **Effective self-presentation**

Return to Task 7.3 and compare the three key features identified above (confident, authoritative and clearly in control of the situation; energetic and enthusiastic; understanding and sensitive) with your list and those aspects you underlined. Discuss with another student teacher how far you agree with the priority given to these three. Set yourself the challenge to convey these three attributes during your next week of teaching. Ask your tutor to give you feedback on your mastery of each. Record your success, or otherwise, in your PDP.

It is worth taking time to check aspects of your self-presentation, for example, use of your voice, the clothes you wear, confidence, your non-verbal communication and your movement in a lesson (see particularly Tasks 5.1 to 5.6). You might also want to check other aspects of how you present yourself – for example, whether you have any habits or mannerisms such as brushing your hair back from your face whilst teaching or the over-use of 'OK', which may detract from your ability to communicate with pupils effectively. You might find pupils spending more time counting how many times you brush your hair back or saying 'OK' than they spend listening to you. Your own habits and mannerisms are the focus of Task 7.6.

Task 7.6 **Your habits and mannerisms**

Early on in your teaching ask another student teacher or your tutor to videotape you teaching one of your lessons. After the lesson watch the videotape and try to detect any habits or mannerisms which could be distracting in lessons and prevent effective communication. Work hard to eliminate or at least reduce any such habits or mannerisms. Ask the same person to videotape you teaching another lesson after you have worked to eliminate any habits and mannerisms and see if there is any difference. Record in your PDP how you reduced/eliminated the habit or mannerism.

Activity 9.5 in Capel, Breckon and O'Neill (2006) focuses on promoting a positive lesson environment.

What impression do the PE facilities create?

The general appearance of the working space is also an important factor in creating an effective learning environment. You need to ensure that the space is clean and tidy and conveys care and attention to pupils and their learning.

It is obviously hard to keep working spaces clean and tidy if a large number of groups and teachers are using the space or if a space is used as a multi-purpose facility, such as lunch served in the main hall of a school followed immediately by a dance or gymnastics lesson. In dance and gymnastics pupils are, for the most part, required to work in bare feet and oftentimes engage in floor work; thus, cleanliness and tidiness is of paramount importance for reasons of health and safety. Further, be mindful of potential hazards to your outdoor working spaces such as a long jump pit littered with drink cans and broken glass as pupils eat their lunch on the playing fields. This situation is made more difficult if a space is let to outside users. If you arrive for a lesson in a space that is unclean or untidy, it is worth cleaning or tidying it up before the lesson starts. You should also mention this to your tutor or Head of Department so that they can take steps to ensure that it does not happen again.

Each time you use a space you must check that it is safe (see also Chapter 9). This requires equipment to be well maintained and in good order. There should not be any equipment left in a working space. Likewise, as your lesson progresses, you should make sure that spare equipment is put away safely and not left lying around. Also, ensure that equipment is put away properly after the lesson so that it is tidy and easily accessible and that the space and the changing rooms are left in a suitable state for the next group.

You can enhance the space by using neat, tidy and well-presented visual displays, such as posters and notices. Ensure, as far as possible, that these are informative, current and meaningful to *all* pupils by, for example, changing the displays seasonally to feature athletic championships, winter sports, the paralympics or Wimbledon; featuring male and female role models from different cultural backgrounds; and, where appropriate, selecting font text that all pupils can read (comic sans for those pupils with dyslexia). Posters are very useful in gymnasiums or sports halls for providing visual displays of skills. Examples of actions and balances are particularly useful when introducing partner work/sport acrobatics. Literacy skills can also be developed by displays of key words associated with an activity or lesson focus. Again, these need to be changed regularly as the activity or focus changes. There are several books and websites that you can refer to for advice on how to create good visual displays. All of these should help to create a positive feeling among pupils about the lesson and about the environment in which they are working as well as aiding pupil learning. Task 7.7 asks you to look at the PE spaces.

Task 7.7 **The PE spaces**

Are the PE facilities in your placement school attractive? Clean? Tidy? Well looked after? Do they invite participation? What can you learn that you can apply when you are in your own school? How can you create an attractive, motivating PE environment in your school? You might like to offer to create a display, for example on an activity or an event, and keep this information in your PDP for reference when you are in your first post.

Purposefulness of your lesson

In a purposeful lesson pupils expect to work, learn and be successful. In order to create a sense of purposefulness you, as the teacher, must create as much time as possible for learning (see time on task in Chapter 6) and not allow time to be wasted. You can achieve this by good organisation and management skills (see Chapter 6) and by establishing a good pace to the lesson. It is important when planning that you look for ways in which you can save time. For example, you can take the register whilst the pupils are changing so that you do not spend too long in the changing rooms before the lesson. You should also make sure that the lesson starts as promptly as possible and that your organisation enables each task or lesson episode, including change from one task or lesson episode to the next, to proceed smoothly and efficiently. You also create a sense of urgency in the lesson, encouraging pupils to do things quickly rather than dawdling, for example, pupils should run to the outside space in which they are working rather than walk along chatting to a friend. They should also have been set a task to start when they get there. Further, you should not allow the pace of the lesson to slow by, for example, taking too long to explain what pupils are to do next or to deal with a minor problem or unnecessary interruption such as a telephone call in the office (you must not leave a class alone to take a call) or spending too long on one task or lesson episode so that pupils become bored, which may cause disruption. Also, you must not take too long to organise pupils. In grouping pupils for example, use a logical sequence of numbers for skill development or small-sided practices such as 2-4-8 or 1-3-6 (see Chapter 6). Reorganising pupils from groups of 3 to pairs for example can take longer and can cause problems when breaking up friendship groups. Task 7.8 looks at the purposefulness of the lesson.

Task 7.8 **Purposefulness of a lesson**

Observe two or three lessons taught by experienced teachers, focusing on the purposefulness of the lesson, for example, how long it takes for pupils to change for the lesson; what techniques the teacher uses and what is said to maintain a good pace to the lesson; how the teacher deals with unnecessary interruptions; how long pupils spend on each task or lesson episode; how long it takes to move from one task to another and how the teacher keeps this time to a minimum.

How do these compare with your own lessons? Ask another student teacher or your tutor to observe one or some of your lessons in relation to the same points. Do you need to change your practice to create a more purposeful lesson or plan more thoroughly for this to happen? Are there aspects of good practice you can adopt in your lessons? Identify what you need to do and try these out in your lessons. Record the teacher's and your own techniques in your PDP to refer to in planning further lessons.

Interpersonal relationships

In a lesson with a positive climate pupils are supported in their learning by a teacher who cares about them and about their learning (see above). You need to know pupils personally in order to build up a relationship with them. You and your pupils must develop mutual respect for each other, accepting each other and valuing each other's viewpoints. All aspects of your teaching are important in showing you value pupils, including such aspects as questioning techniques. Asking open-ended questions, as well as developing pupils' higher order thinking, are useful techniques for valuing pupils' contributions. A teacher may, for example, ask a question such as 'how can you get over a box without putting your feet on it?' If you only want and accept one possible answer 'a vault', you may discount an answer from a pupil who answers the question but does not give the answer you wanted. Hence, the pupil's answer is not valued and the pupil is not given the opportunity to make an effective contribution to the lesson. Try not to totally discount an incorrect answer from a pupil, rather prompt the pupil to think again and guide them to give the correct answer. However, you also need to think about whether the question is worded in the right way.

Interpersonal relationships are central to what has been described as a *humanist approach* to teaching and learning. This places an emphasis on:

■ the 'whole person' (a holistic synthesis of mind, body and feelings);
■ personal growth (the tendency of moving towards higher levels of health, creativity and self-fulfilment);
■ the person's awareness (the person's subjective view about themselves and the world);
■ personal agency (the power of choice and responsibility).

(Kyriacou, 2009: 111)

Although you want to establish a good rapport with pupils, you must not become too friendly with them. Some student teachers on their initial school placement adopt a friendly approach to their pupils and then they have not been able to establish their authority. You must maintain your status as a teacher so that your authority is not undermined and so that pupils do not lose respect for you. If you establish a good relationship with your pupils you can exert your authority when you need to. Siedentop (1991: 132) identified the following components of good relationships:

■ know your pupils;
■ appreciate your pupils;
■ acknowledge their efforts;
■ be a careful listener;
■ include pupils in decisions;
■ make some concessions when appropriate;
■ always show respect for pupils;
■ show honesty and integrity;
■ develop a sense of community, of belonging to the class.

As with all other aspects of your teaching you need to monitor your relationship with your pupils. You can do this by observing pupils' reactions to you and your lessons. If pupils get to class early, change quickly, are enthusiastic, do things quickly and willingly, ask you questions to enhance their learning, follow established rules and routines, treat you and other pupils with respect, help one another without being prompted and feel positive about the class identity, this suggests that you have or are establishing positive interpersonal relationships with your pupils.

Being at ease in your teaching

In a lesson with a positive climate you are likely to be at ease. If you are at ease, your pupils are likely to be so too. When pupils are at ease they are likely to be more confident, able to concentrate on the learning tasks and are more likely to behave appropriately. When you are at ease you are more likely to smile, conveying that you are confident and enjoying the work you are doing with the pupils. This can be aided by using humour effectively.

Using humour

As with other teaching skills, humour must be used appropriately. In the early stages of learning to teach you may wonder whether, when and how you should use humour. However, as you develop as a teacher, you should become more confident. Humour can be used to laugh at yourself when you have said or done something silly, to reassure a pupil who is anxious, to defuse a situation in which there is potential conflict, to laugh with pupils at something they find amusing (as long as that is appropriate for you as a teacher), for example, a hockey ball breaks in two and the pupils laugh about which part to use. Such scenarios reveal the more approachable and human side to your nature.

Although using humour well can be effective, using humour inappropriately can make lessons go terribly wrong. You must not use humour at a pupils' expense, for example to humiliate them through sarcasm. If you use humour too much pupils may perceive you as trying to be their friend, therefore you may become too familiar with pupils (see above). It may also make the lesson and pupils' learning seem unimportant. Thus, effective use of humour can help you to establish a warm, caring, positive climate in your lessons, but if you do not use it effectively, it can destroy your working relationship with your pupils and undermine your authority. It should therefore be used with care and treated as a teaching skill to be developed as you do with any other skill. Task 7.9 looks at lesson climate.

Task 7.9 **Lesson climate**

Observe two or three lessons, each taught by a different teacher. Focus on how the teacher establishes and maintains a positive lesson climate. Record aspects of both verbal and non-verbal behaviour (see Chapter 5) and the responses of pupils to this behaviour. Record examples of good practice in your PDP so that you can incorporate some of them into your own teaching, where appropriate.

The Flanders Interaction Analysis System (FIAS, Flanders, 1960) is an observation schedule which focuses on interactions between teachers and pupils in the classroom and therefore measures classroom climate. The Cheffers Adaptation of the Flanders Interaction Analysis System (CAFIAS, Cheffers, Amidon and Rogers, 1974) is an adaptation of this for use in PE lessons. This has been widely used in studies designed to describe the climate of the gymnasium. If you are interested in this aspect of teaching you may want to obtain a copy of the CAFIAS to gather information as the basis for an assignment on your course.

MOTIVATION

As a teacher you must try to motivate pupils towards learning. Unit 3.2 in Capel, Leask and Turner (2009) covers motivation in detail and you should refer to that chapter for further information.

Motivating pupils is not always an easy task. An understanding of what motivates pupils helps you. Pupils are motivated by activities and tasks that are meaningful, interesting and enjoyable to them. Pupils may be intrinsically motivated in PE to learn or develop a skill, to achieve something difficult, to develop their self-esteem or to have fun. They may be extrinsically motivated by some reward or recognition, such as status, approval, acceptance by peers or teachers. It may be that a few of your pupils are motivated to increase their skill to become professional sportspeople (e.g. footballers) with the large rewards that that can bring (however, it is also important that they remain realistic about the probability of them achieving their goal). The obtainable, appropriate and challenging ILOs you set for pupils should therefore be differentiated to meet the needs of different pupils and be meaningful to each individual.

An understanding of how pupils learn is also important in helping you to motivate them. Pupils' learning is affected by a number of factors, including their previous knowledge and experience of an activity, the relationship with the teacher, the learning situations which the teacher organises, the social context and their motivation to learn. An understanding of theories of learning, for example, Piaget (1962), Vygotsky (1962) and Bruner (1960), helps you to develop teaching tasks which are appropriate to pupils' learning needs, which actively engage them in their own learning and which are motivating for pupils. Piaget's theory (Piaget, 1962), for example, particularly the notion of readiness (i.e. that pupils only learn effectively if their educational experiences are suitably matched to their current level of understanding), can help you to see the need to identify the intellectual and physical demands a task makes on pupils so that it can be matched to pupils' performance. Refer to Unit 5.1 'Ways pupils learn' and Unit 5.2 'Active learning' in Capel, Leask and Turner (2009) and try to apply the information to PE.

Perhaps most important to remember is that the best motivator is success. If you know your pupils you can set appropriate ILOs which allow them to achieve success (Chapters 10 and 11 look at differentiation). You should adopt teaching strategies that actively involve pupils in their own learning and which help them achieve a specific ILO (see also Chapter 10). If the ILOs and tasks are too easy or too difficult pupils' motivation to achieve them is reduced. It is especially important to set obtainable, appropriate and challenging ILOs in PE because pupils' performance is on show, therefore failure in PE is particularly obvious. Physical actions and the success or otherwise of a pupil in accomplishing a task can be seen immediately by the rest of the class, the teacher and anyone else who is able to observe the class. For example, if a pupil cannot perform a forward roll or, in a game situation, when a pupil drops a catch and the opposition gains possession of the ball. Failure in front of a class of peers can be particularly demotivating, especially as it is likely to decrease self-esteem (see below).

This can be made worse by the situation, for example, a hockey lesson on a pitch being overlooked by pupils in a classroom or another 'public' place. Pupils may lose interest in the lesson if they feel conspicuous, for example, if girls wear kit for PE in which they feel embarrassed, they are likely to spend more time worrying about their kit than about achieving the task.

The focus of lessons may also make pupils feel failures. In tennis, for example, teachers have tended to focus on skills and technique, i.e. how to execute a stroke technically correctly, rather than on pupils achieving success by being able to hit the ball over the net. Many pupils find it difficult to maintain a rally using full size courts, rackets and fast tennis balls and are therefore unable to develop the ability to use tactics and strategy to outwit an opponent. Although technique is important, it is also important that the teacher modifies the situation such as using different equipment so pupils can start with a game they are able to play. PE teachers have different viewpoints on this, particularly the balance between skill development and the understanding of a game. How much emphasis should be put on good technique and how much on keeping a rally going? Can pupils enjoy a game of tennis in leisure time without being able to hit the ball correctly each time? You might like to discuss this with your tutor. There is plenty of literature on teaching points for particular skills you might teach and, indeed, you include these in your lesson plans. However, there is also literature that encourages you to see that success can be achieved by adopting a range of approaches to teaching activities. You might like to look at literature on 'games for understanding' (Thorpe, Bunker and Almond, 1986), for example or 'sport education' (Siedentop, 1994). The literature on a health focus in PE also provides an alternative approach for teaching PE (see, for example, Biddle, Cavill and Sallis, 1998; Harris, 2000, Harris and Penney, 1997; Piotrowski, 2000). This places health-related exercise at the core of all physical activity during PE, for life and as a foundation for performance and excellence. You might like to read further about such issues and discuss them with your tutor. In the NCPE 2007 the focus of lessons is on the key concepts and processes. There are also broader goals you need to address.

You therefore need to understand what motivates your pupils and arrange the learning environment so that they are motivated to learn and are successful. An ability to 'read' what is happening during lessons (which requires skills of observation, see Chapter 4) and flexibility in adapting to changing circumstances are important in maintaining motivation. Recognising changes in pupils' levels of motivation or participation for example, requires modification of your teaching strategy, content, material or approach to pupil learning.

To ensure that all pupils are motivated and enjoy positive learning experiences in your PE lessons you might consider the TARGET model outlined by Ames (1992) to create a mastery climate (rather than an outcome climate – see Unit 3.2 in Capel, Leask and Turner, 2009):

T = task: make tasks challenging and diverse
A = authority: give the pupils choice and leadership roles
R = recognition: give recognition to pupils privately and based on individual progress
G = grouping: promote cooperation, learning and peer interaction
E = evaluation: base evaluation on task mastery and individual progress
T = time: adjust time requirements to individual capabilities.

Task 7.10 focuses on motivating pupils.

Task 7.10 **Motivating pupils**

Reflect on the section above and consider for one class you teach, or group of pupils within the class, which is not highly motivated (if there is one), how you can increase pupil motivation in one lesson with the class. Discuss this with your tutor, then thoroughly plan and prepare how to motivate the pupils in the next lesson with this class. Implement this when you teach the lesson, then evaluate how successful your approach was. Store the information in your PDP as evidence of development in this area.

Praise

White (1992: 5) states 'that the majority of teachers believe that being positive, honest and fair with pupils is fundamental to good classroom practice'. If you consider carefully how to use praise to motivate pupils you should receive positive responses from pupils. As a teacher you are a stimulus and praise is used to encourage, to reward, to give a sense of achievement, satisfaction, pleasure, and to establish and reinforce positive behaviour in your lessons.

> It is easy to overlook the occasions for praise, and to react more rapidly to the need to censure. Each lesson, you should try to find some word of praise for a handful of fairly ordinary but commendable things: a well-answered question, the good use of a word, a helpful act.
>
> (Marland, 1993: 23)

Most pupils prefer to be praised rather than criticised. Praise can provide positive reinforcement, make pupils feel better, valued and probably work to achieve more in the lesson. You should use praise when pupils do something well, put effort into their work, show persistence, exhibit appropriate behaviours. Remember that it is important to praise *effort* as well as *achievement*. To be effective praise needs to be positive, encouraging, supportive and valued. Guidelines for delivering effective praise, adapted from Brophy (1981), have been identified as follows:

Effective praise:

■ Is delivered immediately, yet does not intrude on task-related behaviour
■ Identifies specific aspects of behaviour that were well done
■ Provides information about why the behaviour is important
■ Is matched well to the behaviour being reinforced
■ Is related to standard criteria or previous performance rather than compared to other pupils
■ Properly attributes success to effort and ability
■ Includes expectations for continued success and improvement
■ Shows variety, sincerity, and enthusiasm.

(Brophy, 1981, cited in Siedentop and Tannehill, 2000: 87)

There are some problems associated with the use of praise, for example, some pupils get all the praise. Do some pupils never deserve praise and is one pupil's praise another pupil's absence of praise?

The general points to remember when using praise are:

■ do not over-praise as it becomes meaningless;
■ make sure it is earned;
■ don't say it if you don't mean it;
■ if you mean it, *sound* and *look* as though you do: '**SAY** what you mean and **MEAN** what you say'.

Use of praise is covered in Task 7.11.

Task 7.11 **Use of praise**

A pupil's motivation is influenced greatly by your use of praise. Ask your tutor to observe a lesson and identify your use of praise during the lesson. Identify such aspects as the balance between praise to individuals, groups or the whole class. Who gets the praise and how often? What is the balance between praise and censure? Discuss with your tutor how effective your use of praise was and what you can do in your next lesson to increase its effectiveness. Store in your PDP to refer to in developing your use of praise.

The importance of praise to pupils cannot be underestimated (see Unit 3.2 in Capel, Leask and Turner (2009) for further reading on praise and motivation).

Motivating pupils to continue to participate in physical activity

It is one thing to motivate pupils to participate in a PE lesson at school but another to motivate pupils so that they participate in physical activity outside of PE or continue to participate after they leave school. People only continue to participate in physical activity if they are self-motivated, because, for example, they enjoy it, are successful, confident and feel positive about themselves in relation to the activity and can see the purpose of doing it, e.g. for health. Unfortunately, PE teachers have, too often, made pupils feel failures, therefore they lack confidence in their ability. You no doubt know many people who have never undertaken any physical activity since they left school. Do you know why? Ask some of your friends why they do not/have not participated. Was their experience of PE at school a major reason for this? Did they feel that they were not successful at PE? If so, why? Continual failure reduces pupils' self-confidence and self-esteem and decreases the probability that they will participate in physical activity after leaving school. To encourage participation in physical activity once pupils leave school you need to use teaching strategies (see Chapter 10) that help to develop a positive climate in your lessons, which enable pupils to achieve success, to feel confident and to enjoy physical activity, therefore encouraging self-motivation and self-esteem. The notion of promoting motivation to establish positive attitudes to physical activity throughout life is at the heart of the notion of physical literacy (see Chapter 2).

SELF-ESTEEM

Motivation and self-esteem are closely linked. Lawrence (1988) defined self-esteem as a person's evaluation of the discrepancy between his self-image and his ideal self. The important factor in self-esteem is the extent to which the person cares about the discrepancy. PE teachers can lower pupils' self-esteem. As a teacher you should aim to enhance pupils' self-esteem. A positive climate with good interpersonal relationships, in which specific feedback is provided about pupils' performance on a task, along with information and guidance about how to be more successful, in a way which is encouraging and supportive, is more likely to motivate pupils and enhance self-esteem. Self-esteem is enhanced when pupils achieve success and success is more likely if progress is measured

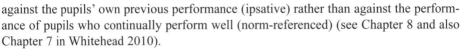
against the pupils' own previous performance (ipsative) rather than against the perform-ance of pupils who continually perform well (norm-referenced) (see Chapter 8 and also Chapter 7 in Whitehead 2010).

Mawer (1995: 122) indicated that:

effective teachers who seek to raise the self-esteem of their pupils will attempt to communicate with pupils in such a way that:

■ they are seen as enthusiastic, relaxed, supportive, encouraging;
■ they show that they value, respect and acknowledge the efforts of their pupils by use of praise and positive specific feedback;
■ their non-verbal behaviour, such as body posture and physical proximity, eye contact, tone of speech, and use of other gestures such as smiling, head nods etc., reflect warmth and a supportive, caring disposition.

Also, pupil self-esteem is enhanced when the teacher:

■ knows pupils well and attempts to share pupils' interests and feelings (*this is not the same as being familiar with pupils*);
■ is prepared to 'give them time' and is a good 'listener';
■ accepts pupils' opinions, ideas and lesson contributions, offers pupils opportunities to make contributions to lessons, and attempts to share decision making with pupils; stresses pupils' present performance rather than dwelling on past perform-ances;
■ has positive expectations of pupils.

Expectancy theory

In order to enhance pupils' self-esteem you need to know and treat your pupils as indi-viduals (see above). Expectancy theory (Rogers, 1982) says that a teacher bases expectations of a pupil on impressions of and previous experiences with the pupil, or even on reports from other teachers. Interactions with the pupil are based on those expec-tations, which in turn influence the way the pupil responds, the response tending to match the teacher's expectations. The expectation is therefore realised. Thus, expectations are a self-fulfilling prophecy because the teacher communicates to the pupil the expectations through, for example, verbal and non-verbal communication, leading the pupil to fulfil the expectations. If you have high, but obtainable expectations pupils are likely to perform well, whereas if expectations are low pupils are likely to perform poorly (this can also relate to good and poor behaviour). Sometimes teacher expectations are based on perceptions or stereotypes, for example, that girls cannot do certain activities such as rugby, that boys should not do dance, or that pupils who are overweight or physically disabled cannot make an effective contribution to a game. They are sometimes based on previous experiences of pupils teachers have taught from the same family. Think of some perceptions or stereotypes of certain types of pupils that may influence what you expect of pupils in a class so that you can find ways to prevent expectancy theory coming into operation. Refer to Martinek's (1991) 'teacher expectancy model for PE' and the 'What's the Use' complex model for further details of expectancy theory in relation to PE (cited in Mawer, 1995: 109–10).

In order to prevent expectations influencing pupils' performance you should:

■ have realistic yet high expectations of all pupils, and set obtainable, appropriate and challenging ILOs and tasks, for them;

■ focus on the pupil's current performance rather than previous performance on an activity or task;

■ avoid comparing one pupil's performance with that of other pupils;

■ use the whole-part-whole method of teaching, i.e. provide an overall picture of what pupils are aiming for, but then break down the activity so that they can practice and be successful on one part at a time before trying the whole activity again;

■ endeavour to motivate all pupils;

■ provide positive, constructive feedback which helps the pupil to improve and raise standards; and

■ include all pupils equally in the lesson, avoiding concentrating on the good performers by adopting an inclusive approach (see Chapter 11).

See Unit 3.2 in Capel, Leask and Turner (2009) for further information about teacher expectations.

Task 7.12 focuses on developing self-esteem or avoiding teacher expectations.

Task 7.12 **Enhancing self-esteem in your pupils**

In one of the next lessons you are planning to teach write an ILO to enhance self-esteem as well as ILOs for content knowledge, skills and understanding. Plan teaching strategies to enhance self-esteem (see Chapter 10), ensuring that all pupils can achieve the ILOs set and differentiating the work to enable their individual needs to be met. Ask your tutor to observe the lesson, identifying how you enhanced self-esteem and if you did anything to reduce self-esteem. Discuss the lesson with your tutor afterwards and incorporate appropriate strategies to enhance self-esteem into future lessons and avoid those which reduce self-esteem.

Write a reflective statement on your teaching and changes you need to make to your teaching to enhance pupils' self-esteem in your PE lessons. Use theory and readings to support your reflection. Record in your PDP as an example of Master's level work.

SUMMARY AND KEY POINTS

A positive climate in your lessons helps to create an environment in which pupils learn, supporting the other aspects of your teaching. In creating a positive climate you need to consider your self-presentation and the presentation of the working space. You also need to consider the purposefulness of the lesson. In a lesson with a positive climate pupils are actively engaged in learning, motivated by obtainable, appropriate and challenging ILOs to enable them to experience success and enhance their self-esteem. Appropriate praise, feedback and guidance provide information and support to enhance further learning. This requires you to differentiate your material to cater for the needs of individual pupils (see Chapter 11) and to treat pupils in a way that shows you are interested in and care about them as individuals and about their progress. Such lessons are

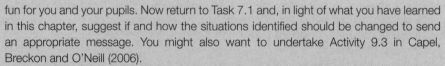

fun for you and your pupils. Now return to Task 7.1 and, in light of what you have learned in this chapter, suggest if and how the situations identified should be changed to send an appropriate message. You might also want to undertake Activity 9.3 in Capel, Breckon and O'Neill (2006).

Check which requirements for your course you have addressed through this chapter.

FURTHER READING

Child, D. (2007) *Psychology and the Teacher*, 6th edn, London: Cassell.
An excellent source text for studying child development and the theories of learning and motivation.

Hardy, C. and Mawer, M. (eds) (1999) *Learning and Teaching in Physical Education,* London: Falmer Press.
A comprehensive handbook to support teaching and learning in PE. Chapter 6 discusses motivation of pupils in PE in relation to how pupils view success and failure.

Marland, M. (2002) *The Craft of the Classroom*, 3rd edn, London: Heinemann Educational.
A readable book that looks at classroom interaction.

The books listed below each include one or more chapters about the classroom environment, classroom climate, creating an effective learning environment and/or strategies for effective teaching and learning, which should provide further underpinning for the aspects of your work introduced in this chapter.

Cohen, L., Manion, L. and Morrison, K. (2004) *A Guide to Teaching Practice*, 5th edn, London: Routledge.

Cooper, P. and McIntyre, D. (1996) *Effective Teaching and Learning: Teachers' and Students' Perspective*, Buckingham: Open University Press.

Kyriacou, C. (2007) *Essential Teaching Skills*, 3rd edn, Cheltenham: Stanley Thornes.

Kyriacou, C. (2009) *Effective Teaching in Schools*, 3rd edn, Cheltenham: Stanley Thornes.

Mawer, M. (1995) *Effective Teaching of Physical Education*, Harlow: Longman.

Rink, J.E. (1993) *Teaching Physical Education for Learning*, 2nd edn, St. Louis, MO: Mosby.

Siedentop, D. and Tannehill, D. (2000) *Developing Teaching Skills in Physical Education*, 4th edn, Mountain View, CA: Mayfield Publishing Co.

8

ASSESSMENT *FOR* AND *OF* LEARNING

Angela Newton and Mark Bowler

INTRODUCTION

Assessment is integral to learning and teaching and thus is an essential part of your role as a PE teacher. You need to recognise where pupils are in their learning, communicate strengths and areas for development and identify the steps required to improve further. This might involve assessing pupil attainment of performance in PE, in their attainment in a variety of roles, and in respect of broader aspects of learning such as their ability to make informed decisions and assess themselves and others. Examples of assessment can range from informal comments such as 'good shot' to the more formal assessment involved in examinations. There are two principal types of assessment. One is known as formative. This type of assessment is designed to help pupils to progress their learning. The other is known as summative and provides information at the end of a lesson or unit of work concerning what pupils have achieved. In one sense formative assessment looks forward while summative assessment looks back. Another way to differentiate between these two types of assessment is to label the first as assessment *for* learning and the second as assessment *of* learning. Both of these types of assessment are covered in this chapter. There is a current consensus that more attention should be paid to assessment *for* learning. Rather than simply telling a pupil that they have attained, for example, a 'good hang position in the air' much more information and guidance is given if the feedback goes further than this and indicates that the pupil performed a good hang position and continues with 'now try and drive your knee up higher in take off to gain more height'. Similarly an examination awarded just a mark gives little guidance as to how pupils can improve their work. Written comments giving feedback on strengths and areas to work on are far more productive and are again an example of assessment *for* learning.

Assessment was identified by the Office for Standards in Education (Ofsted) (2003) as a weakness for student PE teachers. Ofsted (2005, 2008a) also claim that assessment is consistently the weakest part of teaching and learning. This chapter identifies the reasons why we assess and how we do it. It aims to improve your ability to use the principles of assessment *for* learning as well as assessment *of* learning to enable all pupils to achieve their full potential. There are opportunities throughout the chapter to reflect upon and critically analyse assessment in practice.

> # OBJECTIVES
>
> At the end of this chapter you should be able to:
>
> ■ identify the broad principles and purposes of assessment in PE;
> ■ understand the role of assessment *for* learning in improving teaching and learning in PE;
> ■ apply shared intended learning outcomes (ILOs), questioning, feedback and pupil peer and self-assessment in your lessons;
> ■ critically evaluate the success of assessment in helping pupils to achieve their full potential;
> ■ understand the role of assessment *of* learning.
>
> Check the requirements for your course to see which relate to this chapter.

PRINCIPLES AND PURPOSES OF ASSESSMENT

Assessment is an integral part of teaching and learning, whether your focus is formative, as in assessment *for* learning, or summative, as in assessment *of* learning. As with every other part of your work it needs to be done well in order to be effective. Pupils and parents, in particular, are concerned that assessment is carried out rigorously and fairly. This is true both of the very informal assessments you make in a lesson and of the most formal as in giving a final grade or examination mark. Parents may complain if they feel their child's work is being unfairly judged by a teacher; for example, that they always receive criticism of their work, but never praise. Appeals may also be made to awarding bodies against grades awarded by accredited examination courses.

Good assessment adheres to certain principles:

■ it should have a clear purpose and should be fit for that purpose;
■ it is clear what the attainment – practical or written – is being measured against;
■ it should be valid and reliable.

PURPOSES OF ASSESSMENT

Assessment fulfils a number of functions and these are discussed in the next section. Some researchers categorise these functions under two main headings. These are formative and summative. The purpose of formative assessment is to give pupils guidance as to how they can move on from their current stage of understanding or mastery. Typically formative assessment is given in the ongoing teaching situation. No records are kept of the detail of this assessment. Formative assessment is also given in the comments written on a piece of homework or an examination script. The purpose of summative assessment is to record attainment at a particular time, usually the end of a unit, term or year. Summative assessment records learning. This is often a formal process and records are kept of these marks or grades. Summative assessments often appear in pupils' school reports. In both these cases assessment is in the interest of subsequent pupil learning.

As you work through the next section, decide whether the purpose of the assessment described is summative or formative. In order to make this decision you must consider whether the assessment promotes learning (assessment *for* learning) or merely assesses the current level of learning (assessment *of* learning).

Guidance or feedback

Pupils require information about their attainment to help them to understand what you are looking for in their work, to challenge them to greater achievement and to motivate them. This is most likely to take the form of verbal comments to pupils although you may also be required to provide written feedback on occasion, for example when pupils are 'on report' or when you are marking written work.

Diagnosis and evaluation

When first meeting a group of pupils or when beginning a new unit of work you may wish to make a preliminary assessment of the pupils' strengths and needs, in which case you are assessing for the purpose of *diagnosis*. This information guides your subsequent planning. On a lesson by lesson basis you want to know what or how much pupils have learned in a lesson so that you can judge to what extent the ILOs of the lesson have been achieved and then plan the next lesson on the basis of this evaluation. In this case you are assessing for *evaluation*.

Grading and prediction

You may be required to provide grades for an annual report to parents. The grading system may be designated by the school or, in England, may be aligned to National Curriculum levels of attainment. With respect to examination classes you need to grade the work in accordance with the requirements of the awarding body. Many of the sixth-form pupils you teach will be making applications for university. You may need to assess their attainment prior to the completion of application forms to provide a predicted grade and to give information for a reference concerning potential for their chosen course of study. These assessments are for the purposes of *grading* and *prediction*.

Motivation

The nature of the assessment and the way it is communicated to pupils can have a significant effect on their motivation, particularly when it is given publicly. More able pupils thrive on being recognised as running the fastest or jumping the furthest; however for less able pupils it is never appropriate to draw attention to their attainment relative to others. An alternative approach to motivate pupils may be, on occasion, to focus on broader goals, such as how well they can reflect on their work, their leadership skills or their ability to work cooperatively as part of a team. All pupils benefit from positive feedback on effort and application, as appropriate, and on recognition of how much they have improved against previous attainment. Measuring attainment against an individual's previous work is called ipsative assessment and is covered later in this chapter. As you get to know the pupils you realise that individual pupils respond differently to different types of feedback. For example, some may relish a challenge, others may need to be reminded sternly that

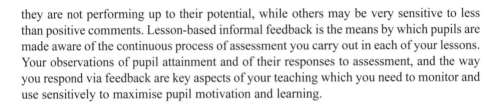

they are not performing up to their potential, while others may be very sensitive to less than positive comments. Lesson-based informal feedback is the means by which pupils are made aware of the continuous process of assessment you carry out in each of your lessons. Your observations of pupil attainment and of their responses to assessment, and the way you respond via feedback are key aspects of your teaching which you need to monitor and use sensitively to maximise pupil motivation and learning.

Selection of pupils for grouping

There may be a school or department policy to group or set pupils according to their ability in PE. You therefore need to provide the relevant information for the groups you teach. These assessments are being carried out for *selection* purposes.

There are other assessment demands made of PE teachers. For example, you may be asked by your head of department or another colleague to conduct trials in an extra-curricular activity in order to select pupils for school teams, or to decide which pupils may benefit most from an invitation to take part in an outdoor activity expedition. On occasion PE teachers may use certain criteria for selection, but the selection process could depend on the teacher making judgements about which pupils perform better than others. The first form of assessment mentioned above is called criterion referenced and the second is known as norm referenced. These types of assessment are explained further later in the chapter. Team selection criteria may not take account of the really keen rugby player who turns up every week at the beginning of the season but does not make the progress or have the necessary physical attributes required for the team. Thus PE teachers have to be clear about how they justify their criteria for team selection. The keen, but non-selected player may lose motivation and self-esteem as a result of the process and you need to consider the effects of such decisions. Self-esteem is addressed in Chapter 7.

Formal reporting

Awarding bodies usually require teachers to assess pupils formally. Examination boards may have elements of teacher-assessed coursework for both practical and theoretical elements. This assessment needs to be planned and carried out systematically and the criteria being used need to be very clearly identified (see assessment *of* learning later in the chapter). Careful assessments of all pupils must be made and recorded in some way. These assessments, collected at intervals from selected units and lessons over a period of time, or from teacher-graded coursework, provide evidence for you to make judgements about pupils. This can form the basis of termly/annual reports to parents.

Task 8.1 asks you to work with another student teacher to observe and analyse assessment in different settings.

Task 8.1 **Observing assessment in action**

In a pair with another student teacher observe a PE teacher in your placement school in at least one curriculum lesson and one extra-curricular session, recording all assessment in each session. Following the observation answer the following questions:

■ what *methods* are used for assessing pupils? This answers the question of how pupils are assessed (e.g. teacher or peer observation, listening to answers to questions, writing down scores/comments, written comments by pupils or assignments);

■ *what* is the teacher assessing? (e.g. attitudes, planning, attainment, knowledge, understanding, evaluation, cooperation);

■ *who* is doing the assessment? Is it always the teacher? Are pupils involved in the process?

■ *why* is the assessment being carried out? Is the purpose to give feedback to the pupils/parents/governors/others? Is it to motivate? Is it to identify the best performers? Any other reasons?

■ *how* are pupils given the results of assessment? Is it through an informal process such as a brief comment giving constructive feedback? Is it through a mark given for a specific attainment or evaluation? Any other ways?

Identify which of your examples involve assessment *for* learning and which involve assessment *of* learning. Some could involve both. Put these observations in your professional development portfolio (PDP) and draw on them when you are planning assessment in your lessons.

MEASURING PUPILS' ACHIEVEMENT

The purpose for which you are carrying out the assessment should determine the yardstick against which you measure achievement. All assessment involves comparison and there are three types of comparison usually associated with assessment:

■ Comparison with the attainment of others (*norm-referenced* assessment).
■ Measurement against predetermined criteria (*criterion-referenced* assessment).
■ Comparison with a previous attainment in the same activity or task (*ipsative* assessment).

Units 6.1 and 6.2 in Capel, Leask and Turner (2009) provide further information.

A race is an obvious example of a *norm-referenced* assessment. Each runner's performance is being judged in relation to the performance in the race of the other competitors. Many school examinations and class tests are also norm-referenced, the aim being to create a rank order of achievement.

Many awarding bodies produce precise descriptors against which pupil attainment is assessed (e.g. General Certificate of Secondary Education (GCSE) practical work). The statements may be associated with a corresponding mark that contributes to a final grade. These statements are the criteria against which pupils' attainment is judged, making the assessment *criterion-referenced*. Awards of many governing bodies (e.g. U.K. Athletics Shine Awards, British Gymnastics Proficiency Awards Scheme) are made on the basis of criterion-referenced assessments.

Where a pupil or athlete is judged to have achieved a 'personal best' then the assessment is being made against previous attempts by that individual to jump, run, swim, etc. This is an *ipsative* assessment. Much informal assessment carried out by both pupils and teachers in lessons is of this nature, for example, when a teacher praises work which is of a higher standard than in previous lessons. Such assessments are made of any aspect of pupil activity or behaviour. When a teacher tells a pupil, 'You have behaved better this lesson than ever before', or a pupil reports that, 'It's the first time I've swum a whole length without stopping', then ipsative assessments have been made.

If you wish to assess for the purpose of *grading* pupils' achievement, for *selecting* pupils or deciding who would benefit most from a particular opportunity, that is *predicting* their future attainment, you may well want to compare pupil attainments and thus are using *norm-referenced* assessment. In making a *diagnosis* of pupils' needs and strengths you need criteria for determining their level of competence. In this case a *criterion-referenced* assessment is most useful. Pupils may well be motivated by the teacher's acknowledgement that their attainment is improving and an *ipsative* assessment provides this. Future improvement of their skill or behaviour is assisted if you are able to offer *guidance* about what the pupils need to work on to develop their attainment further. This is an essential element of assessment *for* learning. The mode of assessment must always be appropriate for what is being measured and why it is being measured. This makes it fit for purpose.

VALIDITY AND RELIABILITY

An assessment is of little value if it does not assess what you want it to assess. If you give a group of pupils a written examination which requires them to show their knowledge of the rules and tactics of basketball it only provides you with information about pupil knowledge of rules and tactics. It does not help you to decide if pupils are able to apply decisions in a game, as no indication is given of their ability to play the game. If an assessment does not provide you with the information that you want then it is not a valid assessment. The assessment may, however, be reliable. This means that the assessment, e.g. a written examination, would achieve the same range of results if the assessment was carried out by another teacher. If you marked a set of examination scripts on another occasion, or if another teacher marked the scripts, the marks awarded to each pupil would be the same as those you gave originally. Good assessments should be both valid and reliable. It is possible for an assessment to be reliable and not valid, as in the case of the basketball examination. Likewise, in a GCSE class studying the skeletal and muscular systems, an essay is set on an aspect of work that is not on the syllabus. The teacher marks all the essays. This would be reliable but hardly valid if the topic was not one to be studied. However, an assessment is not valid if it is not reliable. For example, a situation in which class members were given the responsibility to grade peers against criteria has the potential to be valid but is unlikely to be reliable on account of the lack of knowledge and experience of the pupils. Assessment reliability and validity can be improved with the use of assessment criteria.

It is the case that assessment in the form of assessment *for* learning is integral to and closely related to the normal lesson activity. In this situation, as a teacher, you are likely to use informal methods of assessment very frequently which rely on observation and verbal interaction and take place in the usual working space. This form of assessment is essential in lessons to gather information on a class's overall response and attainment, and is integral to all teaching (see Chapters 4 and 6 on observation and organisation, respectively). However these methods can be unreliable in assessing pupil progress as they often rely on fleeting snap shots of pupils performing. Much more systematic assessment is needed if grades are to be awarded. Written tests which include multiple choice items and are carried out in formal examination conditions with the whole cohort of pupils sitting in the same room and being given identical instructions are far more likely to elicit reliable results. However this type of assessment has limited use. These two examples reveal that the type of assessment must match that which is being assessed.

The perfect assessment is yet to be developed. Validity may be increased by using a number of different assessment methods, for example, direct observation, study of video recordings and written work. You should try to make your assessments as valid and reliable as possible within the overall aim of ensuring that any assessment you use is fit for the purpose you have in mind. Task 8.2 asks you to reflect back on your own experience in PE and consider the reliability and validity of assessment practices to which you were subject.

Task 8.2 **Reflecting on your own assessment experiences**

Consider your own experience as a pupil of being assessed in PE. What assessments took place in your PE lessons? Were you aware of being assessed? Were assessments closely related to normal lesson activity? Do you know on what basis the grade or comment on a report was made? Consider whether the informal/formal methods of assessment that you experienced in PE were valid and reliable. Record your examples of assessment on the diagram below.

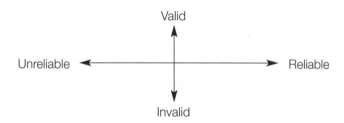

Put these notes into your PDP and consider them when you are planning assessments in your lessons.

THE CONSTITUENTS OF ASSESSMENT *FOR* LEARNING

Assessment *for* learning has been referred to earlier in this chapter. It is useful now to look into this aspect of assessment in more detail. Research led by the Assessment Reform Group (ARG) (2002) into classroom-based practice (e.g. Black and Wiliam, 1998; ARG, 1999) resulted in the production of ten research-based principles of assessment *for* learning to guide practice.

These identify that assessment should:

1   Be considered as part of your planning;
2   Focus on pupil learning;

3   Be a central part of your practice as a teacher;

4   Be regarded as a key professional skill for teachers;

5   Be sensitive and constructive to take account of the emotional impact on pupils;

6   Foster motivation in pupils;

7   Promote understanding of the criteria for assessment and pupil commitment to the goals they need to attain;

8   Provide pupils with guidance about how to improve;

9   Enable pupils to reflect and self-assess so that they can become independent learners;

10   Recognise a full range of educational achievement for all pupils.

(adapted from ARG 2002)

The work of Black and Wiliam and the ARG has had a far-reaching impact throughout education in England. It has significantly influenced The Secondary National Strategy (Department for Education and Skills (DfES) 2005a), formerly the Key Stage 3 National Strategy (DfES, 2002b). This strategy utilises many of the principles of assessment *for* learning and aims to raise standards by strengthening teaching and learning across the curriculum.

THE ROLE OF ASSESSMENT *FOR* LEARNING

As stated above, assessment *for* learning is a type of assessment that promotes pupil learning, understanding and attainment. It refers to feedback that builds from pupils' current level of mastery and identifies how further progress can be made. It is essentially constructive and forward looking. Understandably, it is a vital element of your work as a teacher. Effective use of assessment *for* learning requires good observation skills which give rise to accurate assessment and the provision of effective feedback to pupils. Most of your observations focus on pupils' actions in performance, or contributions whilst adopting different roles such as official, coach or choreographer. They may also focus on pupils' work towards achieving the broader goals of education towards which PE contributes (Chapter 14 looks at broader goals). Many of these actions are fleeting and you have to rely on your ability to observe and judge instantaneously. This is a skill that you need to develop throughout your ITE course and beyond and is linked to your knowledge and understanding of the contexts in which pupils are working. You need to know what you expect to see in pupil attainment and develop the ability to compare this to what you observe. Positioning and the ability to scan your class are other related teaching skills (see Chapter 4 for further guidance on observation). Once you have established sound observation skills, assessment *for* learning helps to determine the progress being made by pupils, indicate their strengths and weaknesses and identify their future needs.

Black *et al.* (2003) found that implementing specific assessment strategies can greatly improve pupil learning and increase enthusiasm and motivation in classroom subjects. These strategies provide a useful framework for your work in assessing for learning. In relation to PE , Spackman (2002) has identified four characteristics of assessment *for* learning that are applicable in our subject. These are shared ILOs, questioning, feedback and pupil peer- and self-assessment. This is a useful text to study.

Shared ILOs

ILOs should be shared with pupils so that they are clear about what is to be learned and why they need to learn it. Statements should model the expectations that guide pupils towards the expected learning. When sharing ILOs in a gymnastics lesson, for example, you might say: 'In today's lesson and during the next two lessons we are going to develop sequences of movement on both floor and apparatus that involve flight and the shapes we can use in flight. Exploring changes in direction and changes in speed helps you to compose more fluent sequences. We aim to produce precise and controlled sequences with some originality.'

It is important when sharing ILOs that the learning is clearly identified, in terms of what pupils will know, understand or be able to do, rather than simply the tasks that the pupils will be carrying out. These ILOs should be revisited throughout the lesson and assessed at appropriate times. When reviewing ILOs, you should ensure that pupils understand how well they achieved the ILOs and the potential they have for further improvement. Guidance for writing clear and differentiated ILOs is in Chapter 3 and also in Chapter 12 of Capel, Breckon and O'Neill (2006), which also has some useful activities (e.g. 12.1, 12.2, 12.3, 12.5, 12.6, 12.7 and 12.8) to help you with assessment.

Questioning

Effective questioning techniques are essential in order to accurately assess pupil knowledge and understanding. Whilst pupil attainment can demonstrate knowledge and understanding, questioning allows a more comprehensive and rigorous assessment, being able to reveal pupils' intellectual grasp of an issue or problem. In the gymnastics example given above teacher questioning would focus on appreciation of what is being learned, that is the effects that changes in direction and speed have on a pupil's composition. For example, questions that might be posed are 'When is it appropriate to increase speed?' or 'At which point in the sequence can changes in direction be made?' Questions should be carefully planned and pupils should be given time to answer; you may even devise a situation in which there is a discussion of the answer with a peer. Both teacher questioning, probing and prompting and peer discussion of questions allow pupils to think about their responses more deeply. (See Chapter 5 on the teacher's use of language for more discussion of questioning techniques.) To ensure that all pupils remain engaged during questioning episodes, a no hands up policy is advisable. This is where the teacher asks all pupils to consider a question and then selects pupils to answer at random. It is also important to foster a supportive environment in which pupils understand that an incorrect answer is part of the learning process.

The questions you use should be directly applicable to what is being learned and appropriate to the cognitive level of the pupils. In addition you need to be clear about the purpose of asking questions, whether a question is being asked for recall, to require pupils to analyse a task or to give pupils the opportunity to make innovative suggestions. A closed question is one that requires a single answer while an open question allows more variable and detailed responses demanding higher order thinking (see Unit 3.1 (pp. 111–18) in Capel, Leask and Turner, 2009). Bloom's *Taxonomy of Learning Domains* (Bloom, 1956) provides a framework from which you can design and evaluate learning and therefore distinguish between lower and higher order thinking skills. Lower order thinking is usually required in answering closed questions while higher order thinking can be activated with open questions. Depending on the nature of the learning you are intending pupils to achieve and thus the domain you are tapping into you need to phrase questions in an appropriate way. Anderson *et al.* (2001) later revised the taxonomy and replaced the nouns used by Bloom with verbs. These describe actions which are easier to measure and therefore help planning, delivery and assessment. Table 8.1 summarises these two categorisations.

For example, a low order (remembering) question might ask pupils if they can recall the name of the muscles in the front of the thigh or the correct learning points for a practical skill or technique. Higher order questions might ask pupils to identify, for example, a movement/part of a skill that requires the use of that muscle (applying) or to design a practice to develop the skill or technique (creating).

■ **Table 8.1** Comparison of Bloom and Anderson's taxonomies

Bloom's taxonomy	Anderson's taxonomy	
Knowledge	Remembering	Lower Order
Comprehension	Understanding	
Application	Applying	
Analysis	Analysing	
Synthesis	Evaluating	
Evaluation	Creating	Higher Order

Task 8.3 is designed to help you to realise the different sorts of question that are used in teaching.

Task 8.3 **Observing and analysing questioning**

Observe a teacher for a lesson in your placement school.

1   Record all the questions that the teacher asks over a 20 minute period.
2   Identify the number of closed and open questions that the teacher uses during the lesson.
3   Evaluate the closed questions and rewrite any you feel could be expressed as open questions.
4   Categorise the level of cognitive demand within the questions using Anderson's taxonomy as a guide.
5   Select one question from either remembering or understanding and consider how it could be made more demanding in order to trigger higher order thinking skills.

Put your observations and notes in your PDP and refer to it when developing questions to use in your lessons.

Feedback

Feedback is one of the most effective aspects of assessment *for* learning when it is focused on learning needs (Black *et al.*, 2003). Feedback should focus on providing information to enable pupils to improve and therefore 'close the gap' between where they are in their learning and where they need to go or be. This involves effective teacher observation, discussed earlier. ILOs should be the focus of all feedback. In PE most feedback is provided verbally. This is commonly divided into descriptive and prescriptive forms (Schmidt and Wrisberg, 2008). Descriptive feedback describes the attainment of a pupil whereas prescriptive also gives the pupil points for improvement. A piece of descriptive feedback might be, 'You contacted the ball with the inside of your foot', while a piece of prescriptive feedback would be, 'You contacted the ball with the inside of your foot – to gain more power you need to use the laces.' Feedback can also be a powerful tool for motivation (see motivation in Chapter 7 and also Unit 3.2 in Capel, Leask and Turner, 2009). Positive, encouraging feedback incorporating the expectation that a pupil is capable of improving motivates the pupil to further effort. On the other hand dismissive, negative feedback can leave a pupil demoralised and with little interest in continuing to work on a task. It is therefore important to ensure that as far as possible your feedback is positive as well as constructive and personalised for the needs of each pupil. Another point to bear in mind is the need to be objective in observing pupils. Try not to let expectations based on previous work influence your judgements. There is a good deal written about teachers' perceptions of pupils and the way that teachers tend to see what they expect to see. This is called the self-fulfilling prophecy (see Chapter 7 and Unit 3.2 in Capel, Leask and Turner, 2009).

It is also necessary to provide written feedback on essays and other projects that pupils who are following examination courses write. Written feedback to pupils should always include comments and not simply a grade. Comments need to identify what has been done well, what needs to be improved and guidance on how to implement changes. Opportunities to discuss and follow up these comments must be planned into your lessons. Feedback is also covered in Chapter 10. Now complete Task 8.4.

Task 8.4 **Critical reflection on research into the effect of feedback on learning**

Review the article by Hattie and Timperley (2007) on 'The Power of Feedback' and consider the impact of the findings in relation to your own practice. In doing this you should reflect on which feedback strategies are most important to you as a PE teacher and which you currently consider to be central to your own development. Put your notes in your PDP as an example of Master's level work.

Hattie, P. and Timperley, H. (2007) The Power of Feedback, *Review of Educational Research*, 27, 1: 53–64.

Peer- and self-assessment

While it is the case that teachers carry out most of the assessment, it is usual for broad education guidelines to recommend that pupils themselves begin to make judgements on their own attainment and progress. In England this expectation is built into both the government concerns with Personal Learning and Thinking Skills (See Chapter 14) and into the National Curriculum for PE in terms of fostering pupil ability in respect of the key process of 'Evaluating and Improving.' As a preparation for self-evaluation, peer-evaluation is a very valuable exercise. However, it is essential to remember that pupil ability to assess themselves or others is in itself a skill that has to be learned, as pupils may not find it easy to critique their own or other's work (see below). The use of criteria sheets is helpful so that pupils know what they are looking for (see the reciprocal teaching style of Mosston and Ashworth (2002) which involves peer-assessment/teaching). Pupils need to develop the trust and confidence necessary to carry out this kind of assessment. You need to plan carefully how you develop this ability. You, as the teacher, also need to learn how to devolve responsibility to the pupils. In situations of self- or peer-assessment it is not the teacher's role to give direct feedback on pupil attainment, rather the teacher should enquire of the pupil how they feel they or their partner is progressing, and what next steps need to be taken for improvement. This is where questioning can be used to good effect (see above, Chapter 5 and Unit 3.1 in Capel, Leask and Turner, 2009). The role of the teacher is also to commend the pupil on astute assessment or to give guidance on how assessment techniques can be improved.

When assessing practical performance, it is easy to see if a peer or self is successful in some activities, e.g. it is easy to see if a ball bowled in cricket is near to the wicket. However, it is not easy to know why it was successful. Peer-assessment should be developed before self-assessment because pupils cannot see themselves perform unless they have access to video playback. Observing and assessing a peer can have a positive effect on pupils' own attainment as it deepens their understanding of the activity/task. The development of visual analysis software provides the opportunity for immediate visual feedback that allows pupils to assess their own and other's attainment more readily (see Chapter 14). Pupils should not be aiming merely to judge each other's work. The peer assessment process should provide pupils with the opportunity to reflect upon the requirements of a performance, and to begin to appreciate the nature and constituents of movement. This can be linked to pupils using proprioceptive feedback to assess self, but they need time and help to develop this.

Developing peer- and self-assessment involves careful planning, time and patience. Pupils need plenty of opportunities to practise this skill. Their ability to evaluate attainment and provide constructive feedback must be developed gradually and with pupil maturity in mind. You might begin by providing pupils with prompts or basic criteria. For instance, pupils may be asked, using a work card or criteria sheet, to identify the strongest aspects of, for example, a performance or piece of written work as well as a key area for development. Eventually you want pupils to make their own decisions about what needs to be improved and also how this progress can be effected.

Using assessment *for* learning to inform teachers' in-lesson decisions

You also draw on assessment *for* learning skills in the ongoing teaching situation to judge the appropriateness of the ILOs of a lesson. This requires good skills, including good observation and sound knowledge of the activity being assessed. If this 'in-lesson' assessment indicates that the ILOs are too ambitious you may need to modify your aspirations for the lesson. This is not unusual even with experienced teachers. Classes sometimes do not respond as anticipated. There is no point in staying with your plans if there is clearly no way that pupils can reach the intended levels of work. Normally this means dropping one ILO or making an ILO less demanding.

Now complete Task 8.5.

Task 8.5 **Action research**

Select one of the four characteristics of assessment *for* learning identified by Spackman (2002, see above) that you feel will improve your practice. Identify two or three goals to focus on in relation to your chosen characteristic, e.g. Questioning: improving the use of open questions; ensuring that all pupils are engaged during questioning; employing higher order questions to stretch more able pupils.

Plan a short unit of work for four lessons and using the action research cycle conduct a small research project aimed at improving your practice. To help you with this, read Chapter 17 and Zwozdiak-Myers, Action research in Capel, Breckon and O'Neill (2006) (Activities 4.1a, 4.1b, 4.2a, 4.2b, 4.3a, 4.3b, 4.3c, 4.3d should also be useful). You may also wish to do some further reading to help identify your goals and to understand the research literature.

After each lesson carefully review and evaluate progress against your goals, making adjustments to your planning as necessary. Some researchers call this plan-do-review (Elliott, 1991). You will find it much easier if your tutor or another student teacher acts as an observer. Evaluate the results and identify how you might apply the findings to other lessons/groups of pupils.

Further guidance on reflective practice is provided in Chapter 17. Put your plans and notes in your PDP.

ASSESSMENT *OF* LEARNING

As indicated at the start of the chapter the purpose of assessment *of* learning or summative assessment is to record attainment at a particular time, usually the end of a unit, term or year. Summative assessment records learning. This is often a formal process and records are kept of these marks or grades. Summative assessments often appear in pupils' school reports. In both these cases assessment is in the interest of subsequent pupil learning.

Assessment *of* learning may be carried out for evaluation, grading, prediction, selection or formal reporting (see earlier in the chapter in the section on purposes of assessment). Assessments for awarding bodies require you to work with specific assess-ment criteria. These will most commonly be for 14–19 examination courses, leadership courses and governing body award schemes. You are expected to make judgements about pupils' learning in order to inform a grade or level or indicate progress towards a goal. Assessment of pupils on a particular unit of work needs to be carried out against the unit objectives. Assessment of an individual, small group or whole group in a lesson needs to be carried out against the ILOs of that lesson.

Although summative assessments are primarily used to confirm learning they also provide an opportunity for you to reflect on your practice and make adaptations for future lessons in the light of the changing needs of your pupils. Summative assessments, such as an in-class test, can also be used to help pupils identify areas which require further development and plan for improvement. When used in this way summative assessments can promote reflective learning. Black *et al.* (2003) refer to this process as the formative use of summative assessment.

BUILDING ASSESSMENT INTO UNIT PLANNING

Having worked through this chapter you should understand fully that assessment is not a 'bolt on' process but is integral to effective teaching and learning. Therefore, it is helpful for you to consider the range of assessment that PE teachers undertake in their day-to-day teaching. As a student teacher you are probably not involved in mapping assessment across units and schemes of work. However, even at this early stage it is useful to be thinking about this (see Chapter 3). You must first be clear about what you want your pupils to learn. This is expressed as your unit objectives. You must also consider the context in which you are teaching. At the planning stage you must clarify which of the unit objectives you are going to assess and record for individual pupils. These objectives are the focus of your evaluation. Once these have been identified you must then decide on the mode of assessment to be used for each objective. All assessment that you intend to carry out should be built into the structure or framework of your units of work and should be carried out throughout the unit.

All objectives from the unit should also be evaluated from a class perspective in order for you to be able to assess the quality of your teaching relative to pupil achievement. This follows the same process as evaluating lesson ILOs, that is an evaluation of what the pupils achieved, material and challenges they should move on to next and how your teaching affected their learning (see Chapter 3).

SUMMARY AND KEY POINTS

After working through this chapter you should now understand the principles and wide range of purposes of assessment, including the need to ensure assessments are valid and reliable. You should also understand the role assessment plays in improving teaching and learning in PE and how it can develop your competence in assessing pupils in your day-to-day teaching, not only in relation to performance but all concepts and processes in PE and broader goals of education. It is recommended that you specifically focus on assessment *for* learning strategies such as shared ILOs, questioning, feedback and peer- and self-assessment, as these enhance pupil learning and improve your teaching.

This chapter has indicated the need for appropriate and specific assessment criteria, whether the assessment is formal or informal. Judgements can then be made and feedback provided in order to move learning forward. You should also be familiar with the need to assess against unit objectives or ILOs of a lesson in order to inform both pupil learning, as well as your own planning and teaching. Given Ofsted concerns about assessment, you should now realise the importance of assessment and be in a position to place it at the centre of the learning process.

Check which requirements for your course you have addressed through this chapter.

FURTHER READING

Black, P., Harrison, C., Lee, C., Marshall, B. and Wiliam, D. *et al*. (2002) *Working inside the Black Box: Assessment for Learning in the Classroom,* London: Kings College.

Black, P. and Wiliam, D. (1998) *Inside the Black Box: Raising Standards through Classroom Assessment,* London: Kings College.

These two publications give detailed information on the use of assessment *for* learning in improving the understanding of how assessment can enhance and improve the teaching and learning process. Although not PE specific, they can add to your understanding of assessment.

Black, P., Harrison, C., Lee, C., Marshall, B. and William, D. (2003) *Assessment for Learning: Putting it into Practice,* Buckingham: Open University Press.

This text is based on a two-year study involving school teachers. It provides a review of the assessment research followed by a discussion on the implementation of the chosen strategies. The strategies are evaluated and guidance for implementing change is provided.

Gardner, J. (ed.) (2006) *Assessment and Learning*, London: Sage Publications Ltd.

This book contains chapters authored by members of the ARG, a group of researchers which ensures policy and practice takes account of current research evidence. The book concentrates on the use of assessment in supporting learning. It provides practice-based theory about assessment in the classroom, developing motivation and assessment in relation to learning theory.

Ofsted (2008b) *Assessment for Learning: The Impact of the National Strategy Support.* Available online at: http://www.ofsted.gov.uk/Ofsted-home/Publications-and-research/ Browse-all-by/Education/Curriculum/English/Primary/Assessment-for-learning-the-impact-of-National-Strategy-support/(language)/eng-GB (accessed 16 April 2009).

This survey reports on the impact of the National Strategy on schools' assessment practice. It comments on the areas that have been successful and have led to improvements in learning and areas that still require development. Some of the strategies mentioned in this chapter are discussed and evaluated.

Wragg, E.C. (2001) *Assessment and Learning in the Secondary School*, London: Routledge-Falmer.

This book looks at the different purposes of assessment, then describes and analyses the different means of assessing progress. Another purpose is to relate assessment to learning. The book is designed to help you reflect on assessment and then take action to improve teaching and learning in your own classroom.

Endnote

The authors would like to acknowledge the significant input of Andrea Lockwood to earlier editions of this chapter.

TEACHING SAFELY AND SAFETY IN PE

Anne Chappell and Will Katene

INTRODUCTION

PE, by its very nature, involves challenges, adventure and inherent risks. Being able to teach safely in PE is a requirement for you to be able to qualify as a teacher. It is worth noting that in a survey of all secondary initial teacher education (ITE) subject inspections between 1999 and 2002, the Office for Standards in Education (Ofsted, 2003: 12) reported that: 'strong features of most PE lessons were the trainees' organisation, control of resources and their high expectations of pupils' behaviour; these were, in part, driven by the safety consciousness of most trainees'.

The importance of teaching safely and safety in PE is highlighted in numerous publications (e.g. Association for Physical Education (afPE), 2008; Beaumont, 2007; Chappell, 2006; Kelly, 1997; Qualifications and Curriculum Authority (QCA), 2007b; Raymond, 1999; Severs, 2003; Whitlam, 2005). As Whitlam (2005: 15) identifies 'totally safe or risk free situations do not occur in PE and school sport because they are practical activities involving movement, often at speed and in confined areas shared with others'. Beaumont (2007: 31) goes on to say that this is what makes PE and school sport 'an exciting and challenging aspect of school life' and that without 'a perceived element of risk, activities...would cease to attract and stimulate...and fail to provide a genuine opportunity for personal and social development', alongside preventing high quality learning through and about the physical. Your role as a PE teacher is to ensure that you develop a culture of teaching safely and safety in PE (and, by implication, pupils learning safely and about safety), thereby, creating and managing a safe learning environment that controls and minimises potential risks and maximises pupils' learning experiences in PE (Raymond, 1999). Every accident or injury that occurs highlights the importance of safe practice and the need to adopt procedures that minimise the likelihood of a recurrence of such incidents. The Free Dictionary (2009, http://www.thefreedictionary.com/safely) defines 'safely' as: 'free from danger or injury'; and 'safety' as: 'the condition of being safe; freedom from danger, risk, or injury'.

The aims of the National Curriculum in England include that young people become 'confident individuals who are able to live safe, healthy and fulfilling lives' and 'stay safe' (QCA, 2008a). Therefore, it is crucial that you plan your lessons to ensure pupils are acquiring appropriate knowledge and understanding of health and safety matters and consider 'what pupils should know' (see afPE, 2008; Beaumont, 2008).

OBJECTIVES

At the end of this chapter you should be able to:

■ understand key health and safety legislation, regulations and policy, as well as your professional responsibilities and issues for maintaining safety in all aspects of teaching PE;

■ develop pupils' knowledge and understanding of, and ability to create and manage, their learning environment to ensure the health and safety of themselves and others;

■ create a safe environment for teaching and learning in your lessons.

Check the requirements for your course to see which relate to this chapter.

HEALTH AND SAFETY LEGISLATION AND REGULATIONS

Given the essential requirement to teach safely and safety in PE, it is necessary for you to acquire an in-depth knowledge and understanding of health and safety issues. This section provides an overview of key health and safety organisations, legislation and regulations (see Figure 9.1 and Table 9.1); your professional responsibilities; issues of teaching safely and safety; how to develop pupils' knowledge and understanding of safety; how to teach pupils to create and manage their learning environment to ensure health and safety of themselves and others. You also need to understand: concepts and principles underpinning safe practice in the different physical activities and teaching environments in which you are teaching; how to assess the safety of specific activities/exercises; the associated safety procedures for specific activities being taught; first aid/emergency procedures; particular medical conditions (e.g. asthma, diabetes, overweight), and know how to plan and/or adapt exercise/activities to minimise risk to pupils with these conditions; class management/organisation skills in relation to the positioning of you, the placement and use of equipment, and the orientation of the activity or exercise. To this end we advise you to read *Safe Practice in Physical Education and School Sport* (afPE, 2008), which looks in depth at safety issues.

It is important for you to recognise that the law provides checklists, procedures and frameworks to safeguard professionals who may be exposed to risks in the workplace. You should, therefore, familiarise yourself with health and safety organisations, legislation and regulations, particularly their interrelationships and interconnections, to better understand your professional responsibility in teaching safely and safety in a PE context.

Task 9.1 (on p. 139) asks you to study the health and safety documentation in your placement school.

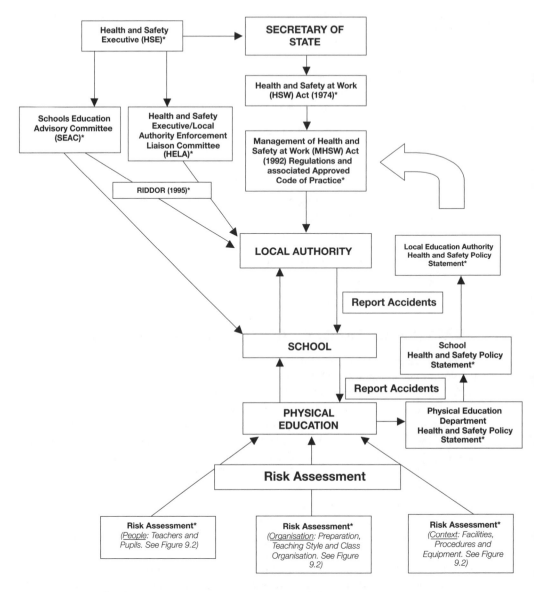

* See Table 9.1 for a description of this organisation, legislation or regulation

■ **Figure 9.1** Overview of health and safety organisations, legislation and regulations (adapted from Elbourn, 1999)

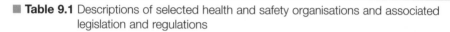

■ **Table 9.1** Descriptions of selected health and safety organisations and associated legislation and regulations

Health and Safety Executive (HSE)	This is a non-departmental public body (NDPB) accountable to the Secretary of State for the Department of Work and Pensions established under the Health and Safety at Work Act (UK legislation, 1974). The HSE's role is to secure the health, safety and welfare of people at work; to protect the public against risks to health and safety arising from work activities; and to control dangerous substances. They are responsible for proposing and setting necessary standards via policy; securing compliance with those standards; and undertaking other forms of activity designed to stimulate or support necessary action on the part of people and organisations that create potential harm (HSE, 2006). This action includes (a) inspecting workplaces (including schools and universities); (b) investigating accidents and cases of ill health; (c) enforcing good standards usually by advising people on how to comply with the law; (d) publishing guidance and advice; (e) providing an information service; (f) carrying out research (Elbourn, 1999: 8).
Schools Education Advisory Committee (SEAC)	This is the HSE advisory committee responsible for advising on the protection of people at work and others (including pupils and members of the public) from hazards to health and safety arising within the field of education.
Health and Safety Executive/Local Authority (LA) Enforcement Liaison Committee (HELA)	HELA's role is to provide effective liaison between the HSE and local authorities (LAs). It seeks to ensure that health and safety legislation is enforced in a consistent way among LAs, and between LAs and the HSE. HELA provides a national forum for discussion and exchange of information on enforcement of legislation. It promotes the achievement of good health and safety standards and practice.
Health and Safety at Work (HSW) Act (UK Legislation 1974)	Health and safety is about preventing people from being harmed at work by taking the right precautions and providing a satisfactory working environment. HSW Act (1974) requires that: (a) employers have to look after the health and safety of their employees; (b) employees have to look after their own health and safety; (c) all have to care for the health and safety of others (e.g., members of the public).
Management of Health and Safety at Work (MHSW) Act (1992) Regulations and associated Approved Code of Practice	'These establish a consistent set of standards for most workplaces including schools, college and universities. LAs (as employers) are required to assess risks to the health and safety of teaching and non-teaching staff, pupils and others who enter the school premises' (Elbourn, 1999: 9).

■ **Table 9.1** continued

The Reporting of Injuries, Diseases and Dangerous Occurrences Regulations (RIDDOR) (1995)	'Reporting accidents and ill health at work is a legal requirement. Those which must be reported include deaths; major injuries; injuries where an employee or self-employed person is away from work or unable to perform their normal work duties for more than 3 consecutive days; injuries to members of the public or people not at work, where they are taken from the scene of an accident to hospital; some work-related diseases; some dangerous occurrences – a near miss, where something happens that does not result in an injury, but could have done. Deaths, major injuries and dangerous occurrences must be notified without delay and over-3-day injuries must be reported within ten days' (HSE, 2007: 2). Schools normally inform LAs of any such occurrences and LAs report these incidents on behalf of the schools. This 'provides information that allows authorities to identify where and how risks arise and, if necessary, to investigate serious accidents and advise on preventative action' (Raymond 1999: 16).
Local Authority Health and Safety Policy Statement	LAs are responsible for producing a broad health and safety policy statement which should ensure that all employees know what is expected of them and what they need to do to discharge their legal liabilities. Additionally, each school is required by their LA to produce a school health and safety policy statement covering local organisation and health and safety arrangements. This is then attached to the LA document to form a complete response to the requirements of the HSW Act (Elbourn, 1999).
School and PE Department Health and Safety Policy Statement	This should include content such as: (a) 'the policy's aims in relation to the law; (b) responsibilities of LA, governing body, headteacher, school health and safety officer and safety representatives; (c) duties and obligations of staff; (d) what is expected of pupils; (e) the composition and duties of a safety committee; (f) arrangements for risk assessments; (g) emergency procedures and fire drills; (h) accident recording and reporting procedures; (i) safety training; (j) security issues; (k) review and monitoring procedures' (Elbourn, 1999: 11). Headteachers are responsible for health and safety matters in a school. Heads of department (HOD) are responsible for the health and safety within their department. Teachers are responsible for the immediate area of their work. If teachers discover a hazard, the law requires them to take all reasonable steps within their power to eliminate this and to refer the matter to their HOD or headteacher, if the limits of their authority preclude a permanent solution. The LA and/or headteacher needs to ensure that PE teachers are: (a) trained in risk assessment and making quality and justifiable decisions; (b) provided with quality information (e.g., predicted data); (c) monitored so that they can learn from their successes and can be helped to minimise the seriousness of harmful outcomes; (d) provided with a framework for making high-quality decisions that minimise the seriousness of harmful outcomes; (e) supported if they follow the LA's/school's decision-making framework, even if harm results (Elbourn, 1999).

■ **Table 9.1** continued

Risk Assessment (People, Context and Organisation)	afPE (2008) provide a useful structural and contextual framework (comprising people, context and organisation) for educating both teachers and pupils in the importance of risk management (see Figure 9.2 and afPE, 2008).

Task 9.1 **Health and safety policy statements and processes in your placement school and PE department**

Familiarise yourself with the health and safety policy statements and processes of both your placement school and PE department.

Find out: (a) who is the school's designated Health and Safety Officer; (b) who is the PE department's designated Health and Safety Officer (or equivalent); (c) who are the certified and trained first aid personnel in the school and in the PE department; (d) where both the first aid box and travelling first aid kit can be found; (e) what risk assessment form is used in the PE department; (f) what form should be filled in to record an accident or injury and where it can be accessed; (g) who is involved and what the stages of the process are in relation to accident forms; (h) the role of the LA in supporting the policy and process of Health and Safety.

Record this information in your professional development portfolio (PDP), for future reference.

PROFESSIONAL RESPONSIBILITIES FOR AND ISSUES RELATED TO TEACHING SAFELY AND SAFETY IN PE

Your professional responsibilities for and issues related to teaching safely in PE include: duty of care and acting in loco parentis; negligence; risk management and control, risk assessment and safety; dealing appropriately with injuries or accidents and accident reporting; first aid training, first aid boxes and travelling first aid kits. Figure 9.2 provides an overview of the factors involved in effective risk management and guides the key considerations for enabling safe working conditions.

Duty of care and in loco parentis

All teachers are responsible for the health and safety of pupils in their care. You should take reasonable care in any situation to: safeguard pupils; anticipate and manage risks to ensure they are at an acceptable level (Whitlam, 2005); and ensure that pupils are not harmed by the actions of themselves or others. This is called 'duty of care'. The term 'in loco parentis', which literally means 'in place of the parent', underpins this duty of care for teachers when responsible for pupils. Whilst pupils are in a teacher's care, some of the privileges of the natural, caring parent are transferred to the qualified teacher. Thus, teachers with this legal responsibility must exercise the same duty of care as a 'reasonably prudent parent', judged not in the context of the home but in that of a school

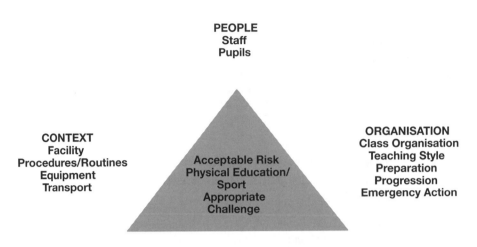

■ **Figure 9.2** The risk-management model (afPE, 2008: 23)

situation. Crucially the 'higher duty of care' is applied in the professional context and qualified teachers, by virtue of their skills, training and experience, are expected to have 'greater insight' and 'awareness of the consequences' of their practice. Teachers are also required to undertake practice, usually in the form of attending courses, which is 'regular and approved' within the profession (afPE, 2008). This includes keeping up to date through continuing professional development (CPD) throughout your career (see Chapter 18 for guidance on CPD).

As a student teacher you cannot legally take on the responsibility for the health and safety of pupils; that responsibility lies with the qualified and experienced teacher in charge of the class/group. When you are teaching, a qualified and experienced teacher must always supervise you in the teaching environment in the same way as they supervise any adult without QTS (afPE, 2008). Likewise, you cannot act as a supply teacher to fill in if the regular qualified teacher is absent. If the qualified teacher is not available, you must not proceed to teach (see Unit 8.3 in Capel, Leask and Turner, 2009). Similarly, if you are running a lunchtime and/or after-school club, you must always have a qualified teacher present.

Negligence

afPE states that: 'Negligence may arise when an individual's actions fall below the standard of care expected in particular circumstances to protect others from the unreasonable risk of harm' (2008: 15). An allegation of negligence requires four elements which relate to: the nature of the responsibility undertaken for the claimant; carelessness by 'act' or 'omission' whilst undertaking that responsibility; resulting injury to the claimant; and information that the potential for the incident could have been foreseen. 'It is the element of carelessness that may impose a liability of negligence. Claims for negligence are normally made against employers. Significant levels of protection exist against allegations of negligence by staff as individuals' (afPE, 2008: 15).

Accusations of negligence can be minimised considerably if it can be shown that:

■ a teacher or coach is sufficiently qualified, experienced and confident to teach the activity and appropriate supervision is provided;

■ teachers keep themselves up to date on health and safety issues and recent developments, through attendance at relevant courses. Furthermore they demonstrate 'regular and approved' practice that operates within policy guidelines;

■ planning takes full account of the people involved, the context of the activity and the associated organisation to ensure that risk management is comprehensive;

■ equipment is used for the purposes that it was intended for and is well maintained;

■ in a manner appropriate to their age, ability and experience, pupils are taught about safety; have safe practice modelled for them; and are always expected to demonstrate safe ways of working;

■ pupils are systematically prepared for the activities being undertaken and the tasks are progressive, ensuring appropriateness for the pupils' experience, ability, age and physical maturity;

■ appropriate footwear and clothing are worn, all adornments are removed, and safety equipment is used where appropriate;

■ any outdoor and adventurous activities or any local or overseas visits, are preceded by prior agreement of parents by means of signed participation documentation (a member of a school's senior management team is normally responsible for providing a suitable form for this purpose);

■ record keeping such as attendance registers, lesson plans and assessment information is efficiently documented and stored. These documents record pupil experience and indicate what they are capable of;

■ regular and accurate risk assessments are undertaken, documented and reviewed;

■ Adults Other Than Teachers (AOTTs) are well informed and given a clear role in the lesson.

(for further information see afPE 2008; and
http://www.teachernet.gov.uk/wholeschool/healthandsafety)

Risk management and control

Risk management is the: 'umbrella term given to the whole process of identifying risks and then taking action to eliminate them' (Raymond, 1999: 49). The law does not expect you to eliminate all risk, but you are required to protect people as far as is 'reasonably practicable' (HSE, 2006: 1). In relation to risk control:

if any significant risk is identified which current practice does not eliminate or minimise, then that risk must be controlled by taking some sort of action…the action may involve: removing the risk completely; trying a less risky option; preventing access to the hazard; re-organising the group, activity or procedure to reduce the likelihood of the hazard causing harm; providing or requiring protective equipment to be used; improving the staff/pupil ratio or providing more information, tuition or training.

(Raymond 1999: 57)

In simple terms the decision about action to be taken or not relates to the manner in which the benefits of an activity 'outweigh the risks' or the 'risks outweigh the benefits' (Beaumont, 2007: 31).

To ensure that you do all that is reasonably practicable to safeguard the health, safety and welfare of pupils, you need to recognise and eliminate the hazards (or anything that can cause harm such as equipment or environment) and reduce the risks (or the chance that someone will be harmed by a hazard). You are expected to foresee a substantial risk and take steps to avoid it or reduce it to an acceptable level. As outlined above, you are also expected to possess a greater than average knowledge and under-standing of the risks involved in the activities you teach and to take precautions in accordance with that knowledge and understanding (afPE, 2008). This can be challeng-ing where practices have been undertaken for many years and are perceived to be the norm and acceptable. It is in this type of environment that you need to be particularly aware. Task 9.2 requires you to carry out an analysis of the risks in setting up and manag-ing a circuit.

Task 9.2 **Risk management**

You have been asked to teach a lesson to a year 8 mixed sex class involving the setting up and use of a circuit of activities. You have been told that the lesson will take place in a gymnasium; the pupils will be using dumbbells and mats, benches, skipping ropes; and will be required to complete as many repeats as possible (in 1 minute) at each station. Pupils will be working in bare feet. The circuit includes push-ups, sit ups, skipping, step ups, shuttle runs, squats, biceps and triceps curls. The warm-up comprises sprint relays, windmills and hurdle stretches.

Using Figure 9.2 and the material covered so far in the chapter, list at least six recommendations to minimise risk. Record your reasons for this selection of recom-mendations and discuss these with your tutor. Record this discussion and put all elements of the observation into your PDP.

Risk assessment and safety

One of the challenges for you is to identify accurately the potential level of risk that an activity poses. Risk assessment 'involves identifying what could cause harm to people and appraising whether sufficient precautions have been taken to prevent or minimise harm' (Elbourn, 1999: 3). Although it might be easy to identify those situations in which risk is most obvious you need to be able to assess all situations in respect of the likeli-hood of accident or injury. Figure 9.2 provides an illustration of an effective method for doing this.

Task 9.3 asks you to complete risk assessments on six of your lessons, using the grading structure from Table 9.2.

Task 9.3 **Risk rating**

Choose six examples of specific activities that you might teach in a PE and/or school sport programme. Use Table 9.2 to calculate a 'risk rating' for each and rank them in order of the highest to lowest rating. Discuss this with your tutor and put your notes in your PDP.

■ **Table 9.2** Calculating a risk rating (Whitlam, 2003: 35)

Hazard severity	Likelihood of occurrence
1. Negligible: near miss/minor injury, e.g. abrasion	1. Improbable: almost zero
2. Slight: injury needing medical attention, e.g. laceration	2. Remote: unlikely to occur
3. Moderate: more serious injury causing absence from school	3. Possible: could occur sometimes
4. Severe: serious injury requiring hospital treatment	4. Probable: may occur several times; not surprising
5. Very severe: permanent injury/fatality	5. Near certainty: expected

Severity x Likelihood = Risk rating

For example, a hockey lesson on dribbling outdoors on an artificial pitch **might** score 1 for hazard severity and 3 for likelihood of occurrence. Risk rating 3.

For example a swimming lesson **might** score 5 for hazard severity and 2 for likelihood of occurrence. Risk rating 10.

To assist you in assessing the risks in your workplace or teaching environment, HSE (2006: 2–5) recommends the following 'Five Steps to Risk Assessment':

Step 1: Identify the hazards (walk around the teaching environment such as the gym and look at what could cause harm; concentrate on significant hazards which could result in serious harm or affect several pupils. Also, ask pupils if they notice anything which may pose a risk).

Step 2: Decide who might be harmed and how (pupils, yourself, PE teacher/tutor, other teachers, public/visitors).

Step 3: Evaluate the risks and decide on precautions (your aim is to make all risks small. If something needs to be done, draw up an action plan and give priority to any remaining risks which are medium or high. In taking action, ask yourself: can I eliminate the risk completely? If not, how can I control the risks so that harm is unlikely? In controlling risks, apply the following principles: (a) try a less risky option; (b) prevent access to the hazard; (c) organise teaching to reduce exposure to the hazard e.g. issue personal protective/adaptive resources/equipment; (d) provide welfare facilities. Failure to take simple precautions can be significantly to your disadvantage if an accident does happen. Remember that if you cannot reduce the risks to an acceptable level then you should not undertake the activity).

Step 4: Record your findings and implement them (you need to be able to show that: a proper check was made; you asked who might be affected; you dealt with all the significant hazards, taking into account the number of pupils involved; the precautions are reasonable, and the remaining risk is low. Keep a written record for future reference or use. It can help you if anyone asks what precautions you have taken. It can also remind you to keep an eye on particular hazards and precautions. It also helps to show that you have done what the law requires if you become involved in any action for civil liability).

Step 5: Review your assessment and update if necessary (it is good practice to review your risk assessment regularly to make sure that the precautions are still working effectively).

(See also afPE, 2008 for detailed guidance and documentation to support this risk assessment process.)

Task 9.4 challenges you to use the five-step risk factor assessment above to assess one of your lessons.

Task 9.4 **Risk assessment of a PE lesson**

Complete a risk assessment of one of your PE lessons, following the 'Five Steps to Risk Assessment' outlined above. Link this assessment to Task 9.3. Discuss the findings with your tutor and put these notes in your PDP.

All LAs and schools should have a risk assessment form. The risk assessment form should prompt the recording of issues associated with people, context and organisation, in relation to the breadth of practice, and whether they pose a 'satisfactory/safe/low risk' or an 'unsatisfactory/unsafe/significant risk'. In cases where a significant risk applies, the form should demonstrate who is affected by the issue and what the proposed risk control consists of (afPE, 2009). It is important that the form is signed, dated and shared with the leadership and management team (Whitlam, 2003), especially where support is required from outside the department to resolve an issue. Task 9.5 asks you to study the risk assessment form in the PE department of your placement school.

Task 9.5 **Risk assessment form**

Look at a completed risk assessment form for the PE department in your placement school for one of the activities you are teaching; one of the facilities that you are working in; and an offsite activity (e.g. a local fixture or a larger scale trip).

Consider the way in which staff have recorded any necessary aspects of risk control where an issue has been identified as being more significant than 'satisfactory/safe/low risk'. What support/action has been sought from outside the department? Discuss this and the associated processes with your tutor. Put these notes in your PDP.

Injuries or accidents and accident reporting

Wherever there is a risk, injuries or accidents are a possibility. If an injury or accident (minor or serious) occurs in your lesson(s), you should not hesitate to act promptly and effectively. It is essential that you understand and implement your placement school's procedures and guidelines for dealing with injuries or accidents. If an injury or accident happens, the priorities are to: (a) assess the situation; (b) safeguard the uninjured members of the class/group; (c) attend to the casualty; (d) inform the emergency services, if appropriate, and everyone who needs to know of the incident (Department for Education and Employment (DfEE), 1998). Increasingly schools have made it accepted practice for staff, particularly PE staff, to use mobile phones or have provided radios/intercoms when they are working at a distance from the school's main building.

It is important that all accidents and injuries (minor or major) are recorded immediately. Some accidents also fall into the category of 'reportable' (HSE, 2005). A reportable accident is defined as one 'which results in death or major injury ... and accidents which prevent the injured person from continuing at his/her normal work for more than three days must be reported within ten days' (HSE, 2005: 1). Major injuries include fractures (other than to the bones of the hands and feet) (for other major injuries and dangerous occurrences see HSE (2005) and also RIDDOR (Table 9.1 above).

All LAs and schools should have their own accident report forms. AfPE recommends that: 'it is important that accidents are recorded on the employer's official report form or accident book as soon as is reasonably possible. This aids the reporting process and is also useful in the event of a liability claim' (2008: 52). These records must be kept for at least three years (Department for Education and Skills (DfES), 2002). However, it has become increasingly valuable for these records to be kept longer in order to ensure that evidence is available in the case where a retrospective claim is made. A detailed accident report would include the information in Figure 9.3.

Together with the accident report, a sketch plan (signed and dated) of where an accident has taken place would be useful as very often people have different views of what took place, where, how and when. Task 9.6 requires you to investigate in your placement school what actions you should take in the event of an accident.

Task 9.6 **Reporting accidents**

Find out what you have to do if an accident or injury occurs whilst you are teaching a PE lesson in your placement school.

What formal guidelines and procedures must be adhered to? Keep a copy of this in your school experience file or PDP for future reference.

First aid training, first aid boxes and travelling first aid kits

afPE (2008) suggests that the minimum first aid requirements for each school are: a person(s) appointed to take charge of first aid arrangements; information for employees about first aid arrangements; well-maintained records of any incidents where first aid is administered; an appropriate number of suitably stocked, identifiable and easily accessible first aid boxes and travelling first aid kits. There should be at least one qualified first aider for every 50 members of staff in each school. Furthermore, it is advisable that all PE teachers and AOTTs receive first aid training appropriate to their teaching responsibilities – including you! (afPE, 2008: 49–54 and 332–5). In the United Kingdom certificates of qualification in first aid are valid for three years, after which time a refresher course and examination is required for re-certification. The regulations for first aid at work were changed by HSE on 1 October 2009. The three-day 'First Aid at Work' and one-day 'Emergency First Aid at Work' (St John's Ambulance) are examples of first

Particulars of the Injured or the Affected Person
Full Name:
Date of Birth:
Gender:
Home Address:
Postcode:
Telephone Number:
Status: Employee/Pupil/Visitor (*please delete as applicable*)
Name(s) of witness(es):

Particulars of the Accident	
Date:	Time:
Description of the events leading to the accident (*continue on an additional sheet if required*):	
Description of the action taken immediately after the accident (*continue on an additional sheet if required*):	

Particulars of the Injury
Was an injury sustained?: Yes/No (*please delete as applicable*)
Cause of injury:
Type of injury:
Part(s) of the body affected:

■ **Figure 9.3** Sample accident report form

Outcome
Was first aid treatment required?: Yes/No (*please delete as applicable*)
If yes, please provide details:
Was a hospital visit required?: Yes/No (*please delete as applicable*)
Date of visit:
Was hospital treatment necessary?: Yes/No (*please delete as applicable*)
Please provide details:
Was time off required following the accident?: Yes/No (*please delete as applicable*)
If yes, how long?:
Was temporary injury sustained?: Yes/No (*please delete as applicable*)
If yes, please provide details:
Was permanent injury sustained?: Yes/No (*please delete as applicable*)
If yes, please provide details:

Risk Management
What action has been taken to avoid/prevent a reoccurrence?:
Recommendations:

Report Completed by
Name:
Date:
Signature:

■ **Figure 9.3** continued

aid courses (for further information on availability of first aid courses, see the Health and Safety Officer at your placement school or university or make enquires at your local sport, leisure and recreation centre). Further guidance on first aid processes for schools is available from the DfES (2002c).

HOW TO DEVELOP PUPILS' KNOWLEDGE AND UNDERSTANDING OF, AND ABILITY TO CREATE AND MANAGE, THEIR LEARNING ENVIRONMENT TO ENSURE HEALTH AND SAFETY OF THEMSELVES AND OTHERS

With reference to teaching safety or developing pupils' knowledge and understanding of creating and managing a safe learning environment, pupils should:

■ learn how to respond appropriately to instructions and signals within established routines and follow rules and codes of conduct in a given activity (e.g. negotiate class rules to ensure a safe teaching environment);
■ learn the importance of being dressed appropriately for the activity/exercise they are participating in (e.g. no jewellery/adornment) and the wearing of protective clothing (e.g. shin pads in football);
■ learn about correct forms of exercise, and how performance and safety are improved when preparation is carried out properly (e.g. performing recommended stretching exercises during warm-up and cool-down phases of a lesson);
■ analyse, plan and carry out tasks safely (e.g. problem-solving activities in OAA);
■ learn the principles of safe partner support (e.g. progressive skills within gymnastics);
■ know the proper use of a range of equipment; the safe handling and storage of equipment and apparatus;
■ create their own apparatus layout to suit the tasks set and are aware of the risks and hazards (e.g. setting out medium and high apparatus to carry out a 'rotation' task);
■ devise, implement and monitor their own, and/or others', exercise and fitness programmes based on the principles of safe and effective exercise (e.g. at Key Stage 4, pupils plan their own exercise programme to improve aspects of their fitness);
■ carry out a risk assessment in a particular activity (e.g. as part of their role as an official, they would check the playing area of a football activity for any pot holes etc.).

In planning activities, it is essential that you not only present an exemplary model of safety management to pupils but also take time to discuss safety thus increasing their awareness and understanding in relation to their safe involvement in physical activities within and beyond school.

A CASE REPORT OF ALLEGED NEGLIGENCE

Below is a case report of alleged negligence (see Swansea Civil Justice Centre, 2002). Other cases are also available (see Raymond, 1999: 97–104 and Whitlam, 2005). This detailed case is presented to highlight some of the complexities of the challenges teachers are faced with in practice, and to help you to understand your professional responsibilities in teaching safely and safety in PE. The case report is presented in the following format to guide you through the important considerations: the relevant parties, evidence available, circumstances of the accident, the issues to be addressed, the facts upon which the expert's opinions are based, the expert's conclusion and lessons to be learned.

The relevant parties

The plaintiff (injured party), Rhian, is a pupil at Dwr-y-Felin Upper School. The defendant (the Local County Council), denies negligence.

Evidence available

Individual statements from Rhian; Rebecca, her partner in the PE lesson; and PE teacher, Mrs S in October 1997.

Circumstances of the accident

One day in Autumn 1997, Rhian participated in her first, year 8, PE lesson. It was the first period of the day, taken by Mrs S, the teacher in charge of the lesson. Towards the end of the lesson, Mrs S asked the class to do headstands in pairs (whilst one pupil performed the headstand, the partner was to give such support as was necessary). Rhian paired herself with another female pupil, Rebecca. Rhian said that neither she nor Rebecca had ever been shown how to perform or support a headstand or had actually been engaged in attempting one. They had not been shown previously, nor did Mrs S demonstrate or give any instruction as to how to do or support a headstand that day. Rhian said that her partner mentioned this to Mrs S but she insisted that they practice full headstands without further demonstration or instruction. They did so. Whilst Rhian was attempting her first headstand, Rebecca was to her side to support her back. Unfortunately, she lost her footing, causing Rhian to move backwards. As a result, she let go of Rhian, who fell, landing awkwardly on her neck and shoulder. Rhian immediately felt a 'click' between her shoulder blades, and felt some discomfort. However, when she looked around the gymnasium looking for Mrs S, she had left the gymnasium and Rhian was unable to find her. Rhian consequently went back to the changing rooms, and got ready for and went to the next lesson without telling any member of staff. However, she went to the school nurse at lunchtime that day because she was still in discomfort. That visit to the nurse was the start of considerable intervention on the part of healthcare professionals, over several months. Rhian suffered a musculo-ligament strain of the soft tissues of the cervical spine. There was stark divergence of medical opinion between two consultant orthopaedic surgeons instructed by each party; Mr G considered that Rhian would suffer indefinite symptoms for an indefinite period. The other consultant considered that symptoms for a period of only 9–12 months were properly attributable to the accident.

The issues to be addressed

Rhian alleges that Mrs S failed to: exercise proper supervision or control over her and the other pupils; instruct her and the other pupils in the proper and safe procedure for carrying out the exercise, in particular, the need to form a secure base with the hands and head on the floor before raising the legs; practice the technique of support appropriately and safely; carry out any proper risk assessment of the activity and demonstrate the exercise in the presence of the class; properly assess the skill level and previous experience of the class; have any proper regard to the relevant publications such as: afPE, *Safe Practice in Physical Education and School Sport*; provide her with a safe place to perform the said activity; and provide sufficient supervision or control of her activities and exposed her to an unnecessary risk of injury.

The facts upon which the expert's opinions are based

Teacher: Mrs S had been a teacher for 12 years, having obtained a degree in Education at a very well-respected College. She had not been involved in any incident in which a pupil had been injured before, or since. Mrs S explained that she began to teach the progressive headstand routine in accordance with the National Curriculum for PE (NCPE) in year 7. However, Rhian did not join the school until Christmas of that year, and therefore missed the first term. Rhian's evidence was that she had never been shown how to do a headstand in any shape or form before 9 October 1997; she had never been in a PE class in which they had been attempted. Rhian's partner said that she had been shown how to perform and how to support a headstand whilst she was in year 7.

Teaching style: Mrs S stated that she demonstrated the various sequential stages leading towards a full, straight-legged headstand, with a pupil (to show method of support) before asking the pupils to perform such a supported headstand. This was confirmed by Rebecca, Rhian's partner; she also confirmed that she fully understood the instructions that had been explained by Mrs S. Whatever Rhian's experience, ability and understanding, her partner fully understood her instruction as to how to support a partner when that partner was attempting a headstand manoeuvre. It was also something which she had done before on many occasions.

Supervision: Rhian's partner, Rebecca, said that Mrs S did not leave the PE lesson and she recalled seeing her at the end of the lesson. Mrs S said that she did not leave the gymnasium and supervised the lesson from start to finish. Mrs S went with the girls to the changing rooms and consequently was available if Rhian had wanted to speak with her about the accident. Mrs S said Rhian did not report any accident.

The expert's conclusion

Mrs S properly instructed Rhian in how to perform a supported headstand and the level to which she should attempt to go: and she properly instructed her partner in how to support a headstand. Further, Mrs S did not leave the gymnasium until the end of the lesson; properly supervising the class throughout the period. That supervision included giving Rhian some individual tuition about headstands. Neither Rhian nor her partner expressed unwillingness to attempt headstands in line with the instructions given nor any tendency to go outside or beyond those instructions. Mrs S was not guilty of any breach of the duty owed to Rhian on 9 October 1997. Insofar as the allegations that Mrs S ought to have prepared for the lesson (and assessed the risks inherent in headstands) in a different way, no findings were made. Had Mrs S acted differently, that would not have prevented the accident that in fact occurred. Rhian suffered an unfortunate accident but the Local County Council (LCC) was not to blame for it. The LCC was not at fault, and was consequently not liable to compensate Rhian for the injury she suffered (Swansea Civil Justice Centre, 2002).

Lessons to be learned

In this case report, the key safety issues were estimations of pupils' sense of responsibility and the level of supervision. It is not so much the activity that causes the accidents, but a combination of factors contributing to accidents. Regardless of differences in pupils' age, the type of school, range of teaching environments and type of activity, Thomas (1994) suggests that there are five factors as to why accidents happen:

1   Bad luck – factors outside the teachers' control.
2   Poor decision making and subsequent reaction to the situation.
3   Lack of adequate and appropriate group management, supervision and organisation.
4   Overestimation of (a) teacher's ability (knowledge, understanding and competence) and (b) pupil's sense of responsibility.
5   Under-estimation of potential risk and hazard.

Thus, a knowledge and understanding of how and why accidents happen can provide a basis for modifying current practice, minimising and anticipating the occurrence of injury or accident and developing a safety culture. In this way PE can continue to offer teachers, student teachers and pupils challenges, adventure and risks safely and in safety. To minimise the risk of alleged negligence, remember to follow the 'Five Steps to Risk Assessment' (see above) and refer to afPE (2008) *Safe Practice in Physical Education and School Sport*.

A CHECKLIST TO SUPPORT YOU IN PROMOTING A CULTURE OF TEACHING SAFELY AND SAFETY IN PE

The checklist below identifies key elements to consider in promoting a culture of teaching safely and safety in PE:

■   Know and understand the current health and safety legislation and regulations (see Table 9.1).
■   Familiarise yourself with the health and safety policy statements of the LA, school and PE department and the procedures and guidelines arising from these documents.
■   Have a good up-to-date working knowledge and understanding of legal and professional responsibilities and your liabilities relating to health and safety and duty of care.
■   Have an in-depth, up-to-date knowledge and understanding of the concepts, principles and safety implications, guidelines and procedures associated with 'people, context and organisation' (see Figure 9.1 above) in relation to your teaching.
■   Ensure that you have a risk assessment framework and receive appropriate training and information updates in order to make accurate and consistent decisions which minimise risk in PE.
■   Carry out regular risk assessments in relation to 'people, context and organisation'.
■   Participate in daily, weekly, monthly and annual risk assessments (e.g. outside

agencies such as the Health and Safety Officer, maintenance 'team', manufacturer) – it is an expectation of school and PE staff.

■ Follow the 'Five Steps to Risk Assessment' (HSE, 2006: 2–5) fully and clinically.

■ Cultivate an ability to perceive and anticipate risks, and become competent in checking for potential hazards. Use this information to make appropriate adaptations to reduce risks to an acceptable level.

■ Plan for all eventualities and especially for emergency action, and ensure that you have first aid training appropriate to your level of responsibility.

Furthermore, as safety in PE is a vast subject and one beyond the remit of this chapter, we urge you to read afPE (2008) as well as checking for regular updates with afPE and other relevant professional associations (see further reading). Now complete Task 9.7.

Task 9.7 **Embedding teaching safely and safety in your teaching**

Write a 3,000 word essay discussing the professional role and responsibility of the teacher in embedding teaching safely and safety as a fundamental aspect of their practice. Consider the challenges faced in undertaking this role and responsibility, and suggest ways of overcoming these.

SUMMARY AND KEY POINTS

This chapter has presented an overview of key health and safety legislation and regulations in England. It discussed some of your professional responsibilities, and issues of teaching safely and safety. The chapter then considered how you can develop pupils' knowledge and understanding of, and ability to create and manage, their learning environment to ensure the health and safety of themselves and others. This was supported with a case report of alleged negligence in a gymnastics lesson to highlight some of the problems teachers face in trying to ensure pupils' safety and the associated accountability. Finally, the chapter provided a checklist to support you in promoting a culture of teaching safely and safety in PE.

It is hoped that this chapter has helped you to approach your teaching with greater knowledge and confidence, rather than uneasiness and concern. We strongly urge you to take responsibility for your own professional development; to keep up to date with recent developments, approved practice and research evidence concerning the provision of health and safety in PE.

Check which requirements for your course you have addressed through this chapter.

FURTHER READING AND RELEVANT ORGANISATIONS

Association for Physical Education (2008) *Safe Practice in Physical Education and School Sport*, **7th edn, Leeds: afPE/Coachwise.**

This key text provides comprehensive up-to-date advice and information for PE teachers and other staff involved in teaching physical education and school sport safely and safety in schools.

Chappell, A. (2006) Safe practice, risk assessment and risk management, in S. Capel, P. Breckon and J. O'Neill (eds) *A Practical Guide to Teaching Physical Education in the Secondary School*, **London: RoutledgeFalmer.**

This chapter provides a range of activities (10.1–10.16) which can be undertaken in the teaching context to support the ongoing development of up-to-date subject knowledge across aspects of health and safety in physical education and school sport.

Raymond, C. (ed.) (1999) *Safety Across the Curriculum*, **London: RoutledgeFalmer.**

This text provides an overview of responsibilities and interpretation of the main legislation and statutory requirements. It offers background information to help you interpret general principles and apply them to your practice.

Whitlam, P. (2005) *Case Law in Physical Education and School Sport: A Guide to Good Practice*, **Leeds: Coachwise/BAALPE.**

This text uses examples from case law to identify and reinforce the principles of good practice and standards of care in physical education and school sport.

Relevant organisations

Association for Physical Education: www.afpe.org.uk

The Association for Physical Education supports the delivery of physical education in schools and in the wider community, seeking to promote and maintain high standards and safe practice in all aspects and at all levels. The website contains regular updates and advice, with links to a helpline for health and safety, and legal advice. They have a health and safety advisory panel who provide frequently asked questions.

Health and Safety Executive: www.hse.gov.uk

The Health and Safety Executive's role is to protect people against risks to health or safety arising out of work activities. They offer information, advice, and training in relation to regulations and codes of practice, inspection, investigation and enforcement. They also provide frequently asked questions.

Endnote

The authors would like to acknowledge the significant input of Geoff Edmondson to the earlier edition of this chapter.

DESIGNING TEACHING APPROACHES TO ACHIEVE INTENDED LEARNING OUTCOMES

Margaret Whitehead with Richard Blair

INTRODUCTION

This chapter is aimed at helping you to understand the complex relationship between the intended learning outcomes (ILOs) of your lessons, the learning tasks and learning environment that you and your students create (Leach and Moon, 1999). It supports the proposal that to achieve any longer term learning aim in respect of a scheme of work, you are required to develop medium-term objectives for units of work and shorter term ILOs for lesson plans (see Chapter 3). Achieving lesson ILOs are the essential building blocks in reaching long-term goals. An appreciation of the key elements of your teaching that impact on achieving ILOs is therefore very important to the whole enterprise of effective teaching of PE. The chapter proposes that the pedagogical knowledge on how you teach is as important as the content knowledge of what you teach (Shulman, 1999). It encourages you to view the significance of combining content knowledge with pedagogical knowledge as the foundation of understanding the importance of all elements of your teaching, whether this is teaching National Curriculum for Physical Education (NCPE) (Qualifications and Curriculum Authority (QCA), 2007a) or classroom-based General Certificate of Secondary Education (GCSE) and General Certificate of Education Advanced (A) level work.

OBJECTIVES

At the end of this chapter you should be able to:

■ understand the relationship between the concepts of teaching skill, teaching approach, teaching strategy, teaching style and the learning environment;

■ understand that teaching strategies are specifically designed teaching approaches comprised of a carefully selected cluster of teaching skills/elements of teaching;

■ understand that the appropriate use of teaching skills is essential to achieving ILOs;

■ appreciate that aims, objectives and ILOs can be achieved only if the appropriate strategy is used;

■ be aware of a range of classifications of teaching approaches, both descriptive and prescriptive;

■ be able to recognise and implement a range of teaching strategies.

Check the requirements for your course to see which relate to this chapter.

TEACHING SKILL, TEACHING APPROACH, TEACHING STRATEGY AND TEACHING STYLE

With reference to how you teach there are a number of concepts or terms that are used in the literature. See Figure 10.1 which charts the relationship between the different concepts.

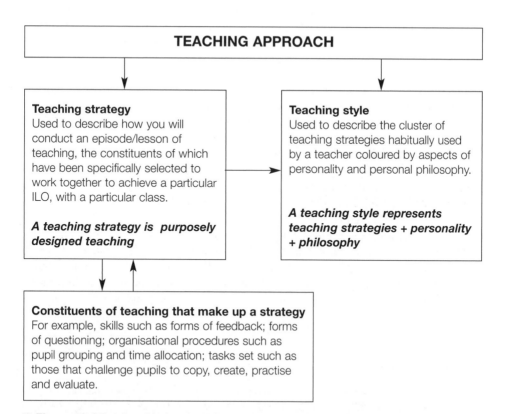

Figure 10.1 Relationship between the concepts of teaching approach, teaching strategy, teaching style and the constituents of teaching

Books on teaching identify a variety of basic teaching skills or elements of teaching such as positioning, organisation and use of voice, that a teacher needs to master to be effective in promoting pupil learning. These skills are covered in various chapters in this book. However, when these skills are combined in teaching there is no consistency in how the resultant patterns of teaching are defined. Throughout this chapter the term approach is used to describe the overall teaching behaviour of a teacher in a lesson. The term approach therefore encompasses the two types of teaching behaviour described in this chapter, being teaching strategies and teaching styles. In this chapter the words strategy and style are used in the following ways.

Teaching *strategy* is used to describe a teaching approach, the constituent elements of which have been selected specifically to work together to achieve a particular ILO with a particular class. This ILO could be concerned with, for example, communication, creativity, precision in movement or teamwork. Research into teaching strategies has been carried out by e.g. Cole and Chan (1994), Joyce and Weil (1996) and Joyce, Calhoun and Hopkins (2002). The work of Mosston and Ashworth (2002) clearly identifies strategies, although, confusingly, they call the types of teaching they describe 'styles'. For examples of strategies and a useful debate on this aspect of teaching see Unit 5.3 in Capel, Leask and Turner, 2009.

Teaching strategies are powerful learning tools that both promote aspects of learning and prohibit others from occurring. A tightly controlled didactic approach, for example, does not foster creativity in dance, nor does an open-ended discovery method result in precision in learning specific techniques such as a swimming stroke or throwing the discus. Likewise, the development of cooperative skills in pupils cannot be achieved if they are always working alone and self-esteem cannot be developed if pupils are always engaged in competitive situations. A *strategy is designed to serve an ILO* and should be planned after the ILOs of the lesson have been identified.

Teaching *style* is used to describe the general method of teacher–pupil interaction and self-presentation used by an individual teacher. Research into teaching styles was carried out by Bennett (1976), Galton and Croll (1980) and Oeser (1955). A teacher's style is made up of those skills and strategies used most often, coloured by his/her personal characteristics. For example, teacher A may have an authoritative self-presentation, use few arm gestures, speak with firmness and precision, seldom using humour and expect, rather than praise, effort. Teacher B may have a relaxed self-presentation, frequently use arm gestures, speak with a quiet voice, often using humour and smiling a great deal.

These two teachers could be equally effective, yet each has developed a different style of working with pupils. It would not be impossible for teacher A and teacher B to design very similar strategies to achieve a particular ILO, but for the nature of their interaction with pupils to be distinctive on account of the way their personal characteristics colour their teaching. Task 10.1 asks you to observe two teachers and note how their style of teaching differs.

Task 10.1 **Observation of teachers' individual styles**

Observe two teachers as they work with pupils and list the behavioural characteristics that each exhibits. How is each style distinctive? The list is likely to include such behaviours as use of humour, use of gesture, amount of interaction with

---

pupils, amount of talking allowed, ways in which order is maintained. Put your notes in your professional development portfolio (PDP).

That every teacher has his/her own style is both to be expected and welcomed as this brings variety and colour into pupils' experience in school. However, it would be un-acceptable to applaud difference *per se*. The strategic element of a teacher's style must be devised on a rational and appropriate basis – related to the ILOs, rather than being a matter of personal preference. In addition there could be situations when the personal characteristics that a teacher exhibits are not appropriate in relation to the ILOs with a particular class. For example, a teacher's preferred relaxed and somewhat humorous approach would not be appropriate in a lesson to introduce throwing the javelin. In another situation such as a year 11 Health-Related Exercise lesson, intended to motivate pupils to plan and implement their own fitness schedule, a teacher's characteristic highly organised and tightly controlled regime would be counter-productive.

The overall ambience of the lesson, being the nature of the interpersonal relation-ship between the teacher and the pupils and between the pupils, is a significant feature of the learning environment. The ambience of the lesson should, at all times, facilitate learn-ing, creating a positive, productive learning experience (Slavin, 2003). The environment should also match the ILOs. For example, in a lesson where you hope to promote inno-vation and imagination 'creating an atmosphere that is conducive to interest and inquiry, and permitting activities that engage students' minds, imagination' (Slavin, 2003: 367) is an advantage. It should also be remembered that the learning environment includes other aspects of the teaching situation such as the nature of the working area, the equipment, the time you have available and, in certain situations, the temperature and the weather. All should be conducive to supporting the pupils in achieving the intended learning outcomes of the lesson.

ELEMENTS OF TEACHING THAT MAKE UP A STRATEGY

In designing a teaching strategy it is important to remember that *all the elements* that make up the lesson plan and its implementation need to be considered in the light of the ILOs you have planned. Elements that need to be considered include:

■ the material to be covered (for example, the swimming strokes);
■ the sequencing and packaging of this material into, for example, a series of progres-sive tasks;
■ the time allocation for each lesson episode;
■ the extent of the responsibility devolved to the pupils (for example, to follow instructions exactly or to interpret guidance according to ability or imagination);
■ the nature of the communication between the teacher and the pupils (for example, teacher questions, work cards, pupil/pupil discussion);
■ the grouping of the pupils;
■ the focus of teacher feedback (for example, on the acquisition of physical skill or the demonstration of cooperation and tolerance);

■ the form and focus of assessment (for example, against previous personal performance or against national standards, formative or summative) (see Chapter 8)
■ the organisation of pupils and equipment in the space (for example, highly prescriptive or leaving room for pupil choice).

Many of these skills have already been discussed in earlier chapters, however the specific
way you implement these in your teaching needs careful thought. For example, the way
questions are framed has an influence on what can be achieved in a lesson, as can the way
pupils are grouped. An understanding that appropriate use and adaptation of teaching
skills is essential to promote/achieve particular ILOs is necessary. Activities 2.2a and
2.2b in Capel, Breckon and O'Neill (2006) are valuable exercises to carry out to appreciate the relationship between ILOs and constituents of teaching. This is exemplified
below through considering the nature of the *learning tasks* set and the specific focus of
feedback, both of which have a significant influence on what is learned. A lesson plan is
somewhat like a jigsaw puzzle with each of the separate pieces selected to make up the
whole. If one piece is missing or the wrong piece selected, the final outcome is inadequate and unsuccessful in terms of achieving ILOs.

Task 10.2 suggests that you observe teaching and begin to identify aspects of planning and teaching that clearly promote achievement of the ILOs. Task 10.3 requires you
to look carefully at your planning to see how far you have selected and designed elements
to match the ILOs.

Task 10.2 **Observation of elements of teaching that facilitate learning**

Remembering that every teacher develops his/her own personal style it is useful to
look more closely at the ways teaching can be planned to achieve a specific ILO.
Read two lesson plans of teachers in your placement school who are working
towards different ILOs. Observe the two lessons being taught and list those
elements of teaching which clearly facilitate the intended learning. Discuss your
observations with the teacher(s) in question and put these notes in your PDP.

Task 10.3 **Selecting elements of teaching to achieve ILOs**

Using your existing lesson plans select four very different ILOs. For each, identify
how one element of teaching from the above list should be used to ensure it is
achieved. For example, if the ILO is that pupils should be able to work together in
creating a gymnastics sequence, an element you identify could be 'communication'
and the specific use of communication that you plan for would be pupil/pupil
discussion. Discuss your thoughts with another student teacher and put these
notes in your PDP.

LEARNING TASKS

Learning tasks form the material of the lesson as it is 'packaged' for pupils to work on. The design of learning tasks is central to achieving ILOs. Critically, tasks should relate to a specific ILO, for example their design might require particular work on or attention to:

■ replication, e.g. tasks requiring pupils copy a model exactly;

■ precision, e.g. tasks requiring attention to detail in performing a skill;

■ developing strength, e.g. tasks that build strength in the arms or legs;

■ experimentation, e.g. tasks that ask pupils to explore gymnastic apparatus;

■ creativity, e.g. tasks that ask pupils to use imagination in developing a motif in dance;

■ intra-group collaboration, e.g. tasks set that demand group discussion and decision;

■ self-evaluation, e.g. tasks that ask pupils to compare their own performance with a set model;

■ evaluation of a peer, e.g. tasks that require pupils to work together to give feedback to a partner;

■ planning subsequent challenges, e.g. tasks that ask pupils to devise how they can progress their own learning.

Also when designing tasks you should consider whether:

■ tasks are to be differentiated in design or outcome. Individual pupils can be given different tasks to work on, to match their level of competence or all members of the class can be given the same task, with different expectations according to their ability. For example, in relation to the latter, all pupils may be asked to complete a gymnastics routine including an inverted movement. The more able may be expected to include a cartwheel while the less able may complete the task satisfactorily using a shoulder stand (see also Chapter 3 on planning);

■ pupils are to be allowed to select which task they tackle;

■ the work set is to be task orientated, that is mastering a particular task; or achievement orientated, being to perform a movement challenge at a higher level than others in the class. See Unit 3.2 in Capel, Leask and Turner, 2009.

In addition tasks must always:

■ be appropriate to the age, maturity, past experience and physical and cognitive ability of the group;

■ accommodate aspects of the learning environment such as the equipment available, the length of the lesson, the working space and perhaps the weather;

■ take account of the characteristics of the class, for example, a group who is often reluctant to take part, a group who is boisterous or easily distracted;

■ take account of how well the class works together in small groups.

Task 10.4 asks you to design tasks to match ILOs.

Task 10.4 **Designing tasks to achieve ILOs**

Design a task to work towards each of the following:

- achieving accuracy of passing the ball in hockey;
- promoting group collaboration in gymnastics;
- developing a motif in dance;
- developing endurance in swimming;
- developing self-assessment in athletics.

Discuss your suggestions with your tutor and put the notes in your PDP.

FEEDBACK

Feedback is a key element of any teaching strategy and should relate directly to the task set, both within NCPE (QCA, 2007a) teaching and classroom-based work in GCSE and A Level. Feedback focuses pupils' attention on the ILO underpinning the task set and provides knowledge of achievement and results. Pupils need to have knowledge of their progress in respect of the ILO. The feedback must, therefore, highlight this aspect of learning and no other. For example, if you are working to promote teamwork in a game, but all your feedback is focused on individual performance of motor skills it is unlikely that you will achieve your ILO. On the other hand, if you want to achieve a polished performance of a sequence, feedback focused on redesigning the content will be distracting.

It is important that when a task is set, the aspect of the work to be focused on by the pupils is made clear and is followed up by feedback explicitly related to that aspect. For example, a particular practice in hockey could have been set to achieve any of the following ILOs:

1   mastery of a new motor skill;
2   use of cooperative skills such as tolerance, communication, flexibility;
3   enhanced creativity/imagination;
4   consistent rule adherence;
5   setting personal goals;
6   supporting a partner's learning;
7   improved movement observation;
8   improved evaluative skills.

Feedback to pupils during and after this practice should be limited to the focus identified. Task 10.5 asks you to consider feedback that matches ILOs from the above list.

Task 10.5 **Matching feedback to ILOs**

Match the following three examples of feedback to the appropriate ILO above and devise an example of feedback for those ILOs not covered. Compare your answers and ideas with those of another student teacher.

a) Well done, Mary, you have scored a goal nearly every time. Do you think the aim that you have set yourself is too easy or too hard?
b) Good, Jason, you kept the ball close to your stick throughout the practice.
c) You are working hard Paul. Which part of the practice do you think you are doing best?

Put your notes in your PDP.

Pupils learn better if there is a clear focus in their thinking, your observation and your feedback. As PE teachers we are sometimes guilty of giving too much feedback covering a wide range of aspects of the task being carried out. Early in your school experiences it is good practice to set a task and to tell pupils that you are coming round to look for one thing, and one thing only. In other words, you give one teaching point. It is generally the case that pupils find it easier to learn one thing at a time and that your observation and feedback is more specific and thus effective if, at any one time, you are looking at one particular aspect of, for example, a movement skill. Feedback must be accurate or pupils will be confused and ill informed. Therefore you yourself must have a clear grasp of what is to be mastered, both to explain the task to pupils and to observe and give feedback. This is important because if the teacher gives incorrect information the feedback can inhibit learning. Appropriate feedback depends on effective observation which is covered in Chapter 4 and, in addition, it is a key feature of the assessment process. The role of feedback in assessment is discussed fully in Chapter 8.

The above discussion has highlighted the importance of linking teacher feedback specifically to the ILOs of a lesson or particular task or episode. Tasks 10.6 and 10.7, respectively, ask you to monitor your own feedback in relation to ILOs and to consider other aspects of your teaching in relation to ILOs.

Task 10.6 **Giving feedback in lessons that matches ILOs**

In one of your lesson plans indicate clearly your ILO for each part of the lesson or task. Ask your tutor to observe the lesson, specifically identifying feedback linked to the stated ILO with a '3' and feedback not linked to the stated ILO with a '1'. Add up your score and discuss your use of feedback with your tutor. Repeat the exercise in another lesson and aim to increase your score. Keep your results in your PDP.

Task 10.7 **Matching other aspects of teaching to ILOs**

Select a lesson that you have already planned but not yet taught, and consider whether either the mode of communication you plan to use in different lesson episodes or the amount of responsibility you plan to give to the pupils helps you to achieve the ILOs. Modify your plan as appropriate, teach the lesson and discuss with your tutor how far your teaching facilitated the intended learning. Keep these notes in your PDP.

THE CLASSIFICATION OF TYPES OF TEACHING STRATEGIES AND TEACHING STYLES

In the 1960s and 1970s approaches to teaching were the subject of much research and lively debate (see, for example, Bennett, 1976; Cox and Dyson, 1975; The Plowden Report (Central Advisory Council for Education, 1967); Galton and Croll, 1980; and Oeser, 1955). Researchers analysed teaching and formulated a variety of classifications of approaches. There were two types of approaches identified. One was concerned to recommend how teaching should take place. These are known as prescriptive classifications and align with teaching strategies. The other type was grounded in observing teachers and recording the ways they taught. These are called descriptive approaches and are closely related to teaching styles.

Teaching strategies

This classification of teaching approaches arises from theories about how teaching should be conducted to promote learning. One useful prescriptive classification to support the planning of teaching in PE was created by Mosston and Ashworth (2002). The underlying philosophy of their work is that effective learning is only achieved via the appropriate interaction between the pupil and the teacher. They call this the O-T-L-O principle, standing for: objectives, teacher behaviour, learning behaviour, outcomes achieved. There are eleven strategies (or styles in their terms) identified and these are grouped into Reproductive and Productive clusters. Reproductive strategies are those concerned with pupils replicating and learning established skills and knowledge, while Productive strategies provide opportunities for pupils to create their own movement responses and develop their own ideas. The strategies form a continuum or spectrum and are ordered in relation to the pattern of pupil and teacher decision making. The strategies start with Command in which the teacher makes all the decisions, move through, for example, Practice, Self Check, Guided Discovery and Divergent Discovery to strategies in which pupils select aspects of the activity they want to work on or investigate. For example, pupils may be free to decide which dance style to use to interpret ideas in a poem, or in a classroom situation pupils may be asked to select which aspect of nutrition to research. It is useful to read Mosston and Ashworth's work and to consider both how the overall strategy realises key outcomes and the way in which the constituents of the strategy contribute to this achievement, for example the questioning techniques and the nature of the feedback recommended. Significantly they are mindful of the broader goals of education (see Chapter 14) as well as the PE-specific goals (see this book's website for more detail of this spectrum: www.routledge.com/textbooks/9780415561648).

However, it is important to remember that the spectrum Mosston and Ashworth describe contains very broad guidelines for the planning of teaching to achieve a particular ILO. Your job as a teacher is to design a strategy tailored to your particular ILO with a particular class. The named strategies in the spectrum do not provide you with ready answers as to how to teach. Rather they give you a useful guide once you have decided on the ILOs of your lesson.

It is valuable here to consider how developing the Key Processes in the NCPE in England (see Chapter 13) would influence your teaching strategy. Figure 10.2 sets out some examples and Task 10.8 asks you to add to these suggestions.

Key Process	Broad strategic approach	Constituent elements
Developing skills in physical activity	Exemplification of the skill by the teacher. Opportunities to practice	Tasks focused on a particular element of the movement. Feedback focused on improvement and performance
Making and applying decisions	Provision of discovery and problem-solving situations, with responsibility devolved to the pupils as individuals or groups	Open tasks. Open questions. Feedback related to imagination and creativity
Developing physical and mental capacity	Challenges set to build physical strength and promote mental perseverance. Pupils setting own goals and practising skills, routines etc.	Tasks that allow pupils to set own goals. Feedback on the choice of goals. Questioning/discussion on progress etc.
Evaluating and improving	Devolvement of responsibility to pupils to evaluate own and others' movement	Provision of criteria sheet with aspects of the movement to be observed. Feedback on the accuracy of observation/self-assessment
Making informed choices about healthy active lifestyles	Information giving and discussion. Providing a range of opportunities to experience different activities	Discussion, encouraging pupil dialogue and communication skills

■ **Figure 10.2** Key Processes and teaching approaches

Task 10.8 **Matching Key Processes to teaching strategies**

Add to the suggestions in the middle and right hand boxes and discuss your proposals with your tutor. Put the completed grid in your PDP.

In considering the notion of a strategy you need to realise that in only very exceptional circumstances do you plan one strategy for the whole lesson. This is because the ILOs to be addressed during the lesson may change. For example, in a lesson taking a 'Games for Understanding' approach (Griffin and Butler, 2005) each part of a lesson needs a different strategy. The focus of the first part of the lesson may be on exploration. This may be followed by discussion of findings and then tasks set to introduce a new movement skill or to improve an existing movement skill. In most lessons the teacher adopts a series of strategies as the lesson progresses and may even implement more than one strategy simultaneously. For example, when groups of pupils need to work towards different ILOs

Dance lesson ILOs: by the end of the lesson pupils have:
a) refined the opening movement phrase in unison;
b) created a duet movement phrase to include unison and canon;
c) appreciated duet relationships in dance.

Intended ILO of lesson episode	Content/material	Teaching strategy
Body preparation (NCPE Key Process: Developing Mental and Physical Capacity)	Warm-up	Whole class directed work
Precision in movement (NCPE Key Process: Developing Skills in Physical Activity)	Opening movement phrase A, as introduced in previous lesson	Peer teaching in pairs with work cards to check accuracy and detail of movement
In pairs, creative development of a motif (NCPE Key Process: Making and Applying Decisions)	Motif selected from opening movement phrase and developed into a duet to include unison and canon.	Problem solving in pairs to develop the motif through discussion, exploration and repetition
Appreciation of duet relationships (NCPE Key Process: Evaluating and Improving)	Newly created duet movement phrase performed by another pair in the class. Video of a dance duet	Observation of peers and small group discussion to identify unison and canon. Whole class observation of a video of a dance duet and discussion with the teacher

■ **Figure 10.3** Possible pattern of strategies that could be used in different sections/episodes of a lesson

and differentiated learning tasks/challenges are required. An example of the use of a series of strategies used in a succession of lesson episodes, one after the other, is shown in Figure 10.3.

Classifications of teaching styles

This classification of teaching is based on the observation of teachers and the subsequent organisation into groups of the types of teachers and teaching witnessed. Each teaching style identified exhibits a cluster of characteristic ways teachers organise their teaching and interact with their pupils. A fairly straightforward descriptive classification of teaching is into two contrasting styles described as traditional and progressive. The elements of each are set out in Figure 10.4.

While this and the other studies referred to above provide valuable insights into teaching it has to be realised that the motivation behind the research was to find out either which approach was the most effective or what learning resulted from the use of a particular approach. They were, in fact, considering teaching from the opposite end to that adopted in this chapter. Our focus is, 'How should I teach to achieve this ILO?', not, as was the researchers' focus, 'What is the outcome of using this approach?'

Traditional	Progressive
1 Subject matter taught in separate 'lessons'	1 Subject matter integrated
2 Teacher provides all the knowledge	2 Teacher guides educational experiences
3 Pupils in passive role	3 Pupils have an active role in learning
4 All curriculum planning carried out by the teacher	4 Pupils play a part in curriculum planning
5 Rote learning and practice favoured ways of engaging with the material	5 Learning often uses discovery techniques
6 Extrinsic motivation using rewards and punishment	6 Intrinsic motivation rather than external rewards and punishments
7 Academic standards important	7 Academic standards not the sole objective
8 Frequent testing	8 Minimal testing
9 Competition used rather than cooperation	9 Includes a good deal of cooperative group work
10 Teaching within the classroom base	10 Teaching within and without the classroom
11 Little emphasis on creative expression	11 Creative expression encouraged
12 Subject matter centred	12 Pupil centred
13 Pupils reliant on the teacher	13 Pupils encouraged to develop independence

■ **Figure 10.4** Traditional and progressive teaching (adapted from Bennett, 1976)

DEVELOPING YOUR OWN PHILOSOPHY OF TEACHING

All teachers are expected to work to government designated curricula and are therefore charged with achieving similar aims. However, as was indicated earlier in the chapter, each teacher has his/her individual style of teaching which is an outcome of his/her unique personality. In addition, as you become more experienced, your teaching may be influenced by your view of the most important values of PE and by your beliefs about, for example, how children learn. These views constitute your philosophy of teaching and colour the way you plan your work and interact with the pupils. While teachers must still work to the guidelines set out in government and school policies, there are opportunities for your personal philosophy to be expressed. For example, if you view the aim of pupils becoming independent learners as a key mission in your teaching, wherever possible you devolve responsibility to pupils. If you believe the learning is best achieved through individual discovery and trial and error, wherever appropriate you use these methods to promote learning. Your philosophy contributes to your personal style of teaching, influencing both the ways in which you characteristically employ a range of teaching skills and the teaching strategies you most commonly use. However, notwithstanding personal philosophies, all teaching must be guided by the ILOs that are congruent with the broader aims of education and PE.

Now complete the Master's tasks 10.9, 10.10 and 10.11. Put these in your PDP as evidence of Master's study.

Task 10.9 **Use of teacher questioning or pupil grouping to achieve ILOs**

In this chapter task setting and feedback have been used as examples of ways the employment of a particular teaching skill needs to be modified according to the ILOs of the lesson, thus contributing to the nature of the teaching strategy employed. Write 500 words on the various uses of either teacher questioning or pupil grouping in achieving different ILOs. Refer to other chapters in this book as appropriate. Share this work with your tutor.

Task 10.10 **Critical consideration of the work of Mosston and Ashworth**

Read Mosston and Ashworth (2002) and carry out a Strengths, Weaknesses, Opportunities and Threats (SWOT) analysis on using this categorisation of teaching strategies as the principal guide to your lesson planning. See this book's website (www.routledge.com/textbooks/9780415561648) for an example of a SWOT analysis. Write a 2,000 word essay entitled 'Critically consider if Mosston and Ashworth's spectrum liberates or limits PE teachers'. Share this work with your tutor.

Task 10.11 **Teaching strategies to achieve the broader aims of education in PE**

Read Chapter 14 on the 'Wider role of a PE teacher' and identify one element of the Every Child Matters agenda (Department for Education and Skills (DfES), 2003) and two of the Personal Learning and Thinking Skills. For each of these broad educational goals make full notes on the constituents of the teaching strategy that would need to be used for its realisation.

Share this work with your tutor.

SUMMARY AND KEY POINTS

This chapter has explained the meanings of some key concepts in teaching with a particular focus on teaching strategies and on selecting the appropriate elements of a strategy to match the ILOs. Teaching strategies are powerful learning tools and must be devised in line with the ILOs of a lesson/part of a lesson. The notion that an ILO cannot be reached without employing the appropriate strategy is very important for you to understand as a PE teacher. It is often claimed that purely through taking part in PE pupils acquire wider educational goals such as independence, communication skills or imagination. This view is itself contentious (see also Chapter 2 and Chapter 1 in Capel and Piotrowski, 2000) but there is a very powerful argument that, while benefits other than enhanced physical skill *can* be acquired in PE lessons, this *will not* happen unless the teacher adopts the appropriate strategy. A strategy comprises a carefully selected cluster of teaching skills and elements of teaching. It is only through the appropriate design and employment of these building bricks that a strategy can successfully deliver the ILO. Notwithstanding your work to employ appropriate strategies, as a student teacher you are beginning to develop your own teaching style. This arises from aspects of your personality and from your developing philosophy of PE. Your teaching style individualises you as a teacher and adds 'colour' to the wide range of teaching strategies you need to use.

Check which requirements for your course you have addressed through this chapter.

FURTHER READING

Hardy, C. and Mawer, M. (eds) (1999) *Learning and Teaching in Physical Education*, **London: Falmer Press.**

Chapter 5 reviews research developments concerning teaching styles and teaching approaches in PE. Emphasis is placed on: the nature and results of studies examining Mosston and Ashworth's spectrum of teaching strategies/styles; approaches to teaching critical thinking skills in PE; direct and indirect approaches to teaching games; and, cooperative teaching and learning in PE.

Joyce, B. and Weil, M. (1996) *Models of Teaching*, **5th edn, Boston, MA: Allyn and Bacon.**

Models are identified to provide a frame of reference for describing a variety of approaches to teaching. These models are grouped into four broad families – social; information-processing; personal; behavioural systems – that share orientations toward human beings and how they learn. Each model is discussed in relation to its underlying theory and educational uses and purposes in real learning situations to encourage reflective thought and inquiry.

Macfadyen, T. and Bailey, R. (2002) *Teaching Physical Education*, **London: Continuum.**

Chapter 4 focuses on Mosston and Ashworth's (2002) spectrum of teaching strategies/styles and provides general guidance when teaching with each approach. It compares the advantages and disadvantages of the direct, teacher-centred teaching with the indirect, pupil-centred teaching and reflects upon why a variety of teaching strategies/styles is important in secondary PE. It then considers other factors which could influence the teacher's selection of instructional method.

Mosston, M. and Ashworth, S. (2002) *Teaching Physical Education*, **5th edn, San Francisco, CA: Benjamin Cummings.**

A valuable analysis of teaching PE with a focus on the pattern of teacher and pupil decision making in different styles/strategies of teaching. A useful chapter on teacher feedback.

Endnote

The authors would like to acknowledge the significant input of Paula Zwozdiak-Myers to earlier editions of this chapter.

PLANNING FOR AN INCLUSIVE APPROACH TO LEARNING AND TEACHING

Philip Vickerman

INTRODUCTION

Teachers have a fundamental responsibility to maximise the learning of all pupils. Teachers are, therefore, required to work flexibly and creatively to design environments that are conducive to learning for all. This involves identifying potential barriers to learning, teaching and assessment, whilst using strategies that offer full access and entitlement to PE. As part of this process you need to develop strategies for working in partnership with pupils, parents, teachers and external agencies to ensure equality of opportunity in PE. A central aspect of this involves active consultation with the pupils themselves, listening to their views, opinions and perceptions of PE.

This chapter provides you with an overview of issues pertinent to an inclusive agenda whilst offering opportunities to reflect upon your practice and learn to use strategies for ensuring equality of opportunity in PE. In England in recent years notions of inclusion and diversity have risen up the agenda to such an extent that there is a plethora of policies, legislation and statutory guidance. The National Curriculum for Physical Education (NCPE) (Qualifications and Curriculum Authority (QCA), 2007a) Statutory Inclusion Statement requires teachers to embrace inclusion and diversity as an integral part of their practice. This requirement is supported by other statutory and policy directives such as: Special Educational Needs (SEN) and Disability Rights Act (Department for Education and Skills (DfES), 2001a), and the Disability Equality Duty (Disability Rights Commission, 2006). Furthermore, with the introduction of the Single Equality Bill (Government Equalities Office, 2008) to tackle entrenched inequalities, the contribution of all pupils and groups is now being signalled as an important part of a modern society. Naturally, this has significant implications for you as a PE teacher in ensuring you meet the full diversity of pupils' needs.

In relation to pupils with SEN, statistical evidence from the Department for Children, Schools and Families (DCSF, 2008a) suggests that 2.8 per cent of pupils across all schools have a statement of SEN and of this 56 per cent are within mainstream schools. However, this does not tell the full picture, as a further 17.2 per cent of pupils with SEN do not have formal statements. Thus, if we combine this data with other diverse and/or marginalised groups (in relation to, e.g. race, gender, English as an additional language, class and poverty to name but a few), the need to have a commitment to supporting inclusive education is well evidenced. This, matched by the increasing focus on the individual within the NCPE (QCA, 2007a) and the Every Child Matters agenda (Her Majesty's Government (HMG), 2005), emphasises the requirement for you as a teacher to embrace this agenda within your strategies for learning, teaching and assessment in order to maximise opportunities for all pupils to participate, perform and reach their full potential. As an example of the practical implications of these policies, PE teachers are required to review the suitability of learning objectives, the nature of activities and the assessment strategies in order to ensure all pupils learn and develop.

OBJECTIVES

At the end of this chapter you should be able to:

■ appreciate the philosophy and practice of inclusive PE that follow from the government's Every Child Matters (2005) and personalisation agenda;

■ identify core values which enable you to plan, deliver and review your strategies for inclusive PE;

■ understand the principles of the NCPE (QCA, 2007a) related to inclusion and its implementation within PE settings;

■ consider a range of learning, teaching and assessment strategies that equip you with the knowledge, skills and understanding to plan and deliver effectively for inclusive PE.

Check the requirements for your course to see which relate to this chapter.

INCLUDING ALL PUPILS IN PE

Avramadis and Norwich (2002) assert that it is important to recognise as part of a modern society that equality of opportunity in all aspects of life, including education, is a social and moral right for all citizens. They propose that schools offer ideal opportunities to learn mutual understanding and respect for diversity. In order for you to begin to consider planning for inclusion in PE lessons, it is essential first to clarify that pupils have a fundamental right to an inclusive education, supported in England through statutory legislation and guidance. In beginning to interpret this, you should recognise that success depends on teachers having an open mind, positive attitude and willingness to modify and adapt learning, teaching and assessment strategies and practices (Morley et al., 2005).

It is crucial to appreciate this does not involve trying to support all pupils in the same way. As Rogers (2007) indicates, in order to facilitate full access to the PE curriculum, you need to develop skills to identify individual pupils' needs, and then devise plans appropriate to their particular circumstances. As such, Mouratidis et al. (2008) and Vickerman (2007) support this view, suggesting equality of opportunity and inclusiveness should focus on celebrating difference whilst creating systems in which pupils are treated equally, but differently. This ensures their particular needs are met through gaining accessibility to all aspects of PE and school sport.

When planning for inclusion, Kasser and Lytle (2005) support the promotion of the social model of disability (Burchardt, 2004) as a means of removing emphasis from pupils with SEN, focusing rather on the roles teachers and non-disabled pupils can play. The social model of disability recognises that often the greatest restrictive factor to a barrier-free PE curriculum is not the pupil who is being perceived as different, but the lack of flexibility and commitment to modify current practices by schools and teachers. Similarly, according to Peters (2004) this view can be applied to all pupils, not just pupils with SEN and in this respect schools and teachers should be proactive in responding to individual pupils' needs in PE, whatever these may be. For example, if a pupil in a wheel-chair struggles to shoot a netball into a high hoop, schools should consider purchasing alternative shooting rings that move up or down. Another example may be where a pupil, because of their cultural beliefs, cannot take part in strenuous physical activity when fast-ing; PE teachers should consider involving them in an officiating or coaching role, in order to ensure they can participate in the lesson. In order to develop an inclusive PE curriculum you should therefore consider strategies that respect difference (Rink and Hall, 2008) and offer other pupils opportunities to value and celebrate diversity.

Planning for inclusion requires responsive and flexible approaches that recognise all pupils are on a continuum of learning in PE (Vickerman and Coates, 2009). Hayes and Stidder (2003) and Vickerman (2007) advocate the need to consider new ways of involving all pupils, drawing on the teacher's skills of experimentation and reflection as well as collaborating with other colleagues and external agencies to maximise learning potential.

You should also consider adopting flexible teaching and assessment strategies (Cole, 2008) to provide opportunities for all pupils to demonstrate knowledge and under-standing. A pupil with cerebral palsy, for example, participating in a games activity involving sending and receiving, may need assistance with modified equipment to help them demonstrate propelling a ball (i.e. a plastic gutter or shoot). In this situation your assessment is particular to that pupil and is in no way comparable with your assessment of others in the class. This personalised assessment enables an SEN pupil to demonstrate individual success and achievement within the PE curriculum (Smith and Green, 2004). An example of modifying teaching in gymnastics may involve restricting or increasing the number of moves in a sequence in order to address the full continuum of learning. Assessment of this task reflects the particular challenge set for the pupil(s).

Furthermore, as part of adopting a systematic process to inclusive PE, schools and teachers should audit their current practices whilst identifying any areas for devel-opment. The Disability Equality Duty (Office for Disability Issues, 2006) is one such method by which schools and teachers are now being expected to review and evaluate the extent to which they are enabling pupils' full access to the curriculum. As part of this approach there is an increasing emphasis on 'hearing the voices of children' (Coates and Vickerman, 2008) or in other words involving pupils in aspects of your planning. In this way pupils' aspirations and interests can be taken into account in devising curricula and lessons. Task 11.1 asks you to reflect on what you have read so far in this chapter, familiarise yourself with key documentation and consider implica-tions for your work in PE.

Task 11.1 **Fundamentals of inclusion**

Based on your reading of this chapter so far make some notes on what you consider as key aspects of inclusion policy and practice that impact on your teaching of PE. Familiarise yourself with government and school policies. Reflect upon what strategies you consider essential to removing barriers to achievement for the full diversity of all pupils in PE. As part of this process you should consider the following questions:

■ Have I read the key government statutory documentation on inclusion?
■ What is the school policy on inclusion?
■ What is the PE department policy on inclusion?
■ In what ways is PE better able or less readily able than other subject areas to cater for pupils with disabilities?

It may be useful to meet your placement school Special Educational Needs Co-ordinator (SENCO) as you carry out this task. Put relevant documents and notes in your professional development portfolio (PDP).

A DIVERSE CONTINUUM OF PUPIL NEEDS

The *Every Child Matters: Change for Children* (DfES, 2003) agenda sets out to ensure every child, whatever their background or circumstances has the support they need to be healthy, stay safe, enjoy and achieve, make a positive contribution, and achieve economic well-being. In order to achieve this, government in England is encouraging more joined-up, multidisciplinary working alongside ensuring children have more opportunities to advocate their views (Fitzgerald, 2005) and opinions about issues that affect them. Furthermore, the Children's Fund, launched in 2000 as part of the *Every Child Matters: Change for Children* agenda (see HMG, 2005) set out to tackle disadvantage and aims to identify at an early stage children who may be at risk of social exclusion, with the intention of matching the help and support they receive to their particular needs, thus enabling them to reach their full potential.

While it is essential that you are fully aware of the statutory requirements concerned with individualised practices in education and recognise the philosophy behind these, this is only the first step in your playing an active part in the process. The key to accommodating all individuals depends on your adapting your practice to cater for the needs of all pupils (see later in the chapter for more detail). This includes the gifted and talented as well as the disabled. Thus, pupils with outstanding potential need to receive appropriate guidance and support within and outside the curriculum. In lessons, these pupils may need more challenging tasks and be required to reach higher levels of achievement. Outside the curriculum you should try to direct them to extra-curricular activity sessions, clubs and coaches where their potential can be nurtured. (See Morley and Bailey, 2006; and Bailey, Morley and Dismore, 2009 for further information on talent development in PE, also Chapter 11 in Capel, Breckon and O'Neill, 2006.)

Another group of pupils who need specific support are those with English as an additional language. These pupils need specific attention. There may be a bilingual support worker to assist or in some situations the pupil can be paired with a bilingual pupil. If you do not have a support worker in the lesson you could increase the use of demonstration or visual images/posters to explain the objectives you are trying to achieve. (See the Physical Education Initial Teacher Training and Education (PEITTE, 2009) website for further guidance.) Pupils who are hearing or sight impaired also need to be accommodated in your lessons so that they can take as full a part as possible, learning and thriving in the PE context. The SENCO in your placement school should be able to give you guidance on supporting these pupils, and others with particular needs.

Other groups who need your consideration are those from non-English cultural family backgrounds, girls and travellers. See Capel and Piotrowski (2000) for a full debate about the needs arising from cultural diversity and the different perspectives and characteristics of girls. See Daniels (2008) for research into catering for the needs of travellers and also Bhopal (2004).

KEY VALUES FOR INCLUDING ALL PUPILS IN PE

In 1992 the National Curriculum for Physical Education (NCPE, Department of Education and Science and the Welsh Office (DES/WO), 1992) identified four key principles related to equality of opportunity. These are *entitlement, accessibility, integration and integrity*. These remain cornerstones upon which the National Curriculum is founded. These principles are readily embraced by the recent introduction of the Every Child Matters agenda (HMG, 2005) and the promotion of personalised learning to ensure pupils gain their full entitlement to the curriculum.

The concept of *entitlement* asserts every pupil's fundamental right to access the PE curriculum. This is of particular relevance to pupils with SEN and has been endorsed by the SEN and Disability Rights Act (DfES, 2001a), Disability Equality Duty (Disability Rights Commission, 2006) and the SEN Code of Practice (DfES 2001b). Indeed, this revised SEN Code of Practice focuses centrally upon the action of schools to implement and deliver inclusive PE. As part of this entitlement, you are expected to take action within the individual school context to plan for inclusive practice in order to facilitate pupils' full entitlement to the curriculum. This recognises the premise of PE teachers adopting positive attitudes and open minds through which potential barriers are minimised via consultation and modification of learning, teaching and assessment strategies (DePauw and Doll-Tepper, 2000).

In terms of *accessibility*, it is your responsibility to ensure PE lessons are barrier free and relevant to the diversity of pupils. This endorses the social model of disability (Burchardt, 2004) which sees it as your responsibility to adjust your teaching in order to accommodate the needs of individual pupils, rather than the pupil being seen as the barrier to participation. For example, a pupil with English as an additional language may require assistance with their communication skills in order to be fully included in your lesson, and the school and the PE department should plan for this in advance.

In relation to the third principle of *integration,* this recognises the benefits of inclusive education and the positive outcomes that can be achieved for all pupils through such approaches. It also begins to address notions of citizenship in which pupils should be encouraged to develop mutual understanding and respect for individual diversity as part of their involvement and participation within a socially inclusive society (Lambe and Bones, 2006). Pupils from different cultural backgrounds could, through the medium of dance for example, learn to appreciate varying traditions and social customs. In this way teamwork, cooperation, mutual understanding, respect and empathy for difference can be addressed in PE (Vickerman and Coates, 2009).

Furthermore, in considering the need to ensure all pupils are integrated into your PE lessons, Wright and Sugden (1999) suggest teaching pupils with SEN should be seen as an extension of your existing mixed ability teaching, in which you differentiate your work. Therefore, as a teacher you should already be developing the necessary skills to facilitate inclusive PE, whatever the need may be, and, as a result, only occasionally require specialist advice and guidance. Thus, the fundamental factor in successful integration is a positive attitude, good differentiation and a readiness to adapt and modify your practice to meet individual pupils' needs.

Finally, in relation to the fourth principle of *integrity*, you are expected to underpin your teaching by valuing the adaptations and modifications you make in order to plan effectively for the inclusion of all pupils. As part of this personal commitment, you should ensure that inclusive PE is of equal worth, challenging, and in no way patronising or demeaning to the individual pupil concerned. Task 11.2 asks you to consider the application of these four principles to your own teaching.

Task 11.2 **Key values for inclusive PE**

Review the four principles of entitlement, accessibility, inclusion and integrity. To address these principles, identify what you consider to be the key actions you should adopt as part of your inclusive learning, teaching and assessment. It may be useful to consider specific pupils or particular physical activities, e.g. swimming, to undertake this task. Discuss your notes with your tutor and then put these in your PDP.

THE NATIONAL CURRICULUM AND INCLUSION

Government directives in England (QCA, 2007a) advocate a world-class curriculum that inspires and challenges all learners which should be achieved through a personalised, imaginative and flexible approach to learning. The NCPE (QCA, 2007a) continues by suggesting inclusion is based upon the active presence, participation and achievement of all pupils in a meaningful and relevant set of learning experiences. An effective, inclusive school should be based upon a whole-school approach to the curriculum in which one of the main purposes is to establish entitlement to a range of high-quality learning experiences for pupils, irrespective of social background, culture, race, gender and/or differences in ability (Hayes and Stidder, 2003).

An inclusive curriculum is one in which all learners see the relevance of the curriculum to their own experiences and aspirations whilst enabling sufficient opportunities to succeed at the highest standard. In doing so, the NCPE (QCA, 2007a) suggests planning for inclusion involves thinking about how the curriculum can be designed to match the needs and interests of the full range of learners including: the gifted and talented; those with learning difficulties and disabilities; learners who are learning English as an additional language; different needs of boys and girls; children who are in care; learners with social, emotional and behavioural difficulties; and those who bring a range of different cultural perspectives and experiences. Thus in responding to meet all pupils' needs in PE, the National Curriculum (QCA, 2007a) Statutory Inclusion Statement identifies four expectations related to: setting suitable learning challenges; responding to pupils' diverse needs; overcoming potential barriers to learning; and devising assessment approaches appropriate to individual pupils and groups of pupils. These represent a practical application of the key principles set out in the 1992 PE curriculum discussed earlier in this chapter. Table 11.1 sets out some examples of how the aspects of the Statutory Inclusion Statement can be realised in your teaching.

PRACTICAL EXAMPLES OF INCLUSIVE PE

So far, we have established a range of principles you need to consider when setting out to include all pupils in PE. We now turn to some examples of learning and teaching that can support this inclusive approach. In reviewing the diverse range of learning and teaching models designed for inclusive PE, all can be simplified to four common factors. These are based around: curriculum adaptation (changing what is taught); instructional modifications (changing how you teach); devising appropriate assessment strategies (adapting how you assess pupils); and human or people resources (looking at changing who teaches or supports adapted aspects of PE).

What is taught

When planning for inclusive PE, it is important to start from the premise of full inclusion (Avramadis and Norwich, 2002), and where this may not be possible, to consider adaptation and/or modification of activities or learning and teaching strategies or both. A central success factor in meeting this is initially to consult where appropriate, with the pupils and/or relevant professionals as part of a multidisciplinary approach (Coates and Vickerman, 2008; Fitzgerald, 2005). This enables you to consider at the planning stage any differentiation that may be required. Careful thought needs to be given to the activities to be covered with respect to those with particular needs. While curriculum planning cannot be designed around the needs of pupils with disability, consideration can be given to the most appropriate activities, where options are feasible. For example, basketball may be more accessible than volleyball for a wheelchair user, and it may be easier to cater for all pupils in sports acrobatics rather than rhythmic gymnastics. In some cases the use of different equipment is the answer to inclusion; alternatively devising a slightly modified form of a game may be the answer. However, in many cases what is taught is best understood by referring to the intended learning outcomes (ILOs) that are planned and the tasks that follow from these outcomes. All pupils are involved in the same activity but the specific outcomes and tasks are differentiated according to the needs of each individual pupil. In fact differentiation, which is the teaching approach designed to include all pupils, is the principal way in which you cater for those with SEN (differentiation is also considered in Chapter 3 and in Chapter 10). In respect of fully inclusive teaching, you may well have to be particularly ingenious and imaginative in creating alternative outcomes and differentiated tasks.

An example of modifying games activities, such as basketball, could be where some pupils may initially require lighter, larger or different coloured balls in order to access the activity. Adaptations to rules may also need to be considered such as allowing a player with movement restrictions five seconds to receive and play the ball. In addition, if utilising such a strategy, it is vital that all members of the group understand the need

■ **Table 11.1** Taking account of the Statutory Inclusion Statement in PE

Aspect of Statutory Inclusion Statement	Interpretation related to planning for effective inclusive PE	What skills, knowledge and strategies do I need to develop?	What resources do I need to help me to succeed?
Setting suitable learning challenges	Ensure that you know what the individual needs of your pupils are. For example, pupils who have coordination difficulties may require shorter-handled racquets or larger balls.	Be clear about the nature of the skill being taught. Recognise different starting points in improving this skill to ensure the pupil succeeds and is motivated to learn and develop.	Discuss strategies with previous class teachers, tutors, the SEN coordinator or disability sport organisations such as the English Federation for Disability Sport.
Responding to pupils' diverse learning needs	Ensure that your learning and teaching environment is conducive to individual pupil needs, and offers entitlement to the curriculum. For example, a pupil who has to keep her legs covered for religious reasons may require flexibility in PE clothing policy.	Check the school PE policy on clothing and ensure it is sufficiently flexible and inclusive to accommodate individual pupil needs. Ensure there are no health and safety implications of e.g. wearing long trousers in the PE activity to be undertaken.	Discuss with the individual pupils concerned how you can be responsive to their individual needs. Discuss the PE clothing policy with relevant parties.
Overcoming potential barriers to learning	Ensure your learning/teaching approach is accessible, and does not restrict opportunities to demonstrate progression.	Ensure that you plan to take a range of equipment into the PE lesson. Ensure there is sufficient space and time for those with disabilities to make progress in the lesson.	Be ready to use a variety of teaching approaches to cater for pupils' responses.
Devising assessment appropriate for individual pupils and groups of pupils	Ensure your assessment is accessible, and does not restrict opportunities to demonstrate mastery and progression. For example, a wheelchair user who cannot demonstrate a run or a jump in athletic activities may require an adaptation of the assessment task.	Recognise the value of baseline assessment. Adopt an open mind to the focus of assessment and consider what the key features are that you wish to assess. Construct an appropriate assessment strategy that involves, for example, verbal rather than physical participation.	At the planning stage identify which principles you want to assess, and how they can be modified or interpreted for the particular pupil concerned. Ensure that the modified assessment has integrity and is still measuring athletic knowledge, skills and understanding.

for such an adaptation in order that they can play to this rule during a game. Modifying the task in dance for a pupil with a learning difficulty could, for example, involve you setting a task of creating a dance routine exemplifying four movement components rather than the six or seven you have required of the rest of the class (Vickerman, 2007). In athletics participation of physically disabled pupils may involve one push of their wheelchair, rather than a jump into the sandpit, or reducing distances to run or travel. Activities may also need to be modified to respond to particular cultural beliefs addressing appropriate kit or being sensitive to pushing people too hard in physical activity when fasting (see Khanifar *et al.*, 2008).

How teaching is conducted

Learning and teaching approaches can be modified in a number of ways. As indicated above, differentiated teaching strategies are the key to your effecting inclusion. Other more specific examples could include the use, by you, of more gestures, non-verbal communication and demonstrations, rather than relying purely on verbal communication. These modifications would accommodate both those with hearing impairment and those for whom English is an additional language. Use of peer support (outlined later in the section on 'who supports learning') is another way that teaching can cater for a variety of needs. A subtle modification of your teaching could also be in respect of the nature of your feedback. With pupils with SEN your feedback is more likely to be directed towards effort and improvement rather than performance *per se*. To achieve this involves astute observation (see Chapter 4 on observation) and empathetic interaction between yourself and the pupil, as well as the encouragement of sensitive interaction between others in the class and the disabled pupil.

Another aspect of modifying learning and teaching approaches could be in relation to a pupil with an emotional and/or behavioural difficulty who may be struggling to fulfil a particular skill on account of an inability to focus and concentrate for any length of time. Through your skilful task setting, encouragement and effective behaviour management the pupil may still remain on task and be motivated to keep trying to raise their physical attainment. While the pupil's movement may not show a great deal of development, the pupil is acquiring valuable experience in application and persistence. Consequently, the pupil is still benefiting from the inclusive PE experience (Fitzgerald *et al.*, 2003), in that their behaviour is much improved, resulting in a determination to remain on task and work towards other learning outcomes.

This last example reveals that work in PE can contribute to achieving wider educational goals as well as PE-specific aims. The notion that there are two ways of looking at learning in PE is supported by Wright and Sugden (1999). They describe two principles of learning: 'moving to learn' and 'learning to move'. They argue that PE has a distinctive role to play, because it is not simply about the education of the physical but involves cognitive, social, language and moral development and responsibilities. One strategy to facilitate inclusion may involve a shift from the traditional (learning to move) outcomes of PE in which skills are taught and learned, to a wider experience of PE (moving to learn) involving opportunities to plan for the social inclusion of pupils across a diverse continuum of learning needs. (See also Chapter 14 on the wider role of PE.) Above all, as the examples outlined show, it is essential that you modify your learning and teaching approaches to cater for the needs of pupils.

As the Statutory Inclusion Statement indicates, responding to the diverse needs of pupils requires PE teachers to acknowledge and respond to difference and diversity amongst pupils, whilst embracing social models of disability through changing learning and teaching styles to fit the pupil rather than the other way round (Burchardt, 2004). Task 11.3 challenges you to devise alternative tasks in the context of two lessons.

Task 11.3 **Designing alternative tasks to cater for pupils with a disability**

In a gymnastics task asking pupils to travel in a variety of directions on large apparatus, create a task for a pupil who can move but is unable to walk or climb.

In a basketball task asking pupils to practise bouncing the ball with both hands, create a task for a pupil who only has use of one hand.

Discuss your suggestions with another student teacher.

Put these notes in your PDP.

For further valuable tasks and more information on differentiation see Capel, Breckon and O'Neill (2006) Chapter 11. Activities 11.6, 11.8 and 11.9 are particularly useful.

Devising appropriate assessment strategies

As a PE teacher you set intended learning outcomes appropriate to the group and the individual pupils that make up the class, recognising that each pupil is on a continuum of learning. Planning alternative tasks is not enough, devising appropriate assessment must also be considered. As a corollary of this, you should also offer alternative methods of assessment which maximise opportunities for pupils to demonstrate knowledge and understanding. Assessment strategies need to go hand in hand with intended learning outcomes. If these outcomes have been modified for a pupil, it is likely that assessment also needs to be modified. If tasks and learning outcomes are clear, devising assessment strategies should follow and not be too problematic.

For example, for a pupil with movement difficulties that make practical participation impossible, an alternative in a gymnastics lesson may be to observe and identify the principles underpinning a particular skill. The assessment here would involve the pupil verbally describing rather than demonstrating the skill.

Another pupil with limited verbal communication may be able to demonstrate a forward roll in gymnastics rather than describe the particular principles of that knowledge, skill or understanding orally. As a result the pupil is still evidencing attainment, but is demonstrating rather than describing the process. A group of pupils who may need special consideration in devising teaching approaches are those with autism (see Durrant, 2009 for coverage of this area).

Who supports learning

All schools have a SENCO and this colleague can give you very valuable information and advice about the needs of individual pupils. Another colleague who may be able to help you is the pupil's form tutor, who may know the pupil and the family well. There may also be other personnel in your placement school who can give support and information. It is useful to ask your Head of PE to whom you might go for guidance.

Depending on the nature of the special need, a pupil may have the support of a Learning Support Assistant (LSA) in PE. These colleagues can be of great assistance. However many LSAs have not had any training in supporting work in PE and it is necessary for you to brief them fully on the role they are to play. This issue is discussed further in Chapter 16 on working with others in PE.

Other support for pupils with SEN can come from their peers. Again, these pupils need careful instruction, however it is often the case that other pupils can enjoy this responsibility and are sensitive, supportive and encouraging. An example could be if you have a pupil with limited vision, you could organise activities such as a 100-metre race in which a fellow pupil stands at the finish line and shouts out the lane number they are in, or a peer runs alongside the pupil for support. It is perhaps wise not to use the same pupil in a support role too often, both because all pupils should be active in PE as far as possible and because this supportive task can be a situation in which all can develop valuable social skills.

Task 11.4 requires you to reflect on some key issues underpinning inclusive practice.

Task 11.4 **Review of inclusive practice**

Reflect on the practical examples for modifying activities for various pupils' individual needs. As part of this reflection identify what strategies you can use to maximise success in learning and achievement whilst minimising barriers to participation whilst also considering the following questions:

■ What are your key principles for planning an inclusive PE curriculum?
■ Who needs to be involved in planning an inclusive PE curriculum?
■ What do you see as the potential challenges and success factors in planning PE lessons that meet the needs of the many, rather than the few?

Put these notes in your PDP.

In summary, these examples demonstrate how the practice of inclusive PE can be delivered if you are prepared to recognise the key principles and values noted earlier in this chapter. A critical success factor is to be flexible and be prepared to try out different learning and teaching strategies to see if they work (Vickerman, 2002). As part of your developing competence in the area of inclusive PE, you should not be daunted by being unsuccessful in your attempts to create barrier-free lessons. The important point is that you learn from your experiences, then try again, rather than restrict yourself to limited learning and teaching strategies.

SUMMARY AND KEY POINTS

Embedding an inclusive approach to your learning, teaching and assessment

It is evident from analysis within this chapter that inclusive PE is a key issue for government, schools and teachers. The philosophical basis of inclusive PE as socially and morally sound is supported through legislation and the development of new practices in the National Curriculum (QCA, 2007a). Your role, and that of schools, is central to the success or failure of the PE inclusion agenda in ensuring the needs of the many, rather than the few, are met within the curriculum. In order to consider how to meet this agenda, there is a need to establish a clear and consistent framework for stakeholders involved in inclusive PE. 'The Eight P's Inclusive PE Framework' (Vickerman, 2002) (see Table 11.2) helps clarify the widely held view of inclusion as a combination of philosophy, process and practice, and draws together a number of key points considered in this chapter. As a result, you are encouraged to use this framework as a basis for considering, planning, delivering and reviewing your emerging practice in inclusive PE.

■ **Table 11.2** Eight P's Inclusive PE Framework

Philosophy – what are the key concepts related to inclusive PE?

Purpose – what are the rationales behind inclusive PE?

Proactive – what challenges am I likely to face in planning and developing an inclusive PE curriculum, and how can they be overcome?

Partnership – who do I need to work with to ensure I succeed?

Process – where is the starting point for my development of inclusive practice, where are the review points and how will I know if I am successful?

Policy – what policies exist in school regarding inclusion?

Pedagogy – what are my own learning and teaching approaches to the development of inclusive PE?

Practice – how can I ensure that I make a difference in practice when I work with the pupils in my class?

The framework encourages you to recognise and spend time analysing, planning and implementing each of the interrelated factors, to ensure you give yourself the best opportunities for creating barrier-free PE lessons for all the pupils you serve (Smith and Thomas, 2006). As such, the first point is to recognise and fully embrace the *philosophy* underpinning inclusion discussed in this chapter as a basic and fundamental human right, which is supported in England through statutory and non-statutory guidance such as the SEN and Disability Rights Act (DfES, 2001a), the revised Code of Practice (DfES, 2001b), the Statutory Inclusion Statement (QCA, 2007a) and the Single Equality Act (Government Equalities Office, 2008). In order to facilitate this process you should embrace a *purposeful* approach to fulfilling the requirements of differentiated learning, teaching and assessment. Consequently, you should spend time examining the principles that form the basis of inclusion, while noting the rationale and arguments for inclusive PE. In order to achieve this you should develop *proactive* approaches to the development and implementation of your inclusive learning and teaching and be prepared to consult actively with fellow teachers, pupils and related individuals and agencies in order to produce a *partnership* approach to your delivery.

Inclusion demands a recognition and commitment to modify and adapt your learning and teaching strategies in order to enable access and entitlement to the PE curriculum, and you have an obligation to undertake this through a value-based approach. The development of inclusive PE must therefore be recognised as part of a *process* that evolves, emerges and changes over time, and it is important to acknowledge that it requires ongoing review by all stakeholders. In conclusion, therefore, it is your responsibility and that of the whole school to ensure inclusion is reflected in *policy* documentation, as a means of monitoring, reviewing and evaluating delivery. The critical success factors however rely on ensuring policy impacts on your *pedagogical* practices. Thus, while philosophies and processes are vital for schools and teachers, ultimately you should measure your success in terms of effective inclusive *practice*, which makes a real difference to the experiences of all pupils in your PE lessons. Task 11.5 challenges you to consider examples of practice against each of the principles in the 8P Framework.

Task 11.5 **Developing an inclusive PE Framework**

Look at the 'Eight P's Inclusive Framework' and from your consideration of the issues raised in this chapter begin to address each of the points in turn. Undertaking this process is designed to help you to clarify the points noted in this chapter, while helping you to create your own learning and teaching framework for inclusive PE. Put your completed chart in your PDP.

Eight P's Inclusive PE Framework	Interpretation of what each stands for in developing your own learning and teaching framework for inclusive PE
Philosophy – what are the key concepts related to inclusive PE?	
Purpose – what are the rationales behind inclusive PE?	
Proactive – what challenges am I likely to face in planning and developing an inclusive PE curriculum, and how can they be met?	
Partnership – who do I need to work with to ensure I succeed?	

Process – where is the starting point for my development of inclusive practice, where are the review points and how will I know if I am successful?	
Policy – what policies exist in school regarding inclusion?	
Pedagogy – what are my own learning and teaching approaches to the development of inclusive PE?	
Practice – how can I ensure that I make a difference in practice when I work with the pupils in my class?	

Task 11.6 asks you to read and critically analyse a text from the recommended reading list.

Task 11.6 **Developing personalised learning**

Read the journal article by Coates and Vickerman (2008) which focuses upon the views and experiences of pupils with SEN in PE. Write a 2,000 word essay critically reflecting upon what learning, teaching and assessment strategies you would adopt to ensure the individual needs of all pupils are met. Share this with your tutor and put it in your PDP as evidence of Master's level study.

Check which requirements for your course you have addressed through this chapter.

FURTHER READING

Capel, S. and Piotrowski, S. (eds) (2000) *Issues in Physical Education*, **London: Routledge.**

Chapters 2, 3 and 4 look at, respectively, issues concerned with gender, special educational needs and cultural diversity. As well as debating policy issues in respect of different groups of pupils the chapters also give guidance as to how you might cater for pupils with particular needs.

Coates, J. and Vickerman, P. (2008) Let the children have their say: children with special educational needs and their experiences of physical education – a review, *Support for Learning***, 23, 4: 168–75.**

This paper is a review of literature on listening to the voices of pupils with SEN related to their experiences of PE. The paper is worth reading to gain insights into empowering young people who may be marginalised and the barriers and challenges they face in gaining access and entitlement to PE.

Hayes, S. and Stidder, G. (2003) *Equity and Inclusion in Physical Education*, **London: Routledge.**

This book offers a comprehensive overview of a range of issues related to including diverse groups in PE. The book specifically addresses a multiplicity of issues related to social class, race, ethnicity, gender, sexuality, SEN and ability and is a valuable resource for all working to include pupils in PE.

Winnick, J. (2005) *Adapted Physical Education and Sport*, **Champaign, IL: Human Kinetics.**

This book offers a range of theoretical and practical strategies for inclusion in physical activity. It provides an extensive resource for reviewing differentiated strategies for including a range of pupils in physical activity.

Young, D., Johnson, C., Steckler, A., Gittelsohn, J., Ruth, R., Saunders, P., Saksvig, B., Ribisl, K., Lytle, L. and McKenzie, T. (2006) Data to action: using formative research to develop intervention programs to increase physical activity in adolescent girls, *Health Education and Behaviour*, **33, 1: 97–111.**

This research paper offers recommendations, interventions and strategies designed to enhance girls' engagement in physical activity. The paper also identifies preferences and barriers to participation and is a useful resource for teachers in developing inclusive PE.

USING INFORMATION AND COMMUNICATIONS TECHNOLOGY TO SUPPORT LEARNING AND TEACHING IN PE

Gary Stidder and Susan Capel

INTRODUCTION

The expectation that teachers are able to use information and communications technology (ICT) effectively to support learning and teaching in all subjects is here to stay. It is also likely that within the next five years you will be using technology that has yet to be invented. Thus, the knowledge and skills you require as a teacher working in schools today includes the ability to use ICT confidently in subject teaching, professional activities and administration as an integral part of professional practice rather than as a bolt-on extra.

The focus in any scheme or unit of work and in any lesson must be on the pupils learning (rather than the teacher's teaching) and therefore in relation to ICT, the focus must be on whether its use enhances the achievement of objectives and intended learning outcomes (ILOs). Thus, you need to make informed decisions as to whether a specific resource should be used to support pupils in achieving a specific ILO. This chapter is designed to help you to develop your knowledge and understanding of how you can use ICT specifically through PE to enhance pupils' learning. The value and benefits that ICT can provide PE teachers are discussed, including practical application within lessons. Specific examples of ICT to support learning and teaching are available on this book's website (www.routledge.com/textbooks/9780415561648). The chapter then briefly considers the use of ICT in supporting administration within PE. Finally, the chapter focuses on you looking at your own development of ICT knowledge and skills.

OBJECTIVES

At the end of this chapter you should be able to:

- make informed decisions about how you can use ICT specifically in PE to enhance pupils' learning;
- plan the use of ICT to achieve ILOs and enhance pupils' learning;
- understand potential value and benefits, but also some potential limitations and pitfalls (including relying on 'gimmicks and gadgets') in order to engage pupils in purposeful learning;
- use ICT to support PE administration;
- understand the importance of developing your own ICT skills and be able to identify how to go about this.

Check the requirements of your course to see which relate to this chapter.

USING ICT TO ENHANCE PUPILS' LEARNING IN PE

There is no doubt that ICT is changing the ways in which young people lead their lives and is influencing their educational development. Within schools, well-planned lessons which incorporate the use of appropriate ICT with a focus on pupil activity and providing pupils with 'hands-on' opportunities to use ICT can develop pupils' existing knowledge and skills and enhance learning. ICT skills learned in one subject can be transferred into other subjects. This is particularly relevant for PE teachers where the Department for Education and Skills (DfES) have stated:

> PE teachers will not need to teach ICT capability but can exploit new opportunities for pupils to apply and develop the capability that they already have, to enhance their learning in PE. Consequently, the focus of the lesson remains firmly rooted in PE and teachers are not burdened with the need to teach ICT.
>
> (DfES, 2004c: 8)

Thus, the focus in planning the use of ICT in your lessons should be on whether it enhances pupils' learning. Two aspects of this are particularly important to consider.

First, 'ICT should only be used where its use is justified as a method of achieving the stated learning outcomes for any lesson' (Bennett and Leask, 2009: 53). There must be a clear rationale for using specific ICT resources in PE lessons. Thus, you need to focus your planning on the ILOs for the lesson and to consider whether ICT resources can enhance the effectiveness of the pupils' learning. In considering ILOs in PE it is particularly important to consider those related to the practical aspects of the subject. It is important that the level of physical activity is maintained; after all, PE lessons are the only place where we can be sure that all pupils undertake some physical activity.

Second, you need to consider the value of ICT for particular tasks. The use of ICT should allow the pupil to achieve something that could not be achieved without using ICT and/or to learn it more effectively and efficiently.

In short, the key questions are: will using ICT in a particular lesson enhance pupils' learning, or can the lesson ILOs be achieved in other ways? Are you confident that using

ICT is appropriate for the lesson? (see also Blair, 2006: 86–7 (particularly Activities 8.5, 8.6 and 8.7) in Capel, Breckon and O'Neill, 2006).

There are many values and benefits of using ICT in learning and teaching. Properly planned and appropriate ICT which is geared to support pupil activity can be motivating for pupils, many of whom may be enthusiastic users of ICT. Thus, the main value and benefit is in enhancing pupils' learning.

However, there are also limitations and pitfalls in using ICT in learning and teaching. The pupils/teacher may not have adequate knowledge and skills to use ICT effectively. It may not be properly planned and appropriate and may not be geared to support pupil learning. Teachers may rely on gimmicks and gadgets which entertain rather than enhance pupils learning. In such situations, the least that using ICT can do is to have no effect on enhancing learning; however, it might even detract from learning.

Planning to use ICT to achieve ILOs and enhance pupils' learning

Planning to use ICT in lessons is integral to planning any lesson. When ILOs have been identified, consideration is given to a range of aspects of the lesson, including whole class learning activities and how these are differentiated for pupils of different abilities, learning points, teaching styles and strategies, organisation, the learning resources (including ICT) to enhance pupils' learning, and assessment of pupils learning.

Thus, prior to starting planning, it is important to know what ICT resources are available to enhance pupils' learning. There are many forms of ICT that can be used in the various environments in which you teach. The British Education and Communications Technology Agency (Becta) (http://schools.becta.org.uk/index. php?section=cu&catcode=ss_cu_skl_02&rid=1701) provide a definition of ICT from the Qualifications and Curriuclum Authority (QCA):

> Information and communications technologies (ICT) are the computing and communications facilities and features that variously support teaching, learning and a range of activities in education. Such ICT-related activities include, for example, the use of:
>
> ■ broadcast material or CD-ROM as sources of information in history;
> ■ microcomputers with appropriate keyboards and other devices to teach literacy and writing;
> ■ keyboards, effects and sequencers in music teaching;
> ■ devices to facilitate communication for pupils with special needs;
> ■ electronic toys to develop spatial awareness and psycho-motor control;
> ■ email to support collaborative writing and sharing of resources;
> ■ video-conferencing to support the teaching of modern foreign languages;
> ■ internet-based research to support geographical enquiry;
> ■ integrated learning systems (ILS) to teach basic numeracy;
> ■ communications technology to exchange administrative and assessment data.

In PE, resources include, for example, computers, the internet, cameras, DVD, portable media players, motion analysis systems, timing devices, interactive whiteboards and various curricular resources, alongside other more traditional and established types of technology such as televisions and video.

Some specific packages are also available. On this book's website (see www.routledge.com/textbooks/9780415561648) there are descriptions of some of these types of ICT and some consideration of how these can enhance pupil learning in a range of practical contexts/range of activities (those included are: cameras; mobile phone cameras; motion analysis software; film editing; portable media players; interactive whiteboards; voice projections systems; developing FUNctional skills through physical education; games consoles; Nintendo 'Wii Fit'; dance mat systems; pedometers; pupil response systems; Archos; the use of ipods; podcasting; the virtual learning environment (VLE); video conferencing; YouTube). There are also examples of ICT to support learning and teaching in PE available on the Becta website (http://schools.becta.org.uk/index.php?section=cu&catcode=ss_cu_ac_phy_03).

Task 12.1 asks you to undertake an audit of ICT available in your placement school.

Task 12.1 **Audit of ICT available in your placement school**

Carry out an audit of the range of ICT available in your placement school to enhance learning opportunities for pupils and/or your teaching of PE. Talk to the PE teachers to identify ways in which it is used to enhance learning and teaching in PE. Store your observations in your professional development portfolio (PDP) as an aide-memoire for planning your own lessons.

In addition, prior to including any ICT in lessons, you need to consider the extent to which pupils are competent users of the ICT you plan to use in your lesson. Pupils' experience of ICT varies considerably and it is vital, therefore, that they have the skills, knowledge and understanding to benefit from the use of ICT in the lesson.

Becta (http://schools.becta.org.uk/index.php?section=cu&catcode=ss_cu_ac_phy_03&rid=9267) state that:

The following are skills which pupils should have learned by the end of Key Stage 2 and may be particularly relevant to the use of ICT in PE at Key Stage 3:

■ using simple search techniques
■ entering data into a database and presenting the information as a simple graph or table
■ combining text, graphics and sound to develop ideas
■ using datalogging equipment to monitor changes
■ identifying patterns revealed by simple models and simulations
■ using email
■ recognising the need for quality and accuracy in their work
■ using different software to create displays, presentations, posters and stories
■ recognising the value of ICT for particular tasks
■ describing how ICT can be used in situations outside lessons.

Once you have decided to include ICT in a lesson, you know what ICT is available and know the pupils' level of knowledge and skill in using this, you then need to consider how to introduce the use of ICT. Sufficient introductory tasks and progressions need to be planned that stimulate and encourage pupils to engage with the learning. Without such preparation the use of ICT may have little or no effect.

Further, it is important to consider both the learning activities/lesson episodes and the key elements of teaching into which you can incorporate ICT better to enable the ILOs to be achieved. In the revised National Curriculum for PE (NCPE) in England (QCA, 2007b: 195) the curriculum opportunities offered to pupils should include the use of ICT as a means of improving individual and group performance and tracking progress. The NCPE states that ICT should be used by teachers and pupils to: 'Record and review performances and record data for the purposes of personal improvement' (QCA, 2007b: 195). Bennett and Leask (2009: 15) provide some guidance as to the types of ICT that can be used to support some learning activities/lesson episodes. This is reproduced in Table 12.1.

■ **Table 12.1** Some guidance as to the types of ICT that can be used to support some learning activities/lesson episodes in PE

Finding things out	Recording/analysing performance, internet sources (e.g. records)
Developing ideas	Planning sequences/tactics
Making things happen	Modelling sequences/tactics, sporting simulations
Exchanging and sharing information	Reporting events, posters, flyers, web/multimedia authoring, video, digital video
Reviewing, modifying and evaluating	Website evaluation, presentation of performance statistics, event diaries, performance portfolios

Thus, with appropriate planning, the use of ICT may support the ways in which you, for example:

Learning activities/lesson episodes

■ improve individual and group performances;
■ track progress;
■ record and review performances;
■ record data for the purposes of personal improvement.

Key elements of teaching into which you can incorporate ICT

■ communicate information to pupils on the lesson, challenge or task, e.g. video of a game if pupils have never seen the game; picture of the position pupils are aiming to achieve in a handstand. Resource based dance relies on video of choreographed pieces;
■ provide opportunities for pupils to gain a better understanding of the nature of movement, in lieu of demonstrations, e.g. video for whole class to observe and discuss;
■ analyse movement;
■ introduce a new skill or game;
■ challenge the most able;
■ support those requiring particular help;
■ encourage pupils to take responsibility for their own learning;

■ provide feedback on pupil performance/participation, e.g. hand-held cameras or video for immediate viewing. This is particularly useful in skills where a pupil cannot see her/himself or see the effect of her/his movement;

■ provide opportunities for peer assessment and self-assessment, e.g. use of video/camera to discuss feedback to peer or self;

■ provide pupils with the means to record work to be taken up again in later lessons, e.g. videoing dance motif to be developed next lesson. Video of own performance to remind on key points to improve;

■ prepare a presentation;

■ provide worthwhile tasks for pupils off-practical, e.g. task to look up a website or to use video or camera to support work in lesson.

These apply to both the practical aspects of teaching PE and to classroom-based activity, e.g. when teaching examinations classes (e.g. General Certificate of Secondary Education (GCSE), General Certificate of Education Advanced (A) Level, BTech, 14–19 Diplomas in Sport and Active Leisure) to pupils in the 14–19 age range (see Chapter 13). Examples of some learning activities/lesson episodes and key elements of teaching into which you can incorporate ICT in lessons and the ICT which can support them are given in Figure 12.1. This is part of Task 12.2, which you should undertake now.

Task 12.2 **ICT which can support aspects of learning and teaching in PE**

Complete Figure 12.1 recording the usefulness or not of a learning activity/lesson episode or key elements of teaching (some examples of learning activities and key elements are given on the list on pages 187–188). Spaces are left for you to add further examples of learning activities/lesson episodes or key elements of teaching for which any form of ICT might enhance pupils' learning, or the effectiveness and efficiency of your teaching. The list of resources on this book's website (www.routledge.com/textbooks/9780415561648) may be useful in completing this task. Discuss similarities and differences on your completed figure with another student teacher and/or your tutor and add/change as appropriate. Store this information in your PDP to draw on as appropriate in your lesson planning.

Task 12.3 asks you to consider the use of ICT in planning and delivering lessons in a slightly different way.

Task 12.3 **Using ICT to enhance pupils' learning in PE**

Using Figure 12.1, consider whether a specific type of ICT might enhance pupils' learning, or the effectiveness and efficiency of your teaching. Discuss your completed figure with another student teacher and identify similarities and differences. Store the information in your PDP for future reference.

Learning activities/lesson episodes or key elements of teaching	Work cards, whiteboards	Cameras/video	Software	Gadgets	Others (please identify)
	Whether useful/not useful and reason	Whether useful/not useful and reason	Whether useful/not useful and reason	Whether useful/not useful and reason	Whether useful/not useful and reason
Improving individual and group performances					
Tracking progress					
Record and review performances					
Record data for the purposes of personal improvement					
Communicating information					
Provide opportunities for pupils to gain a better understanding of the nature of movement					
Analysing movement					
Introducing a new skill/game					
Challenging the most able					
Supporting those needing particular help					
Provide feedback on pupil performance/participation					

■ **Figure 12.1** Examples of ICT which can support some learning and teaching activities in lessons

189 ■

Learning activities/lesson episodes or key elements of teaching	Work cards, whiteboards	Cameras/video	Software	Gadgets	Others (please identify)
	Whether useful/not useful and reason	Whether useful/not useful and reason	Whether useful/not useful and reason	Whether useful/not useful and reason	Whether useful/not useful and reason
Encouraging pupils to take responsibility for own learning					
Preparing a presentation					
Provide worthwhile tasks for pupils off-practical					
Provide opportunities for peer assessment and self-assessment					
Provide students with the means to record work to be take up again in later lessons					
Other learning activities or key elements (list as appropriate)					

▪ **Figure 12.1** continued

USING ICT FOR ADMINISTRATION IN PE

There are many potential applications for using ICT to support administration in PE. Some of these potential uses are outlined below, starting with your own administration and progressing to the administration of a PE department. It is important that you think carefully about the use of ICT in administration, particularly whether it enables you to undertake your administration more efficiently and effectively. You should not use ICT simply for the sake of it.

The first aspect of administration links directly to enhancing pupils' learning – your planning.

Planning

ICT can allow you to write, modify and update units of work and lesson plans on a regular basis. In addition, teaching materials such as worksheets and reciprocal teaching cards can be produced, revised and therefore be matched to meet the needs of different classes and of individual pupils. Equally, your planning can be informed by incorporating ideas from online teaching materials such as the QCA (www.qca.gov.uk) and those listed on www.teachernet.gov.uk or www.standards.dfes.gov.uk. These resources are available to teachers and student teachers in order to support you in enhancing pupils' learning.

Pupil information

ICT can be useful in the registration and monitoring of pupils' daily attendance. Laptop and palm top computers allow attendance and absence to be recorded and monitored in each lesson. Information about pupil attendance and absence in each lesson can be used within the PE department to track non-participation or absence but is also used more widely across the school as a useful device for tracking particular patterns of attendance or absence.

ICT can also be used to record other information about pupils. This includes information related to medical and parental consent forms. A central database can store information about pupils that may be particularly relevant to PE staff, such as whether pupils have certain allergies or medical conditions that may potentially affect their participation in PE, such as diabetes, asthma or epilepsy and other recording and reporting – school reports, assessment results.

Assessment, recording and reporting

There are a range of ways in which ICT can be used to support assessment, e.g. it can be used to record pupils' achievement against ILOs (making a permanent record of the performance, which would otherwise be observed and lost). This can be analysed after the lesson (by the pupils as well as the teacher) and reports made. When writing a report for parents, the teacher, therefore, has evidence to which she/he can refer. Pupils can also submit homework tasks electronically through the virtual learning environment for marking and/or feedback from the teacher. These can be marked electronically and then recorded by the teacher. Podcasting is another way that teachers can provide feedback to pupils on their progress (see this book's website for details: www.routledge.com/textbooks/9780415561648).

Furthermore, parents can be contacted via electronic mail or text messaging about their child's progress, which does away with the need to send letters home either by post or with the child. However, you must check school policies on this as well as ensuring that parents have access to the relevant ICT.

Extra-curricular activities

Extra-curricular activities are integral to the work of all PE departments, providing opportunities for pupils to engage in extra-curricular and school activities. School activities include sports days, sports festivals and swimming galas, each of which enables schools to celebrate the achievements of their pupils. These can be one of the highlights of a school's sporting calendar. Most schools also have an extensive programme of inter-school competitions. Databases of awards, sports days/festivals, swimming galas, school teams, extra-curricular programmes can be effectively planned through the use of ICT. ICT can also be used to sort pupils into groups/teams. Inter-school sports fixtures can be arranged through email. In this respect, ICT is available for teachers to produce professional programmes of events and then record competitors results onto a spreadsheet. Software is available to calculate times and scores and produce updated and final results very quickly. These can be printed off and taken away at the end of the event and entered on to the schools website along with pictures of competitors and award ceremonies. Further, announcements about successes can be put on the school intranet or internet. (Note: pupils could do these analyses in lessons such as mathematics, enhancing the learning opportunities available, see above.) Likewise, ICT can be used to support other aspects of the administration of extra-curricular activities, for example, producing termly and yearly timetables of activities, scheduling of practices, assigning pupils to teams, printing team sheets with ease, contests, match results, recording results of tournaments.

Traditionally, telephone, fax and post have been the means by which PE staff organise inter-school events. Whilst these are perfectly acceptable forms of communication, electronic mail and mobile phone technology, including text messaging and video conferencing, can be used, where appropriate, to organise fixtures or plan off-site visits (including overseas school trips). In addition, contact details for other schools can be kept electronically in an address book and updated accordingly and used to produce mailing lists which may assist in making fixtures and other related sporting events.

ICT can also be used for other administrative tasks, such as staff records, administrative appointments, suppliers and equipment inventory, as well as to track the condition and availability of facilities. Task 12.4 is designed to enable you to find out how ICT is used to support administration in your placement school and Task 12.5 aims to help you consider how ICT can improve your administration

---

Task 12.4 **Audit of ICT to support administration**

Repeat Task 12.1 by carrying out an audit of the range of ICT used in your placement school to support administration. Talk to the PE teachers to identify ways in which it is used to make administration more efficient and effective. Store your observations in your PDP as an aide-memoire for doing your own administration.

Task 12.5 **Consider ways in which ICT can improve your own administration and the administration of the PE department in your placement school**

Use Figure 12.2 to identify ICT which will help to make the various administrative activities that you undertake as a PE teacher, and that are undertaken across a PE department, more effective and efficient and then consider your own knowledge, skill and confidence in using that ICT and what development you need. Undertake that development, recording your progress in your PDP.

Administrative activity	Useful ICT applications which increase effectiveness and efficiency	Knowledge and skill of each application	Confidence in using each application	Plan to develop knowledge, skill and confidence in each application
Keeping records of pupils, attendance, absence and participation				
Medical information about pupils, including allergies				
Communicating with parents				
Extra-curricular activities (use specific examples)				
Planning tournaments etc.				
Other departmental administration (please list)				

■ **Figure 12.2** Using ICT to support administration in PE

DEVELOPING YOUR OWN SKILLS AND CONFIDENCE IN USING ICT

Research by Stidder and Hayes (2006) found that student PE teachers are frequent users of ICT and are confident in applying the use of ICT within their teaching as and when they feel it is appropriate and are prepared to incorporate its use in other aspects of their professional role. For example, many student PE teachers indicated that they were able to use spreadsheets (44 per cent), assessment software (73 per cent), digital photography (70 per cent) and video (95 per cent) as well as produce worksheets (100 per cent) and other resources using a range of ICT applications within their placement schools. Most recently, the Office for Standards in Education (Ofsted, 2009: 58) found that PE teachers had good opportunities to discuss the progress of pupils in depth and share data, increasingly through the use of ICT. Consequently, the majority of work was planned appropriately for different abilities and pupils were able to make good progress.

ICT can only be a useful tool for enhancing learning and teaching if used correctly and effectively. This means that you need both knowledge of, and skills to use, ICT. You also need to continue to learn new skills. One aspect of knowledge and skills is the judgement to use ICT appropriately.

In order to ensure that your ICT knowledge and skills enable you to use ICT effectively to enhance pupils' learning you should audit your strengths and weaknesses in the use of basic ICT skills. In order to do this, we suggest that you complete Task 1.4.1 in Capel, Leask and Turner (2009), using the table in the text or on the companion website (available at: www.routledge.com/textbooks/9780415478724). Changes to working practices and technology can sometimes be uncomfortable but are, nevertheless, inevitable and there are many opportunities for you to develop your ICT skills to enable pupils to improve their learning. Find out what types of training are available to enable teachers to use ICT both in learning and teaching and in administration (you can start by referring to the section using ICT for professional development in Unit 1.4 in Capel, Leask and Turner, 2009).

Reflective practitioners are professionals who keep up with the times and predict the changes to come. To coin a sporting phrase 'there are people who are ahead of the game' and in this respect you may wish to consider the final reflective task. To this end you can also use ICT to support this. For example, ICT enables participation in online discussion groups to share ideas and good practice and it provides access to research and inspection evidence. Now complete Task 12.6.

Task 12.6 **Using ICT in your teaching**

Critically review and evaluate research on using ICT in PE (start by referring to the suggested reading list at the end of this chapter). Compare this with the policy and practice you have observed/experienced at your placement school. Highlight ways in which it can enhance or detract from learning and teaching in PE. Store this information in your PDP and refer to it when selecting ICT to use in learning and teaching and in your administration.

Tearle *et al.* (2005) found that whilst the potential for the use of ICT in PE is considerable, the actual practice and resource provision was found to be unplanned and the potential was often unrealised. The research findings indicated that many of the specific ICT resources which are of most benefit to PE are quite distinct from the needs and potential contributions to ICT in other subject areas. The researchers concluded that the potentially valuable role of ICT in PE needed to be more visible and widely promoted outside the subject area and that proactive effort including institutional support and training was needed to realise the potential of ICT in PE.

It is important to acknowledge, however, that there will be challenges in meeting these requirements. For example, Ofsted (2004) reported that whilst student teachers bring with them increasing levels of ICT competence, the opportunities to develop these skills in schools is often restricted by the lack of good ICT provision. Ofsted (2004: 4) have reported that the contribution of ICT to raising pupils' achievements remains unsatisfactory in one third of schools and that access to specialist computer facilities remains a problem for many PE departments. Subsequent reports (Ofsted, 2008c) also identified that these issues still persist and that the use of ICT remains inconsistent across the curriculum whilst there is limited use of ICT in practical lessons.

SUMMARY AND KEY POINTS

Whilst there are many advocates of the use of ICT in learning and teaching across all subject areas there may also be some cynics who believe that the abbreviation 'ICT' stands for 'It Causes Trouble'. This chapter has looked at the use of a range of ICT to support and enhance learning and teaching and administration in PE. It has also looked at how you can develop your own skills – and hence confidence – in using ICT. There have been many new innovations that have particular relevance to PE. The first step in assessing the application of ICT in PE is for you to decide whether it is suitable in supporting good practice in learning and teaching and then when to use it and how to introduce it. Remember that, as with any new teaching and learning strategy, pupils need guidance as to how to use ICT. An over-emphasis on using ICT in PE lessons at the expense of the 'physical' and 'practical' aspects of PE potentially can do more harm than good with respect to pupils' learning. You may overcome some of this by linking with other subjects. For example, pupils may collect information about health in PE but analyse that in biology. The results can then be used in both subjects. Likewise, pupils may collect data about, for example, times of a run and analyse that in mathematics. Again, the results can then be used in both subjects. Your professional judgement should be used to make decisions about the use of ICT to support and enhance the achievement of ILOs and provide opportunities to explore and enhance understanding. Nonetheless, ICT does have many advantages in enhancing learning in PE in schools.

The use of ICT within PE will continue to be an integral part of many future developments and initiatives that are likely to emerge as technology becomes more advanced and accepted as part of mainstream learning and teaching. A key question for you to consider in respect of the use of ICT is whether pupils might achieve or learn something different or more effectively and efficiently by incorporating this into your lessons and whether this may challenge, stimulate and engage pupils to a greater extent. If it does, use it; if not, don't.

Check which requirements for your course you have addressed through this chapter.

FURTHER READING

Ofsted (Office for Standards in Education) (2004) *2004 Report: ICT in Schools: The Impact of Government Initiatives*, (www.ofsted.gov.uk), May 2004, London: HMI 2196.
> This report draws upon evidence from PE from visits to secondary schools between 2002 and 2003. There are examples of good professional practice where ICT has been introduced to enhance learning and teaching in PE.

Ofsted (Office for Standards in Education) (2009) *PE in Schools 2005/08: Working Towards 2012 and Beyond*, April, Reference number: 080249 (www.ofsted.gov.uk).
> This is the latest UK government report which highlights strengths and weaknesses of PE learning and teaching in both primary and secondary schools. It provides examples of ways in which teachers have used ICT innovatively for teaching, learning and assessment in physical education.

Stidder, G. (2004) The use of information and communications technology in PE, in S. Capel (ed.), *Learning to Teach Physical Education in the Secondary School: A Companion to School Experience*, 2nd edn, London: Routledge, pp. 219–38.
> This chapter considers ways in which PE teachers might introduce the use of ICT to support their teaching and enhance pupils' learning. It also provides some guidance on when it might be appropriate to use ICT in secondary school PE.

Stidder, G. and Hayes, S. (2006) A longitudinal survey of PE trainees' experiences on school placements in the south-east of England (2000–2004), *European Physical Education Review*, Autumn, 12, 3: 317–38.
> This ten-year study of student PE teachers' statutory experiences of school-based training in secondary schools provides information as to the extent to which student PE teachers incorporate the use of ICT into their daily practice.

Tearle, P., Golder, G., Moore, J. and Ogden, K. (2005) The use of ICT in PE in the Exeter Initial Teacher Training Partnership, available online at: http://www.ttrb.ac.uk/attachments/515557e2-a1a6-4e2d-a92d-fc44179625c9.doc.
> This report highlights the key findings and recommendations from a project that investigated ways in which ICT has been used in a PE–ITT partnership. It highlights the extent to which student PE teachers have incorporated the use of ICT into their practice during both school and university-based parts of the course.

Acknowledgements

We would like to acknowledge the help and support of Kevin Morton (Seaford Head Community College), Craig Bull (Hayesbrook Specialist Sports College), Andy Gore, Sam Carter and Ben Gould (University of Brighton) for their assistance in researching the information on this book's website (www.routledge.com/textbooks/9780415561648).

NATIONAL CURRICULUM 2007

Margaret Whitehead and Susan Capel with Andy Wild and Suzanne Everley

INTRODUCTION

A National Curriculum was introduced in England as a result of the Education Reform Act (ERA), 1988 (DES, 1988). The National Curriculum for Physical Education (NCPE) was introduced in 1992 (Department of Education and Science/Welsh Office (DES/WO), 1992). Since then, the NCPE has been revised three times: 1995 (Department for Education (DfE), 1995); 1999 (Department for Education and Employment/ Qualifications and Curriculum Authority (DfEE/QCA), 1999); and 2007 (QCA, 2007a). These changes have resulted in significant changes to curriculum requirements. This chapter interprets the NCPE 2007.

OBJECTIVES

At the end of this chapter you should be able to:

- understand the NCPE 2007 (QCA, 2007a);
- consider the implications of the Programme of Study in the NCPE for PE in schools;
- understand the implications of NCPE for both teaching strategies and teaching content;
- critically examine PE curricular to consider how far they fulfil NCPE requirements;
- understand what high-quality PE might look like.

Check the requirements of your course to see which relate to this chapter.

AIMS OF PE

The government's aim, as spelled out in *Every Child Matters* (ECM) (Department for Education and Skills (DfES), 2003), is for every child, whatever their background or their circumstances, to have the support they need to:

- be healthy;
- stay safe;
- enjoy and achieve;
- make a positive contribution;
- achieve economic well-being.

The philosophy of ECM underpins the National Curriculum in England and all subjects are expected to make a contribution to achieving the key elements of ECM. Work in all curriculum subjects, including PE, is therefore required to ensure that pupils make progress in becoming:

- successful learners who enjoy learning, make progress and achieve;
- confident individuals who are able to live safe, healthy and fulfilling lives;
- responsible citizens who make a positive contribution to society (QCA, 2007a).

Each subject, through the teaching strategies it adopts and the subject matter it studies, makes a distinctive contribution to achieving these overarching aspirations. The contribution of PE to meeting these broad curriculum aims are set out in the Importance Statement in the NCPE – a statement that prefaces the Programme of Study for each curricular subject. This statement for PE states that:

> PE develops pupils' competence and confidence to take part in a range of physical activities that become a central part of their lives, both in and out of school.
>
> A high-quality PE curriculum enables all pupils to enjoy and succeed in many kinds of physical activity. They develop a wide range of skills and the ability to use tactics, strategies and compositional ideas to perform successfully. When they are performing, they think about what they are doing, analyse the situation and make decisions. They also reflect on their own and others' performances and find ways to improve them. As a result, they develop the confidence to take part in different physical activities and learn about the value of healthy, active lifestyles. Discovering what they like to do, what their aptitudes are at school, and how and where to get involved in physical activity helps them make informed choices about lifelong physical activity.
>
> PE helps pupils develop personally and socially. They work as individuals, in groups and in teams, developing concepts of fairness and of personal and social responsibility. They take on different roles and responsibilities, including leadership, coaching and officiating. Through the range of experiences that physical education offers, they learn how to be effective in competitive, creative and challenging situations.
>
> (QCA, 2007a)

Now complete Task 13.1.

Task 13.1 **Using the Importance Statement in your planning and teaching**

Refer to Chapter 2 where the aims of PE arising from the Importance Statement are listed. Select any six lesson plans you have taught in the last two weeks and carry out an audit of the intended learning outcomes (ILOs) specified in your planning. Tally the number of times you have addressed one of the above aims through an ILO. Discuss this audit with your tutor and consider if you need to review your ILOs.

Store this in your professional development portfolio (PDP) and repeat this task at a later stage of your course.

The Importance Statement claims a great deal for PE. If all of this is to be achieved, then it is important to consider how the NCPE is constructed to realise these aims.

In studying the Importance Statement there are two fundamental messages. The first message focuses on the pupils. Much of the statement describes how PE can impact on the all round personal development of the individual pupil. Issues covered include promoting pupils' confidence, fostering personal and social development, encouraging pupils to make decisions and to reflect on their performance. The second focuses on content, and is concerned with the breadth of experience pupils have in, for example, competitive, creative and adventurous situations. The rationale for this breadth is so that pupils can discover their interests and aptitudes and develop the confidence to make some form(s) of physical activity part of their lives. It is worth reflecting that while this second message appears to be about content, in fact its priority is again the pupils, ensuring they have a rich and varied experience.

There is no doubt that the National Curriculum as a whole and the NCPE specifically is pupil centred. The material covered provides the context for pupils to learn, develop and mature. Learning in each subject does, of course, introduce pupils to specific subject-related skills and content, but more importantly it guides pupils to learn how to learn, to work effectively with others and develop independence – that is they aim to foster the aspirations of the ECM philosophy. All teachers are, therefore, teaching children rather than teaching their subject *per se*. What does this mean for PE? It means that we must always think of the pupil first and see the different activities as contexts in which we can help them to grow as people.

ACHIEVING THE AIMS OF PE WITHIN THE NATIONAL CURRICULUM

Guidance on achieving the aims of PE as described in the Importance Statement is set out in the Programme of Study. This comprises four elements. First, *Key Concepts* and *Key Processes*. Key Processes relate directly to Key Concepts and are designated as the essential experiences pupils must have to come to understand the Key Concepts. Working to promote these two elements relies on using appropriate teaching approaches. The other two elements are entitled *Range and Content* and *Curriculum Opportunities*. These look particularly at the activities that provide the contexts for the Key Processes to be experienced and thus the Key Concepts to be understood. Working to realise these elements relies on selecting appropriate physical activities within the curriculum.

The Programme of Study in the NCPE 2007 is based on four Key Concepts and five Key Processes. These are examined below.

Key Concepts

The four Key Concepts in the NCPE are:

■ Competence
■ Performance
■ Creativity
■ Healthy, active lifestyles.

COMPETENCE

The concept of competence addresses those factors that concern both physical and mental skills. In relation to the physical, it refers to both large/whole-body (e.g. walking, running, throwing, rolling) and fine motor skills (e.g. handling a piece of equipment). Skills are not learned in isolation. Rather, pupils need to be able to select when to use specific skills, tactics, strategies and compositional ideas in different types of physical activity – both those which are familiar as well as unfamiliar contexts. Thus, consideration needs to be given to the cognitive capabilities of pupils, as well as the application of mental qualities that are required for pupils to continue to apply themselves in respect of a physically demanding activity. The demands here may, for example, be meeting the challenge of the need to persist, as more complex skills are developed; remaining mentally alert to changing environments; or continuing in sustained exercise.

PERFORMANCE

The concept of performance requires that pupils are not only able to achieve but that they can refine and improve this performance within challenging contexts to achieve specific goals. As teachers you should strive to encourage a desire to engage in activities of different natures (e.g. competitive, adventurous and creative), individually and in teams/groups. You need to move beyond encouraging pupils simply to take part in such activities, towards developing their genuine interest and commitment to participate. There are clear distinctions between doing something because you have to and doing it willingly; the willing participant is more likely to progress to pursue the activity as a natural part of their lifestyle and thus engage in lifelong activity.

CREATIVITY

The concept of creativity involves the direct expression of imagination and problem solving. Pupils should be encouraged to explore and experiment to produce efficient and effective outcomes. Creativity in PE is far broader than choreographic challenges in dance and compositional tasks in gymnastics. Problem solving and initiative are needed in many aspects of outdoor and adventurous activities (OAA) as well as in devising strategies in game play. An outstanding games player is not only skilful but is also creative and imaginative. Pupil exploration in finding ways to perform skills is also a form of creativity. What is discovered may not be new to the activity but it is new to the pupil. A solution found by a pupil can sometimes be more readily learnt/adopted than one issued by the teacher.

HEALTHY, ACTIVE LIFESTYLES

Pupils should have an understanding of the physical, social and mental benefits of appropriate physical activity and the crucial part that this has to play in their leading a healthy lifestyle. Through this concept, therefore, links need to be made with pupils' lives beyond the classroom; we are not being asked to make them fit and healthy on a temporary basis resulting from the activity they have done within the lesson, but rather as a long-term result of what they actually take away *from lessons* in terms of learning.

Key Processes

The five Key Processes are the essential skills and processes for pupils to learn in order to make progress with respect to the four Concepts. These are:

■ Developing skills in physical activity
■ Making and applying decisions
■ Developing physical and mental capacity
■ Evaluating and improving
■ Making informed choices about healthy, active lifestyles.

DEVELOPING SKILLS IN PHYSICAL ACTIVITY

This requires the various large/whole-body and fine motor skills to be refined and adapted into specific techniques for different sports and dance forms and for different purposes. For example, the skill of striking can be refined to play badminton, cricket, hockey, rounders, tennis; the skill of throwing can be refined for use in a range of team games, for throwing events in athletics and for throwing the hoop in rhythmic gymnastics.

MAKING AND APPLYING DECISIONS

In order to improve their performance pupils need to plan and implement the skills, being able to select and use tactics, strategies and compositional ideas effectively in a range of competitive, creative and adventurous contexts. When the circumstances of a game or situation change, pupils need to be able to refine and adapt their plans and ideas. They also need to recognise hazards and risks and be able to make decisions about how to control any risks to both themselves and others (Chapter 9 looks at teaching safety to pupils in PE).

DEVELOPING PHYSICAL AND MENTAL CAPACITY

Developing physical capacity refers to developing physical strength, stamina, speed and flexibility to enable pupils to cope with the demands of different activities. Mental capacity refers to developing mental determination to succeed – including having the confidence to have a go, the determination to face up to challenges and keep going, expressing and dealing with emotions and the desire to achieve success for both self and others.

EVALUATING AND IMPROVING

In order to improve all aspects of their performance it is important that pupils are able to analyse their own and others performance of, for example, skills, tactics, strategies, co-operating in team situations, compositional ideas and making independent decisions. Pupils need to be able to assess physical and mental aspects of these challenges, identify strengths and weaknesses, deciding what they need to do to improve their performance and taking action to improve in future performances.

MAKING INFORMED CHOICES ABOUT HEALTHY, ACTIVE LIFESTYLES

Pupils should be able to identify the types of activities to which they are best suited; the types of roles (such as performer, leader, official) they would like to take on; and be able to make choices about their involvement in physical activity outside of PE lessons, so that they become involved regularly in physical activity.

The relationship between Concepts and Processes is not wholly straightforward. However, Table 13.1 is one interpretation of this relationship. As indicated above, the Concepts and Processes rely on teaching approaches for their realisation. Suggestions of these implications are set out in the right-hand column of Table 13.1.

■ Table 13.1 The relationship between Key Concepts and Key Processes and implications for teaching approaches

Key Concepts that pupils need to understand	**Key Processes** pupils need to experience to grasp key concepts	**Curriculum implications** – some examples of modes of teaching needed to realise Key Concepts/Processes
Competence	Developing physical and mental capacity	Set tasks to introduce and establish whole-body and fine manipulative skills
	Developing skills in physical activity	Set tasks that work to develop strength, stamina, speed and flexibility in a variety of activities
	Making and applying decisions	Enable pupils to appreciate the demands of different activities and to understand the relationship between e.g. skills/techniques and tactics/choreographic principles
		Encourage pupils to set themselves realistic targets, appreciate challenges they are facing and have confidence to persevere
		Support pupils in developing the skills needed to work effectively with others in competitive and cooperative settings
Performance	Developing skills in physical activity	Provide a challenging and supportive environment to motivate pupils to work hard on improving skills across a wide range of activities e.g. competitive, creative, as an individual and as part of a group

	Making and applying decisions	Promote pupil confidence and positive self-esteem, thus fostering enthusiasm to participate, by use of differentiation
	Evaluating and improving	Encourage pupils to take responsibility for their own learning
Creativity	Evaluating and improving	Adopt teaching methods that demand imagination, discovery and problem solving in all activities
	Making and applying decisions	Decisions devolved to pupils can be concerned with e.g. skill performance, deployment of tactics, compositional/ choreographic ideas and expeditions
	Developing physical and mental capacity	Devolve responsibility to pupils where safe to do so
Healthy, active lifestyles	Making informed choices about healthy, active lifestyles	Provide opportunities to experience a wide range of different activities and roles in these activities
		Encourage reflection on personal strengths, weakness and interests
		Encourage participation in physical activity beyond the curriculum, both to further competence and to experience different activities
		Give attention to, and encourage discussion of, issues related to HRE (Health-Related Exercise)
		Discuss/explain physical/social/emotional reasons why they should participate in physical activity

As you can see from the right-hand column in Table 13.1, in order to engage pupils in Key Processes your teaching needs to, for example:

■ provide a supportive and motivating setting for learning (see Chapter 7 and also Unit 3.2 in Capel, Leask and Turner, 2009);
■ devolve responsibility to pupils;
■ encourage pupils to set their own tasks;
■ set discovery tasks (pupils finding an answer for themselves rather than being told), problem-solving tasks (pupils challenged to solve a particular problem, e.g. in choreographing dance or following a route in OAA) and open-ended tasks (pupils being free to select the area of activity on which they will work);
■ create situations in which pupils evaluate and critically consider their own and others' movement;
■ provide models of skills/techniques to be mastered;

- set challenges for pupils to practice/refine/develop skills/techniques;
- set tasks that involve pupils in developing strength, speed, stamina and flexibility;
- challenge pupils to apply skills/techniques in e.g. a game or choreographic situation.

With reference to this list and to Table 13.1, carry out Task 13.2 to identify what else your teaching needs to include to achieve all the aspirations of the NCPE.

Task 13.2 **Identifying what else your teaching needs to include to foster development of the Key Concepts and engage pupils in the Key Processes of the NCPE**

The list above is derived from Table 13.1. Read through the explanatory notes for Key Concepts and Key Processes and list what else your teaching needs to address to cover all requirements of the NCPE – for example, to promote pupil confidence. Make suggestions as to how aspects of your teaching can achieve these aspirations. For example, to promote confidence you need to provide positive feedback and show enthusiasm for individual progress, however small. See Chapter 7 for examples. Discuss these notes with your tutor and then put them in your PDP.

The second part of the Programme of Study looks at Range and Content and Curriculum Opportunities.

Range and content

The range and content of the NCPE outlines the breadth of the subject that you can draw on in order to teach the Concepts and Processes. It is suggested that PE should include at least four of the following activity types.

- Outwitting an opponent
- Accurate replication of actions, phrases and sequences
- Exploring and communicating ideas, concepts and emotions
- Performing at maximum levels
- Identifying and solving problems
- Exercising safely and effectively.

OUTWITTING AN OPPONENT

This involves overcoming an opponent or opponents in face-to-face individual and team competition. Invasion games, net/wall games and striking games are included here, as are combat activities. Another example could be middle- and long-distance races where tactics may be important.

ACCURATE REPLICATION OF ACTIONS, PHRASES AND SEQUENCES

Repeating actions, phrases or sequences of movement precisely is important in a range of activities, including dance, diving, gymnastics, synchronised swimming, trampolining.

EXPLORING AND COMMUNICATING IDEAS, CONCEPTS AND EMOTIONS

Activities in which how well ideas, feelings, concepts or emotions are communicated in relation to artistic merit or choreography include different dance styles.

PERFORMING AT MAXIMUM LEVELS

Activities in which the best score or time is measured, either in direct competition or by comparing scores at different times, include running or swimming races or throwing events in athletics, having a high score in archery or a low score in golf.

IDENTIFYING AND SOLVING PROBLEMS

A range of outdoor and adventurous activities (OAA) such as orienteering, life saving, water sports and camping is particularly relevant here.

EXERCISING SAFELY AND EFFECTIVELY

This includes activities in which the aim is to provide experiences of health, well-being or fitness, many of which may be individual activities, such as jogging, aerobics, aquarobics.

Curriculum opportunities

The NCPE 2007 also identifies Curriculum Opportunities which are integral to pupils' learning and enhance their engagement with the Key Concepts, Key Processes and with the Range and Content of PE. Pupils should be provided with opportunities to be involved in a broad range of activities which together develop strength, stamina, suppleness and speed of the whole body, allow them to perform as individuals, in a group or team in competitions or performances outside class. In addition to performing, pupils should experience other roles, including leadership and officiating. Further, they should be able to use ICT to help improve their performance and to track their progress (ICT is covered in Chapter 12) and be able to make links between PE and other curriculum subjects.

The NCPE documentation concerned with Curriculum Opportunities also charges you, as teachers, to ensure that steps are taken to encourage pupils to continue with activities in extra-curricular time and outside the school setting. To achieve this you need, first, to ensure that pupils are motivated and get satisfaction and enjoyment from their work in curriculum PE. Second, you should alert pupils to activities occurring in extra-curricular time. Ideally these activity settings allow the most able to develop further, the less able to improve and for all to experience a wider range of activities than can be provided in curriculum time. Your goal should be that *all* pupils take part in some extra-curricular activity. Third, you need to inform pupils of opportunities in the local area where they can take part in a range of activities. As far as possible you should know your pupils and support them in decisions to take part in this additional participation.

Table 13.2 sets out some examples of how Range and Content and Curriculum Opportunities can be covered through work in various physical activities.

■ **Table 13.2** The relationship between physical activities, Range and Content and Curriculum Opportunities

Some examples of Range and Content to be found in physical activities	Some examples of range of Physical Activity	Some examples of Curriculum Opportunities provided by different activities
Accurate replication; Identifying and solving problems	Gymnastics	Individual/group work
Accurate replication; Identifying and solving problems	Sports Acrobatics	Group work
Accurate replication; Exploring and communicating ideas, concepts and emotions; Identifying and solving problems	Dance – creative	Use of ICT; Links with other subjects; Individual/group work
Accurate replication; Exploring and communicating ideas, concepts and emotions; Identifying and solving problems	Dance – street	Use of ICT; Individual work
Accurate replication	Dance – national	Links with other subjects; Group work
Performing at maximum levels; Exercising safely and effectively	Aerobics	Links with other subjects
Accurate replication; Performing at maximum levels	Athletics – field	Use of ICT; Experience different roles; Individual work
Accurate replication; Performing at maximum levels	Athletics – track	Use of ICT; Experience different roles; Individual work
Performing at maximum levels; Exercising safely and effectively	Circuits	Use of ICT; Links with other subjects
Performing at maximum levels; Exercising safely and effectively	Weight training	Use of ICT; Links with other subjects; Individual work
Performing at maximum levels; Accurate replication	Individual sports, e.g. golf, archery	Individual work; Experience different roles
Outwitting opponents; Accurate replication; Identifying and solving problems	Invasion games	Team work; Experience different roles
Outwitting opponents; Accurate replication; Identifying and solving problems	Net/wall games	Team work; Experience different roles
Outwitting opponents; Accurate replication; Identifying and solving problems	Striking/fielding games	Team work; Experience different roles

▨ **Table 13.2** continued

Some examples of Range and Content to be found in physical activities	Some examples of range of Physical Activity	Some examples of Curriculum Opportunities provided by different activities
Outwitting opponents; Accurate replication; Performing at maximum levels	Individual sports, e.g. fencing, judo, karate	Experience different roles; Individual work
Accurate replication; Performing at maximum levels; Exercising safely and effectively	Swimming strokes	Individual work
Accurate replication	Life saving	Group work
Accurate replication; Exploring and communicating ideas, concepts and emotions; Exercising safely and effectively	Synchronised swimming	Individual/group work
Identifying and solving problems; Exercising safely and effectively	Orienteering	Use of ICT; Links with other subjects; Group work
Identifying and solving problems; Exercising safely and effectively	OAA	Use of ICT; Links with other subjects; Group work
Identifying and solving problems; Exercising safely and effectively	Water sports	Individual/group work

Using Table 13.2 now carry out Task 13.3

Task 13.3 **Delivering Range and Content and Curriculum Opportunities through different physical activities**

Using Table 13.2 consider how far a year's programme for a Class 9, consisting of Health-Related Exercise, Games and Athletics, would cover all the Range and Content and Curriculum Opportunities spelled out in the NCPE. Suggest what, in your view, might be needed to ensure full coverage.

Discuss your suggestions with another student teacher and put these notes in your PDP.

DRAWING UP CURRICULUM PLANS TO ADDRESS ALL ASPECTS OF NCPE

Once you start teaching, it is likely that you will be involved in discussions about curriculum plans and when you are in a position of responsibility you have the task of devising curriculum plans for each key stage. Curriculum plans should be based firmly in NCPE requirements and therefore should have as their underlying rationale that pupils experience opportunities to develop the Key Concepts and Key Processes. In any year all Key Concepts and Key Processes need to be addressed. The next step is to decide on the Range and Content of activities you are going to use to provide pupils with these experiences. The NCPE indicates that at least four of the six Range and Content activity types should be included in Key Stage 3, and at least two in Key Stage 4. You should also map through the Curricular Opportunities you need to provide via the activities selected.

Table 13.3 shows how this process might be conducted. The table provides a grid to be completed (as, for example, the curriculum for Year 9 is being compiled).

Using Tables 13.1, 13.2 and 13.3 complete Task 13.4.

Task 13.4 **Curriculum planning for Year 9**

Study Tables 13.1 and 13.2 and complete the empty boxes in Table 13.3 (the table can be downloaded from this book's website, www.routledge.com/textbooks/ 9780415561648).

Check back to earlier sections in this chapter to ensure that you have an adequate Range and Content of activities and that all Curriculum Opportunities are covered. Presume you are fortunate in having all facilities available and staff to teach all activities. Indicate if you are teaching girls, boys or mixed groups.

Carry out the same process for Year 11.

Discuss your completed grid with your tutor and put it in your PDP.

The activities selected in a particular school, of course, have to take into account a number of factors. Perhaps the most fundamental is the facilities available in any one school. Indeed, the Office for Standards in Education (Ofsted, 2002a) indicates that in most schools, the availability of facilities and resources is a significant influence on how the curriculum is planned and delivered. Outdoor games may be dominant in a curriculum if there is limited indoor space for activities such as gymnastics and dance; likewise, swimming may not be included in schools which do not have their own or easy access to a swimming pool elsewhere because of the time/cost/supervision issues of travel. However, there may be other factors influencing the choice of range and content, including teachers' backgrounds, experiences and perceived strengths and weaknesses as well as the historical and traditional content of curricular and extra-curricular activities. Notwithstanding these considerations the curriculum should offer breadth and balance in both the activities covered and in the time given to each type of activity. Similarly there must be breadth and balance in the experiences pupils have in respect of developing their mastery of Key Concepts and Key Processes.

Where facilities and staff strengths are very significant in planning it may be necessary to devise a curriculum starting with the activities and then to map through how the Concepts, Processes and Opportunities can be catered for through involvement in the content selected. In cases such as this, particular attention needs to be given to the selection of work within an activity (such as opportunities for creative work in gymnastics if dance cannot be provided) and to the teaching strategies employed (such as including problem solving in a games situation, if OAA is not feasible). Both these are important to ensure full coverage of the Concepts and Processes.

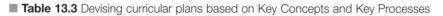

■ **Table 13.3** Devising curricular plans based on Key Concepts and Key Processes

Planning Grid for Year 9

Key Concepts/ Processes	Modes of teaching, teaching approaches/ strategies, e.g.	Physical Activities	Range and Content	Curriculum Opportunities
Competence Developing physical and mental capacity Developing skills in physical activity Making and applying decisions	Provide models of skills/ techniques to be mastered Set tasks that involve pupils in developing strength, speed, stamina and flexibility Challenge pupils to apply skills/techniques in e.g. a game or choreographic situation			
Performance Developing skills in physical activity Making and applying decisions Evaluating and improving	Provide models of skills/techniques to be mastered Set challenges for pupils to practice/refine/develop skills/techniques Encourage pupils to evaluate their movement and take responsibility for their own learning			
Creativity Evaluating and improving Making and applying decisions Developing physical and mental capacity	Set discovery, problem-solving and open-ended tasks Create situations in which pupils evaluate and critically consider their own and others' movement Devolve responsibility to pupils where safe to do so			
Healthy, active lifestyles Making informed choices about healthy, active lifestyles	Provide a supportive and motivating setting for learning Encourage pupils to set own targets Work with individuals in discussing strengths and interests			

Table 13.4 is an example of how this may be done. The selection of Key Concepts, Key Processes and Content is likely to differ in each year and Key Stage. In addition, the Content may be used to give pupils experiences in respect of different Concepts. For example, in games, early work may focus on performance and competence and later work on creativity. In OAA early experience may be concerned with exercising safely and later experience may be about identifying and solving problems. In compiling a curriculum plan it is essential that all Key Concepts and Key Processes and the resultant teaching approaches/strategies are fully addressed.

Using Table 13.4 as an example now complete Task 13.5.

▓ **Table 13.4** Devising curriculum plans around selected activities

Activity	Aspects of Range and Content covered, e.g.	Curriculum Opportunities provided, e.g.	Key Concepts, e.g. (see Table 13.1 for Key Processes and teaching approach/strategy implications)
Year 7 (6 hour blocks per term/activity)			
Term 1			
Gymnastics Invasion games	Accurate replication Outwitting an opponent	Individual Team	Performance Performance
Gymnastics Net/wall games	Accurate replication Outwitting an opponent	Individual Team	Creativity Competence
Term 2			
Dance – creative Orienteering	Exploring ideas Exercising safely	Individual/group Individual/group (ICT)	Creativity Healthy active lifestyles
Dance – creative Health-related exercise activities	Exploring ideas Exercising safely	Individual/group Individual	Creativity Healthy active lifestyles
Term 3			
Athletics OAA	Maximum levels Exercising safely	Individual (ICT) Group	Performance Healthy active lifestyles
Swimming Striking/fielding	Accurate replication Outwitting an opponent	Individual Team	Performance Competence

■ **Table 13.4** continued

Activity	Aspects of Range and Content covered, e.g.	Curriculum Opportunities provided, e.g.	Key Concepts, e.g. (see Table 13.1 for Key Processes and teaching approach/strategy implications)
Year 8 (6 hour blocks per term/activity)			
Term 1			
Sports acrobatics Invasion games	Accurate replication Outwitting an opponent	Group Team	Performance Competence
Sports acobatics Health-related exercise activities	Accurate replication Exercising safely	Group Individual (ICT)	Creativity Healthy active lifestyles
Term 2			
Dance – country Circuits	Exploring ideas Exercising safely	Group Individual (ICT)	Performance Healthy active lifestyles
Dance – country Invasion games	Exploring ideas Outwitting an opponent	Group Team	Creativity Competence
Term 3			
Swimming Striking/fielding	Accurate replication Outwitting an opponent	Individual Team	Performance Competence
Athletics Water sports	Maximum levels Exercising safely	Individual (ICT) Group	Performance Healthy active lifestyles

Weighting of Key Processes
Outwitting an opponent 36 hours 25%
Accurate replication of actions, phrases and sequences 36 hours 25%
Exercising safely and effectively 36 hours 25%
Exploring and communicating ideas, concepts and emotions 24 hours 17%
Performing at maximum levels 12 hours 8%

Task 13.5 **Mapping Key Concepts, Key Processes and Curriculum Opportunities on to an existing Key Stage curriculum plan**

Obtain a copy of a curriculum plan for Key Stage 3 or 4 and carry out an analysis as exemplified in Table 13.4. Discuss you analysis with another student teacher.
    Record this in your PDP.

ACHIEVING THE ASPIRATIONS IN THE IMPORTANCE STATEMENT

A question you may well ask is 'How do I know whether the learning experiences I am providing for pupils in PE are being successful?' What criteria can I use to evaluate if pupils are developing in respect of the ECM aims? To help you to answer this question the Department for Education and Skills (DfES, 2004d) state that when schools are providing high-quality PE, pupils:

1   are committed to PE and sport and make them a central part of their lives – both in and out of schools;
2   know and understand what they are trying to achieve and how to go about it;
3   understand that PE and sport is an important part of a healthy active lifestyle;
4   have the confidence to get involved in PE and sport;
5   have the skills and control that they need to take part in PE and sport;
6   willingly take part in a range of competitive, creative and challenge-type activities, both as individuals and as part of a team or group;
7   think about what they are doing and make appropriate decisions for themselves;
8   show a desire to improve and achieve in relation to their own abilities;
9   have the stamina, suppleness and strength to keep going;
10   enjoy PE, school and community sport.

(DfES, 2004d)

HOW IS PUPILS' LEARNING MEASURED?

In any curriculum plan it is essential to know how pupils' attainment is measured. The attainment target and the level descriptions are central to the NCPE. The range of levels within which the majority of pupils are expected to work at the end of the key stage are:

Range of levels within which the great majority of pupils are expected to work		Expected attainment for the majority of pupils at the end of the Key Stage	
Key Stage 1	1–3	at age 7	2
Key Stage 2	2–5	at age 11	4
Key Stage 3	3–7	at age 14	5/6

Thus levels relevant to most pupils at Key Stage 3 and 4 are set out in the descriptors of Level 3–8. Together, they demonstrate the progression and continuity which is central to enhancing pupils' learning and against which pupils' attainment is measured.

Chapter 3 looks at the increasing expectations and demands made on pupils as they progress through the NCPE key stages.

The level descriptions cross-reference directly to the five Key Processes, and therefore direct you to adopt a holistic approach in teaching and learning. See Chapter 3 for further discussion of progression and continuity. Carry out Task 13.6 to track progression in two Key Processes.

Task 13.6 **Tracking progression in two Key Processes**

Locate a copy of NCPE level descriptors 3–8 (see http://curriculum.qcda.gov.uk/key-stages-3-and-4/subjects/physical-education/). Select a Key Process and chart the progress identified from Level 3 to Level 8. Select another Key Process and repeat this mapping.

Discuss your notes with another student teacher who has also carried out this task. Put your notes in your PDP.

DEVELOPING YOUR TEACHING WITHIN THE NCPE 2007 (OR OTHER) FRAMEWORK

Murdoch (2004) suggested that new education initiatives can be problematic and that some are not readily accepted, nor adopted in practice. She expressed the view that since 1992 the concept of teaching a process-based rather than product- or activity-based curriculum has been central to curriculum discourse and NCPE programmes of study have been presented to reflect this focus. This means that teaching should be seen as engaging pupils in a variety of carefully chosen learning processes, rather than teaching being viewed as having the overarching goal of a class producing a predetermined product, for example mastering a particular skill, technique or tactic. She goes on to say that it would appear that some PE teachers have not embraced, nor widely adopted, the process-based model; pedagogical application centres, still, on the activity and the associated skills that are necessary to play different sports or participate in specific physical activities. Indicators in many schools – in the form of sport/activity specific units of work – suggest this to be still the case. In effect we are asking an age-old question once more: Do PE teachers primarily teach physical/sports activities or do they teach pupils? It is interesting to note that from as far back as 2000 Penney and Chandler (2000) have urged the profession to develop curriculum planning structures that focus on the key processes rather than a structure which subsumes the processes and overrides it with a focus on activities.

The NCPE 2007 is again presented to direct you, as teachers, to having pupil learning at the forefront of your thinking with the physical activities providing the context for this learning. As indicated by Murdoch, the profession has been urged to make this move in previous curricular guidance, however, some teachers have found it problematic to follow this recommendation. While there are certainly teachers whose work is distinctly pupil centred, others still tend to focus on teaching the activities. With the very clear focus in the NCPE 2007 documentation on pupil learning and a process model, it is expected that you, entering the profession in 2011 and beyond, will play a major role in spearheading this focus. This means that you may need to look beyond how you were taught in school and some of the teaching currently occurring in schools. You need to adopt a different approach, using the NCPE as your rationale. It is accepted that this is a subtle change, as in some ways you cannot promote pupil learning unless they are engaged in an activity and you cannot teach an activity without at the same time fostering pupil learning. Perhaps the key to developing a process-based, pupil-centred approach is to focus more on charting the progress of individual pupils across all Key

Concepts/Processes, rather than assessing learning outcomes in the context of the class achieving particular skills/techniques/tactics. The notion of the importance of catering for individual needs is at the heart of the ECM philosophy and the government priority of an inclusive curriculum. Now complete Tasks 13.7 and 13.8.

Other chapters in this book, e.g. Chapters 10 and 14, focus on developing your teaching to enable you to meet this challenge.

Task 13.7 **Process-based and product-based curricula**

With another student teacher discuss what you understand by a process-based curriculum and how this differs from a product-based curriculum. It is useful here to read Penney and Chandler (2000). Have a similarly focused discussion with a qualified teacher and critically appraise any differing views that are expressed. Have these discussions changed, in any way, your own opinions?

Record your discussions and your views in your PDP as evidence of Master's level work.

Task 13.8 **The contribution of PE to achieving the aims of the National Curriculum**

The essence of a compelling learning experience is that it is engaging, challenging and enriching for pupils and contributes to their becoming successful learners, confident individuals and responsible citizens.

Focus on your school-based experience(s), and in the form of a 2,000 word essay critically examine the contribution that PE can make to realising the aims of the National Curriculum.

Keep this essay in you PDP as evidence of Master's level work.

SUMMARY AND KEY POINTS

Together, the Importance Statement, the Key Concepts and Key Processes, Range and Content and Curriculum Opportunities of the NCPE 2007 provide specific guidance in respect of teaching PE. In addition, they allow a certain degree of flexibility in planning curriculum provision, to enable schools and teachers to be responsive to the interests and learning needs of pupils, and to work within the facilities and expertise of the school. Schemes of work, units of work and lessons planned and taught within the NCPE 2007 should focus on working towards Key Concepts and Key Processes, using activities as the context for learning, rather than as an end in themselves. This means that, ideally, your planning, both long term and short term, should start with the learning experiences that the pupils are to have in relation to the Key Concepts and Key Processes. Once this has been decided you should consider which activities best provide the context(s) for these experiences.

The NCPE sets out a pupil-centred, process-based model. At the heart of all your work are the pupils, their confidence in their abilities, their determination to make progress and their motivation to be involved in a range of physical activities in and outside school. Your long-term goal as a PE teacher is for all pupils to adopt physical activity as a lifelong habit. This can only be achieved if each pupil is treated as an individual on their own personal journey in becoming more physically competent and confident. Teaching is not only pupil centred, it also needs to be personalised.

When it is taught well, PE clearly has the potential to have life-changing effects, not just on the individual, but it can also have a positive impact too on school, community and society in general. It is salutary to be reminded that the memories for many people of their school-based PE lessons are all too often tarnished by negative experiences. It would be worrying if the following quotes were to refer to your PE lessons: 'horrendous lessons on the sports field...'; 'wearing kit that made me feel and look stupid...'; 'standing around a lot and feeling cold most of the time...'; 'being told to do things, but never being shown how, or told why...'; 'waiting my turn in long queues and then being ridiculed in front of my peers...'; 'being ordered through the showers seemed like a form of public humiliation...'.

The message behind these negative comments is the need to see PE experiences through the eyes of the pupils.

You need to be perceptive, empathetic and responsive. The National Curriculum urges you, as teachers, to facilitate compelling and high-quality learning experiences. To enable all pupils to have these experiences demands the sort of teaching that puts the pupils at the heart of the enterprise. Your teaching needs to reward individual effort and celebrate progress, however small. NCPE challenges you to judge your work as a teacher not on the quality of the game of hockey played by class 8R on a Wednesday morning but by how far each pupil has moved in mastering the Key Concepts and Key Processes that form the underpinning rationale of the curriculum.

Check which requirements for your course you have addressed through this chapter.

FURTHER INFORMATION

You may need to review more fully the NCPE programme of study (QCA, 2007a). This is available at: http://curriculum.qcda.gov.uk/key-stages-3-and-4/subjects/physical-education/index.aspx.

In addition, the following three websites provide useful resources/information:

http://curriculum.qcda.org.uk
http://curriculum.qcda.gov.uk/key-stages-3-and-4/organising-your-curriculum/
http://www.newsecondarycurriculum.org

FURTHER READING

Murdoch, E. (1997) The background to, and developments from, the National Curriculum for PE, in S. Capel (ed.), *Learning to Teach Physical Education in the Secondary School: A Companion to School Experience*, London: Routledge, pp. 252–70.

Murdoch, E. (2004) NCPE 2000 – where are we so far?, in S. Capel (ed.), *Learning to Teach Physical Education in the Secondary School: A Companion to School Experience*, 2nd edn, London: Routledge, pp. 280–300.

These two chapters look at the development of the NCPE in England from 1992. They are included on this book's website (www.routledge.com/textbooks/9780415561648).

Penney, D. and Chandler, T. (2000) Physical education: what future(s)?, *Sport, Education and Society*, 5, 1: 71–87.

This article looks at alternative approaches to curriculum PE.

WIDER ROLE OF A PE TEACHER

Margaret Whitehead and Jes Woodhouse

INTRODUCTION

As well as PE-specific aims and objectives, PE also contributes to the educational enterprise as a whole. It is to be expected that in starting your initial teacher education (ITE) you are concerned very much with the teaching of PE, the content you are to cover in lessons, the organisation you need to put in place and the teaching approaches you decide to use. This, of course, is at the heart of your work. However, as a teacher, not just a PE teacher, you have wider responsibilities in respect of the school and the pupils. This chapter is designed to help you to appreciate these responsibilities and to understand how you can fulfil this wider obligation.

> ## OBJECTIVES
>
> At the end of this chapter you should be able to:
>
> - understand the ways in which the aims of PE align with broad curriculum aims;
> - be aware of the ways that PE can contribute to these broader aims;
> - be able to critically consider the role of PE in contributing to the educational enterprise as a whole.
>
> Check the requirements for your course to see which relate to this chapter.

HELPING PUPILS TO LEARN HOW TO LEARN

It is probably true to say that many student PE teachers are drawn to the subject because of their love for physical activity and sport. In this light, it is only natural that much of your initial focus falls upon the teaching of physical activity and sport. As time goes on, and your vision broadens, you will feel comfortable with the teaching of PE. Eventually, there should come a time when you take the next step and understand the concept of educating pupils in the context of PE, which then sets you up for the very important shift to helping pupils to learn through experiences in PE. It is then a relatively short step to the realisation that your role, first and foremost, is that of helping pupils to learn, or better, to learn how to learn. Your contribution to this aim is of benefit to pupils across the school curriculum and beyond into life after school. Your role in helping pupils to learn and make progress in PE is merely one aspect of helping pupils to learn how to learn.

It can take time to embrace fully this wider responsibility, but an understanding of the contribution PE can make to the achievement of broader educational aims is a help-ful first step. Once you begin planning lessons with intended learning outcomes (ILOs) that identify both PE-specific and more generic aims, you are on the way to developing the breadth of vision that underpins truly high-quality teaching.

To provide a background to discussing this twofold responsibility of PE teachers, this chapter uses the current broad educational priorities in England. This serves as an example of the broader educational aims and the ways that individual subjects can contribute to the all round education of young people. Most countries have similar broader educational aims and it is helpful for you to identify these early in your ITE. Figure 14.1 is designed to show how the Key Concepts and Processes identified in the latest National Curriculum for Physical Education (NCPE, Qualifications and Curriculum Authority (QCA), 2007) in England, link to the broader aims of the school curriculum as a whole. Of course, there will be times when you are helping pupils develop skills and knowledge that are very specific to participation in physical activity but it is important to recognise that a wide range of skills and qualities and a great deal of knowledge that can be acquired in PE, can be applied in education as a whole (see also Chapter 2). Your awareness of this potential of PE not only enables you to become a much more versatile and responsive PE teacher, it should also help you realise the true value of the subject as a learning medium for all pupils. This is of particular significance for pupils who struggle in other areas but thrive in PE. You also become aware of the ways that pupils' experiences across other curriculum subjects can influence their ability to learn in PE.

From Figure14.1 you should be able to identify fairly easily the clear threads that tie the Key Concepts and Processes underpinning PE to the Personal, Learning and Thinking Skills (PLTS). Furthermore you should be able to locate the relationship between the PLTS (see Qualifications and Curriculum Development Authority (QCDA) website) and the educational aims propounded within broader curriculum documentation, and how these all contribute to the key components that underpin the UK government policy related to children and young people, which in England is currently termed *Every Child Matters* (ECM) (Department for Education and Skills (DfES), 2003).

Figure 14.1 can be read from top down or bottom up. Starting from the top, the government ECM policy tasks schools to enable all pupils to enjoy and achieve, to make a positive contribution to society, to be healthy, to stay safe and in the long term have the skills to secure their own economic well-being. Arising from these five outcomes schools are expected to work towards achieving three aims, being to develop pupils as success-ful learners, confident individuals and responsible citizens. As an adjunct to these aims the government drew up a list of PLTS that need to be fostered. These skills refer to the ability to be reflective learners, independent enquirers, creative thinkers, self-managers, effective participators and team workers. As a corollary of these overarching directives

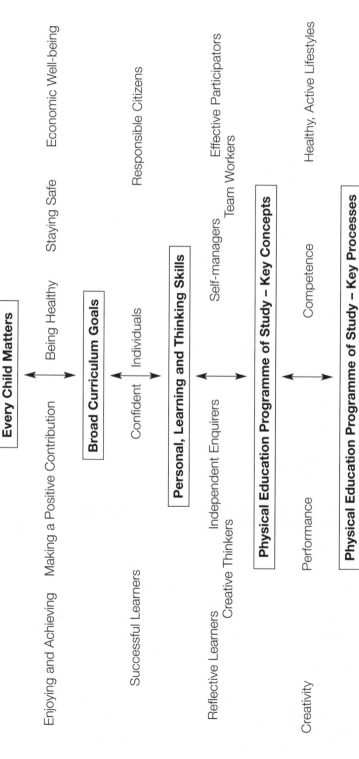

■ **Figure 14.1** The relationship between the goals of Every Child Matters and the aims of PE

there were two considerations in planning the NCPE, one concerned with ensuring that the subject contributes as fully as possible to the broad curriculum aspirations and the other to identify the unique contribution PE can make to pupils' education. The Key Concepts and Processes were the outcome of this deliberation. (See Chapter 13 for a detailed discussion of the NCPE (QCA, 2007a.)

Figure 14.1 can also be read from the bottom up. Task 14.1 challenges you to read it in this way and to identify how the Key Concepts and Processes in PE can be seen to contribute to broader curriculum aspirations.

Task 14.1 **How PE can contribute to broader curriculum aims**

Look at Figure 14.1 and identify the relationships between PE Key Concepts and Processes (there is more detail of these in Chapter 13) and the three sets of broader curriculum aspirations. Construct a flow chart for at least two of the PE Key Processes, mapping, for each, its contribution to four stages/levels set out above in Figure 14.1. Discuss this with another student teacher who has carried out this task. Put this chart and a résumé of your discussion in your professional development portfolio (PDP).

ACHIEVING BROAD CURRICULUM AIMS IN PE

The next two sections set out ways that broad curriculum aims can be achieved in the context of PE. As you can see, the principal focus is on planning how to deliver the lesson and how you effect the plan in the teaching situation. It is indeed more often through the way PE is taught that broader aims can be achieved – that is, *how* you teach. Of course, *what* you teach is also important and there is a paragraph at the end of each section which identifies the activity settings that might most readily support the wider learning under discussion.

CONTRIBUTING TO THE ACHIEVEMENT OF THE BROAD CURRICULUM AIMS IN PE

All teachers, whatever their subject area, are expected to make a contribution to the broad aims of education, and there is no doubt that PE teachers can play a part in helping all pupils to move towards achieving these aims. In England these aims are to enable all pupils to become successful learners, confident individuals and responsible citizens.

Pupils who are *successful learners* enjoy their learning, make progress, achieve within their potential and are motivated to learn. While it is hoped that all pupils become successful learners in PE, it is valuable to consider the key steps we need to take to ensure this actually occurs. There are two areas to consider, one is in the planning and one is in the teaching of lessons. In planning it is important that tasks build from the current achievements of pupils. Within the lesson pupils should be challenged to make progress through progressively demanding tasks. This is, in fact, not as easy as it appears as pupils are at slightly different stages in learning. The corollary of this is that you need to plan tasks that cater for the range of abilities in the class. This approach is known as differentiation and is an important element of all planning. (See Chapter 11 on inclusive approaches to teaching.) Planning to enable all pupils to succeed is also referred to as mastery learning (Bloom, 1976). Mastery learning is a term used to focus attention on the achievement of a task by an individual rather than judging achievement against that of others. Characteristically here pupils are working on tasks appropriate to their level of ability and assessment is ipsative, that is against the pupil's previous performance. Mastery learning can be a valuable element of differentiation. Further discussion of effecting differentiation can be found in Chapters 3, 10 and 11.

With reference to ensuring all pupils are successful learners, as you teach a lesson, it is important to be vigilant, observing how pupils are responding to the tasks set (see Chapter 4 on observation). Pupils who are succeeding should be praised and encouraged to tackle more challenging tasks, while those who are having difficulty should be supported with guidance and perhaps a simplification of the task. Above all you, as the teacher, should be encouraging and quick to reward pupils for effort and progress. Teacher feedback to individuals is key to promoting and maintaining learning and motivation. Feedback should be positive, informative and specific to the task at hand. The importance of different forms of feedback is discussed in Chapters 5 and 10. This planning and ongoing support in lessons can, and should, be taking place whatever practical activity (or indeed theoretical/classroom-based aspect of PE) is being taught. See Figure 14.2 for some examples of the basic principles underlying this teaching.

Pupils who are *confident individuals* are described as being prepared to try new challenges and to take initiative. They make decisions and defend their own views. In addition they have the ability to live safe, healthy and fulfilling lives. Both teacher planning and teaching and the physical activity contexts (for example, gymnastics, competitive games or outdoor and adventurous activities (OAA)) in which pupils take part are important in working to achieve this aim. With respect to planning you need to give pupils the opportunity to tackle new challenges and to engage in problem-solving situations in which they have to rely on their own initiative and resources. Situations in which pupils need to discuss solutions help them to be articulate, expressing and defending their own views. These could include tasks with pupils working on their own or in pairs to create a dance or gymnastic sequence. Alternatively group tasks could be given, such as devising set play strategies in games, solving a problem in an outdoor expedition or formulating a route in an orienteering exercise.

In teaching PE lessons that aspire to develop confident individuals, pupils need to be given the time and space to explore and experiment. Additionally the teacher needs to be patient and show a belief in the pupils' ability to solve the problem or master the task. An acceptance of pupil ideas, and a willingness to discuss these, is an asset, as is genuine appreciation of solutions proposed by individuals. The recognition of an individual's contribution to group discussion and group problem solving is also to be recommended. Throughout all lessons where there is an element of risk, time should be taken to alert pupils to safety issues (see Chapter 9 for a detailed discussion of safety issues). Where appropriate, devolvement of responsibility with respect to risk control may be given to pupils. As a teacher who knows a class, you are able to judge how far and when this responsibility can be given to pupils. If you are in any doubt over this issue it is best to ask advice from your head of department.

Physical activity contexts in which the goal of nurturing confident individuals can be furthered are many and various. OAA provides excellent opportunities for pupils to take the initiative, encounter new challenges and solve problems. Any activity involving

ECM	Characteristics	Examples of planning to promote disposition	Examples of teaching to foster disposition	Examples of contexts in which disposition could be fostered
Successful Learners	Enjoy learning Make progress Achieve within their individual potential Show motivation to learn	Plan steps to improve work Mastery learning Differentiation	Positive atmosphere Encouragement Observe and respond to individuals	All PE contexts
Confident Individuals	Be prepared to try new challenges Be able to make decisions Be able to defend own views Have the ability to live safe, healthy and fulfilling lives	Plan new experiences Plan open-ended tasks Allow for discussion Plan input on safety and health issues	Show belief in pupils' ability Encourage Accept individual ideas Reward appropriate communication skills Permeate as appropriate	OAA, Gymnastics, Dance, Competitive games Group planning tasks OAA, HRE
Responsible Citizens	Be aware of others' needs as well as own Be trustworthy Realise different roles are needed for a group to function effectively Have the ability to make a positive contribution to school/family/ society	Plan group activities Devolve responsibility Identify different roles in group tasks	Reward caring behaviour Reward appropriate behaviour Reward respect for others' roles Teacher sets a good example of appropriate behaviour	Group activities Off-site situations, e.g. camping Group activities in which there are a number of key roles to be played, follow up discussion of these

■ **Figure 14.2** Achieving ECM aims through PE

problem solving and/or group work provides a rich context for realising this goal. Similarly, any activity in which there are safety risks, such as some events in athletics, can provide a setting to develop pupils' awareness of and response to potential hazards. See Figure 14.2 for some suggestions for promoting the development of confident individuals in your teaching. Task 14.2 asks you to think of specific activity contexts that foster the development of confident individuals.

Task 14.2 **PE situations to promote confidence in pupils**

1   Make a list of challenges in OAA that depend on pupils taking initiative.
2   Make a list of group tasks in gymnastics and in athletics that demand negotiation between group members.
3   Make a list of physical activity contexts that have no health and safety risks.

Share these lists with another student teacher and then put them into your PDP.

Pupils who are *responsible citizens* are aware of others' needs as well as their own. They are trustworthy and realise that different roles are needed for a group to function effectively. Furthermore, they have the ability to make a positive contribution to the class, the school and the community. The planning and teaching of PE can both contribute to achieving this broad educational aim. The contribution principally centres around group work and pupils taking different roles and having different responsibilities in relation to group challenges. An example of this type of work is exemplified in the concept of *Sport Education* (Siedentop, 1994). Here pupils work in groups on a long-term project such as the preparation to take part in a tournament. The group assigns each member with a clear role, which could be, for example, team captain, referee, oversight of equipment needed or schedule planning for practices. Roles could involve leadership, planning, recording or liaison with other groups. Above all pupils need to be aware that to make a group function effectively all must play their part. Planning for such experiences should include a range of group activities in which participants face familiar or novel challenges. You must plan tasks in which it is safe to devolve responsibility, judging carefully what pupils should be able to do. Ideally careful planning of specific roles that different pupils are to adopt, ensures that all have the experience of taking on a range of different responsibilities.

In the teaching situation teacher observation and feedback needs to focus on how well the individuals are taking and using responsibility and how far they are sensitive to and accommodating the needs of others. Appropriate support, guidance and praise should address these areas of pupil endeavour. For example, if a pupil has been assigned a leadership role you may need to observe carefully how far this individual is being successful and step in to give support, perhaps reminding pupils of the responsibilities you have delegated to members of the group.

As in respect of promoting confident individuals, the nurturing of responsible citizens can be incorporated into a number of physical activity contexts. Any aspect of PE involving group work that demands collaboration and accommodation is a useful context for developing sensitivity to others. Group work that requires problem solving, discussion and allocation of roles is also valuable, as are situations in which responsibilities are devolved to group members. However, this does not happen without being planned and taught. There are many settings in PE where these challenges are part of the activity. For example, in team building in games, choreography in synchronised swimming and group challenges in OAA.

Chapter 7 in Capel, Breckon and O'Neill (2006) has a useful section on moral development and Activities 7.6a. and 7.6b are valuable. Further examples in respect of supporting pupils in becoming responsible citizens through PE are to be found in Figure 14.2. Task 14.3 challenges you to observe and identify the ways that individuals in groups work together on a task (setting up groups is covered in Chapter 6).

Task 14.3 Recognising how pupils work together

Observe three situations in PE in which pupils are asked to collaborate in groups. Examples could be: a group charged to set up their own arrangement of apparatus in gymnastics, a group asked to create a synchronised swimming sequence and a group set the challenge to devise a circuit to develop stamina.

Observe the pupils as they work. Note down the part that each individual plays. Are there leaders in the group? Are there those who are hard to please? Are there those who take little part in the enterprise and accept the ideas of others?

Consider what feedback you might give to the group and/or individuals to develop the ability of the group to work together. Discuss these ideas with your tutor and put your thoughts in your PDP.

PROMOTING PERSONAL LEARNING AND THINKING SKILLS (PLTS) IN PE

In order to realise the achievement of the broad aims of education, the government in England has identified six PLTS (see further reading for website) that all areas of the curriculum are expected to take steps to develop as they work with pupils. These skills are expressed as aspirations through which pupils should become Independent Enquirers, Creative Thinkers, Reflective Learners, Team Workers, Self-managers and Effective Participants. These are closely related to the broad aims and point towards the skills pupils need to acquire to achieve the aims. In most cases mastering PLTS depends on the way that the pupils are engaged in their learning, in other words the methods of teaching adopted by the teacher. Lesson planning, teaching and appropriate physical activity contexts are discussed below in respect of the first three skills named above.

The characteristics that *independent enquirers* exhibit are suggested as the ability to identify questions and problems, the confidence to explore ideas, the motivation to analyse and evaluate issues and subsequently to support answers and conclusions found.

There are many situations in PE in which becoming familiar with and mastering the material of the subject can be achieved through pupil investigation rather than teacher direction. Lesson plans that include setting problems and challenges give pupils the experience of using their own initiative and should develop the confidence to rely less on the teacher and more on their own endeavour. The teaching strategies of Guided Discovery, Convergent Discovery and Divergent Discovery would be valuable in this context. A wide range of examples of using these styles can be found in Mosston and Ashworth (2002). Planning for this type of enquiry should always leave time for discussion.

In the teaching of these lessons your role is less of an instructor and more of a guide. Having set the problem or challenge, you should leave plenty of time for the pupils to develop their own work. Keen observation shows you where sensitive support is needed. Teacher feedback should reward the individual's effort, supporting, as far as appropriate, pupil suggestions. In interacting with the pupil you should show respect for pupil ideas, thus giving pupils confidence in the value of their own input to the lesson. During the time set aside for discussion you should be patient and encouraging, praising effective solutions and suggesting ways that other solutions can be modified and made more pertinent.

Most PE contexts can accommodate this type of teaching. Forms of discovery learning are, however, not appropriate in situations in which there are high-risk safety factors. See Figure 14.3 for the basic principles underlying this teaching.

Task 14.4 asks you to identify situations in PE in which types of discovery learning would be appropriate.

Task 14.4 **Discovery learning in PE**

Discuss with another student teacher specific situations in which it would be appropriate to use teaching approaches to encourage independent enquiry on the part of the pupils, in three of the following areas: dance (e.g. selecting a poem on which to base a solo dance), gymnastics (e.g. discovering how to increase the speed of a turn), athletics (e.g. experiment with ways to pass the baton in a relay), games (e.g. ways of deceiving an opponent), and HRE (e.g. plan a group circuit to support the promotion of flexibility and stamina for a physical activity of your choice). Record your ideas in your PDP.

Creative thinkers are described as being able to generate ideas, adopt innovative approaches and respond effectively in novel situations. In a sense creative thinking develops from independent enquiry, building from the confidence to suggest solutions into the capacity to create new ideas.

Planning to promote creative thinking must include opportunities in which pupils are free to explore, innovate and create. Open-ended tasks and divergent teaching approaches (see Mosston and Ashworth, 2002) are likely to be the most effective. These situations are those in which there is no set answer to a task or problem and pupils are expected to use their own imagination and initiative. For example, the challenge to create a gymnastic or dance sequence exemplifying certain moves or relationships, the challenge to map out a route between two fixed points that can be followed unobtrusively, or the challenge to devise a secret sign language in relation to set plays in games. Time must be allowed in planning for trial and error experiences and for creativity to develop and blossom.

In the teaching situation you need to make it clear that novel ideas put forward by pupils are not only desirable but also valued. Throughout the process you can give guidance by questioning and prompting, to help pupils think widely round the problem set.

Personal, learning and thinking skill	Examples	Examples of planning to promote skill	Examples of teaching to promote skill	Examples of contexts in which skill could be fostered in PE
Independent enquirers	Identify questions/ problems Explore issues Analyse and evaluate Support conclusions	Plan situations in which Discovery (Guided, Convergent or Divergent) is appropriate Leave time for analysis and discussion	Reward individual effort/ideas Support new exploration Support self-evaluation Question views	All PE situations in which any form of Discovery (Guided, Convergent or Divergent) is appropriate. This could include athletics, life saving and martial arts
Creative thinkers	Generate ideas Ask questions Work with others in generating and solving problem Adapt to new ideas	Plan situations in which new thinking is demanded, by individual and group Give time for trial and error	Accept all appropriate ideas Welcome debate Reward group dialogue Reward good new ideas	All PE situations where open-ended tasks are appropriate, e.g. gymnastics, dance, OAA, team planning in games
Reflective learners	Assess self and others Set goals for their own work Review progress Invite feedback	Introduce learners to assessment criteria and AforL Devolve this responsibility gradually Reward honest debate	Set an example of AforL/ positive approach to assessment Support/reward self-assessment	All PE situations where it is appropriate to self-assess and set personal goals

■ **Figure 14.3** Promoting PLTS through PE

The teacher should accept all ideas that are appropriate and reward effort and application even where little has been created. Pupils need to realise that becoming a creative thinker is a process that takes time and that early attempts may be less successful or innovative. Above all you need to convey to pupils that they are capable of generating ideas and that this is not the sole preserve of the teacher. It is possibly worth saying that effective innovation only occurs in situations in which the pupils are already equipped with the necessary knowledge and experience to engage in a particular creative challenge. Creativity is very often the result of novel ways of combining elements of a task. For example, pupils may be asked in a synchronised swimming lesson to create a sequence including a number of moves. The creativity here is evident in the innovative ways that one move flows smoothly into the next and the order in which the moves are performed.

Creative thinking in PE can be fostered in activities such as dance and gymnastics where compositions are devised by pupils. In team games there are opportunities for planning new tactics and formations and in OAA there is ample opportunity to find new solutions to challenges and to invent responses to novel situations. See Figure 14.3 for further examples of aspects of teaching to promote creative thinkers.

Pupils who can be described as *reflective learners* are able to stand back and assess their own learning. They can review their progress and set their own goals. In addition, they welcome feedback from others and are willing to consider any advice or guidance.

Planning teaching to encourage reflective learning requires that clear guidance is given in respect to what is to be learned. This specification needs to be followed up by opportunities for pupils to assess themselves against these targets. The teaching strategy of Self-check (Mosston and Ashworth, 2002) is designed to accommodate this approach. It is useful to note that it can be valuable for pupils to experience Reciprocal Teaching before embarking on assessing themselves. In reciprocal teaching peers work together, usually with a criteria sheet, and evaluate each other's work against these criteria. In a self-assessment situation it is often useful for pupils to have a criteria sheet to refer to. This is a situation in which ICT can be valuable in the form of video or still photography. These types of technology can enable the pupil to see exactly how they are performing. (See Chapter 12 for a discussion of ICT in teaching PE.) Where ICT is employed time needs to be built into the lesson so that it can be used to full effect. Examples of situations in which pupils can begin to take responsibility for self-assessment could include reference to video recording in improving a dance motif, a gymnastic skill or a trampolining move or situations in which pupils are considering the effect of different tactics in running a long-distance race. Equally a pupil could be asked to reflect on the part they played in a competitive game situation, identifying personal strengths and areas to be developed.

In lessons adopting a self-assessment approach your role as the teacher is to support the pupils as they make judgements about their progress. Encouragement and recognition of pupil effort is essential. You should promote a positive 'assessment for learning' approach (see Chapter 8), which, rather than always looking for deficiencies, is focused on how improvements can be made. It is valuable to devise a system of record keeping so that pupils can build from previous work when they return to lessons in the future. In preparation for significant devolvement of responsibility to pupils for assessing their progress, it is valuable to engage frequently with pupils in a dialogue asking them to share how they feel they are progressing. This exercise can be carried out between pupils working in pairs. The practice of ending a lesson with a recapitulation of what has been worked on and learnt can also act as a preparation for later devolvement of the responsibility for self-assessment. Task 14.5 involves your observation of an experienced teacher helping pupils to become responsible for their own and others' learning.

Task 14.5 **Devolving responsibility for assessment to pupils**

Observe a lesson during which the teacher is devolving elements of assessment to pupils. Record the support given to learners and the feedback given by the teacher. Note key teaching approaches that enabled this devolvement of responsibility to be effective.

Discuss with the teacher in what ways pupils had been prepared in previous lessons to take on this responsibility. Put the record and the notes in your PDP.

The development of reflective learners can take place in every PE context as learning is at the heart of all PE and it is always appropriate to work with pupils in assessing their progress. The abilities that are fostered in reflective learning are a key element of learning how to learn. Honest self-assessment and planning for further appropriate experiences in order to gain knowledge and understanding helps to equip pupils to face the wide range of challenges that they will encounter throughout life. Further examples in respect of promoting reflective learners in PE are to be found in Figure 14.3.

Teaching approaches that contribute to promoting *Team Workers*, *Self-managers* and *Effective Participants* are closely related to those which have been described in respect of some of the ECM aims. Task 14.6 below asks you to complete a simple chart for these three PLTS. It is suggested that you consider if any of the teaching methods and contexts recommended in respect of the ECM aims could be applied to this task.

Task 14.6 **Promoting PLTS through PE**

Complete a grid, as set out below, for each of the skills related to becoming Team Workers, Self-managers and Effective Participants referring to the suggestions made with respect to achieving the ECM aims. Before completing each grid it would be useful to consider the specific characteristics that a pupil with the skill in question would demonstrate. Discuss your completed grid with your tutor, justifying your selection of planning, teaching and contexts. Compare your completed grid with the ideas in Figure 14.4 on this book's website (www.routledge.com/textbooks/9780415561648). Put the completed charts in your PDP. *One example is given below:*

Skill	Examples of planning to promote skill	Examples of teaching to promote skill	Examples of contexts in which skill could be fostered in PE
Team Workers	*Challenges set for groups to create or problem solve*	*Observation and feedback to the group and individuals, encouraging use of communication and listening skills*	*Group planning for a synchronised swimming sequence*

Task 14.7 is designed to encourage you to look back at all the PLTS and to consider how they might be developed in the teaching example specified.

Task 14.7 **Identifying PLTS in a HRE setting**

Within a Health-Related Exercise unit of work, pupils have been challenged to develop, implement and monitor a personal exercise programme designed to improve cardiovascular and muscular endurance. Consider carefully how pupils are likely to be involved in the task and, with reference to the sections above, identify PLTS which could well be developed by the pupils and consider how far the aims of ECM may be addressed.

Discuss your ideas with another student teacher who has also carried out this task and put your notes in your PDP.

EXAMPLES OF PE LEARNING ACTIVITIES THAT CAN PROVIDE OPPORTUNITIES FOR ADDRESSING BROAD EDUCATIONAL AIMS

Examples now follow of PE learning activities that can readily be utilised to enable pupils to develop a wide range of skills, qualities and knowledge shown in Figure 14.1 and discussed above. You can see how it is often a combination of teaching method and content that facilitates the achievement of a variety of multiple ILOs. This understanding ultimately helps you use, select and develop a wide range of approaches in planning and teaching lessons. After each of the examples a task (14.8 and 14.9) is suggested to encourage you to look in more detail at the teaching in each situation.

Example 14.1

Consider a class of pupils divided into small groups, tasked with developing a simple motif into a small group dance. They need to work collaboratively, be creative and make decisions about the way in which the motif is developed. Along the way, they need to evaluate their performance and consider ways in which it might be improved. In addition to this, they are working on their performance skills and, as result of the whole process, are developing their physical capacities as well as experiencing ways of learning.

This relatively simple task requires pupils to encounter most of the Key Processes in PE, for example, being creative and making decisions, evaluating and improving and developing skills. At the same time they are addressing the Key PE Concepts of Creativity, Performance and Competence.

In addition the way that the pupils are involved in their learning involves their using a range of PLTS. For example, they need to think creatively, reflect on their learning, be an effective team worker and collaborate with others. With sensitive guidance from the teacher all pupils should make progress towards all the ECM aims, namely, becoming Successful Learners, Confident Individuals and Responsible Citizens.

Task 14.8 **Giving feedback in a lesson focused on developing creativity**

With reference to Example 14.1 discuss with your tutor which aspects of pupil response feedback in the lesson should be addressed, e.g. group collaboration, creativity, self-assessment. Put these notes in your PDP.

Example 14.2

A group of pupils following a programme of Sport Education need to evaluate performance and make decisions about the skills needing to be developed to enable effective participation in a forthcoming tournament. Given the need for them to organise not only the ways in which their skills and tactical knowledge might be improved, but also the organisation of and officiating within the tournament, there is clearly enormous scope to develop both physical capacity and PLTS. Sport Education provides a good opportunity for pupils, as they collaborate together, to practise the PLTS of team workers and effective participants. As they review progress, they are also involved in reflection and, possibly, creative challenges, such as problem solving. These experiences should also feed forward into supporting pupils as Successful Learners, Confident Individuals and Responsible Citizens.

Task 14.9 **Devolving responsibility in a Sport Education context**

With reference to Example 14.2 discuss with your tutor ways in which you can ensure that every member of each group has the opportunity to experience different roles within the group enterprise. Put your notes in your PDP.

FURTHER CONSIDERATIONS

It should be borne in mind that pupils do not achieve the broader curriculum aims without a clear learning focus or appropriately structured learning activities. An academic review conducted by Bailey *et al.* (2009) examined critically the claims made for the potential of PE in developing physical, social, affective and cognitive skills, qualities and knowledge. The review served to confirm the *potential* of PE, but was less supportive of any genuinely strong developmental benefit beyond the enhancement of physical skills. This may well be due in part to the tendency of PE teachers to espouse the potential social, affective and cognitive benefits accruing from the PE experience whilst maintaining a very heavy focus in their lessons on the acquisition of physical skills. Whilst these physical skills clearly underpin the subject and represent its unique contribution to the curriculum, you are not helping young people towards a future of a full, effective and worthwhile life if you neglect to pay attention, as appropriate, to the broad aims of education.

It may be the case that in order to promote some of these broader aspirations in the context of PE, elements of a lesson may be less focused on the practical activity and more concerned with, for example, creativity or team work. However, this is seldom a threat to achieving PE-specific aims as the 'non-physical' skills and abilities being fostered have a clear beneficial effect on progress in PE. Of course a balance needs to be struck between the range of challenges set for pupils in a lesson. It would very seldom be appropriate to devote a whole lesson to non-physically active work. On the other hand, to disregard the responsibility to work towards pupils achieving broader aims would be denying them a range of valuable opportunities that cannot be replicated in any other subject area. Furthermore the acknowledgement of the responsibility PE teachers have to play a significant part in pupils' total experience of education recognises the holistic nature of each of us as humans.

Being aware of this, and gradually letting this area of your responsibility appear clearly in your planning and your provision of related learning experiences, assists you greatly in becoming a valuable and valued member of the education community. You will feel able to contribute more fully to supporting the ethos of the whole school through your work within a PE context. As a teacher you have a responsibility to nurture broader curriculum aims beyond the PE department. You may well have a tutor group and may also have the responsibility to lead sessions with your tutor group on personal, social, health and economic education (PSHE education). Throughout all your dealings with pupils it is essential that you keep the broader aims of education in mind, setting a good example yourself and encouraging and recognising progress in areas such as effective collaboration and self-management.

Task 14.10 comprises a range of tasks which are designed to help you with Master's level work.

Task 14.10 **The contribution of PE to broader educational goals**

■ Read and critically analyse the Bailey *et al*. (2008) article (see further reading). Discuss your views with another student teacher. Record areas of agreement and disagreement

■ Carry out a SWOT analysis on the benefits or otherwise of PE contributing to broader curriculum aims. This is a square divided into four equal squares, headed Strengths, Weaknesses, Opportunities, Threats (an outline grid is on this book's website (www.routledge.com/textbooks/9780415561648). Present and defend the content of your SWOT chart in a meeting with your tutor.

■ Write an essay of 2,000 words on the dangers of PE being valued *only* in the context of the subject being a means to ends beyond the mastery of physical competence.

Put all these records in your PDP. These notes could well be referred to in writing an application for a job and subsequently attending an interview.

SUMMARY AND KEY POINTS

This chapter has shown that the aims of PE are closely aligned to many of the broad curriculum aims and that PE can play a significant part in the achievement of these aspirations. Specifically the chapter has looked at ways that PE can foster the underlying principles of the UK government's ECM policy and can play a significant part in promoting PLTS. Success depends on thoughtful planning and on sensitive delivery of lessons. PE is a powerful context for enabling pupils to learn how to learn. There is a wealth of opportunities in PE to develop, for example, creativity, independence and team work. Work in many contexts in PE has the potential to make a significant contribution to achieving the broader aims of education. You have the opportunity to make a real difference to the all round education of pupils, far beyond the confines of the gymnasium and the sports field.

Check which requirements for your course you have addressed through this chapter.

FURTHER READING

Bailey, R., Armour, K., Kirk, D., Jess, M., Pickup, I. and Sandford, R. (British Educational Research Association (BERA) Physical Education and Sport Pedagogy Special Interest Group) (2008) **The educational benefits claimed for physical education and school sport: an academic review**, *Research Papers in Education*, 24, 1, March: 1–27.
This detailed paper looks at the research into the benefits of PE, specifically at Physical, Affective, Social and Cognitive areas of development.

Capel, S. and Piotrowski, S. (eds) (2000) *Issues in Physical Education*, London: Routledge.
Chapter 1 provides a useful discussion concerning PE achieving broader aims. Chapter 9 looks at issues surrounding helping pupils to work effectively in competitive and cooperative settings.

Gardner, H. (1993) *Frames of Mind – The Theory of Multiple Intelligences*, 2nd edn, London: Fontana.
Gardner's theory of multiple intelligences can be helpful both in encouraging you to extend your view of the concept of intelligence and in coming to recognise how 'non-kinesthetic' intelligences might be developed through a predominantly kinesthetic medium.

Leaver, B.L. (1997) *Teaching the Whole Class*, 4th edn, Thousand Oaks, CA: Corwin Press.
Once you have developed a wider appreciation of the potential for learning inherent within PE, Leaver's clearly written guide to teaching the whole class can help you on two major fronts. First, it provides practical help as you look to respond to the range of learning needs and influential factors you meet within any group of learners. Second, and more relevant to the subject of this chapter, as you come to appreciate the range of pupil characteristics and skills to which you have to adapt your teaching, so you come to appreciate the potential of your teaching to develop within pupils' characteristics and skills that you might have thought at first were not related to PE.

Mosston, M. and Ashworth, S. (2002) *Teaching Physical Education*, 5th edn, Columbus: Merrill Publishing Co.
This book covers a variety of teaching strategies that can be valuable in promoting broader educational aims.

Penney, D. and Chandler, T. (2000) **Physical education: what future(s)?**, *Sport, Education and Society*, 5, 1: 71–87.
This article challenges the appropriateness of a focus on physical activities in PE and recommends a broader approach. The two articles below are shortened versions of this more complex paper, but are useful introductions to the issues discussed.

Penney, D. (1999) PE in changing times, is it time for a change?, *British Journal of Physical Education*, 30, 2: 4–6.

Penney, D. and Chandler, T. (2000) A curriculum without connections?, *British Journal of Teaching Physical Education*, 31, 2: 37–40.

It will be easier to appreciate and grasp the connections between PE and wider educational goals if you are able first of all to make connections and see the potential for transferability of learning within the subject itself. This journal article by Penney and Chandler provides a clearly written first step in this regard.

Website for further discussion of PLTS: http://curriculum.qcda.gov.uk/key-stages-3-and-4/skills/plts/index.aspx

14–19 ACCREDITED QUALIFICATIONS

Gill Golder

INTRODUCTION

In England, Wales and Northern Ireland accredited qualifications in PE have developed significantly over the past two decades and are now a key aspect of the work of PE departments to consider when designing their curriculum. Some of the reasons for the development of 14–19 qualifications were highlighted in the Children's Plan (Department for Children, Schools and Families (DCSF), 2007), which identified the changing economy as a driver to ensure that young people have the right skills to move into further or higher education or into work; setting a target that by 2015 all young people will stay on in education or training to 18 and beyond. The Department for Education and Skills (DfES) (2005b: 4) highlighted:

> The 14–19 reforms will give all young people the opportunity to choose a mix of learning which motivates, interests and challenges them, and which gives them the knowledge, skills and attitude they need to succeed in education, work, and life.

Leney (2003) suggests that the development of the 14–19 curriculum is not just a UK phenomenon. Reform of education and training systems in all European countries reflects the different kinds of skills and knowledge that people will need for the future in their personal, social and economic activities. The 14–19 reforms share three goals widely found in almost every national and international policy document on qualifications frameworks. They should:

- be transparent in terms of what they signify and what must be achieved;
- minimise barriers to progression, both vertical and horizontal;
- maximise access, flexibility and portability between different sectors of education and work and different sites of learning.

(Young, 2003: 224)

In England, Wales and Northern Ireland three public service agreement targets (DCSF, 2008b) shape the range of qualifications, structure of learning and accountability of opportunities. These are to:

- ensure that, until at least their eighteenth birthday, all young people participate in education and training that stretches and challenges them to achieve their potential and go on to further or higher education or skilled employment;

■ give young people the knowledge and skills that employers and the economy need to prosper in the twenty-first century;

■ close the achievement gap so that all have an equal opportunity to succeed, irrespective of gender, race, disability or background.

This chapter first examines the developing 14–19 curriculum (DCSF, 2008c) and the place of the Qualifications and Credit Framework (QCF) within it (pp. 235–239); second it discusses the range of accredited qualifications available in PE within the 14–19 curriculum (pp. 239–242); and third it considers the implications of accredited qualifications in PE on teaching and learning approaches (pp. 242–250).

With the 14–19 reforms comes a need for you to prepare for the diversity of teaching and learning environments and opportunities you may face both in school placements and in your future career. You need to reflect on the professional knowledge, skills and attributes you need to meet the diverse 14–19 curriculum, develop your professional knowledge to plan, deliver and assess the 14–19 curriculum and build your professional skills to meet the needs of all pupils through interactive, challenging and engaging learning opportunities.

OBJECTIVES

At the end of this chapter you should be able to:

■ have an overview of the 14–19 reforms in England, Wales and Northern Ireland;

■ understand the 14–19 curriculum and the place of the QCF within it;

■ understand the diversity of accredited qualifications available in PE and PE-related areas within the 14–19 curriculum;

■ be aware of teaching and learning approaches for theoretical and practical aspects of accredited qualifications in PE;

■ understand the range of assessment procedures for accredited qualifications.

Check the requirements for your course to see which relate to this chapter.

THE 14–19 CURRICULUM AND THE QUALIFICATIONS AND CREDIT FRAMEWORK (QCF)

The DCSF (2008c) has the aim that the 14–19 education and skills reforms makes learning after the age of 14 years a more engaging experience for young people by giving them a wider choice of learning opportunities. One aim of these reforms is to increase participation in formal education at age 17 from 75 per cent to 90 per cent over a ten year period. To achieve this aim, a new entitlement has been developed to provide the right learning opportunities for all young people aged 14–19 years.

The entitlements for 14–19 year olds are incorporated into the QCF, which is designed to be inclusive and simple to understand. It provides a simple way to recognise and accredit qualifications in England, Wales and Northern Ireland. It does this by attaching importance to achievement through the award of credits for units (i.e. parts of a full qualification) and full qualifications. The European Qualifications Framework (EQF) for Life Long Learning has a similar function, enabling European countries to link their qualifications systems to one another. The development of the QCF is at the heart of a major reform of the qualifications system, especially vocational qualifications, as it aims to make both the system and the qualifications offered more relevant to the needs of employers and more flexible and accessible for young people. This is achieved by enabling young people to follow flexible routes to gain full qualifications and to achieve qualifications in small steps.

The DCSF set out the entitlement for all young people, aged 14–19 years, to the right learning opportunities. The statutory requirements of this entitlement are that all young people study, as part of the new secondary curriculum, the Key Stage 4 core of English, mathematics, and science and the foundation subjects of information and communications technology (ICT), PE and citizenship. In addition, all pupils study religious education, sex, drug, alcohol and tobacco education and careers education. They should also have opportunities for work-related learning and enterprise, and the opportunity to study at least one of the arts, design and technology (D&T), the humanities or modern foreign languages (MFL). The final element of the entitlement is that all pupils develop functional skills in English, mathematics and ICT and personal learning and thinking skills (PLTS). These are incorporated into the secondary curriculum, the General Certificate of Secondary Education (GCSE) and General Certificate of Education Advanced (A) levels, Diplomas, Foundation Learning Tier and Apprenticeships.

At the heart of this reform of the 14–19 curriculum is the opportunity for young people to gain qualifications in one of four routes of learning:

■ General qualifications: GCSE, A level (comprising Advanced Supplementary (AS) level (the first three units representing the first half of an A level course of study, the second half (known as A2), comprising another three units of study), and Advanced Extension (AE), comprising a single piece of work requiring a high degree of planning, preparation, research and autonomous working alongside their A level), and International Baccalaureate (IB) (IB Middle and IB Diploma). There is also a Welsh Baccalaureate. General qualifications are designed to provide candidates with knowledge and understanding of their chosen subject.

■ Diplomas: available at three levels, Foundation (equivalent to 5 GCSEs at grade D and below), Higher (equivalent to 7 GCSEs at grade C–A*) and Advanced (equivalent to 3.5 A levels). These are designed to combine theoretical study with practical experiential learning of a range of widely applicable skills and knowledge, set within a 'specialised' context, e.g. Sport and Active Leisure. There is a Progression Diploma (equivalent to 2.5 A levels).

■ Foundation learning tier: high-quality credit-based qualifications at entry level and level 1. These are designed to increase participation, achievement and progression for pupils working below level 2.

■ Apprenticeships: one to four year courses where apprentices learn on the job, building up knowledge and skills, gaining qualifications such as the National Vocational Qualification (NVQ), Key Skills or Business and Technician Education Council

(BTEC) and earning money at the same time, e.g. Apprenticeship in Leisure, Travel and Tourism. These are designed to give pupils knowledge and skills for specific employment yet also transferable skills across different sectors.

Throughout their 14–19 education pupils are entitled to information, advice and guidance to help them make the most suitable choices.

General and Diploma qualifications are generally taught in schools and therefore are covered in more detail later in this chapter. BTEC and Oxford and Cambridge Regional (OCR) First and National qualifications and some NVQ qualifications are currently offered in schools. As the 14–19 entitlement develops it is intended that BTECs will continue to be available through the Additional and Specialist Learning component of the Diploma (these vocational subjects currently offered in schools are explored later in this chapter and within Apprenticeship frameworks. For further information about foundation tier learning and apprenticeships, refer to http://www.dcsf.gov.uk/14-19/).

The intention of the routes is to give pupils the opportunity to combine qualifications and tailor their learning programmes to meet their specific needs. To support this, there is flexibility built into the entitlement and, in turn, flexibility in progression within and between routes. Schools and colleges are able to provide opportunities for their pupils to study qualifications that do not fall under the four routes, providing there is clear rationale to maintain pupils' interests or re-engage them in learning. This flexibility between routes to respond to individual needs is shown by an example. A year 10 pupil (aged 14–15 years) could be following National Curriculum core (English, mathematics and science) and foundation subjects (including PE), alongside a higher diploma in Sport and Active Leisure. This may be built upon by additional specialist learning, e.g. Sports Coach UK leaders awards or complemented by studying a qualification in another subject, e.g. GCSE in French.

The 14–19 accredited qualifications studied in schools and colleges are predominantly between entry level and level 3 of the 8 level QCF (see Figure 15.1). The higher the level the more difficult the qualification, with qualifications at the same level being considered broadly similar in terms of the demand they place on the individual e.g. Advanced Diploma in Sport and Active Leisure and A Levels.

The majority of accredited qualifications studied by 14–19 year olds are between entry level and level 3. Figure 15.1 shows the levels and qualifications at each level, as well as how credits could be gained for part of a full award at levels 1 to 3. At each level these credits are split into three separate qualification categories (award, certificate and diploma) based upon the number of units completed (the size/duration). For example, a GCSE at grade B, where over 370 guided learning hours have been completed, would be a full level 2 qualification; whereas an NVQ at level two, where units worth up to 120 guided learning hours have been completed, would be a level 2 'award'. Pupils who have completed 1 out of the 4 units at A level would have completed approximately 95 guided learning hours at level 3 (for more information see http://www.qcda.gov.uk/8150.aspx).

The Qualifications and Curriculum Authority (QCA) (England), the Department for Education, Lifelong Learning and Skills (DELLS) (Wales) and the Council for the Curriculum Examinations and Assessment (CCEA) (Northern Ireland) (2006) suggest that there are benefits of the QCF for learning providers (schools, colleges, and workplaces), employers and young people. Learning providers benefit by being able to design

QCF Level (lowest at bottom)	Examples of qualifications in each level (Note: levels 4-8 are part of the framework of higher education)			
Level 8	Doctorate and specialist qualifications			
Level 7	Master's degree Postgraduate certificates and diplomas			
Level 6	Honour's degree Graduate certificates and diplomas			
Level 5	Diploma of higher education and further education Foundation degrees Higher National Diplomas			
Level 4	Certificate of higher education			
Level 3	A levels (including AS, A2 and AE) IB Diploma Advanced Welsh Baccalaureate Advanced Diploma (and shorter progression diploma) NVQ level 3 BTEC or OCR National Diploma	Credits can be awarded for completion of part of these qualifications within the credit framework. For every ten guided learning hours completed a 'unit' can be claimed		
		'Awards' are given for 1–12 units therefore up to 120 guided learning hours	'Certificates' for 12–36 units therefore up to 360 guided learning hours	'Diploma' is the full level two qualification with 37 or more units therefore 370 or more guided learning hours
Level 2	GCSEs Grades A*–C IB Middle Intermediate Welsh Baccalaureate Higher Diploma NVQ level 2 BTEC or OCR First Diploma			
Level 1	GCSEs Grades D–G Foundation Welsh Baccalaureate Foundation Diploma NVQ level 1 BTEC or OCR Introductory Diploma			
Entry level	Entry level certificate			

■ **Figure 15.1** The qualifications in the Qualifications and Credit Framework (QCF)

more personalised programmes to suit individuals, which, in turn, have knock-on effects for retention and progress. Credits and qualifications are logged on an individual achievement record enabling learning providers to track progress and set suitable learning challenges. Employers benefit by gaining access to in-house training approved within a QCF, helping employees gain credit for achievements on employer-led programmes. Now complete Task 15.1.

Task 15.1 **The 14–19 curriculum**

Search accredited qualifications in the National QCF, using the website search engine below. Find five different qualifications at each of entry level, level 1, level 2 and level 3: http://www.accreditedqualifications.org.uk/index.aspx.

Obtain a copy of the 14–19 curriculum and range of qualifications available in your placement school. What is offered as part of the 14–19 curriculum and at what levels?

Compare what is offered in your placement school with what is offered in another school in which another student teacher is placed. Store your findings in your professional development portfolio (PDP).

THE DIVERSITY OF ACCREDITED QUALIFICATIONS AVAILABLE IN PE AND PE-RELATED AREAS WITHIN THE 14–19 CURRICULUM

The breadth of 14–19 accredited qualifications in which PE sits is vast. The content of PE in core curriculum is governed by key concepts and processes outlined in the National Curriculum for Physical Education (QCA, 2008b) (Chapter 13 covers the National Curriculum in England), and the wider goals to which PE contributes (see Chapter 14). The range of accredited PE qualifications which fit into the entitlement of the QCF and which are generally taught in schools is outlined below (i.e. general qualifications, the diploma and vocational qualifications).

General qualifications

General qualifications in PE include the *GCSE*, short and full courses and *A level* (AS, A2 levels and AE). The examination awarding bodies (i.e. AQA (Assessment and Qualifications Alliance), Edexcel, OCR, CCEA (Northern Ireland Council for the Curriculum, Examinations and Assessment) and WJEC (Welsh Joint Education Committee)) publish detailed specifications of the content which must be covered within these qualifications. Pupils engage in a wide range of topics and issues as they study for general qualifications, including biomechanics, elite performance, historical and sociocultural effects, physiological and psychological effects on performance. In these pupils are expected to demonstrate their knowledge and understanding of the subject content specified in the curriculum and, to a certain extent, are also expected to apply the specified content through illustration and exemplification. The range of assessment is explored in more detail later in the chapter, but includes a variety of types of coursework (e.g. analysis of performance in GCSE PE, synoptic assessment in A2, applied learning projects in the diploma), examinations and practical performance elements (e.g. personal competence and performance is assessed in both GCSE Dance and GCSE PE, in a range of activities, sports or individual pursuits). In addition to the subject-specific content, pupils are also expected to use and develop their functional skills (English, mathematics, ICT) and PLTS whilst displaying positive attitudes and attributes to learning (Chapter 14 covers the wider aspects of learning). Now complete Task 15.2.

Task 15.2 **Compare examination specifications for GCSE**

Obtain a copy of the GCSE PE specifications from two different awarding bodies (AQA (www.aqa.org.uk), Edexcel (www.edexcel.com), OCR (www.ocr.org.uk), CCEA (www.ccea.org.uk) or WJEC (www.wjec.co.uk):

■ identify the differences in percentage of marks given for the following components: coursework, final examination and practical;
■ with reference to the structure of the examinations, examine how and when different components of each specification are assessed;
■ with reference to the content of the curriculum, identify which theoretical aspects are examined, what practical options are available and how the coursework is selected.

You can repeat this exercise for A level examinations from the same awarding bodies. Record this in your PDP.

In addition to traditional general qualifications the *International Baccalaureate (IB)* is now offered by a number of schools in England, Wales, Scotland and Northern Ireland (along with 134 other countries). The IB is a continuum of education, consisting of three individual programmes, with the middle years programme aimed at 11–16 year olds and the Diploma programme at 16–19 year olds. It aims to enable pupils to become inquiring, knowledgeable and caring young people who help to create a better and more peaceful world through intercultural understanding and respect (more details can be found on http://www.ibo.org/). The curriculum represents the best from many different countries rather than the exported or imported national system of any one; it is currently accessible in a wide variety of schools (national and international; public and private), in 131 countries.

The middle years programme requires pupils to study subjects from eight subject groups through five areas of interaction: approaches to learning, community and service, human ingenuity, environment, and health and social education.

For the IB Diploma programme pupils study six subjects selected from different subject groups. Normally, three subjects are studied at higher level (courses representing 240 teaching hours) and the remaining three subjects are studied at standard level (courses representing 159 teaching hours). Central to the philosophy of the IB Diploma programme and forming the compulsory core are: an extended essay; theory of knowledge (TOK); and Creativity, Action, Service (CAS). The extended essay offers the opportunity to investigate a topic of individual interest, and acquaints pupils with the independent research and writing skills expected at university. The TOK is interdisciplinary in nature, designed to provide coherence by exploring the nature of knowledge across disciplines and encouraging an appreciation of other cultural perspectives. CAS encourages involvement in artistic pursuits, sports and community service work, thus fostering their awareness and appreciation of life outside the academic arena.

The *Welsh Baccalaureate Qualification (WBQ)* combines personal development skills with existing qualifications such as GCSEs, A levels and NVQs to make one wider award.

The Diploma

The *Diploma in Sport and Active Leisure* combines theoretical and practical learning to equip young people for further or higher education and long-term employability. The blend of learning is intended to be more motivating and engaging for some pupils than either purely theoretical learning in general qualifications or occupationally specific learning, as in vocational courses. Each diploma is made up of three components. *Principal Learning* develops the knowledge, skills, understanding and attitudes associated with the Sport and Active Leisure sector, including social, political, economic and environmental dimensions of the industry. *Generic Learning* develops the general skills for learning, employability and personal capability that can be applied within the subject or sector and more widely. This comprises three *functional* skills (English, mathematics, ICT) and six *PLTS* skills (independent enquiry, creative thinking, reflective learning, team working, self-management and effective participation). *Additional and/or Specialist Learning* enables pupils to deepen learning within the Sport and Active Leisure Sector and/or to broaden their curriculum by taking complementary qualifications for a successful progression pathway. The Diploma is taught at three levels, foundation, higher and advanced with a shortened progression diploma available at level 3; in this a pupil would study the principal and generic learning but not the additional or specialist learning.

The Sport and Active Leisure Diploma has three interrelated themes which underpin all levels:

■ Theme 1: Sport and active leisure and the individual.
■ Theme 2: Sport and active leisure and the economy.
■ Theme 3: Sport and active leisure and the community.

It is the intention of the diploma routinely to make connections between these different themes and modules within themes and between work-based learning and learning in the classroom. This notion of connectedness is built upon the theories of applied learning and experiential learning (see below). You might want to undertake Task 15.3, which is designed to help you to analyse the implications of undertaking this qualification.

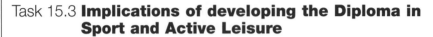

> ## Task 15.3 Implications of developing the Diploma in Sport and Active Leisure
>
> Review the content and intended forms of delivery of the Higher Diploma in Sport and Active Leisure, with particular focus on principal learning.
>
> - What implications could this have on your practice and teaching in general?
> - What structures will schools need to adopt for this qualification to work?
> - What new forms of practice will schools have to adopt if they adopt this qualification?
>
> Compare your reflections with those of another student teacher, then put in your PDP.

Vocational qualifications

Currently running alongside the four learning routes are vocational qualifications. Once the full offer of Diploma qualifications and Apprenticeships are available in 2013 these qualifications will only be available as additional or specialist learning in the Diploma or as part of an apprenticeship. However, at present, a range of vocational qualifications such as NVQs at levels 1 to 3 and BTEC or OCR Introductory (level 1), First (level 2) and National Diplomas (level 3) (these qualifications are known more commonly as BTEC when awarded by Edexcel) may be studied. Introductory, First and National diplomas are specialist work-related qualifications for the sport and leisure industry for working in, for example, public and private sector fitness clubs and leisure and health centres. These may be studied in, for example, the level 1 Introductory Certificate in Sport and Leisure, the level 2 First Diploma in Sport (Exercise and Fitness), and the level 3 Sport (Performance and Excellence). The qualifications are developed alongside the National Occupational Standards (NOS) to provide preparation for employment, further vocational study, or career development for those already in work.

NVQs are work-related, competence-based qualifications. Pupils studying these courses engage in work-related skills specified in the NOS across the active leisure and learning sector, e.g. Activity Leadership, Operational Services, Outdoor Recreation and Playwork. They are expected to demonstrate relevant sector-specific knowledge and understanding, use skills and apply knowledge and understanding to relevant tasks. Gaining a NVQ facilitates entry into, or progression in, employment, further education and training.

DEVELOPING MODELS OF APPLIED LEARNING FOR 14–19 YEARS OLDS

The development of the 14–19 accredited qualification pathways aims to do justice to the variety of ways young people develop, taking into account that: 'as individuals mature, their need and capacity to be self-directing, to use their experience in learning, to identify their own readiness to learn, and to organize their learning around life problems increases ... rapidly' (Knowles *et al.*, 2005: 62).

The concept of applied learning is at the heart of the 14–19 reforms, and hence of the entitlement to the right learning opportunities and support for all young people. The QCA (2006) define applied learning as:

> acquiring and applying knowledge, skills and understanding through tasks set in sector or subject contexts that have many of the characteristics of real work, or are set within the workplace. Most importantly, the purpose of the task in which learners apply their knowledge, skills and understanding must be relevant to the workplace.
>
> (QCA, 2006: 26)

Applied learning methods include strategies that integrate job-related or practical examples into the classroom. Applied learning provides the means for pupils to put into action the theory they are learning by engaging them in real-world situations. This involves hands on problem solving (e.g. scenario work, where pupils have to work within the boundaries of a preset context e.g. imagine they are an elite coach and they have to design a training plan for an elite athlete), cooperative or team-based activities (e.g. co-planning and running a sporting/leisure activity for a specific population), lessons that require the use of different forms of communication or interaction (e.g. presenting a multimedia project on the globalisation of sport) and projects that ask pupils to apply knowledge and skills from several domains to produce a product of some kind (e.g. planning a marketing campaign for a local sports club). Theoretical understandings and knowledge required to complete a task are drawn out from the context, which also provides the opportunity to use and apply what has been learnt. Implications of this for teaching are that teachers have to use experiential learning strategies. This is an educational strategy that connects classroom theory with practice in the real world, in which learning occurs through active involvement in what is being studied. Experiential learning comprises a spiral of experiencing, reflection, generalising, applying or replanning and transferring learning (based on Kolb's 1984 cycle). Thus, through experience, knowledge, skills and understanding in different contexts are progressively developed. The process of reflection prompts pupils to think about and draw out lessons learnt from their experience. When generalising, new insights are developed and decisions made as to how and where they can use what they have learnt, drawing conclusions from past and present experiences. Applying or replanning requires the use of new knowledge, skills or understanding in a particular context before transferring learning to new contexts. Figure 15.2 illustrates this in the context of the Diploma in Sport and Active Leisure.

Thus, the teaching approaches used to support learning on these qualifications needs to be considered carefully. This book focuses largely on teaching in the practical context. However, your ability to teach effectively to enhance pupils' learning in the classroom and their ability to apply theory to practice in both classroom and practical contexts is very important to engage pupils in their theoretical, applied and experiential learning.

The principles of teaching and learning in these contexts are the same as in practical contexts; thus, the material in this book is very relevant. However, it is important that teaching in a classroom does not become 'chalk and talk'; rather that it is active learning. This is covered in Unit 5.2 in Capel, Leask and Turner, 2009. Further guidance is also given in the further reading at the end of this chapter.

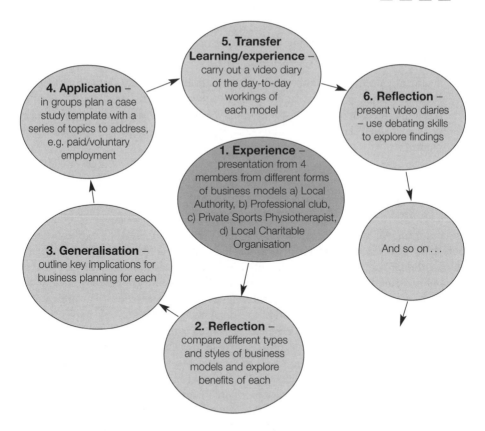

■ **Figure 15.2** An example of a project using experiential learning based on the higher theme 2 Sport and Active Leisure and the Economy, module 2.5 Business in the Sport and Active Leisure Industry

TEACHING AND LEARNING APPROACHES USED IN THE 14–19 ACCREDITED QUALIFICATIONS: A PEDAGOGY FOR THE 14–19 CURRICULUM

> I never teach my pupils; I only attempt to provide the conditions in which they can learn.
>
> (Albert Einstein)

The DfES (2007) defines pedagogy as the act of teaching and the rationale that supports the actions that teachers take. What works in terms of pedagogical approach is dependent on a range of factors. The breadth of content of 14–19 accredited qualifications, not just subject-specific (with their mix of practical, theory and applied learning) but also generic, the range of young people likely to be following the 14–19 curriculum, their motivation and previous experiences and what you are trying to achieve in any one lesson/part of a lesson support the notion that different approaches to teaching and learning are needed to provide a challenging and stimulating learning environment for all pupils.

As in planning practical lessons, from the aims and content of the larger scheme of work (the curriculum of the qualification being studied), learning should be planned into units of work, which form the basis from which individual lessons are planned. Within these, consideration needs to be given to pupils' previous learning, the intended learning outcomes (ILOs) of the particular session, the whole class learning activities and how these are differentiated, the learning (or teaching) points, the organisation and management and the teaching strategies to be used. Learning should be active to engage pupils in their learning. A prerequisite of learning is to set the challenge at the appropriate level, enabling pupils to become more independent learners. In addition, pupils should be engaged in the process of learning so that they can see what they have achieved and how they have made progress.

The structure of classroom-based lessons would also follow the same general structure of practical lessons, i.e. introduction and warm-up; main part and conclusion, although different terminology may be used, e.g. starters and plenaries. Some starters and plenaries are considered in the next section.

Starters and plenaries

As for the introduction and warm-up of a practical lesson, carefully planned starter activities are important in teaching. These are used for a variety of reasons, but predominantly they develop early levels of engagement and motivation by injecting a sense of pace and challenge and, building on prior knowledge, provide a foundation for the introduction of new topics. Teachers use a wide variety of starter activities to achieve this aim, but they all have certain aspects in common: they should contribute directly to the lesson ILOs; take account of the range of individual needs; show progression over time; have clear and concise instructions; and are referred back to at the end of the lesson for consolidating learning.

An equally successful tool for enhancing learning is the plenary (as is the conclusion in a practical lesson). It helps pupils crystallise, understand and remember what has been learned and provides a signpost for future learning. As with starter activities, teachers use a wide range of plenary activities. However, all plenary activities should be designed to suit the lesson and its ILOs and encourage reflection on what has been learned and how. Figure 15.3 exemplifies different starters and plenary activities for a range of ILOs and 14–19 qualifications. Task 15.4 asks you to look at starters and plenary activities for your lessons.

Task 15.4 **Starter and plenary activities**

Observe teachers working with classroom-based groups studying for one of the qualifications in the 14–19 framework. Note down the ILOs set, the type and purpose of starter activity and the type and purpose of plenary activity. Provide examples from three different qualifications, if possible.

Plan your own starter and plenary activity to teach one aspect of one of the qualifications taught at your placement school.

Put your findings into your PDP, use and evaluate when appropriate to develop these further.

Intended Learning Outcome	Starter activity	Purpose of activity	Plenary activity	Purpose of the activity
To be able to describe strategies to improve both short-term memory storage (chunking) and long-term memory storage. (OCR GCE Physical Education section B)	Play 'Kim's Game': 15 every day items on a tray; students study tray for 20 seconds. Remove tray, students recall items	To start discussion on what strategies people used to remember items	Body Pegs activity. Attach one strategy for improving retention and retrieval to 7 different major body parts attach a word and action to it	Develop pupils' strategies to organise and remember what they have learned
Describe nutrition, including nutritional requirements and common terminology associated with nutrition (Edexcel Level 3 BTEC National in Sport and Exercise Sciences unit 12)	Supermarket 'top trumps' – hand out a food packet with nutritional information on to each student. They compare nutritional information, scoring a point for each item e.g. daily saturated fats	To create a climate of interaction and involvement	Ready, steady, cook. Provide groups with a shopping bag of packeted food with nutritional information on, they have 5 minutes to decide what they would include and exclude to create a balanced diet	Draw out application of what has been learned
Develop an understanding of specific exercise or training programmes including advantages and disadvantages (AQA GCSE Physical Education unit 3)	Pupils are asked to match up cards carrying the name of a piece of fitness training equipment with the card containing the main muscle group it works	To develop subject specific vocabulary to be used in the lesson and understanding of existing knowledge of definitions	With a partner create one circuit training card with details of the exercise, the muscle worked and the repetition options to use in a practical context next lesson	Help pupils to change what they have learned into a form which they can communicate

■ **Figure 15.3** Examples of starter and plenary activities for three different qualifications

Interactive activities

Getting pupils to engage in learning can be as simple as ensuring that the learning environment is safe and conducive to learning and where physical and emotional needs are taken into consideration. However, interactive teaching strategies and active learning facilitate learning by involving pupils in thinking about, discussing and using ideas through a range of problem solving, guided discovery or self-directed tasks rather than more teacher-directed activities. For interactive teaching to impact most effectively on learning the teacher needs to be knowledgeable, enthusiastic, well resourced and progressive, e.g. know and understand the specification requirements (curriculum), meet the needs of the pupils (know the pupils) and create relevant resources to support your teaching and pupils' learning (understand the nature of learning). Interactive tasks need to be appropriate to the abilities and learning styles of the pupils, thus, you should not always rely on one teaching strategy to impart knowledge but engage pupils in the learning process by varied and appropriate approaches. For example, for a pupil-led approach you might set a class debate on different views of drugs in sport, asking pupils to research and present their view, then defend their position; for a more guided discovery approach you may ask pupils to practise and perform a range of skills in different activities and then decide where on the open-closed continuum each lies; for a teacher-directed approach you may lead pupils through a range of physiological tests to enable them to make links with the anatomical systems.

Interactive learning comes in a variety of forms but can include some or all of the following:

■ Teaching methods ally closely with the aims of the 14–19 qualification being followed, the objectives of the unit of work, ILO of the lesson/lesson episode and the nature of the pupils.

■ Lessons include a variety of learning opportunities for pupils and keep interest sustained and the pace of the lesson moving.

■ Teaching applies theory to practice, e.g. make theory come to life by relating it to physical activity that pupils do, or they can observe, using role play and simulation.

■ Tasks are varied and able to attract and sustain the attention of pupils, e.g. look at interactive approaches rather than the traditional 'chalk and talk', e.g.: (1) *Human model* – in teams of three write down the names of major bones, muscles or joints on sticky labels. Have one as the model and stick labels to the correct part of the body; (2) *Note taking* – use different frameworks to help pupils take notes, e.g. structure maps, explosion charts, flow charts, lists, identifying key words (see, for example, Unit 5.2 in Capel, Leask and Turner, 2009).

■ Tasks are challenging and motivating, reinforcing prior learning, e.g. build on prior learning by using ongoing assessment of pupils' knowledge and understanding and use assessment to develop challenging and motivating tasks. (Assessment *for* learning is covered in Chapter 8.)

■ Tasks are differentiated to suit the pace of learning, e.g. create supporting resources that take into account the learning needs of pupils, their reading abilities, and their preferred style of learning (e.g. task cards, visual representations, hands-on resources) (differentiation is covered in Chapter 11).

■ ICT is used to enhance and empower pupils' learning, e.g. analysis software, multimedia materials to develop critical enquiry (see Chapter 12).

■   Tasks provide opportunities for pupils to develop their functional skills (English, mathematics, ICT), key skills (Working with Others, Improving Own Learning and Performance and Problem Solving) and PLTS and can help pupils develop competencies for other accredited qualifications (see Chapter 14).

■   Learning is not restricted to formal lesson environments but is enriched, enhanced and extended by learning outside the classroom, e.g. involvement in work-based learning, leadership or volunteering activities.

Task 15.5 focuses on developing learning challenges.

Task 15.5 **Designing learning challenges**

Access http://content.yudu.com/A12ml1/16-19wboard/resources/
index.htm?referrerUrl=%20

Consider how a digital resource can be used to set challenging and interactive learning activities that enable an ILO to be achieved, which recognise the needs of the pupils and which draw upon some of the ideas noted above.

Plan a lesson or episode to achieve a specific ILO to use this or a similar type of resource.

Put your results into your PDP.

Although the focus of classroom-based work in this chapter is the 14–19 curriculum, it can be applied when it is necessary to teach a core PE class in a classroom (e.g. when the weather is wet and no indoor practical space is available).

Further guidance on classroom-based lessons, active learning, applied and experiential learning are given in the further reading and in Unit 5.2 in Capel, Leask and Turner (2009).

ASSESSMENT OF THE 14–19 ACCREDITED QUALIFICATIONS

The principles that guide assessment *for* learning (see Chapter 8) should underpin learning and ongoing assessment for 14–19 accredited qualifications. Assessment *for* learning activities should be a natural part of teaching; thus, when used effectively and appropriately this should maximise learning potential for pupils.

However, assessment *of* learning (summative assessment) is a key feature of all 14–19 accredited qualifications. This assessment can be either externally or internally assessed. An externally assessed component is usually a written examination marked by awarding body examiners. Internally assessed work (often called coursework) is normally completed over a longer period of time and tests types of knowledge, skills and understanding which are more difficult to assess under examination conditions. Internally assessed coursework can be set in three ways:

1   by the awarding body;
2   by teachers and then approved by the awarding body; or
3   by teachers according to guidance in the specification.

The assessments should enable pupils to demonstrate knowledge, skills and understanding in a variety of ways. Internally assessed work is marked by teachers and the accuracy of this marking is checked by awarding body moderators. Figure 15.4 outlines the main types of internally assessed coursework used in 14–19 accredited qualifications.

Type of Coursework	Description	Example of Qualification
Assessment of Practical Performance	Candidates are required to perform effectively under applied conditions in their selected activities, using tactics or compositional techniques, observing rules and conventions.	GCSE, AS and A2
Personal Exercise Programme	Candidates show application of knowledge and understanding by planning, performing and evaluating a health-related exercise programme to improve performance.	GCSE, AS and A2
Analysis of Performance	This provides a link between application of skills and the appreciation of the factors affecting participation and performance, which lead to an improvement in performance.	GCSE
Extended Essay	In-depth research into a specific topic of interest intended to promote high-level research and writing skills, intellectual discovery and creativity.	A2, IB Diploma
Synoptic Assessment	Combination of knowledge, understanding and skills from different units studied.	A2, Diploma
Oral Presentation	Candidates demonstrate knowledge, skills and understanding through a presentation using different formats, e.g. video, PowerPoint, debate.	IB, Diploma
Applied Learning Projects/Work-based Learning	Candidates complete specific enquiry tasks whilst working within an employment context or simulated environment.	Diploma
Portfolios of Evidence	A portfolio of evidence shows that candidates are competent and knowledgeable in their work role and have an evidence basis showing their achievements against unit criteria.	Vocational Qualifications, e.g. NVQ, BTEC
'Signed-off' Units	Units are 'signed off' when candidates show that they have an underpinning knowledge, understanding and work-based performance to make sure they can demonstrate competence in the workplace.	Diploma, NVQ, BTEC

■ **Figure 15.4** The main types of coursework in PE or PE-related 14-19 accredited qualifications

Further consideration is given to assessment in 14–19 qualifications in Unit 6.2 in Capel, Leask and Turner (2009). Now complete Task 15.6.

Task 15.6 **Types of assessment on 14–19 qualifications**

Find out the types of assessment which are included on the 14–19 qualifications in your placement school. Ask your tutor what formative assessment (assessment *for* learning) they undertake to help pupils to work towards the objectives of the course and specific aspects of summative assessment.

Observe the assessment taking place and/or read the outcomes of the assessment (e.g. some of the coursework submitted by pupils at different grades) or the teacher's report on practical assessments.

Record your findings in your PDP.

SUMMARY AND KEY POINTS

This chapter has looked at the 14–19 curriculum in England, Wales and Northern Ireland and the place of the QCF within it, the range of accredited qualifications available in PE within the 14–19 curriculum and the implications of accredited qualifications in PE on teaching and learning approaches. The qualifications and certificates towards which pupils are working are the product of their engagement and can act as a passport to further or higher education, training or employment. If qualifications are to be credible to the world at large and result in pupils who develop the knowledge, skills and attitudes they need to succeed in education, work and life, then they need to do as Seltzer and Bentley (1999: viii) say:

> To thrive in an economy defined by innovative application of knowledge, we must do more than absorb and feed back information. Learners and workers must draw on their entire spectrum of learning experiences to apply what they have learned in new and creative ways.

It is your responsibility to facilitate learning, motivate and enthuse young people to want to learn, not only to achieve the qualifications and certificates for which they are studying, but also to achieve functional skills, key skills, PLTS and other wider goals of education. Together, these provide the skills for young people, with the help of teachers and careers advisers, to make their own informed choices about their future.

Implications for you, as a student teacher, lie in your responsibility to develop:

- subject content knowledge per se to be able to deliver the content of specific qualifications;
- knowledge of individual characteristics and development to be able to respond to the diverse needs of all pupils and challenge them to meet their potential;
- your pedagogic knowledge to accrue a wide array of teaching and learning strategies that engage pupils in the process of learning; and
- your attitudes to appreciate how the 14–19 accredited qualification fits into the wider educational landscape.

Check which requirements for your course you have addressed through this chapter.

FURTHER READING

These readings are designed to help you specifically with classroom-based lessons.

Best, B. and Thomas, W. (2007) *The Creative Teaching and Learning Toolkit*, **New York: Continuum.**

This text contains a mixture of printed and downloadable resources and practical strategies aimed at creating learning activities that engage and motivate pupils.

Bowkett, S. (2007) *100+ Ideas for Teaching Thinking Skills*, **New York: Continuum.**

This text contains a range of ideas and activities aimed at designing challenging lessons to keep pupils interested and developing their thinking skills.

Silberman, M. (1996) *Active Learning: 101 Strategies to Teach Any Subject,* **Harlow: Allyn and Bacon.**

This text provides a wide range of instructional strategies to engage pupils in learning for any subject. Specific, practical strategies include ways to get pupils active from the start through activities that build teamwork and immediately get them thinking about the subject matter.

Sutherland, R., Robertson, S. and John, P. (2008) *Improving Classroom Learning with ICT*, **Abingdon: Routledge.**

This text examines ways in which ICT can be used in the classroom to enhance teaching and learning in different settings and across different subjects. Case studies provide exemplification.

WORKING WITH OTHERS TO ACHIEVE THE AIMS OF PE

Margaret Whitehead and Karen Pack

INTRODUCTION

As was set out in Chapters 2, 13 and 14, PE has the potential to achieve a wide range of subject-specific aims and to contribute to wider educational aims. For example, as a PE teacher you work to foster, in every pupil, the motivation, confidence and competence to continue physical activity throughout life. In addition, you take steps to help pupils develop into successful learners and confident individuals. In order to meet these challenges you need to work in partnership with a range of colleagues who bring particular skills and experience into the school. The resources and staff in any PE department are unlikely to be able to cater for the wide range of needs and interests presented by the pupils. It would be true to say that, unlike 20 years ago, PE departments can no longer be self-sufficient entities. It therefore follows that the effective collaboration with colleagues from within the department and the school, as well as from outside the school, is a significant part of today's PE teacher's job. This chapter aims to alert you to some of the people you may work with and some of the ways to make best use of their support.

While many of these responsibilities are not those that usually involve either student teachers or newly qualified teachers (NQTs) it is important that you become aware of the working context into which your career will take you. This chapter aims to alert you to this aspect of your work and help you to understand the nature and realities of these various partnerships. The responsibilities of some of the PE personnel mentioned in the chapter are set out in Chapter 18, which considers continuing professional development (CPD). The objectives below exemplify some of the partnerships that you will need to foster.

OBJECTIVES

At the end of this chapter you should be able to:

■ understand how you can work with colleagues in PE curriculum time;

■ understand how you can work with others, for example coaches, in the context of extra-curricular activities;

■ understand how you can work with other members of the school community;

■ understand how you can work with local colleagues such as the Partnership Development Manager (PDM), School Sports Coordinators (SSCos) and Primary Link Teachers (PLTs) in the context of School Sports Partnerships (SSPs) and Sports Colleges;

■ understand how you can work with others in the community in a wide range of activity settings.

Check the requirements for your course to see which relate to this chapter.

WORKING WITH COLLEAGUES IN PE CURRICULUM TIME

This section looks briefly at the importance of working with colleagues in the PE curriculum time to:

■ ensure all members of the department share and act in line with a common philosophy;

■ make best use of colleagues from outside the PE department who contribute to PE lessons;

■ keep lesson and pupil records to achieve continuity of experience for pupils;

■ make best use of Learning Support Assistants.

The first area in which it is important to work with others is in respect of PE curriculum time. The department will have agreed aims for PE in your school and overall schemes of work to achieve these aims. Chapter 3 discussed the planning of schemes of work and units in PE. These are usually devised by the members of the PE department working together. All personnel working in the department need to appreciate the underlying aims of the department and work to the planned schemes and units of work. On a week by week basis all staff need to keep full records, both of material covered in lessons and units, and of pupil progress. Charting pupil progress is a crucial element of collaboration, both to ensure that staff are aware of individual pupils' strengths and where each may need particular help and to plan for continuity of experience for all pupils. This information is particularly important where staff from outside the department play a part in curriculum work. Teachers from other departments within the school, e.g. a mathematics teacher with a particular expertise, such as a coaching qualification in badminton, may be used, as well as experts, such as coaches, from outside the school. In these cases the PE staff need to ensure that these practitioners are fully aware of the material they are to cover, the objectives of units of work and intended learning outcomes (ILOs) of lessons and the nature of the classes they are to teach. While these personnel may be conversant with PE-specific aims it may be the case that they are less aware of the wider curricular aims. Guidance may be needed to alert these people to the contribution that teaching method, as well as content, makes to achieving these wider goals. This issue is addressed in Chapters 2 and 10.

Learning Support Assistants (LSAs) may join a lesson to assist a pupil with special needs. The PE knowledge and experience of LSAs vary, but all will benefit from prior information concerning the work to be covered and some guidance on how this can be adapted for individual pupils. In all cases, LSAs should be aware of the ILOs of a lesson. In some instances the teacher may design specific tasks for a pupil with disabilities and these tasks need to be explained carefully to the LSA. Time set aside before each lesson to discuss the role of the LSA in a lesson is essential and is always welcomed by LSAs. Task 16.1 is designed to alert you to the ways best use can be made of LSAs in PE.

Task 16.1 **Making best use of LSAs in PE**

Observe a lesson in which an LSA is working with a pupil in PE.

Record how the teacher briefs the LSA before the lesson, how the LSA supports the pupil, how the teacher monitors this support and any discussion that takes place after the lesson between the teacher and the LSA. Discuss the role of the LSA in the lesson with the teacher in question. Put your findings in your professional development portfolio (PDP).

Above all, every teacher should keep full records of the work that has been delivered and keep records of pupil progress. These should be readily available for easy reference. These records are essential for the creation of pupil reports and as evidence against which to assess how far the department has achieved its aims. All involved in curricular teaching should also share significant incidents, as appropriate, with the department. These could be concerned with, for example, the persistent absence of a pupil, difficult confrontations with or between pupils and particular progress or promise. An openness to discuss work and time set aside to collaborate with others is always important.

All members of the PE department are likely to be involved in the planning of the staffing of curricular work and decisions are usually taken on the grounds of providing the best possible experience for pupils. Each practitioner working in curriculum time should enhance the quality of work in the department. While it is principally the role of the Head of Department to ensure intra-departmental cohesion and consistency, and to brief practitioners from outside the department, all the PE staff have a role to play in these matters. In order to make best use of all colleagues, information about the lesson, particularly the ILOs, should be made available and discussed well before the lesson takes place. In any agreement to call on staff from outside the department to work in curricular lessons, time must be set aside for thorough briefing of these colleagues.

WORKING WITH OTHERS IN THE CONTEXT OF EXTRA-CURRICULAR ACTIVITIES

This section looks briefly at working with:

■ qualified adults known as Adults other than Teachers (AOTTs);
■ staff from other departments who have a particular interest or expertise;
■ coaches, dance animateurs and other appropriately qualified practitioners with particular expertise;
■ personnel in off-site provision, e.g. clubs, leisure centres, stables, dry-ski centres;
■ other adults who give assistance in relation to taking pupils to events away from school.

Chapter 13 in Capel, Breckon and O'Neill (2006) is a useful reference here and completion of Activity 13.4 would be valuable.

Table 16.1 lists the range of practitioners identified above, who most frequently support the PE staff in extra-curricular time. Against each practitioner the following considerations are identified:

■ the rationale for involving them in extra-curricular work;
■ the roles they may play in this work;
■ the advantages and disadvantages of their involvement;
■ the skills needed by the PE staff to make best use of these additional colleagues.

Table 16.1 needs careful study and Task 16.2 asks you to critically consider the table and discuss its content with an experienced member of the PE staff.

Task 16.2 **A critical analysis of Table 16.1**

Study Table 16.1 and discuss the entries in two of the columns, in respect to each of the groups of people identified, with an experienced member of the PE staff.

   Record in your PDP any changes that the member of staff would like to make to the table.

In most cases this additional help allows for smaller group teaching, opportunities for pupils to experience a new activity and/or a wider range of activities and for opportunities for pupils to work with practitioners with high-level expertise. In addition, support from other adults can be invaluable in the supervision of pupils during off-site matches, trips and expeditions. However, as indicated in Table 16.1, there are also challenges in bringing others into work in extra-curricular activities as well as a range of responsibilities that must be enacted by PE staff in respect of this extra help. The best way for student teachers to appreciate ways of working with these practitioners is to observe how experienced staff interact with them, giving support and guidance and setting examples of how to work appropriately with pupils. Task 16.3 asks you to find out about the qualifications of one group of practitioners who may play a part in extra-curricular work – AOTTs – and then to observe how an experienced teacher makes best use of this additional support.

■ **Table 16.1** Working with others in the context of extra-curricular activities

Working with others in extra-curricular time	Rationale for involvement of other practitioners/adults	Role of other practitioners/adults	Advantages/disadvantages of involving other practitioners/adults	Skills needed by PE staff to work with other practitioners/adults
Adults Other Than Teachers (AOTTs)	AOTTs can support PE staff where there is a great deal of organisation to be carried out and they can work alongside the teacher in situations where there are large groups to manage	Essentially AOTTs act in a supporting role alongside qualified teachers or coaches. Under the guidance of the teacher AOTTs may help with the organisation and carry out some delegated teaching tasks	AOTTs provide valuable support where large group management and organisation are concerned. Pupils may be able to work in smaller groups and at appropriate levels if more adults are on hand. *Possible problems: if AOTTs are given too much teaching responsibility, if they have no understanding of the activity being taught and if they have not followed AOTT training*	PE staff will need to brief, support and encourage AOTTs, giving them confidence to play a positive role in lessons. PE staff should never give AOTTs responsibilities beyond their agreed role and capability
Staff from other departments in the school	Members of staff will have expertise in a particular physical activity	Members of staff may bring knowledge and experience not found among the PE staff or may enable an additional session to be run in an activity	Members of staff may provide additional opportunities for pupils to be introduced to a new activity or be challenged to make progress in an activity in which they have some experience. *Possible problem: if member of staff has no coaching qualifications*	PE staff may need to give guidance on class management skills in PE. Tactful intervention may be needed
Coaches/animateurs from other providers, e.g. National Governing Bodies and Local Arts Council	Practitioners will bring a high level of expertise in a specific activity to the PE department	Practitioners may work with high-level performers or may be responsible for introducing an activity to pupils	Practitioners will be very experienced and have a coaching qualification. *Possible problem: if practitioners have little experience in respect of motivating and managing groups of pupils*	PE staff may need to supervise lessons in the early stages and may need to give guidance on class management skills. Tactful intervention may be needed

■ **Table 16.1** continued

Working with others in extra-curricular time	Rationale for involvement of other practitioners/adults	Role of other practitioners/adults	Advantages/disadvantages of involving other practitioners/adults	Skills needed by PE staff to work with other practitioners/adults
Personnel at local leisure centres and sports clubs	Personnel will enable pupils to experience a range of activities not available at the school	Personnel will manage the pupils in the Centre or Club ensuring they take part in particular physical activities	Personnel will add to the range of activities in which pupils can be involved. Pupils will become familiar with Centre/Club to encourage Lifelong Physical Activity. *Possible problem: if personnel have little experience in managing and motivating pupils*	PE staff will need to visit Centre/Club to assess all aspects of health and safety. PE staff will need to visit periodically to check appropriate pupil behaviour and effective management by staff. PE staff may need to stop using a facility if it is unsatisfactory
Adults to support school expeditions and trips, e.g. away matches locally or further afield	These adults will enable trips to take place as staff/student ratios are laid down for these activities	Adults will undertake supervisory roles during travel and free time. Adults will provide Duty of Care role for the school in these settings	Adults will enable trips etc to take place and be an extra pair of hands for regular help or emergency assistance. *Possible problems: if adults get 'too close' to the pupils, take on too much responsibility or take unilateral decisions outside school policies*	PE staff will need to brief these adults fully in relation to their Duty of Care, emergency procedures, and school policies for trips, e.g. size of groups for pupils leaving centre in free time, permission to go swimming etc.

Task 16.3 **The role of AOTTs**

1   Search out and read documentation about AOTTs, who they are and how they are trained. The afPE website should be useful here (http://www.afpe.org.uk/).
2   Replicate Task 16.1 with respect to an AOTT who is playing a part in extra-curricular activities.

Put your findings in your PDP.

A group of people who could also contribute to extra-curricular work (and indeed curriculum lessons) who have not been specifically identified in Table 16.1 are older pupils who may have taken a Community Sports Leaders Award (CSLA) course or who may be interested in having work experience in the PE context. The practice to involve these young people is to be encouraged. It is usual for these helpers to adopt a role similar to that of AOTTs.

WORKING WITH OTHER MEMBERS OF THE SCHOOL COMMUNITY

This section looks briefly at the need to ensure that the PE department:

- is fully integrated into the school;
- is involved in developing school policy and in planning school initiatives;
- is seen to play a part in delivering broader educational goals such as Personal Learning and Thinking Skills;
- is able to articulate the value of their subject to other staff;
- is involved in cross-school care of and support for pupils;
- collaborates with the school Special Educational Needs Coordinator (SENCO);
- cooperates fully in completing all school records;
- works closely with school ancillary staff.

It has often been the case that the PE department and its members have been seen as somewhat separate from the rest of the work of the school. This situation is in no way desirable but has been perpetuated partly on account of the physical location of the department, away from the main school buildings. PE staff may seldom use the school staffrooms and may have less time to interact with other members of staff because of the variety of organisational tasks they have to undertake, not least those surrounding health and safety (see Chapter 9).

However, it is very important that the PE staff play a full part in the life of the school, in devising school policies, in whole-school planning and in respect of working with others to achieve school aims (see also Chapter 2). For example, PE staff can play a significant part in initiatives in England concerning Assessment for Learning and 'Learning 2 Learn' (Black *et al*., 2003; Spackman, 2002). In addition PE can make a contribution to achieving the goals set out in the government's Every Child Matters philosophy (Department for Education and Skills (DfES), 2003) as well as in realising the development of Personal Learning and Thinking Skills (see Chapter 14). In some instances, such as organising a 'Healthy School Week' or a 'Learning to Work Together' event, there is no reason why PE staff should not take the lead.

PE staff are sometimes reticent in coming forward to assert the importance of their subject in the education of the whole child. This is unfortunate as the subject has much to offer all pupils, with some pupils benefiting particularly from work in PE. In this context it is important that you should be able to articulate the unique and significant contributions that the subject can offer in the total education of pupils. PE teachers need to contest the too widely held view that their subject is no more than a 'recreational extra'. There are numerous grounds on which the subject can justify its place in the curriculum. These have been discussed in Chapter 2 on the aims of PE and in Chapter 14, which is concerned with the whole-school goals to which PE can make a contribution. Task 16.4 challenges you to articulate the importance of PE in the school curriculum.

Task 16.4 **Articulating the importance of PE**

Discuss with another student teacher how you would justify the inclusion of PE in the school curriculum. Chapters 2, 13 and 14 of this book should give you some guidance. See also Chapters 1 and 2 in Capel, Breckon and O'Neill (2006). Share your deliberations with your tutor and note your discussion. Put the records of this exercise in your PDP. These notes could be useful to you in writing letters of application and preparing for a teaching job interview.

Another way in which PE staff need to be involved in whole-school issues is concerned with the care and support of pupils, particularly those who may confront difficulties. On a general level it is important that PE staff keep full records and cooperate readily with school procedures of report writing and meeting parents. In respect of pupils with problems, PE staff should, where possible, be involved in case study meetings, as it is sometimes found that in this subject area some pupils, such as those who have behavioural difficulties, display particular problems, such as truancy and aggressive behaviour, or may, in fact, present no problems, being committed and enthusiastic in this subject area. The PE department needs to work closely with the school SENCO as this colleague has detailed knowledge of the needs of individual pupils. In some cases there may be key issues to accommodate in respect of some pupils.

As PE staff are very much involved in after-school activities it may be necessary to liaise closely with staff in other departments that use after school time, such as those in the drama and music departments. Use of facilities and expectations of pupils to attend these sessions may be issues to negotiate.

One other area in which the PE teacher needs to work with others in the whole-school setting is with respect to key support/ancillary staff such as the caretaker, the ground staff and school secretaries and administrators. These individuals play critical roles in the functioning of the PE department and need to be kept fully informed of the plans and requirements of the subject. It is often the case that the caretaker is the only person on site after school hours and is the contact for parents collecting pupils after matches. It is therefore valuable for staff taking teams away from school to keep in contact with the caretaker about travel information. Task 16.5 is concerned with the way that ancillary staff are kept fully informed of, and are involved in, departmental activities.

Task 16.5 **Working with ancillary staff**

Take time to explore how ancillary staff, such as caretakers and ground staff, in your placement school are kept informed of, and are depended on, in mounting various departmental activities. This could include the running of tournaments, the presentation of a gymnastics or dance performance or the establishment of a scheme to allow parents to use school facilities such as the swimming pool. Identify two key strategies that you feel are most valuable. Put your findings in your PDP. Add to these notes any further experiences you have in working with ancillary staff.

To achieve all these challenges of collaboration, PE staff need to think carefully in allocating their time, ensuring that departmental needs do not always override school responsibilities. As a PE teacher you need to understand the contribution that PE can make to pupils' education and be able to explain and justify this to other staff. Above all you, as well as all PE teachers, should make every effort to be fully part of the school community, particularly in connection with catering for pupils with special needs. PE staff need to plan well ahead, appreciate situations from others' perspectives and be as flexible as possible in negotiation. Time should be taken to meet with and discuss plans with others. Where colleagues feel they are valued as part of a team they are likely to be helpful and supportive.

WORKING WITH LOCAL COLLEAGUES IN THE CONTEXT OF SCHOOL SPORT PARTNERSHIPS (SSPs) AND SPORTS COLLEGES

This section looks briefly at working with:

- schools in a SSP;
- personnel with particular responsibilities in the partnership;
- PLTs;
- local special schools;
- local schools outside the partnership.

In your school experiences you may have worked in a Sports College or in a secondary school that is one of a family of schools, the work of which relates to that of a Sports College. One feature of this arrangement is that there are a number of personnel who hold specific posts in the family and who have particular roles in respect of all the schools in the family. It is unusual nowadays for PE departments in the UK to function in isolation from other schools. As you work in your placement schools and subsequently take up a full-time job, it is important to relate effectively with the wide range of colleagues in these partnerships.

Collaboration with schools in the family provides a forum to share ideas, to work together to find solutions to problems and to organise activities and events for pupils. In addition, families of schools can work together to foster links with the community, to bid for initiative funding and to plan continuing professional development (CPD) opportunities for staff. There are few negative aspects of this arrangement, however PE staff need to ensure that time spent in collaborative work is in the best interests of their pupils.

Each family of schools has a PDM and a number of School Sport Coordinators (SSCo) (see also Chapter 18). In addition, the family may have Directors of Specialisms and Competition Managers.

In short, the role of these colleagues is to ensure that the pupils and staff in the family of schools have the best possible opportunities in respect of PE. All these practitioners bring a wealth of experience to the family and their job is to work with staff to raise the quality of PE for all pupils. Where staff are out of school on courses these colleagues can often cover the work in school. You are strongly encouraged to seek out these individuals and to learn about their roles. In some cases it may be possible to shadow a colleague for a day. This is excellent as it gives you a real insight into the nature of their responsibilities. Task 16.6 asks you to shadow one of the partnership personnel and to record the tasks undertaken.

Task 16.6 **Investigating the role of a PDM or SSCo**

Make arrangements via your Head of Department to spend a day shadowing either a PDM or SSCo. Keep a full record of the day and put these notes in your PDP.

Primary schools are also members of the families of schools and each has a member of staff with responsibility for PE. These colleagues are known as PLTs and have a number of roles. They are tasked with ensuring high-quality PE experience for pupils in their school and for supporting the generalist primary teachers in teaching the subject. PLTs work closely with the PDM and the SSCos to make sure there is a smooth transition for pupils between primary and secondary school. This often takes the form of visits to the secondary school by primary pupils, where these pupils are taught by secondary staff. In addition, when PLTs work alongside secondary colleagues, information can be shared both about the nature of the PE experience in the primary school and about the progress and potential of the individual pupils.

There may be a Special School within the family of schools, or a Special School in the local area, with which there is collaboration. It is often the case that Special Schools benefit from some use of mainstream facilities as well as drawing on PE expertise within the family of schools. Other schools in the partnership can benefit from the expertise in the Special School in respect of adapting PE for pupils with special needs.

Finally there may be local independent schools or secondary schools outside the family with which collaboration takes place. The system of twinning an independent school with a maintained school can offer additional opportunities for pupils. This may relate to use of facilities, sharing staff expertise and setting up fixtures. In addition there may be situations in which CPD can be jointly set up and/or meetings take place to share good practice. Task 16.7 requires you to find out the nature of partnership collaboration in the family of schools in which your placement school is situated.

Task 16.7 **Inter-school collaboration**

Find out from your Head of Department the range and nature of the inter-school collaborative arrangements the school has established. Discuss the benefits and difficulties (if any) of these relationships. Put a record of the discussion in your PDP.

As a student teacher it is important that you are aware of the range of PE colleagues within the family of schools and in the locality who are all working to enhance the quality of PE experience for the pupils. The expertise of these colleagues is extensive and in many ways they are there to help and support you. They have up-to-date knowledge of the policies and initiatives from, for example, the Youth Sport Trust and Sport England. Time given to talk to these colleagues is always informative. Once you are in a post, working with these colleagues will be a key part of your job, not least to keep abreast of developments and opportunities for the pupils and for yourself.

WORKING WITH OTHERS IN THE COMMUNITY IN A WIDE RANGE OF ACTIVITY SETTINGS

This section looks briefly at working with:

- local authority personnel such as Sports Development Officers;
- PE Advisers:
- personnel in local leisure facilities and sports clubs.

As has been seen from the section above there is a range of local school-based PE and sport personnel – the roles of whom are to work within families of schools to enhance the quality of PE locally or regionally. In addition to these practitioners there is a range of other people in the local authority and in the local community who provide opportunities for physical activity outside school. It is important both that you are aware of these practitioners and that you are proactive in developing productive relationships with them.

Some local education authorities have a PE Adviser. This colleague is there to support all PE teachers, particularly NQTs. Advisers are fully conversant with the education policies of the authority and how these impact on PE. Advisers are a valuable source of information and support and it is very much in your interests to make contact with this colleague, where the post exists, when you have a permanent teaching position.

While each local authority has its own structure and operational patterns with respect to recreation, physical activity and sport, there are usually a number of Sports Development Officers employed within the organisation. The specific roles of these individuals vary but all have a responsibility to enhance out-of-school opportunities for physical activity for members of the community. All have a budget to spend on programmes, thus making collaboration with them potentially useful. If, for example, your school swimming pool is out of action, or Year 10 girls have asked for a particular activity to be on offer over a holiday period, it may be possible to organise short- or long-term arrangements with Sports Development personnel.

It is also useful for PE teachers to have knowledge of local sports clubs and leisure centres and to take time to visit these facilities and talk to those in charge. In some cases clubs may have been awarded 'Club Mark' which indicates that they have robust systems in place that cater for young people. This is valuable for all pupils but perhaps most important for pupils who have talent in a particular activity. It is unlikely that the school can foster outstanding ability in a particular activity and close collaboration with a club and/or a coach is often the best way forward. In addition, opportunities for groups of pupils to visit and take part in activities in out-of-school hours may be able to be arranged. Planned visits with pupils to clubs and leisure centres are very good ways to introduce young people to activities and opportunities that are available. While the PE teacher has no direct responsibility for pupils' out-of-school physical activity, a key aim of any PE department is to encourage participation in physical activity as a lifelong habit. By introducing pupils to local sports clubs and leisure centres you can help to make these places familiar and thus encourage pupils to continue with physical activity after they leave school.

To develop this aspect of collaboration you need to research facilities available in the local area and set time aside for meetings. You need to appreciate the varied responsibilities of personnel in clubs and centres and be willing to negotiate joint ventures with imagination and tact. Task 16.8 asks you to find out where local sports clubs are to be found in the area near your placement school and to find out how a pupil can become a member of one of these clubs.

Task 16.8 **Investigating a local sports club**

Take time to research clubs local to your placement school at which coaching is available to support young people with particular talent. Make contact with at least one club to find out the steps you would need to take to arrange for a pupil to become a member. Put these findings in your PDP. Add to these notes any relevant experience you have throughout your initial teacher education course.

SUMMARY AND KEY POINTS

This chapter has surveyed a range of examples of personnel with whom the PE department may collaborate. You are also likely to come into contact with others with whom you will need to develop an effective working relationship. Working with others crosses a wide field from close involvement in-house with school policies and practices, to frequent dialogue with other teachers, and from working jointly with other schools and clubs, to drawing on the expertise of key personnel such as PDMs and local coaches.

The fundamental purpose of all these collaborative exercises is to ensure that every pupil is working to their potential and is having the appropriate range of experiences. These experiences may be concerned with nurturing talent, providing opportunities for involvement in a wide range of physical activities, giving extra support for pupils with special needs or helping to prepare all pupils for participation once they leave school. Task 16.9 asks you to consider the advantages and disadvantages of working with others.

Check which requirements for your course you have addressed through this chapter.

Task 16.9 **Advantages and disadvantages of working with others**

Read and discuss with another student teacher Waring, M. and Warburton, P. (2000) Working with the community: a necessary evil or a positive change of direction?, in S. Capel and S. Piotrowski (eds), *Issues in Physical Education*, London: Routledge.

Write a 2,000 word essay critically considering the advantages and disadvantages of involving a range of non-PE department colleagues in the work with pupils.

Put your discussion and the essay in your PDP. Both pieces of writing could be useful in the context of a teaching job interview.

FURTHER READING

Capel, S., Breckon, P. and O'Neill, J. (eds) (2006) *A Practical Guide to Teaching Physical Education in the Secondary School*, London: Routledge.
Chapter 13, 'Working with others', looks at a range of practical issues in this area.

Capel, S. and Piotrowski, S. (eds) (2000) *Issues in Physical Education*, London: Routledge.
Chapter 10, 'Working with others in the community: a necessary evil or a positive change of direction?', is a valuable and thought-provoking chapter.

Websites with information about Sports Colleges and SSPs

http://www.youthsporttrust.org/page/specialist-sport/index.html
This connects to a page on the main corporate website which includes both an overview of Sports Colleges and SSPs and a diagram used to illustrate how schools and personnel work together.

http://www.youthsporttrust.org/page/publications/index.html
This address has a diagram and an overview of Youth Sport Trust's work with SSPs within annual reviews.

http://ssx.youthsporttrust.org/subpage/sspwelcome/index.htm
This is a resource for SSPs and contains a number of case studies and tools for good practice.

TEACHER AS A RESEARCHER/ REFLECTIVE PRACTITIONER

Paula Zwozdiak-Myers

INTRODUCTION

In recent decades, the concepts *enquiry* and *research* have increasingly become embedded within discourse concerning teacher professional development, particularly in relation to performance management, raising educational standards and school improvement planning. Teachers who ask searching questions about educational practice, which arise from their own professional concerns and situational contexts, demonstrate a commitment to continuous learning by seeking new ideas, evaluating and reflecting on their impact, and trying out new practices and ways of working to improve their own effectiveness in the teaching environment. This approach to professional development exemplifies and underpins the concepts of the teacher as *a reflective practitioner, as an extended professional and as a researcher*. These concepts are closely related, with Stenhouse (1975) arguing that the outstanding feature of *extended professionals* is their capacity and commitment to engage in autonomous self-development through reflection, systematic self-study and research.

Central to your development as a teacher is your capacity and commitment to observe and analyse what is happening in your own lessons and to use your professional judgement both to *reflect* and *act* upon these observations and analyses in order to improve pupil learning and your teaching. This enables you to make informed judgements, which are derived from an evidence base, about the effectiveness of both.

This chapter introduces you to key concepts associated with the teacher as a researcher and reflective practitioner. It also considers how you can make the most of the observation opportunities and experiences incorporated into your course. These include *observation by you* of teaching conducted by your tutor and other experienced teachers and *observation of your teaching* by your tutor and other teachers. Other information-gathering techniques are introduced in the context of describing the nature of a method of research often used in teaching – that is *Action Research*.

OBJECTIVES

At the end of this chapter you should be able to:

■ understand what is meant by the teacher as a reflective practitioner, an extended professional and as a researcher;

■ understand the role of reflective teaching in developing your expertise as a teacher and improving the quality of pupil learning;

■ have some insight into the range of questions which can be addressed through lesson observation;

■ know about some techniques available for gathering information about teaching and learning in PE lessons – including Action Research.

Check the requirements for your course to see which relate to this chapter.

THE TEACHER AS A REFLECTIVE PRACTITIONER, AN EXTENDED PROFESSIONAL AND AS A RESEARCHER

While reflective practice is currently very much part of what is expected of teachers, there has long been a concern for teachers to take responsibility for their own learning and development. The work of key writers in the field such as Dewey (1933), Schon (1987), Hoyle (1974) and Stenhouse (1975) warrants study (see Activity 3.1 in Capel, Breckon and O'Neill, 2006). Dewey identified particular orientations, notably the attitudes of *open-mindedness*, responsibility and whole-heartedness, that he proposed are prerequisites to *reflective action*. He built on this and suggested that *reflection* is associated with a particular mode of thinking, which involves turning a subject over in the mind to give it serious consideration and thought. He identifies five phases or states of thinking: *problem*, *suggestions*, *reasoning*, *hypothesis* and *testing*. Schon's (1987) conceptualisation of the *reflective practitioner* originated in earlier work (Argyris and Schon, 1974). An element of his writing describes two concepts associated with reflection that are useful to you at this stage of your career. These are *reflection in action* and *reflection on action*. Reflection in action occurs in the ongoing teaching situation as you survey the class, picking up possibly unexpected responses, which may need an alteration to the lesson as planned. Such expressions as 'thinking on your feet', 'reading the class' and 'keeping your wits about you' aptly portray reflection in action. Reflection in action is a skill that develops over time as your observation improves and you accrue a range of experiences that can inform how you deal with the unexpected. Being ready to modify plans if pupils do not respond as you had anticipated is discussed in Chapter 4 and responding to off-task behaviour was discussed in Chapter 6. Reflection on action involves looking back on action some time after the event. This type of reflection highlights the need for you to think carefully about the outcomes of your teaching and capacity to enhance pupil learning through rigorous and systematic evaluation procedures. This reflection has been discussed in the context of lesson evaluation in Chapter 3 and Chapter 8, and is returned to later in this chapter.

Hoyle (1974) introduced the notion of the teacher as an extended professional, that is, a teacher who is demonstrating professionalism beyond the baseline of competence in teaching. He describes this teacher as characteristically:

- showing a high level of classroom competence;
- exhibiting a pupil-centred approach;
- having a high level of skill in handling pupils and understanding them;
- deriving great satisfaction from working with pupils;
- evaluating own performance in terms of perceptions of changes in pupils' behaviour and achievement.

Building on Hoyle's (1974) work, and focusing very much on the *teacher as a researcher*, Stenhouse (1975: 143–4) identifies five key attributes to characterise extended professionals as they research their own practice. Extended professionals:

- reflect critically and systematically on their practice;
- have a commitment to question their practice as the basis for teacher development;
- have the commitment and skills to study their own teaching and in so doing develop the art of self-study;
- appreciate the benefit of having their teaching observed by others and discussing their teaching with others in an open and honest manner;
- have a concern to question and to test theory in practice.

These attributes have resonance with many of those aspects of teaching that this book has been introducing to you and on which you have been working. However, your concern with improving your teaching has, to date, been focused on acquiring the basic skills of teaching and has probably been driven by the need to match up to the expectations of your tutor. For example, you may have been encouraged to work on smooth transitions in your lesson management or use pupils more in providing demonstrations. What has been described above, however, is, significantly, led by the teacher's own interest and desire to become ever more effective in promoting pupil learning. Genuine commitment to teacher development arises from critically constructive self-reflection and considered response and has the potential to develop into more systematic research into teaching. This chapter now reviews those aspects of your initial teacher education (ITE) course that lay the ground for your development as a reflective practitioner and then turns to introducing you to Action Research as one procedure to carry out research into teaching.

PREPARING TO BE A REFLECTIVE PRACTITIONER IN YOUR ITE COURSE

At the heart of reflecting on teaching and of research into teaching is a concern to ensure that pupils learn as a result of your teaching. Much of your ITE course requires you to observe, identify and understand the many and complex relationships between learning and teaching. The teacher behaviours, skills and strategies you have been practising have this one goal in mind, for example planning, observation, communication, organisation and assessment. The step beyond the execution of these skills in themselves is to judge if they are effective in promoting learning. Remember that taking a reflective stance on your teaching applies both to the teaching of activities in NCPE (2007) and to classroom-based work in General Certificate of Secondary Education (GCSE) and General Certificate of Education Advanced (A) Level courses.

There are at least three ways that you can learn first hand about the relationship between learning and teaching. The first is to observe other teachers and to identify what they do and the effect of their actions. Numerous tasks have been set throughout this book to encourage you to observe teachers at work, see, for example, Tasks 4.1, 6.1, 10.2 and 14.1. The second is to receive feedback on your own teaching from your tutor or another teacher. This feedback is usually focused on how far what you did fostered learning. The third way to learn about the effect of teaching on learning is to conduct a constructively self-critical analysis of your lessons. You will already be familiar with this process through your lesson evaluation.

All three methods mentioned above concerning learning about teaching and about pupil learning depend on some form of observation followed by systematic reflection. Chapter 4 looks in detail at the *why*, *what* and *how* of observation. As observation lies at the heart of becoming a reflective practitioner, practising and acquiring the skills of observation are very important and you are recommended at this stage to reread this chapter.

LEARNING THROUGH OBSERVING OTHER TEACHERS

Observing experienced teachers is very valuable and much can be learnt from this exercise. Remember it is a privilege to be present in a lesson; as you move into your career there are seldom opportunities to observe others teach. It is always useful to observe a number of teachers as this helps you to realise that there are many different ways of promoting pupil learning, managing pupils and conducting teaching. As you do these observations you are undertaking the role of what in research is known as a 'non-partici-pant' observer. This means that you play no part in the lesson, sitting unobtrusively in a position from which you can see the whole class, or pupil(s) in question.

In setting up an observation of your tutor or another teacher it is important that an appropriate procedure is adopted. For example, the first step is to talk to your tutor (or another teacher) to confirm their willingness to be observed. Following this you need to explain what aspect of teaching you are particularly interested to observe. In your early weeks this may be organisation of the pupils in the space or allocation of time. Later in the course you may want to observe pupil learning and see how the teacher caters for the range of different abilities in the class. Alternatively, you may be interested in how the teacher devolves responsibility to pupils. It is valuable at this stage to gather information about the class and the lesson to be observed (see below).

Once you have decided and agreed the focus of the observation you need to draw up a simple observation instrument (to be covered later in this chapter) to direct your attention to key aspects of teaching or pupil learning. For example, your instrument may enable you to document how the teacher uses praise, or it may guide you to observe a small number of pupils and chart their progress in achieving intended learning outcomes (ILOs). You must share this instrument with the teacher in question. If you have the opportunity, it is useful to practise using the instrument, possibly with a video-recorded lesson.

After you have observed the lesson you should arrange to meet the teacher to go through what you observed and discuss this fully with him/her. You will, of course, thank the teacher for allowing you to observe the lesson.

Background information for undertaking an observation

Background information about the class and lesson is important in undertaking any lesson observation. This can be collected from the teacher using a sheet such as that shown in Figure 17.1 (this is available on this book's website (www.routledge.com/ textbooks/9780415561648) for ease of completion).

Class............................ Class size............................. Boys/girls/mixed ....

Year/Key Stage............................. Time................................... Room ....

Teacher .... Date ....

Observer ....

Activity being taught...

Length of Unit of Work......................... Lesson number within this Unit ....

What are the intended learning outcomes of this lesson?

1. ....

2. ....

3. ....

You may want to add other information appropriate to the observation.

■ **Figure 17.1** Background information for lesson observation

Observation focus

It is important that there is a *focus* for any observation in order to obtain maximum information. What you decide to observe depends on the stage of your ITE course, the teaching skills you are finding particularly challenging, for example voice variation, or perhaps an aspect of pupil learning that you are being encouraged to put into effect, such as skill progression. See Chapter 4 on other ideas about what to observe.

What you observe could include:

■ the lesson plan and stages of the lesson from the moment the pupils arrive to their dismissal from the changing rooms at the end;
■ how the teacher ensures safe participation by the pupils at all times;
■ the teacher's use of such skills as verbal and non-verbal interaction, positioning, use of praise and reprimand;
■ how the pupils respond to the challenges set by the teacher;

- ■ how pupils of different abilities are catered for;
- ■ why pupils move 'off task';
- ■ how often pupils ask questions;
- ■ how well the pupils work together in groups.

The observation in Task 17.1 is focused on how aspects of teaching foster pupil learning through engaging in National Curriculum for Physical Education (NCPE) 2007 (Qualifications and Curriculum Authority (QCA), 2007a) Key Processes. These Key Processes are discussed in Chapter 14.

How an observation takes place in a lesson depends on the focus of the observation. If, for example, you are observing a specific management activity, you need to scan the whole environment rather than concentrate on the activity in which pupils are participating. You therefore need to be able to observe all pupils including those furthest from you. In some situations you may want to focus on one or a few pupils, for example, if a pupil is having particular difficulty or is not on task and beginning to misbehave. On the other hand, if the teacher is promoting group work you may observe just one group. Further discussion of how to observe can be found in Chapter 4.

Devising an observation instrument

As indicated above much can be learnt from observation if you have made a record of what you have observed. Systematic documentation of teacher and pupil behaviour is a key aspect of research, and any work you do during your ITE course helps to prepare for future reflective investigations. Recording observation is best done on a pre-prepared observation instrument. This instrument does not have to be a complex document, but one that directs attention to the specific issue at hand as it is all too easy to get distracted by some of the other numerous events that occur in a lesson! Care and attention need to be put into its design to ensure that it is clear and easy to complete. Time taken to map out an instrument is invaluable in facilitating observation. At this stage in your learning to teach it is advisable to keep the instrument simple. Examples of simple observation instruments can be found on this book's website (see www.routledge.com/textbooks/ 9780415561648). Activity 4.3c in Capel, Breckon and O'Neill (2006) includes two simple and useful observation instruments.

Task 17.1 outlines an observation exercise to match teacher behaviour to pupils working to achieve NCPE 2007 Key Processes. A simple observation instrument is provided in Figure 17.2. Figure 17.3 is an example of a completed observation carried out to match teaching with NCPE 2007 Key Processes.

Task 17.1 **An observation schedule for looking at the purpose of tasks set by the teacher**

Observe a lesson taught by your tutor or another teacher, using the observation schedule in Figure 17.2 below. Identify the ILOs of the lesson with the teacher before the lesson. During the lesson listen carefully to the teacher and try to relate the tasks set to these ILOs. Since in England these ILOs are related to Key Processes of the NCPE 2007, make a decision as to whether or not the tasks set are related to three of these processes: *developing skills in physical activity; making*

---

and applying decisions; and evaluating and improving. These processes are inter-related and any one task may appear in more than one column. An example is provided (Figure 17.3) to show what a completed schedule might look like for a gymnastic lesson. The ILOs have been included together with the related National Curriculum Key Processes. Discuss the lesson with your tutor afterwards to check your interpretation of events in the lesson. Put the completed observation in your professional development portfolio (PDP).

Part of lesson (see Chapter 3 for identification of parts of a lesson)	Developing skills in physical activity	Making and applying decisions	Evaluating and improving

■ **Figure 17.2** Observation schedule for Task 17.1

Observing experienced teachers at work and discussing with them, in depth, what you observed helps you to recognise different aspects of teaching and how these relate to learning. You identify and appreciate the appropriate application of a wide range of teaching skills. Furthermore, you begin to learn how to analyse teaching and deduce the reasons for and causes of events in the lesson; in other words you engage in answering the question 'why', in respect of the way the lesson was taught and how it developed. In talking to the teacher after the lesson you have the opportunity to hear first hand how the teacher perceived the events in the lesson and to come to understand how decisions were made in the teaching situation that took account of pupil responses. In addition, you can debate other ways that the lesson might have been conducted and how the next lesson can take account of the progress or otherwise of the pupils' learning. In this debate you need to listen carefully to what the teacher says, as she/he is sharing with you the process of reflection that you are expected to develop in your ITE course. The cognitive processes of analysis and deduction in which you engage here are a valuable foundation for becoming a reflective teacher.

LEARNING THROUGH OTHERS OBSERVING YOUR TEACHING

Throughout your ITE course you are likely to have a teacher observing all or part of your lessons. As a student teacher you should not be left alone in sole charge of a lesson, particularly in a potentially hazardous subject such as PE. On many occasions the

Intended learning outcomes
By the end of this lesson pupils will be able to:

■   perform a variety of rolling movements from work cards demonstrating body tension and clarity of body shape *(develop skills in physical activity)*;
■   plan and perform a sequence on apparatus to include a jump, roll and weight on hands movement, making the end of one movement the beginning of the next *(make and apply decisions)*;
■   use criteria provided by the teacher to give verbal feedback to a partner on their rolling sequence using appropriate terminology, e.g. tension, tucked, stretched *(evaluate and improve)*.

Part of lesson	Developing skills in physical activity	Making and applying decisions	Evaluating and improving
Introduction and warm-up	Teacher reinforces quality in running actions		Pupils identify improvements that would benefit others as well as themselves
Development of skill or topic *Floor work*	Pupils all perform same rolling movements – they work towards goals, showing initiative, commitment and perseverance		Pupils set personal goals with success criteria for their development and work
	Pupils choose starting and finishing positions from work cards	Pupils select and apply three rolls to a small sequence – they connect their own and others' ideas and experiences in inventive ways	Pupils asked to observe each other's sequence and provide constructive support and feedback using specific criteria – they also learn to deal positively with praise and criticism
Apparatus	Pupils practice transition from jump on bench to roll on floor		
		Pupils plan sequence to include jump, roll and weight on hands movement – they try out alternative possibilities and follow ideas through	Pupils evaluate experiences and learning to inform future progress

■ **Figure 17.3** Example of completed observation schedule used in a gymnastics lesson

Part of lesson	Developing skills in physical activity	Making and applying decisions	Evaluating and improving
			Questions/answers on quality in jumping, rolling and taking weight on their hands – pupils analyse and evaluate information, judging its relevance and value
Conclusion	Pupils put away apparatus and then practise weight on hands movements		Pupils identify improvements that would benefit others as well as themselves

■ **Figure 17.3** continued

observing teacher takes notes on your teaching in order to support your developing expertise; these are then discussed with you after the lesson. These feedback documents are very important and should be kept either alongside the lesson to which it refers or in a clear section of your PDP. In the early stages of your course these documents provide key information on your progress. Once you are established in your school placement you are encouraged to take more responsibility for your own learning, particularly in respect of the overall expectations in your gaining Qualified Teacher Status (QTS). As the onus moves to you for your development as a teacher, you begin to practise the critical self-reflection inherent in adopting a research approach to pupil learning and approaches to teaching. Your weekly meetings with your tutor look at your course expectations and it is likely that in discussion, priorities for you to work on are agreed. It is therefore appropriate for you to ask your tutor or observing teacher to give you specific feedback on a particular focus. The provision of a simple observation sheet for the teacher to use ensures that you receive the information you need. Examples of foci could include:

■   your picking up and responding to early signs of off-task behaviour;
■   your use of praise or assessment for learning;
■   how pupils respond to your challenge to solve problems;
■   how effectively pupils use ICT to promote learning;
■   whether your teaching encourages progression in pupil mastery of a skill.

Task 17.2 requires you to select a focus for observation and to devise an instrument to be used in observing your teaching.

Task 17.2 **Developing an observation schedule**

Select a teaching skill you need to work on to develop your teaching ability. Using the information in this chapter, in Chapter 4 and examples on this book's website (see www.routledge.com/textbooks/9780415561648), devise an observation schedule to focus on your use of this teaching skill. Activity 4.3c in Capel, Breckon and O'Neill (2006) includes two simple and useful observation instruments.

Ask your tutor to use the observation schedule to observe your use of this teaching skill in a lesson. Explain how the observation schedule should be used. Discuss the effectiveness of the observation schedule after the lesson and adapt if necessary. Also discuss the outcomes of the observation with the observer. Work to develop your ability in using the teaching skill, then repeat the observation using the same (or revised) observation schedule. Put the completed observation in your PDP.

An essential follow up to this observation is time to discuss the teaching with the observer. In some cases you may realise what you did or did not do, but in other cases you may not be aware of events. Listen carefully to all the advice given and learn as much as you can from this feedback. In your teaching being observed by another teacher and the subsequent discussion after the lesson your ability to reflect critically is enhanced through your observer engaging in a debate with you. You are likely to be asked to evaluate the lesson as a whole and conduct a constructive self-criticism of your teaching, identifying your strengths and areas for improvement. Significant here are the ways in which your teaching is related to pupil learning. You may be asked to explain and justify aspects of your teaching and to ponder if, with the benefit of hindsight, you might have adopted a different approach. Together with the observer you may identify aspects of your teaching that were effective and how you can embed these into your teaching and in addition reflect on and think about how a problem might be avoided in the future. More broadly you may debate the relationship between learning and teaching and together weigh the potential value of implementing different approaches to promote learning. You may be challenged to be imaginative and innovative in respect of future planning. In short in situations where you are observed there is the opportunity for you to develop the valuable reflective skills of honest self-appraisal, in-depth analysis of the events of the lesson, identification of your strengths, intelligent conjecture of the causes of problems and flexibility in devising solutions.

LEARNING THROUGH SELF-REFLECTION ON YOUR OWN TEACHING

As your ITE course progresses you are expected to take more and more responsibility for your own development as a teacher. Your tutor's feedback is likely to be prefaced by questions such as 'How far did the pupils achieve the ILOs?', 'Which aspects of your teaching were most effective in promoting learning?', 'Where do you think you could make improvements in your teaching?', 'What issues should you take into account as you plan the next lesson?'. You are expected to be alert to all aspects of your teaching, particularly its effect on learning, and be able to reflect on these after the lesson. In other words you are expected to be beginning to become a reflective professional. Indeed your progress in the latter part of your ITE course may well be judged very much on your ability to take ownership of your development as a teacher and the ways that your teaching promotes pupil learning.

The lesson evaluations that you have been completing throughout the course are, of course, the forerunner of documenting your reflection on your teaching. As indicated above, the key questions to be asked and answered in lesson evaluation are:

■   *What* did the pupils achieve/learn or not achieve/learn?
■   *Why* did they achieve/learn or not achieve/learn. In other words why did this learning take place/not take place? What aspects of my planning/teaching were effective/less effective, e.g. was it too difficult, was there not enough time etc.?
■   *How* should I plan/teach in the next lesson to accommodate these findings? What do I continue to do next time or what do I need to do differently to promote learning, e.g. differentiate more/better, provide more specific feedback etc.?

These questions can lead to different patterns of thinking. For example, the question 'What did the pupils learn?' requires you to conduct a form of evaluative thinking. Here you need to compare the progress pupils made with the ILOs of the lesson. On the other hand, when you ask the question 'Why did learning take place/not take place' you are involved in a more analytical consideration. This might focus on your planning or your teaching. Both types of thinking are important when you begin to conduct research into teaching. In fact in asking yourself these questions you are carrying out *reflection on action* – a key characteristic of a reflective professional and of carrying out research into your teaching.

Reflection on action (see above) enables you to reconsider what is worth doing and alternative approaches to what you are doing in your lessons, thus developing sensitivity to what you are doing and how. The basis for reflecting on what happens in your lessons is your knowledge about, and understanding of, for example, whether outcomes for pupils' learning were met, the appropriateness of content you planned or the effectiveness of the teaching approaches you used. Spending a few minutes at the end of a lesson reflecting on what you did, what worked, what did not work, what might have worked better and what you might do next time enables you to gain insight and learn from your mistakes. This relies on your observation in the lesson and your powers of recall of the lesson. To enhance the effectiveness of reflecting on your lessons you need to develop techniques to help you recall events. As soon as possible after the lesson, 'relive' the events which took place, before you forget what you saw. Jot down the main events of the lesson, particularly if there was any deviation from the lesson plan or if there were any 'critical' incidents which occurred, or take more extensive notes. You should draw on your experience of similar situations in the past and observation and feedback by your tutor. See Activity 3.2c in Capel, Breckon and O'Neill (2006) for an example of reflection on action.

Using video can be a valuable way to record your teaching and pupil learning, to allow you to reflect on the lesson more fully. It can also be used to assist observation of pupils (see Chapter 4 for observation of pupils). It has the advantage of allowing you to focus on any number of aspects of the learning and teaching process. The main problem with using this technique is the disruptive influence it may have on the pupils. For this reason it is better to video over a period of time to allow pupils to become accustomed to the process. It is also difficult to record dialogue, particularly outside on a windy day. Wet weather can also cause problems. Task 17.3 is an example of a use to which video may be put. The purpose of this task is for you to compare your perspectives of a lesson with those of another student teacher.

You must note that the videoing of pupils is a sensitive issue and you should not video pupils without permission. Your school should have a policy on this and therefore you need to discuss it fully with your tutor before commencing.

Task 17.3 **Analysing a teaching episode using video**

Arrange through your tutor permission for one of your lessons to be videotaped (discuss with your tutor first). After the lesson watch the video and record what was happening during the lesson. Ask another student teacher to do the same. Compare the similarities and differences between your two records. Try to find out why the differences have occurred. Do the same task for a videotaped lesson taught by the other student teacher.

This task should make you aware that different people see the same lesson differently, depending on the perspective being taken. If you leave the observation open (as above) the differences may be more marked than if you focus the observation in the lesson. You may want to observe the two videotapes again with a specific observation focus in mind, for example, where was the student teacher positioned during the lesson? Did the pupils achieve the ILOs? What time did pupils spend on task? In so doing, you may want to use a focused observation schedule. Put your observations and discussions into your PDP.

By regularly engaging in constructive self-criticism through systematic reflection on your own teaching you gain valuable experience of asking yourself searching questions as to why learning did or did not occur in your lesson. You are challenged to recall how the pupils responded to your teaching and to make an honest appraisal of your planning and how you conducted the lesson. Your awareness of the effect of different teaching approaches on learning is heightened and you become more perceptive of the many variables to be found in the teaching situation. In the interests of maximising pupil learning you are drawn into interrogating your practice and to hypothesising a range of ways you could develop your teaching. This involves a creative and imaginative approach as well as a willingness to refer to theory to inform and support your decisions. You learn to stand back from your teaching and be an honest judge of your practice. As you become more experienced you observe the different responses from individual pupils and begin to appreciate that you need to make a range of subtle modifications to your teaching to cater for all pupils. You become ever more alert to all aspects of pupil learning and your teaching, and persistently search for better ways to promote learning. In all these ways you are developing the essential dispositions in becoming a reflective teacher.

The practices discussed above that have been part of your ITE course, that is, observing other teachers, learning from the observation of your teaching by others and the expectation that, through critical self-reflection you take responsibility for your own progress, all lay the ground for you to become a reflective teacher. This is an attitude of mind that is expected as part of your professional responsibility. It is an attitude that should permeate all your work. With this approach to your teaching you are likely to continue to grow and develop as a teacher and become more effective in promoting pupil learning. This analytical and evaluative attitude and approach forms the basis of any research into teaching. You are encouraged to build on these dispositions and to become involved in research into teaching. This research can be a small-scale exercise you conduct on your own, part of a school initiative or part of an assessed course or qualification. The process of Action Research is the classic procedure for research into teaching and the next section explains this procedure in some detail.

ACTION RESEARCH

The commitment to learn from practice and to improve practice are characteristic principles of Action Research, as is the concern to generate and produce knowledge. Reflecting on practice is a core component of Action Research and an important vehicle through which you can gain greater insight, understanding and awareness of your professional growth and development as a teacher, identify possible avenues for alternative practice, gain a greater sense of autonomy over your own work and begin to internalise the processes associated with the art of self-study.

Action Research is the most commonly used and most highly developed approach to interrogating and improving your own teaching. You may be involved in a small-scale Action Research project as part of your ITE course, however, it is more likely that you will be involved in this form of research after you have qualified as part of continuing professional development (CPD) that is organised by your school or in relation to a CPD course you attend. (See Unit 5.4 in Capel, Leask and Turner, 2009 for further detail of research as part of CPD.) Action Research is now widely used as an element of 'Learning at Work' which is an option in much study at Master's level. While this is a highly structured exercise many of the processes you have experienced during your ITE, as have been outlined above, have prepared you to undertake this work.

The term Action Research refers to a process that teachers use to investigate their own practice and answer questions about the quality of learning and teaching. This process incorporates analysing and evaluating information about a particular experience, occurrence or situation after the event. This form of critical self-reflection can be viewed as 'the systematic and deliberate thinking back over one's actions' (Russell and Munby, 1992: 3). It has also been described by Carr and Kemmis (1986: 162) as a 'self-reflective spiral of cycles of planning, acting, observing, reflecting then re-planning, further action, further observation and further reflection'. A simplified version of McKernan's (1996: 29) model of Action Research, as shown in Figure 17.4, exemplifies the various stages of this process.

This model illustrates an important feature of Action Research, notably, the cyclical nature of an ongoing process to improve the quality and effectiveness of practice. The first stage is shown in the wide vertical arrows in the diagram, headed with 'Identify research area/goal'. Once this has been identified the next step is to conduct a literature search into the area. This search establishes current theories related to the area and any research that has been carried out into the area. As a result of this literature search you develop an action plan, which outlines the different teaching approaches that you anticipate you will use, the data you will collect and the instruments you will use to gather this

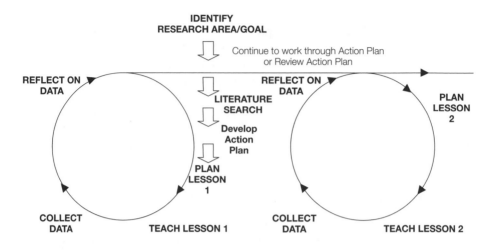

▨ **Figure 17.4** Action Research model (adapted from McKernan, 1996)

data. In the light of the class you will be teaching you plan the first lesson, drawing from the cluster of approaches you have already identified. You teach the lesson and you or an observer gather data, as you teach and possibly after the lesson, through a way of capturing pupil response to the teaching. You then interrogate the data in much the same way as you analyse a lesson evaluation and reflect on and decide how you will teach the following lesson. According to the nature of the data you may stay within your original Action Plan or you may decide to modify this. As Figure 17.4 shows, you then plan and teach the next lesson, collect and reflect on data and so the cycle continues.

Cohen, Manion and Morrison (2007: 192) suggest 'ideally, the step-by-step process is constantly monitored over varying periods of time'. Here they alert you to the fact that you do not solve a problem or unpack all aspects of an issue in one lesson. Rather in each lesson you try a particular combination of elements of teaching. Successful elements should be retained and built upon whereas less successful elements should be modified or discarded in the light of your reflection. This relies on your skills of observation, reflection and evaluation. Systematically reflecting on data gathered, lesson-by-lesson, to consider why particular outcomes were realised in the light of a particular strategy is the hallmark of Action Research.

The focus of your Action Research

Action Research characteristically starts by identifying a perceived issue or problem in a lesson. This may be identified through your lesson observations, information gathering, reflections and evaluations. Common foci for Action Research in PE include:

- ▪ solving a particular issue or problem related to promoting pupil learning, for example, raising pupils' self-esteem, improving social cohesion in a class, improving your mixed ability teaching, finding different ways of achieving differentiation in your lessons;

■ monitoring your own performance in an area that needs developing, for example, not praising pupils enough, not using demonstrations effectively, having a monotonous voice;

■ enabling pupils to achieve a particular ILO, such as using ICT to effect;

■ achieving a particular goal, for example, promoting creativity, getting boys and girls to work together more effectively, using particular learning resources (for example, teaching cards for use in reciprocal teaching) or teaching strategies.

Further information and details of how to engage in Action Research can be found in section 4.3c in Capel, Breckon and O'Neill (2006).

Before undertaking Action Research you need to understand fully the ethical implications and implement these throughout. For example, if you are on your ITE course, you should tell your tutor what you intend to do and the sort of information you are going to collect and check that your tutor is in full agreement with all aspects of your investigation. Once you are qualified you will need the approval of your Head of Department and possibly other senior members of staff. If collecting information from other people you must be sure they know why you are collecting it and that you have their full agreement and permission to collect the information. You must also maintain confidentiality. For further detail about these and other ethical considerations refer to the guidelines in Capel, Leask and Turner (2009, Unit 5.4) and Bell (2005, Chapter 3).

Information-gathering techniques

As Cohen, Manion and Morrison (2007) indicate, a central feature of Action Research is the gathering of data that provides a record of the outcomes of your teaching in relation to pupils' learning. This data needs to be analysed in detail to decide on your next steps in the process. The gathering of data is therefore an important aspect of this research. The information you gather by observation or using other information-gathering techniques are of two types:

■ *quantitative* techniques: any method which produces data that can be reduced to a numerical form and can be analysed statistically (for example, a record of the number of times an event occurs). Quantitative data is normally collected in a structured format using some type of rating scale, for example, those recording: *duration* (a record of when an event starts and when it finishes, e.g. by using a stop watch, e.g. pupils' time on task); *interval* (a record of what event occurs in a set period of time, e.g. non-verbal behaviour); or an *event* (a record of the number of times an event occurs in a lesson, e.g. a demonstration). 'Closed' questions on questionnaires can also be quantitative;

■ *qualitative* techniques: any method used to gain insight rather than statistical analysis, for example, unstructured observations, personal perceptions about what is observed, reflective journals/diaries, some rating scales, documents, interviews, and 'open-ended' questions on questionnaires.

Quantitative and qualitative data can be gathered through observation as well as other data collection techniques such as keeping field notes/diaries, using questionnaires and conducting interviews. See Capel, Breckon and O'Neill (2006) Activity 4.3a which asks you to consider the strengths and weaknesses of different data collection techniques.

OBSERVATION INSTRUMENTS

These are useful, structured frameworks for recording lesson observations. The advantage is that they can be constructed to focus the observation on a particular issue and can be used to provide either quantitative or qualitative information. Samples of observation schedules available, samples of which are on this book's website (see www.routledge.com/textbooks/9780415561648) and in Activities 4.3c and 9.2 in Capel, Breckon and O'Neill, 2006. Hopkins (2002) provides examples of observation schedules and checklists developed by teachers who were concerned with gathering information on a variety of issues and Underwood (1988) includes schedules for analysing aspects of learning/teaching in the PE context. Alternatively you can develop your own schedule for a specific purpose.

FIELD NOTES AND DIARIES

Very often field notes are used as a first step prior to narrowing down the focus of an investigation. They are particularly relevant for observations designed to allow you to describe events in a lesson, either considering the whole range of events that occur (for example, recording your general impressions of a teaching environment), or describing all events in a broadly defined area of concern (for example, pupil behaviour). Such observations are designed to enable you to identify any issues or problems and to determine what you want to look at in more detail. You can then collect information systematically to focus further investigation on the issue or problem. McKernan (1996) distinguishes between three types of field notes/diary you can maintain in educational research:

- intimate journal – a personal diary to record events on a day-to-day basis;
- log book – used regularly to summarise key happenings and events;
- memoir – entries made infrequently which allows time to reflect on events and interpret them more objectively.

In a sense the PDP you are keeping throughout your ITE course can be seen as the forerunner to more focused research-based field notes and diaries. Your lesson evaluations are an example of a form of diary or log book. Field notes are particularly useful if you wish to undertake a case study of an individual pupil or group of pupils, for example, if you are involved in a 'shadowing' exercise. In such instances observations and field notes are made over a period of time and can then be collated in a diary. This can then be used to reflect on and analyse patterns over a period of time. It is always important to maintain confidentiality and avoid direct reference to individuals and specific schools within your field notes.

QUESTIONNAIRES

These can be a useful means of acquiring information about learning and teaching from the perspective of the teacher and/or the pupils. By asking pupils specific questions about the lesson, for example, you can gather valuable information about the impact of your teaching on the pupils. The way your questions are constructed is of considerable importance to the effectiveness of your questionnaire. As Burton (2007: 153) suggests, your questions should be:

■ *clear* – questions are constructed simply and combining questions must be avoided;

■ *concise* – to minimise ambiguity and avoid information overload;

■ *accessible* – the language must be appropriate for your participants and compli-cated grammar such as double-negatives should be avoided;

■ *unbiased* – questions must be structured impartially and leading questions that can bias responses must be avoided.

Several types of question can be incorporated into your questionnaire, providing varying degrees of quantitative and/or qualitative data. *Closed questions*, for example, give your pupils definitive choices and limit their responses to a 'yes' or 'no' type of format whereas *open-ended* questions can elicit a phrase or comment and may be more illumin-ating, but rely on the language ability of the pupil.

The questionnaire in Figure 17.5 would be quick to administer and provide you with quantitative and qualitative data about a lesson. It includes both closed and open-ended questions.

Question	Circle the answer that best matches your view
Do you enjoy PE lessons?	Usually/Sometimes/Never
How much of this lesson did you enjoy?	All of it/Some of it/None of it
How successful do you think you were in what you were asked to do?	Very successful/Quite successful/Not at all successful
How much did you learn in this lesson?	Very much/Something/Not much
How active do you feel you were in this lesson?	Very active/Quite active/Not active enough
How much equipment did you have?	Enough/Not enough
How much help did you get from the teacher?	Enough/Not enough
	Answer the question in your own words
Write down anything you particularly enjoyed about this lesson	
Write down anything you feel could make this lesson better	

■ **Figure 17.5** An example of a simple questionnaire on pupils' perceptions of learning

If care is taken in their construction, questionnaires can be easy to administer and provide a large amount of information. One problem is that in a normal teaching situation ques-tionnaires take time to give out, complete and return. Another problem is that they depend on whether or not the pupils have the ability to understand the questions. When constructing a questionnaire or selecting one already developed, ensure that the language is at the right level for the pupils and is jargon free so that they understand exactly what you are asking. There is also a danger that pupils may not be truthful, but try to please the teacher by writing the type of answer they think the teacher wishes to hear. Bell (2005) provides detailed guidance on designing and administering questionnaires.

INTERVIEWS

There are three main types of interview: structured, semi-structured and unstructured.

- *Structured* interviews allow you to work through an interview schedule and are usually composed of closed questions, which direct the response options of those you interview. With such limited flexibility, however, your data may lack evidence that is pivotal to your research, as the questions you ask might not offer a sufficient range of responses to gain a fully comprehensive overview of the topic.
- *Semi-structured* interviews offer a more flexible style, which can be used to collect information equivalent to that of structured interviews. You begin by identifying a number of key questions that not only elicit specific types of response, but also act as prompts. Further probing can be used to ensure that those interviewed understand the question. A technique described by Oppenheim (1992) as 'funnelling questions' helps you to gain more information about an area of interest by pursuing further questions around the same subject area or theme.
- *Unstructured* interviews are the most flexible style and can allow you to gather complementary evidence. This approach is generally used to explore an area in preliminary research, for people with access to specialised information. However, the success of such interviews relies heavily upon the dexterity and expertise of the interviewer, for example, when the interviewer poses informed questions and adapts to the situation by reacting perceptively to new leads as they arise during the interview.

Although interviews are usually undertaken on a one-to-one basis you can interview your research participants in groups. The main advantage of group interviews is that they can elicit rich data as your participants listen to one another. Further benefits identified by Cohen, Manion and Morrison (2007) include: people are often less intimidated, feel more at ease and can freely engage in discussion; they are less time consuming than individual interviews; and, subsequent individual interviews can explore issues which arose from the group interview. The major disadvantages of group interviews, as Fontana and Frey (2000: 652) identified, are that 'the results cannot be generalised, the emerging group culture may interfere with individual expression ... the group may be dominated by one person and "groupthink" is a possible outcome'.

Using information gathered

An important point to note is that the information you collect is only the starting point for your investigations. It should be used to inform your reflections, evaluation, discussions with your tutor or other teachers, and to determine any action to be taken, for example, developing, implementing, monitoring and evaluating a solution. Perceptive reflection on the data is essential to understand reasons for the effectiveness or otherwise of particular teaching and to plan for the next lesson in the Action Research cycle.

Task 17.4 gives you guidance in conducting a mini Action Research project of your own.

> ## Task 17.4 **An Action Research project**
>
> An Action Research project may be part of your coursework. If not, undertake this task.
>
> Identify an issue you want to address, a problem you want to solve, for example an aspect of your performance you want to monitor or a specific aspect of pupil learning you want to improve, with a view to improving your own practice or pupil learning. Through conducting a literature search identify what other writing/research has been carried out into the issue in question. Decide the best methods of collecting information and design your research instruments (if necessary enlist the support of your tutor or another student teacher; it is often helpful to undertake Action Research in pairs). Arrange appropriate lesson(s) for the information to be collected. Analyse the information and try to come to some conclusions. In the light of your results consider how you might modify your practice. Try to change your practice as appropriate and monitor the changes made. Repeat the information collecting at a later date to determine how successfully you have modified your practice. Put the outcome of this investigation in your PDP.

There are two more Master's level tasks on this book's website (see www.routledge.com/textbooks/9780415561648).

THE VALUE OF RESEARCH INTO YOUR TEACHING

By conducting research in this way you are investigating aspects of educational theory. You are coming to appreciate the complex ways in which theory and practice are related and to realise that while there is much common ground in teaching, every situation creates a specific context for using theory to inform practice. As you work in this way you come to understand the range of elements that influence 'good practice', for example the school context, the social dynamic in a class and the way pupils perceive the activity/subject you are teaching. You apply the outcomes to your own teaching and/or pupil learning in order to address an issue, solve a problem or achieve a particular goal. You may then look at the same issue, problem or goal in more depth or from a different perspective, or move on to another focus. You can also share your findings with others, for example, you could write an article for a professional journal (such as *Physical Education Matters*) or present a paper at a conference to share your findings with others.

A number of opportunities currently exist for teachers to undertake research as detailed in Chapter 18 and you are encouraged to consider engaging in this work once you are established in your first teaching post. Your professional association, the Association for Physical Education (afPE), is also active in encouraging research. Their Research and Development Working Group identify areas of research which are currently of particular relevance to PE in the United Kingdom. They can provide guidance and some relevant initial readings, and suggestions for possible research questions to be explored in the area. The afPE website provides links to some other websites that may help you in relation to research (see http://www.afpe.org.uk).

SUMMARY AND KEY POINTS

This chapter has tried to help you to 'see' what is happening in order to 'read' the complex situations you encounter in the learning and teaching environment, both in NCPE (2007) activity settings and in the classroom. It is widely acknowledged that observing experienced teachers teach is one of the best methods of gaining insights into the learning and teaching process. The problem is that time spent in school, and in lesson observation, can be wasted if there is not a clear focus. In this chapter some techniques for focusing your observations and obtaining relevant information have been identified. The chapter has also introduced you to the need to reflect on your observations and critically analyse 'what' you are doing and importantly, to be able to justify 'why' you are doing it. Only by adopting a critical stance are you able to respond in a rational, reflective and professional way to the many factors which no doubt impinge upon pupil learning and your teaching of PE throughout your professional life. Undertaking Action Research should help you to identify issues and address problems identified through observation, reflection and evaluation. This means thinking critically about what you are doing, finding ways of systematically investigating it and making sense of your investigations. As you gain experience, confidence and learn to challenge, communicate, explore ideas you become a better teacher and match up to Stenhouse's (1975) description of an extended professional.

Check which requirements for your course you have addressed through this chapter.

FURTHER READING

Bell, J. (2005) *Doing your Research Project: A Guide for First-time Researchers in Education and Social Science*, 4th edn, Maidenhead: Open University Press.

This book is designed for people who are undertaking small-scale research projects. Part 2, 'Selecting methods of information collection', provides examples of information collecting techniques.

British Educational Research Association (2004) *Revised Ethical Guidelines for Educational Research,* Southwell: BERA. Available online at: http://www.bera.ac.uk.

This publication is essential reading for helping you to consider the ethical implications of research you might undertake.

Burton, N., Brundett, M. and Jones, M. (2008) *Doing Your Education Research Project*, London: Sage.

This book discusses the nature of practitioner-based research in relation to professional development. It provides useful guidance on designing your research project and data-gathering techniques.

Capel, S., Breckon, P. and O'Neill, J. (eds) (2006) *A Practical Guide to Teaching Physical Education in the Secondary School,* Abingdon, Oxon: Routledge.

Chapter 3 provides a range of practical activities to help develop your capacity and understanding of how to engage in reflective practice. Chapter 4 is designed to develop your understanding of the principles and procedures of Action Research and recognise its potential within the context of teaching and learning.

Capel, S., Leask, M. and Turner, T. (2009) *Learning to Teach in the Secondary School: A Companion to School Experience*, 5th edn, London: Routledge.

Unit 5.4 offers further advice on practitioner research, reflective practice and evidence-informed practice.

Hopkins, D. (2002) *A Teacher's Guide to Classroom Research*, 3rd edn, Buckingham: Open University Press.

This book is a good starting point for anyone wishing to research their own practice. It contains practical ideas and examples of a variety of information collection techniques in addition to guidance on each aspect of the research process.

Koshy, V. (2005) *Action Research for Improving Practice – A Practical Guide,* London: Paul Chapman.

This book provides step-by-step advice on how to undertake Action Research from choosing a topic, devising your plan of action, gathering and analysing data to writing up your project or dissertation. It also offers advice on how to set up small-scale research projects in schools for improving practice.

CONTINUING PROFESSIONAL DEVELOPMENT IN PE

Susan Capel

INTRODUCTION

Your professional development as a teacher should be viewed as a lifelong learning process. This process begins whilst you are a student teacher, extends into your first/induction year of teaching as a newly qualified teacher (NQT) and continues throughout your teaching career. Lawrence, Taylor and Capel point out that this lifelong process of learning, commonly known as continuing professional development (CPD), 'helps you continue to learn and develop professionally throughout your career' (2009: 443). CPD has been defined as consisting 'of reflective activity designed to improve an individual's attributes, knowledge, understanding and skills. It supports individual needs and improves professional practice' (Training and Development Agency for Schools (TDA, http://www.tda.gov.uk/teachers/continuingprofessionaldevelopment/what_is_cpd.aspx). Thus, ongoing CPD is essential for and integral to effective teaching and, hence, to effective pupil learning.

You must take responsibility for your own professional development. Many of you are following a structured initial teacher education (ITE) course on which your progress is assessed through both practical assessment of your teaching and written assessments which, if you are learning to teach in England, is likely to be at Master's level. At the end of your ITE course in England your career entry and development profile (CEDP) (http://www.tda.gov.uk/induction) is the beginning of active planning for your future career, identifying appropriate areas for development and activities and/or experiences appropriate to achieve these. During your induction period support is provided by an induction tutor, whilst as your teaching career progresses you are supported by school managers. The greatest asset of any school is its teachers and continued support for their professional development and well-being is central to raising standards of teaching, learning and assessment.

As well as recognising the importance of CPD you need to consider carefully both the focus and type of CPD which you undertake. The focus may be, for example, development of teachers' knowledge and/or teaching skills, but may also embrace a number of other foci and activities, including critical thinking, reflective practice, intellectual development, personal, moral and political dimensions of teaching as a professional activity. As regards the type of CPD, this may include a variety of activities, including formal accredited and non-accredited courses (either longer term (such as a Master's course) or short-term courses); teacher appraisal; involvement in action research projects; reading current research and inspection evidence; independent learning; attending conferences; critical observation of peers and your teaching being observed; collaborative practices such as peer teaching; demonstrations with teachers as pupils; analysis of individual differences such as learning styles and preferences. One of the most common types of CPD activity has been the one-off short course. However, this type of CPD has been criticised. For example, Armour and Yelling (2002) found that much CPD tends to take place at specific times, is often off-site, involves one-off attendance at training courses with minimal follow-up, entails limited dissemination of information to teachers in school, and provides limited opportunities and/or support to enable teachers to apply new learning 'in the classroom'.

More effective is CPD which is substantial and sustained over time; makes connections between new learning and existing practice; is well resourced financially and in relation to staffing. Garet *et al.* (2001) stress the importance of engaging teachers in active learning: actively engaging in meaningful planning, practice, discussion and debate (e.g. observing and being observed). The General Teaching Council for England (GTCE, 2007b) identifies the characteristics of effective CPD as:

- having a clear focus on pupil learning;
- involving teachers in identifying their needs;
- being grounded in what is known about effective adult learning.

This includes:

- sustained access to coaching and mentoring;
- a range of opportunities for observation and feedback as part of collaborative and collegial working practices;
- opportunities for teachers to change practice, carry out research and engage in reflective practice;
- modelling of preferred practice (e.g. active learning) both in classrooms and in adult learning situations;
- sustained structured and cumulative opportunities for practising what has been learnt.

This chapter considers CPD, starting with aspects of your ITE course, then the transition from student teacher to newly qualified teacher (NQT), induction into your first school and into teaching (both immediate and during the first year of teaching) and CPD beyond the first year.

OBJECTIVES

At the end of this chapter you should be able to:

- maintain an accurate record of evidence of your professional development through the use of a portfolio of professional development;
- apply for your first teaching post;

- make the transition from student teacher to NQT;
- make best use of your induction;
- recognise some of the CPD opportunities available to you as a teacher and set goals for CPD early in your career.

Check the requirements for your course to see which relate to this chapter.

We suggest that you read Unit 8.2 in Capel, Leask and Turner (2009) alongside this chapter.

DEVELOPING AND MAINTAINING YOUR PROFESSIONAL DEVELOPMENT PORTFOLIO (PDP)

A PDP is an accumulative record of your progress and development during your ITE PE course. Indeed, we have asked you to store information from the tasks throughout this book in your PDP. It documents your performance in relation to the requirements to qualify as a teacher, your strengths and successes and areas for development and gives examples of your work that is part of your ITE course. It contains evidence of your developing professional knowledge and judgement to complement your knowledge for teaching. Benefits of building a PDP include enabling you (and others) to reflect upon, discuss and record both your achievements and professional development needs, thereby identifying and monitoring your progress and development; and it can form a strong platform from which to consider your professional development needs during your first few weeks as an NQT. Your higher education institution (HEI) is likely to provide you with a framework for building your PDP. If not, below is an example of what you might include in your PDP.

- curriculum vitae (including relevant certificates/awards) (you can find information on a CV in Unit 8.1 (pp. 430–1) in Capel, Leask and Turner (2009));
- needs analysis/audit (1 per term);
- action plans (2–3 per term);
- school-based subject tutor and HEI tutor observation notes and/or written reports from observations of your teaching; reflections on lesson observations;
- notes of weekly meetings with your school-based subject tutor;
- record of evidence of achieving the standards to qualify as a teacher;
- PE and professional studies written assignments and related activities/tasks;
- notes/reflections on HEI-based work; on tasks undertaken as you read this book; on any aspect of your course as it happens;
- reflections on professional development undertaken outside your course and evaluations of their impact on pupils' learning;
- reflections on/evaluations of other aspects of teaching and learning and your development as a teacher in the broader school context;
- any other items you identify as appropriate/important to you.

Your PDP is a valuable document to take with you for interview for your first teaching post (and in England to inform your self-evaluation tool). It is also useful to have throughout your teaching career (e.g. preparation for your formal appraisal or perform-ance management-related interview). Aspects of your PDP may be incorporated into a professional development record (PDR), such as the one developed by the Professional Development Board (PDB) for PE in England (which is available from the Association for Physical Education (afPE)). Task 18.1 asks you to start keeping your PDP.

Task 18.1 **Your professional development portfolio (PDP)**

If you are given a PDP on your ITE course, keep it up to date and organised. If you are not given a PDP, devise one yourself using the framework identified above along with any other information that you feel is appropriate. Regularly identify, monitor, record and reflect critically on your progress and development; particularly your achievements, professional development needs and action plans.

DEVELOPING YOUR KNOWLEDGE FOR TEACHING

Before reading the next section, complete Task 18.2.

Task 18.2 **Knowledge for teaching**

List that knowledge you think, at this stage of your development as a teacher, you need to be able to teach effectively to promote pupils' learning. Compare your list with that of another student teacher.

After reading the next section of the chapter, return to your list and compare with the knowledge identified below. If it is different, why do you think that is so?

Store your reflections in your PDP.

Teaching should be viewed as a knowledge-based profession, as opposed to a compe-tence-based profession. High-quality or expert teaching is not merely a matter of acquiring teaching skills; it also requires a range of knowledge.

There are many different classifications of knowledge for teaching (see, for example, Hoyle and John 1995; McIntyre, 2005; Wilson, 2009). One commonly used classification of knowledge you need to develop to be an effective teacher is Shulman's (1987) model of knowledge bases for effective teaching. This is offered here as a valuable framework for CPD. Shulman (1987: 8) describes the knowledge bases required by teachers as:

1   *Content Knowledge* (sometimes called subject matter knowledge): the amount and organisation of knowledge in the mind of the teacher. This includes substantive structures (the factual information and explanatory frameworks that are used both to make sense of information and to guide inquiry in the subject) and syntactic structures (the variety of ways in which the basic concepts and principles of the discipline are organised, and the ways in which truth or falsehood, validity or inva-lidity, are established).

2   *General Pedagogical Knowledge*: those broad principles and strategies of class-
     room management and organisation that appear to transcend subject matter.
3   *Pedagogical Content Knowledge*: the combination of content and pedagogy that is
     the distinctive body of knowledge for teaching a particular subject and that makes
     the subject comprehensible to others. It includes, for any given subject area, the
     most useful forms of representation of ideas, the most powerful analogies, illustra-
     tions, examples, explanations and demonstrations and how particular topics,
     problems, or issues are organised, represented, adapted to the diverse interests and
     abilities of learners and presented.
4   *Knowledge of Learners and their Characteristics*: empirical or social knowledge of
     learners (knowledge of children of a particular age range); and cognitive knowl-
     edge of learners (knowledge of child development and context-bound to a
     particular group of learners).
5   *Curriculum Knowledge*: the text, materials and programmes that serve as 'tools of
     the trade' for the teacher.
6   *Knowledge of Educational Contexts*: factors which affect development and class-
     room performance, ranging from the workings of the group or classroom, the
     governance and financing of schools, to the character of communities and cultures.
7   *Knowledge of Educational Ends, Purposes and Values (and the philosophical and
     historical grounds)*: the purposeful activity of teaching, both in the sense of short-
     term goals for a lesson or series of lessons and in the sense of long-term purposes
     of education.

This knowledge for teaching is not comprehensive. For example, Turner-Bisset (1999)
added knowledge of self. Teaching demands a large investment of self, therefore the self
is a crucial element in the way teachers themselves understand the nature of the job and
is an important requisite for reflection at the higher levels. Further, it is also important to
recognise that the knowledge (and skills) you develop does not stand in isolation; rather,
the knowledge (and skills) are interacting and it is this which underpins effective
teaching.

In addition, it is argued by Turner-Bisset (1999) that, as student teachers, you use
fewer knowledge bases at any one time than experienced teachers; tend to adopt whole-
sale lessons modelled by experienced teachers without adapting the lessons for a
particular group of learners or educational context, without reflecting on the content
knowledge or pedagogical content knowledge or without a very clear understanding and
knowledge of educational ends, purposes or values; and often want an abundant reper-
toire of ideas for lessons to make a good impression on school staff and pupils and to
have lessons which go well, without management or discipline problems (Chapter 17
looks at the importance of critical reflection in your planning – not only teaching something because it has always been taught that way). Thus, you continue to learn and
develop after qualifying as a teacher.

Now return to Task 18.1 and compare your list with the list above. It is likely that,
like many other student teachers, you have identified content knowledge, pedagogical
content knowledge and curriculum knowledge (in England the NCPE). You may not have
included other aspects of knowledge needed for teaching. If not, it is important to understand the range and breadth of knowledge you need to know and be able to apply in
developing your teaching.

You have arrived on your ITE course with different experiences and understandings of PE compared with others on your course. You have a range of strengths and professional development needs in terms of practical experience and knowledge in a subject as complex as PE. In order to identify and address knowledge strengths and professional development needs, your HEI is likely to ask you to complete a needs analysis/audit. The starting point is to encourage you to identify and assess your strengths and needs and plan how you are going to develop your strengths and redress gaps in your knowledge. This audit is likely to include a system for reviewing your progress and identifying the action you need to take to enable you to consolidate, develop and monitor these knowledge bases during your ITE course (say half-way through and at the end), first/induction year of teaching and throughout your teaching career.

Figure 18.1 provides one method of recording evidence of your knowledge strengths and identifying the action you need to take to develop further. Now complete Task 18.3.

Task 18.3 **Reviewing your knowledge of the subject**

Complete the grid shown in Figure 18.1 (an empty grid can be found on this book's website; www.routledge.com/textbooks/9780415561648) by identifying:

■ The type of evidence that you can list to indicate ability at each of the three times during the course;
■ The action you need to take to develop your knowledge.

This grid does not include all the knowledge you need to develop. Add further areas to the grid, as appropriate.

   Use this as the basis for your development during both your ITE course and induction year. Remember that on your ITE course you might not be able to develop all knowledge bases/aspects of your teaching at the same time, therefore, identify your priorities. Store this in your PDP.

Towards the end of your ITE course you need to find a teaching post. The next section looks at applying for your first teaching post.

APPLYING FOR YOUR FIRST TEACHING POST

One of many challenges facing you during ITE course is securing your first teaching post. It is important that you give careful consideration and attention to this process. There is a wealth of information to guide and support you in this process, much of which provides a common framework for obtaining your first teaching post. For example:

■ *deciding where you want to teach;*
■ *looking for suitable vacancies* (e.g. where and when teaching posts are advertised and whether a post is right for you);
■ *applying for a teaching post* (e.g. sending for details; information about the post; how to use the person specification; writing successful job applications and covering letters; writing a CV; choosing referees; criminal records bureau clearance, criminal convictions);

Content knowledge	Strengths that you bring to your ITE course (i.e. 3 or 4 (see * below), plus evidence you can offer to indicate knowledge)	September/Winter Term areas for development (i.e. activities you grade 1 or 2 (see * below))	Action you need to take to develop ability	December/Spring Term areas for development (i.e. 1 or 2 * below)	Action you need to take to develop ability	March/Summer Term areas for development (i.e. 1 or 2 * below)	Action you need to take to develop ability
Safe practice in activities included in curriculum in which you are teaching	3 = Canoeing (BCU UKCC Level 1 Certificate in Coaching Paddlesport) 4 = Athletics (Coaching Level 2 Core; much experience in coaching all ages in most events); Swimming (ASA_UKCC Level 3 Certificate for Coaching Swimming)	1 = rugby, gymnastics	Undertake some rugby training. Need to attend gymnastics course and/or observe and assist with gym clubs				
Confidence in **playing/ performing** and **demonstrating**	3 = dance 4 = hockey, netball, swimming	1 = gymnastics, tennis, rugby	Play more tennis and rugby				
Knowledge of **teaching/learning points** of activities included in the curriculum in your placement school	3 = dance, outdoor and adventurous activities 4 = athletics, swimming	1 = gymnastics	More experience in dance. Ask for some on timetable after half term. Much more gym needed				

Tactical knowledge and knowledge of rules. List of activities in which you have a good working knowledge of the rules	3 = volleyball 4 = hockey, netball	1 = tennis, rugby 2 = basketball	Attend courses in rugby and basketball. Read the latest rule books		
Officiating awards. List governing bodies for which you have attained awards			Take officiating course in hockey, netball		

* Score yourself on a range of activities included in the curriculum for PE, according to your confidence in your knowledge and understanding in these areas and how confident you are performing them and demonstrating to others:

1 = no experience/knowledge/confidence/performance;
2 = little experience/knowledge/confidence/performance;
3 = good experience/knowledge/confidence/performance, but little valid evidence;
4 = extensive experience/very good knowledge/very confident/very skilled performer, with evidence.

IMPORTANT

Remember that while the above chart refers to activity-specific strengths and areas for development, in England your teaching should use the activities as contexts for learning, with the teaching directed towards helping pupils master the Key Concepts and Key Processes in NCPE (see Chapter 13).

■ **Figure 18.1** Review of knowledge for teaching: knowledge strengths in different physical activities and identification of the action you need to take to develop further in relation to your timetable each term

- *interviews* (e.g. preparing for an interview; the interview itself; withdrawing from an interview; interview expenses);
- *if you are offered the post* (e.g. deciding whether you want the post; starting salary; accepting the post);
- *getting feedback from a school in which you have been unsuccessful in getting a job* (useful advice can sometimes be gained concerning the school's perception of your strengths and weaknesses).

For further details of how and where to obtain information on applying for your first teaching post, we suggest you read Unit 8.1 in Capel, Leask and Turner (2009). Other useful sources are listed in the further reading at the end of this chapter. If, however, you are not successful in securing a permanent job, consider supply teaching. Task 18.4 is designed to help you with one aspect of getting a job: your CV.

Task 18.4 **Curriculum vitae**

Either write, or update, your curriculum vitae (see p. 430 in Capel, Leask and Turner (2009) for information about the content and format for a CV). Discuss this with another student teacher or your tutor to identify your *strengths* both in relation to your practical teaching and your knowledge and your *professional development needs*. Check that these match with your current audit and that you have a clear plan for development.

Put your CV and audit in your PDP.

TRANSITION FROM STUDENT TEACHER TO NEWLY QUALIFIED TEACHER (NQT)

Successfully completing your ITE course and securing a teaching post is just the start of your development as a teacher. You are likely to have mixed feelings at this stage: relief at having passed the course and qualifying as a teacher; confidence and belief in your ability to solve any problem you are faced with; but also fear of failure. As you face the reality of teaching as an NQT, you may find you lose your confidence and cannot solve every problem. It is important to recognise that this is a normal part of your development as a teacher. The continued support you receive as an NQT (and subsequently through-out your teaching career) is designed to support you through this, to help you to continue to identify professional development needs to continue to improve your effectiveness as a teacher.

As a start in successfully making the transition from student teacher to NQT you will no doubt want to visit the school before you formally take up your first teaching post. Indeed, most schools encourage this. This usually takes place towards the end of the summer term and enables you to spend some time getting to know the teachers with whom you will be working and to collect useful documentation (for example, your timetable, copies of schemes of work and examination syllabuses, dates of fixtures, the staff handbook). In addition, you may be invited to visit the school when pupils meet their form teachers for the following year. If you are taking on duties of a form teacher, this is a valuable opportunity to meet your form/tutor group informally. You may also be invited to assist with sports day or a similar school event run by the PE department.

These preliminary visits can be a valuable boost to your confidence by providing an opportunity to ask those questions which only occurred to you after the interview. You can also ensure that you have the resources necessary to guide your thinking and preparation for the term ahead. If you are to make best use of this time, it is well worth doing some preparation for the visit by making a checklist of the questions you wish to ask, resources you need to collect, people you need to meet. Some of these are listed in Table 18.1.

■ **Table 18.1** Checklist of questions to be asked and information to be collected from a preliminary visit to your school

---

■ Curriculum: What exactly will you be teaching?
■ Pupils: Numbers in classes? Names of classes? Basis for organisation of groups? Other.
■ Procedures: For the changing rooms? Registers? Marking? Rewards and sanctions? Other procedures.
■ Resources: What facilities does the school have? Are facilities elsewhere used (e.g. the town's recreation centre)? If so, how do you get there? Where is the equipment stored? How do you access it? What resources are there for theory lessons?
■ Extra-curricular activities: When do these take place? What part will you be expected to play? What is the schedule of matches for the year?
■ Dates: of terms? Any special events? In-service days?
■ Clothing: Are there any special requirements?
■ People to meet: Head of department and staff teaching in the PE department; Head and deputies; induction tutor; head of year or house.
■ Useful contacts: Names and telephone numbers.
■ Any other information.

One of the people you will probably meet either on your preliminary visit or at the start of your first term is the school's induction tutor. This is likely to be a senior member of staff, often one of the deputy heads.

As an NQT, you will have some successes and some failures and will soon realise that you cannot solve every problem or change the world. As a result, your confidence may decrease and you may not be fully effective until you are settled in the school and the job. A supportive induction tutor and a well-structured induction programme should help you make this transition. (Chapter 1 in Capel *et al.* (2004) gives further information about the transition from student teacher to NQT and on your immediate professional needs.)

Task 18.5 asks you to look at this transition whilst you are on your ITE course.

Task 18.5 **Preparing for the transition from student teacher to NQT**

Talk to any NQTs in your placement school. Find out the differences, as they perceive them, between being a student teacher and an NQT. What preparation did they make before starting in the post? What help have they found particularly useful and why in making the transition?

Record in your PDP how you could use these experiences during your own induction year.

INDUCTION

Once you have qualified as a teacher and begun your teaching career, you will begin to consolidate what you have already learned on your ITE course and build on your achievements to date. Further, you may begin to understand the importance of some of the material you covered on your ITE course, which you did not understand at the time; indeed, many student teachers find that they did not understand the importance of some of the knowledge on their ITE course or how it all fitted together to support their teaching and it is only when they start to teach that they understand its importance and how it fits together. A well kept PDP is therefore vital in supporting this.

This next stage begins with your induction period. Induction can be divided into two main parts: immediate induction into the school and the job, which gives you vital information to help you through the early days; and ongoing induction throughout the first year; providing the link between ITE and CPD. Immediate induction is covered in Unit 8.2 in Capel, Leask and Turner (2009). The next section focuses on ongoing induction. The aim of the induction period is to ensure that all NQTs are supported throughout the first/induction year of teaching after they have been awarded QTS. Your induction period should provide you with an individual programme of professional development and monitoring. In England, during your induction period, TDA (http://www.tda.gov.uk/partners/induction.aspx) have indicated that you can expect:

1   an *induction tutor* who works with you to plan an effective individualised induction programme incorporating a range of development opportunities;
2   a *reduced timetable*. It is recommended that your timetable is no more than 90 per cent of that which another mainscale teacher (who does not receive a responsibility payment) is expected to teach at the same school. This time is in addition to any non-contact time and can be used for activities that specifically contribute to your induction programme;
3   an *individualised induction programme* of monitoring, support and assessment. This should be planned by you and your induction tutor and should reflect: your strengths and professional development needs and priorities (specified as objectives); the demands of the specific post in which you are starting your teaching career; and the requirements you need to meet at the end of induction (in England, the core standards (see http://www.tda.gov.uk/teachers/induction/corestandardsand assessment/corestandards.aspx). The support you require to meet these objectives

includes identifying who will be responsible for what, and when activities will take place. It is important that you understand the purpose of the programme and what it will involve;

4   *a programme of professional development opportunities.* In collaboration with your induction tutor, you will need to plan other professional development opportunities, for example: opportunities to observe the teaching of experienced teachers; planning with the department and school; visits to schools and settings beyond your own workplace; more formal training events and courses; working alongside others and becoming involved in planning within the department or school; meeting with your induction tutor to review your progress and consider your development;

5   *observation of your teaching* during the first four weeks and then approximately every six to eight weeks by your induction tutor and/or by others as appropriate *with follow up review meetings* whereby you and your induction tutor review the lesson and your progress against your objectives and revise your objectives and action plan if necessary. The first observation should take place during the first four weeks of the first term and then occur at least once per half-term;

6   *termly formal assessment meetings* towards the end of each term, involving you, your induction tutor and/or headteacher for a formal assessment. The main focus of these meetings is to review your current progress towards meeting requirements of induction (in England, the core standards);

7   *reports on your progress.* After each of the first two formal assessment meetings, the headteacher should make a report to the Local Authority (LA) or other appropriate body (e.g. in England to the Independent Schools Council teacher induction panel (ISCtip)) on your progress towards meeting the requirements to pass induction;

8   *additional support in cases of difficulties.* If you are in danger of not meeting the requirements of induction by the end of the induction period, further support should be planned and arranged as soon as possible. In England, the LA/ISCtip should be informed and should equally check that this support is in place. Unsatisfactory progress at one stage of your induction programme does not mean that you will inevitably fail to complete the induction period successfully. It is important that all parties work positively to help you overcome any shortcomings;

9   *a named contact at the LA/ISCtip.* If you have any concerns about the content or administration of your induction programme, you must first use the school's procedures for raising professional concerns. If your concerns go beyond the school or are not addressed, you should contact the named induction contact in the LA/ISCtip, details of whom should have been given to you at the beginning of your induction period;

10 *a recommendation on completion of induction.* After the formal assessment meeting towards the end of the induction period, your headteacher will make a recommendation to the LA/ISCtip about whether you have met the requirements for induction. The LA/ISCtip will decide whether you have met the requirements of satisfactory completion of the induction period, and will write to you, your headteacher and the GTCE to communicate this decision.

There is further information on induction in Unit 8.2 (pp. 443–52) in Capel, Leask and Turner (2009).

CPD THROUGHOUT YOUR TEACHING CAREER

Progression and continuity in teaching from your ITE PE course to the induction period signifies the first stage of your CPD. Similarly, satisfactory completion of the induction period should provide a strong base for taking on greater responsibilities for your own CPD throughout your teaching career. In the final assessment meeting of your induction period, you target areas for development for your second (and early) years of teaching. The focus and type of CPD you pursue depends on a number of factors: what aspects of your teaching need to be developed in order to improve your future practice; how can you best go about improving your practice in the area(s) that really needs developing; and your future career plans and aspirations. You need to devise a programme of CPD activities to meet your own individual improvement and development needs.

As a start, you should be well acquainted with the continuous and cyclical process of planning, teaching and reflection/review to improve your teaching performance both intuitively and through a systematic self- and assisted appraisal as part of your induction period. In addition, both internal (teacher appraisal/performance management) and external (Office for Standards in Education (Ofsted) inspections) quality assurance mechanisms should be in place at your school to assess the quality of your teaching and the extent to which you are engaged in regular and systematic reflection on your own practice. The TDA (http://www.tda.gov.uk/teachers/continuingprofessionaldevelopment/what_is_cpd.aspx) identify three possible sources of CPD:

■ within school, e.g. coaching and mentoring, critical observation of other teachers and your teaching being observed, feedback on lesson observations, collaborative planning and teaching, shadowing, sharing good practice, whole-school development events;
■ school networks, e.g. cross-school and virtual networks;
■ other external expertise, e.g. external courses and further study offered by a range of providers, including higher education institutions and subject associations.

Some CPD activities are discussed below to help you in the process. These are appraisal and performance management; award and non-award bearing courses in education and PE; involvement with ITE as a subject tutor; and other CPD activities. This list is not exhaustive and you should identify CPD opportunities which suit your own individual learning needs.

Appraisal and performance management

Appraisal and performance management are part of making explicit teacher accountability and are crucial to the school's performance management arrangements. The information recorded in your PDP during your induction year should inform your induction review meeting at the end of your induction period. Targets set at your induction review meeting form the basis of your annual review, part of the performance management process. Appraisal normally consists of observation of your teaching and an appraisal interview. An appraisal interview should provide you with valuable dialogue. It may start with discussion of your observed teaching performance, then progress to your performance over the past year (particularly in relation to pupils' progress). In addition to your teaching, other topics may be discussed, for example, pastoral work, curriculum development work, administrative activities and management and membership of committees and working parties. In all of these areas you discuss your strengths and areas for development, CPD undertaken to address these or ways in which any identified needs might be met, e.g. by attending conferences, studying for a higher degree or other opportunities for CPD within the school.

Master's level and award bearing courses in education and PE

In developing your knowledge for teaching, those of you learning to teach on a one-year Postgraduate Certificate of Education (PGCE) course in England are likely to be studying for Master's level credits (you are likely to have 60 Master's level credits at the end of your course), as well as working towards meeting the standards you need to achieve to gain qualified teacher status at the end of your course. The Master's level aspect of the course is designed, at least in part, to support your development as critical educators, which Furlong identified as being able to 'educate pupils to think critically about knowledge and about values, to recognise differences in interpretation, to develop the skills needed to form their own judgements in a rapidly changing world' (Furlong, 2007). The Master's level aspect of the course enables you to take a critical approach to your own professional education and development.

To continue your progress and development from your ITE course, particularly in relation to linking theory to practice and critical analysis and reflection, you might wish to study for the additional credits to obtain a Master's Degree in Education or in PE. A higher degree should, for example: support your development as an autonomous professional; support your ability to define and evaluate complex educational issues drawing on national and international perspectives; deepen your knowledge and understanding of your specialist subject to enable you to analyse policy, theory and practice, and strive for excellence in teaching and learning; and equip you with the methodological knowledge needed to select appropriate methods to conduct research (see Chapter 17). It may also enhance your chances of promotion to middle and/or senior management positions, such as head of department, head of year or deputy headteacher.

It is likely that your HEI will have designed its Master's course(s) to follow on from your ITE course, perhaps with a module you can take as an NQT that helps you to develop your expertise and professional knowledge within the context of PE. In addition to providing CPD this also gives you the opportunity to return regularly to the HEI during your first year of teaching to discuss issues and to seek answers to specific questions from other NQTs or HEI tutors. You may then be able to take modules which support your development in an area which you have identified as part of your career development (e.g. specialist subject modules to become an advanced skills teacher, or expand into other areas such as leadership and management, special educational needs or other aspects of work). Master's courses in many HEIs allow you to use your school-based experiences to inform your learning, and some may have a focus on learning at work. Thus, there are a range of opportunities for continuing your learning through a Master's degree. As far as a teaching career is concerned, it is highly desirable for you to undertake modules as and when appropriate to your individual professional development needs.

As well as taught Masters' courses, there are research opportunities leading to a Doctor of Education (EdD), Master of Philosophy (MPhil) or Doctor of Philosophy (PhD). Contact your local HEI for further information.

Non-award bearing courses

The National College for Continuing Professional Development (NCfCPD) is run by afPE to 'play a major role in providing leadership for PE and those who deliver it, raising and protecting professional standards and enabling the Association to develop systematic accreditation systems to ensure appropriate preparation, experience and qualification; to promote safe and ethical delivery; and to share exemplary practice' (http://www.afpe.org.uk/public/ncfcpd_info.htm). The College provides CPD courses, consultancies and support options to support all PESS (PE and School Sport) staff in their professional development.

The Department for Children, Schools and Families (DCSF) and the Department for Culture, Media and Sport (DCMS) in England are jointly responsible for the Physical Education, School Sport and Club Links (PESSCL) National Strategy, which is designed to support, enhance and transform PE and school sport with the aim of offering all young people aged 5 to 16 the opportunity to participate in five hours a week of high-quality PE and sport (three hours for 16–19 year-olds). This is expected to be: at least two hours of high-quality PE and sport at schools – with the expectation that this will be delivered totally within the curriculum; and an additional two or more hours beyond the school day delivered by a range of school, community and club providers. The strategy comprises nine interrelated strands (specialist sports colleges; school sport coordinators; Professional Development; Step Into Sport; Club Links; Gifted and Talented; Sporting Playgrounds; Swimming; the Qualifications and Curriculum Authority (QCA) PE and School Sport Investigation). The professional development programme provides a number of modules which are available to PE teachers in maintained and special schools in England. You should familiarise yourself with this programme (see: http://www.teachernet.gov.uk/teachingandlearning/subjects/pe/nationalstrategy/Professional_Development/).

The PDB for PE in England exists to ensure that there is high-quality CPD for all PE teachers, for the benefit of pupils and to raise standards in PE and school sport (PESS). A list of courses which have been awarded a kite-mark or licence is available at: http://www.afpe.org.uk/public/pdb_current_awards.htm.

You might be interested in extending aspects of your content knowledge in PE by undertaking National Governing Body (NGB) awards in your specialist sport/activity. This might lead to you working with gifted and talented pupils at your school or at county, regional and national level. Alternatively, you might wish to take courses in sports/activities in which your content knowledge is not as strong (see, for example, 'Coaching for Teachers' courses).

Involvement with ITE as a subject tutor

One of the features of a healthy teaching profession is the fact that its members are actively involved in recruiting and educating the next generation of teachers. It is likely that, once you are established as a teacher, you will be able to share your expertise with student teachers through the role of subject tutor. Many teachers report that this is a rewarding and satisfying, but demanding, CPD activity. However, although student teachers need quality academic and emotional/pastoral support as they learn how to teach, they are also a valuable resource in offering new insights, visions and ideas related to current practice in PE, encouraging the subject tutor to reflect critically on his/her own practice.

Your own individual development needs

As an NQT you spend the first couple of years in teaching establishing yourself. However, once you have settled into your first teaching post, and as you grow in experience and confidence, you will probably want to develop areas of expertise and take on posts of responsibility, either within the subject area or department or within the school. There are several routes you might wish to follow, depending on your strengths, professional development needs, interests and possible career developments. For example, you may wish to remain in the classroom and support other teachers to develop their teaching further (in England this is an Advanced Skills Teacher; the requirements that demonstrate your excellence in the classroom can be accessed from http://www.teachernet.gov.uk/ast).

You might become involved with PE curriculum development projects such as assessment in PE (see Chapter 8) or 14–19 accredited qualifications in PE (see Chapter 15). A range of CPD opportunities are available in relation to each of these. For example, in the latter, if you are involved with teaching and/or examining PE at General Certificate of Secondary Education (GCSE) or General Certificate of Education Advanced (A) Level you may work as a marker or moderator for an awarding body – for which training is provided.

A common career development for PE teachers is one which utilises their skills of organisation and management. You may wish to become head of a PE department. To do this you would normally be expected to have gained at least three years' experience and have a proven record of good teaching, organisation and interpersonal skills. It is expected that you will have undertaken additional award and non-award bearing courses covering a range of aspects including subject development and middle management skills.

Other career development opportunities that you might want to pursue are those that are related to sports colleges and the school sports coordinator programme (see also Chapter 16). There are several roles which are part of partnership working with Specialist Sports Colleges, including Partnership Development Manager (usually located in a sports college with responsibility for managing the partnership and the links with other PE and sport organisations) and School Sport Coordinator (each secondary school in the partnership has a school sports coordinator with responsibility for developing after school sport, intra- and inter-school competition in the school and in a family of 4–5 primary schools). There is also a Primary Link Teacher within each of the primary/special schools in the partnership whose role is to improve PESS within the primary or special school. On this book's website there is both a list of current PE and school sport posts and a diagram to show the collaboration between schools in the Coopers Company and Coborn School Partnership which is coordinated by the Partnership Development Manager (see www.routledge.com/textbooks/9780415561648). Other roles within a School Sport Partnership may include Competition Manager, Further Education Sport Coordinator and Director of Sport. Again, a range of training opportunities are available.

There are a range of other posts which you might want to work towards which may be broader than PE, including Key Stage Coordinator. You may wish to extend the time you spend on the pastoral aspect of schools by undertaking the teaching of pastoral programmes in the school, attending conferences and courses for teachers interested in pastoral issues. These experiences could lead you to become assistant year/house tutor and then head of year/house.

It is important to recognise that, just as when you started your first post, when you take up a new responsibility or post, you go through a period of transition as you adjust to the new situation. You are likely to adjust more quickly if you have identified areas for development in a new post. This enables you to undertake appropriate CPD (and any formal qualifications or requirements) to develop an understanding of the role and the skills you need to carry out the role successfully. There are many CPD opportunities, for example, short or long courses, a higher degree or a further professional qualification and being involved in development and change activities in the school.

Although not discussed in detail here, a valuable opportunity for CPD is provided through involvement in school development planning. Discuss with your tutor the school development plan and how you might be involved in this in relation to your development targets and your career aspirations.

Other CPD activities

The activities identified above only consider a sample of possible CPD activities. There are numerous other types of CPD activities which enable you to develop your knowledge, e.g. reading current research and inspection evidence; attending conferences; collaborative practices such as peer teaching; demonstrations with teachers as pupils; analysis of individual differences such as learning styles and preferences.

We also strongly advise that you keep up to date with educational issues. A good way to do this is to read regularly the *Times Educational Supplement (TES)*, which is available in many school staffrooms.

PROFESSIONAL ASSOCIATIONS

It is also crucial that you are aware of the importance of joining a professional association. This may be any one of the teachers' unions. As a PE teacher you have a particular need and responsibility to ensure that you have adequate insurance cover and ready access to professional advice. You will be aware of highly publicised incidents where tragedy has befallen pupils involved in PE or physical activities. In these instances, LEAs, schools and individual teachers have, on occasion, been taken to court. See Chapter 9 for information about teaching safely and safety in PE. AfPE is the association for PE teachers in the United Kingdom and also provides insurance for PE teachers should you wish to take out an extra premium which provides extra cover against personal liability for PE teachers. AfPE also provides much information, resources etc. to support your developing teaching skills (see http://www.afpe.org.uk/).

Now complete Task 18.6.

Task 18.6 **Monitoring and evaluation**

In order to continue to learn in the teaching situation, as well as get the most out of your CPD, you should seriously consider maintaining the active, reflective approach to learning that you started during your ITE course. When you start teaching, monitor and evaluate your development as a teacher against specific objectives identified for development and continue to question what you are doing and identify alternative approaches (see Chapter 17). Record your progress in your PDP. Discuss this informally and/or through the appraisal process.

SUMMARY AND KEY POINTS

This chapter has discussed the importance of CPD and what it means; examined CPD during your ITE PE course, particularly: the PDP; knowledge development; applying for your first teaching post; and transition from student teacher to NQT. It looked at CPD during your first/induction year of teaching as an NQT and concluded by looking briefly at CPD throughout your teaching career, highlighting key CPD activities such as appraisal and performance management, embarking on award and non-award bearing courses, involvement in ITE as a subject tutor and other CPD activities. It focused on the importance of CPD to address your own individual development needs.

In order to continue to develop as a teacher and improve the effectiveness of your teaching, CPD is ongoing throughout your career. In conclusion, three key areas that have been discussed in this chapter that are worthy of serious consideration are reinforced/identified. First, in order to improve the effectiveness of both your teaching and pupils' learning experiences in PE, it is essential that you implement a continuous and cyclical process of planning, teaching and critical reflection/review. Second, it is a difficult task to develop the highly complex range of knowledge bases needed to be an effective teacher, and it is unlikely that you will develop these fully by the end of your ITE course. Thus, in order to support your ongoing development into an effective teacher able to facilitate learning, you need to engage in substantial and sustained CPD activities over time; making connections between new learning and existing practice; and engaging in active learning (meaningful planning, practice, discussion and debate (e.g. observing and being observed)). Third, ongoing CPD activities help you to retain (or even recapture) a thirst for learning (and encourage this in the pupils you teach) and maintain a love of your subject and passion for teaching, giving you enthusiasm, freshness and energy for teaching and learning – particularly when you find yourself burdened with paperwork, pupil indiscipline and misbehaviour or Ofsted inspections.

We wish you many enjoyable years as a teacher, continuing to be excited by the challenges inherent in this career by maintaining the development of your teaching and enhancement of pupil learning.

Check which requirements for your course you have addressed through this chapter.

FURTHER READING

Association for Physical Education

Information about the PDB and PDR, as well as other information about CPD, can be obtained from afPE (http://www.afpe.org.uk/).

Capel, S., Breckon, P. and O'Neill, J. (eds) (2006) *A Practical Guide to Teaching Physical Education in the Secondary School*, London: Routledge.

This book includes a range of activities designed to support your development as a PE teacher.

Capel, S., Heilbronn, R., Leask, M. and Turner, T. (2004) *Starting to Teach in the Secondary School: A Companion for the Newly Qualified Teacher*, 2nd edn, London: RoutledgeFalmer.

This book is designed for the newly qualified teacher, so should be a valuable resource in the first and early years of teaching. Chapter 1, Heilbronn, R. (2004) 'From trainee to newly qualified teacher: your immediate professional needs' is of particular interest.

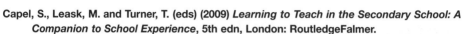

Capel, S., Leask, M. and Turner, T. (eds) (2009) *Learning to Teach in the Secondary School: A Companion to School Experience*, **5th edn, London: RoutledgeFalmer.**

Unit 8.1 provides a comprehensive five-stage approach on how to obtain your first teaching post: deciding where you want to teach; looking for suitable vacancies; selecting a post which interests you and sending for further details; making an application; preparing for and attending an interview; accepting a post (pp. 425–42).

Unit 8.2 looks at continuing professional development. It looks at: your PDP; transition from student teacher to NQT; induction (immediate and ongoing); CPD beyond the first year (pp. 443–52).

Capel, S. and Piotrowski, S. (eds) (2000) *Issues in Physical Education*, **London: RoutledgeFalmer.**

This book covers a range of issues in PE which should be of value to you in critically reflecting on PE and also in supporting Master's level assignments you undertake.

General Teaching Council for England (GTCE) has much material on CPD, including:

GTCE (General Teaching Council for England) (2007a) A Personalised Approach to CPD, January 2007, available online at: http://www.gtce.org.uk/network/personal_cpd/ personal_cpd_project.pdf.

GTCE (General Teaching Council for England) (2007b) Making CPD better: bringing together research about CPD, *Teacher Professional Learning Framework TPLF 07*.

There are a range of organisations that produce material to help you find your first teaching post. These include teacher unions, such as: National Union of Teachers (NUT) (http://www.teachers.org.uk); National Association of Schoolmasters Union of Women Teachers (NASUWT) (http://www.teachersunion.org.uk); the Association for Teachers and Lecturers (ATL) (http://www.atl.org.uk/); Voice (http://www.voicetheunion.org.uk/); The Educational Institute of Scotland (EIS) (http://www.eis.org.uk/).They also include the Association of Graduate Careers Advisory Services (AGCAS) (http://www.agcas.org.uk/) and the Times Educational Supplement (TES) (Annual) *First Appointments Supplement* (http://www.tes.co.uk).

These include information about such things as: finding the right post – sources of vacancies and searching for jobs, applying for teaching posts, writing your CV, suggestions on how to make effective written applications and how to prepare for an interview, interviews, accepting the post, what to do if you are unsuccessful this time, salary matters and what to expect when you start your first post. In addition, the *TES* provides weekly term-time advice for teachers and practical help with ICT, curriculum subjects and careers in education, as well as the largest selection of education job advertisements.

Endnote

The author would like to acknowledge the significant input of Jean Leah, Will Katene and Gill Watson to earlier editions of this chapter.

APPENDIX: LEARNING OUTSIDE THE CLASSROOM – DAY VISITS AND RESIDENTIAL FIELD WORK

Tim Hewett

Learning outside the classroom has significant learning benefits for participants and school visits take place beyond the classroom for a wide variety of reasons. Many such visits involve members of the PE department and they may even involve students as temporary members of the department whilst on school experience! A visit to an international sporting event, an outdoor and adventurous activities residential or a sports exchange/tour can all take you outside the confines of the school grounds, perhaps to another part of the county or country, or maybe even abroad. As a student teacher, or newly qualified teacher, you will not be expected to lead such a visit, but the experience that you may gain from assisting is widely recognised as being of substantial benefit. However, before committing to help to run a visit you should ensure that you feel confident that you can carry out the responsibility that will be placed on you. In order to do this it is obviously important to clarify at the outset what exactly your role would be, with whoever is organising the trip.

One further word of caution; you should carefully examine your own motives for wishing to involve yourself in the trip. If you are attracted solely by the chance to see a big match, or have always fancied a go at rock climbing or perhaps would like a 'free' ski trip, then you should probably think again! The level of commitment required on all such visits is high, as is the level of responsibility on the staff team. The amount of supervision that is required will probably mean that you will have little opportunity to pursue the activities for yourself. Be under no illusion, such trips are hard work and demanding, but of course they can also be particularly rewarding. Many teachers have found that taking their pupils beyond the classroom enhances their working relationships with them a good deal. This is, in turn, of benefit to relationships on return to school, not only with those particular pupils who attended the trip, but also often with a wider spread of pupils.

Is it worth the risk?

Some trainee teachers have concerns regarding their liability in relation to risks associated with learning outside the classroom; such concerns are often fuelled by the negative reporting in the press of adventure activities. Staff do have a duty of care towards young people, but that does not mean that we should isolate them from risk entirely. It is widely accepted that 'wrapping them in cotton wool' denies them the opportunity to develop their own risk management skills; such skills are an important part of everyday adult life.

The government, and governor and headteacher associations have all gone on record to support teachers who embark on learning outside the classroom. Exercise common sense, follow guidelines and fulfil your responsibility to keep young people safe but at the same time ensure that you enable them to learn to manage risks for themselves.

Taking responsibility

Like so many other teaching situations it is neither feasible nor desirable to lay down prescriptive legislation to cover all eventualities in planning and delivering educational visits. What follows could be considered as a set of guidelines that will be of use during your school experience as well as later in your career. You will find that your school has guidelines, as has the LEA, and it is obviously important that you follow these procedures when planning and delivering such events.

When you are responsible for running an off-site activity the following are the areas you should consider.

Why are we going?

Whilst a great deal of important planning needs to be undertaken, much of which will focus on the practical issues concerned with the health and safety of the pupils and the smooth running of the trip, it is very important to be clear at the outset of the aims of the event.

Indeed the 'Why?' is of fundamental importance and will inform almost every aspect of the organisation and delivery of the trip. It may be that the visit is part of a unit of work from the PE curriculum or forms part of some cross-curricular theme. It may be targeting a particular group of pupils with special needs or is an element of a PHSE programme. Whatever the aims, everyone involved should be clear of what the trip is for. If the pupils think they have signed up for a holiday, they may get a rude awakening which in turn will present the staff with untold problems!

It is not uncommon to involve the pupils in the setting of objectives for such events and indeed the planning also. Such involvement can increase the potential for achieving the learning outcomes.

What next?

Once the aims are clear some more decisions can be made; who is going, when and where are they going and what are they going to do when they get there? Some of these issues are obviously linked but once agreed it is possible to move to the practical issues of how all this is to be organised. A key member of school staff to work with here is the Educational Visits Coordinator (EVC). As the name suggests, his/her role is to undertake overall coordination of the school's programme of visits; this individual will help with the approval process and the paperwork to be completed.

In the limited space in this text not all planning issues can be addressed, but below are some points that you may wish to consider in relation to the identified aims.

Who is going?

■ Year group?
■ Tutor group?
■ Target group?
■ Open to any pupils?
■ Pupils, and/or staff from other schools?
■ Which staff will go?
■ Will there be any other adult helpers?
■ What will the arrangements be for those pupils not attending?

When will you go?

■ Term time?
■ Holiday?
■ Weekend?
■ Early, middle or late in the module programme?
■ How does the proposed trip fit the school's programme of other visits?
■ What is your workload at the proposed time?
■ Do you have other commitments?

Where will you go?

■ Is the venue suitable in order to achieve objectives?
■ Proximity – journey time/cost?
■ Do you have previous experience of the area?
■ Is there relevant information available regarding the area?
■ If residential – what sort of accommodation?

What will you do when you get there?

■ Are the planned activities suitable in order to achieve objectives?
■ Can you manage such activities?
■ Possibility for differentiation?
■ Environmental considerations?

Other factors

■ All the above will be influenced by the costs involved and your pupils' ability to meet them. What is the school's policy on charging?

How will you make it all happen?

Once decisions have been made on the above then the detailed planning can begin! Much of the practical organising of visits relies on the application of common sense, this will be reflected in school and LEA guidelines, which you should follow. As a professional educator you are, or are becoming, an effective organiser, but it is worth remembering that the consequences of getting it wrong away from school are generally higher than when you deliver a poorly planned school-based lesson. You should not underestimate the level of responsibility that you are taking on. The next section, which makes no claim to be definitive, outlines a number of important things that will need to be undertaken.

Approval

Before signing up pupils for the 'big event' or sending off any deposits, clearly approval will need to be sought from the headteacher, and in some cases the governing body and the LEA. Who gives approval depends on the nature of the planned trip, generally if adventurous activities are involved the LEA will need to be contacted. If your school is grant maintained, however, the decision will lie with the headteacher and governing body alone. Refer to your school guidelines for the correct procedure.

Parental consent

Consent in writing will need to be sought from the pupils' parents for any visit or journey that is not part of the everyday routine of the school. In order for them to give their consent they will want to know what is planned. The information that they require might include:

■ Dates and times of departure and return.
■ Destination, with address and contact telephone number if possible.
■ The aims of the visit.
■ Details of activities to be undertaken.
■ Names of group leader and accompanying staff.
■ Method of travel.
■ Code of conduct, relating to expected standards of behaviour.
■ Financial arrangements, to include charges/voluntary contributions, methods of payment, cancellation arrangements and advice on pocket money.
■ Insurance, what cover has been arranged.
■ Clothing/footwear/equipment requirements. Prohibited items.

The above list identifies a good deal of the practical planning that will have to be completed. For some visits such planning can prove complex and time consuming. There is a need to be realistic in the time allowed for such planning. Some events will need to be arranged over a year ahead of the date of departure!

Pupil information

Along with the parental consent form for the pupils, there is also a need to collect specific information about each member of the party, including staff. Such information might include:

- Personal details, full name, address, date of birth, etc.
- Next of kin contacts, work and home.
- Medical details, e.g. current medication, allergies, potential ailments, doctor's name and address.
- Special dietary needs on moral, health or religious grounds.

Pre-visit preparation

There is always a need for some preparation with the pupils prior to departure, if only to establish where they need to be and what they need to bring. Codes of behaviour, group organisation, objective setting, skill acquisition, menu planning are just some of the issues that may also need addressing and may involve preparation sessions spread over some weeks or even months.

Post-visit reflection by pupils and staff

A review of the pupils' experiences of the visit is essential if the learning is to be maximised. The review starts by reflecting on what was done and goes on to look at what was learnt and finally to transfer the learning. Finding time for reflection is often difficult, so planning a review session into the programme is important. There is sometimes a temptation to set review and reflection aside for more pressing matters, however, this is to undermine all the hard work of organising and delivering.

Some form of evaluation, by staff, of the visit itself and the effectiveness of the planning is also clearly of benefit, particularly if there is an intention to repeat the visit.

Providers

Schools often make use of day and residential centres as part of their educational visits programme. Such contracting out may range from the employment of individual specialist staff on an 'ad hoc' basis to the use of a large commercial activity centre or a tour company. Choosing the right provider is an issue that requires considerable enquiry, one certainly has to go beyond the glossy brochure! Clearly the quality of the provision and the price are key issues, but as a starting point it should be clear that the course they offer fits the aims of your programme. For example, do they offer an off-the-peg package or are they prepared to work with you to tailor a course to suit your needs? Being able to talk to another teacher who has already made use of the centre could be particularly informative!

Providers of adventure activities are required to be licensed under the Adventure Activities Licensing Scheme. In order to obtain a licence all areas of their operation are inspected, including management systems, staff expertise, suitability of equipment, safety procedures and many other health and safety arrangements. Schools offering adventure activities to their own pupils will not need to be licensed but will need to follow LEA guidelines.

Before you go!

Away from your normal teaching environment it may be appropriate to adopt a more relaxed style but do not forget that you are still the teacher and your interactions with pupils and colleagues will be watched, and talked about. You should always remember the responsibilities that come with being a teacher!

It should be clear from this section that being involved in educational visits involves a high level of commitment and responsibility, as well as a good deal of hard work. However, do not be daunted, the benefits for your pupils and your own professional development are many. Teaching beyond the classroom can be a most rewarding experience!

Task A.1 **School procedures for educational visits**

Obtain a copy of both your school's policy document and the LEA guidelines, if appropriate, on educational visits and from these find out the following:

■ What are the procedures for gaining approval for a visit that includes adventurous activities?
■ What is the school's policy on charging for educational visits? Is there any facility for offering assistance towards the cost of a visit in the case of hardship?
■ What insurance cover does the school and/or LEA have in place for educational visits? Do either recommend additional cover for visits abroad or for visits concerned with adventurous activities?
■ What are the insurance implications for staff of using their own cars to transport pupils on educational visits?

Task A.2 **Choosing a provider**

Obtain details of the LEA's residential centres along with details of a commercial centre that offers courses suitable for your pupils. For a suitable hypothetical course of your own choosing, devise criteria to judge what is on offer, and then evaluate the centres in the light of your criteria.

Further resources

Learning Outside the Classroom website: http://www.lotc.org.uk/

Institute for Outdoor Learning website: http://www.outdoor-learning.org/index.htm

The Active Reviewing Guide: http://reviewing.co.uk/

REFERENCES

afPE (Association for Physical Education) (2008) *Safe Practice in Physical Education and School Sport*, 7th edn, Leeds: afPE/Coachwise.

afPE (Association for Physical Education) (2009) *Generic Risk Assessment for Physical Education*, afPE Health and Safety Advisory Panel Meeting Papers, 25 March 2009.

afPE (Association for Physical Education) publications: http://www.afpe.org.uk/public/ncfcpd_info.htm.

afPE (Association for Physical Education) website: http://www.afpe.org.uk/.

AGCAS (Association of Graduate Careers Advisory Services): http://www.agcas.org.uk/.

Alexander, R. (2008) *Essays on Pedagogy*, Abingdon: Routledge.

Allen, F. and Taylor, A. (2009) Active learning, in S. Capel, M. Leask and T. Turner (eds) *Learning to Teach in the Secondary School: A Companion to School Experience*, 5th edn, London: Routledge, pp. 267–84.

Allen, M. and Toplis, R. (2009) The student teacher's role and responsibilities, in S. Capel, M. Leask and T. Turner (eds), *Learning to Teach in the Secondary School: A Companion to School Experience*, 5th edn, London: Routledge, pp. 21–35.

Almond, L. (ed.) (1997) *Physical Education in Schools*, 2nd edn, London: Kogan Page.

Ames, C. (1992) Achievement goals, motivational climate and motivational processes, in G.C. Roberts (ed.), *Motivation in Sport and Exercise*, Champaign, IL: Human Kinetics, pp. 161–76.

Anderson, L.W., Krathwohl, D.R., Airasain, P.W., Cruikshank, K.A., Mayer, R.E., Pintrich, P.R., Raths, J. and Wittrock, M.C. (eds) (2001) *A Taxonomy for Learning, Teaching, and Assessing – A Revision of Bloom's Taxonomy of Educational Objectives*, New York: Addison Wesley Longman Inc.

Argyris, C. and Schon, D. (1974) *Theory into Practice: Increasing Professional Effectiveness,* San Francisco, CA: Jossey Bass.

Armour, K. and Jones, R. (1998) *Physical Education Teachers' Lives and Careers. PE, Sport and Educational Status*, London: Falmer Press.

Armour, K.M. and Yelling, M. (2002) Looking with 'fresh eyes': Ways forward for CPD in physical education, paper presented at the Annual British Educational Research Association Conference, University of Exeter, September 2002.

Arnold, P.J. (1988) *The Curriculum, Education and Movement*, London: Falmer.

Assessment Reform Group (ARG) (1999) *Assessment for Learning: Beyond the Black Box*, Cambridge: University of Cambridge School of Education.

Assessment Reform Group (ARG) (2002) *Assessment for Learning: 10 Principles*, Cambridge: University of Cambridge, Assessment Reform Group.

ATL (the Association for Teachers and Lecturers): http://www.atl.org.uk/.

Avramadis, E. and Norwich, B. (2002) Teachers' attitudes towards integration and inclusion: a review of the literature, *European Journal of Special Needs Education* 17, 2: 129–47.

REFERENCES ■ ■ ■ ■

Bailey, R. (2002) Questioning as a teaching strategy in physical education, *The Bulletin of Physical Education*, 38, 2: 119–26.

Bailey, R. (2005) Evaluating the relationship between physical education, sport and social inclusion, *Educational Review*, 57, 1: 71–90.

Bailey, R., Armour, K., Kirk, D., Jess, M., Pickup, I. and Sandford, R. (British Educational Research Association (BERA) Physical Education and Sport Pedagogy Special Interest Group) (2008) The educational benefits claimed for physical education and school sport: an academic review, *Research Papers in Education*, 24, 1: March: 1–27.

Bailey, R., Morley, D. and Dismore, H. (2009) Talent development in physical education: a national survey of policy and practice in England, *Physical Education and Sport Pedagogy*, 14, 1: 59–72.

Beaumont, G. (2007) Health and safety, *Physical Education Matters*, 2, 1: 31.

Beaumont, G. (2008) Cotton wool kids: risk and children, *Physical Education Matters*, 3, 3: 10–11.

Becta (The British Education and Communications Technology Agency) website: What is ICT. Available online at: http://schools.becta.org.uk/index.php?section=cu&catcode=ss_cu_skl_02&rid=1701 (accessed 8 September 2009).

Becta (The British Education and Communications Technology Agency) website: Pupil entitlement to ICT: Physical education. Available online at: http://schools.becta.org.uk/index.php?section=cu&catcode=ss_cu_ac_phy_03.

Bell, J. (2005) *Doing your Research Project: A Guide for First-time Researchers in Education and Social Science*, 4th edn, Maidenhead: Open University Press.

Bennett, N. (1976) *Teaching Styles and Pupil Progress*, London: Open Books.

Bennett, R. and Leask, M. (2009) Using ICT for professional purposes: an introduction, in S. Capel, M. Leask and T. Turner (eds), *Learning to Teach in the Secondary School: A Companion to School Experience*, 5th edn, London: Routledge, pp. 47–62.

BERA (British Educational Research Association) (2004) *Revised Ethical Guidelines for Educational Research*, Southwell: BERA. Available online at: http://www.bera.ac.uk.

Best, B. and Thomas, W. (2007) *The Creative Teaching and Learning Toolkit*, New York: Continuum.

Bhopal, K. (2004) Gypsy travellers and education: changing needs and changing perceptions, *British Journal of Educational Studies*, 52, 2: 47–64.

Biddle, S., Cavill, N. and Sallis, J. (eds) (1998) *Young and Active? Young People and Health-Enhancing Physical Activity – Evidence and Implications*, London: Health Education Authority.

Black, P., Harrison, C., Lee, C., Marshall, B. and William, D. (2003) *Assessment for Learning: Putting it into Practice*, Buckingham: Open University Press.

Black, P. and Wiliam, D. (1998) *Inside the Black Box: Raising Standards through Classroom Assessment*, London: Kings College.

Black, P. and Wiliam, D. (2002) *Working Inside the Black Box: Assessment for Learning in the Classroom*, London: King's College.

Blair, R. (2006) Planning for pupils' learning in broader dimensions of the curriculum 2: key skills and the use of information and communications technology, in S. Capel, P. Breckon and J. O'Neill (eds), *A Practical Guide to Teaching Physical Education in the Secondary School*, London: Routledge, pp. 80–8.

Bloom, B.S. (ed.) (1956) *Taxonomy of Educational Objectives: The Classification of Educational Goals. Handbook 1: Cognitive Domain*, New York: Longmans Green.

Bloom, B.S. (1976) *Human Characteristics and School Learning*, New York: McGraw-Hill.

Bowkett, S. (2007) *100+ Ideas for Teaching Thinking Skills*, New York: Continuum.

Brown, G.A. and Edmondson, R. (1984) Asking questions, in E.C. Wragg (ed.), *Classroom Teaching Skills*, London: Croom Helm, pp. 97–120.

Bruner, J.S. (1960) *The Process of Education*, New York: Vantage.

Burchardt, T. (2004) Capabilities and disability: the capabilities framework and the social model of disability, *Disability and Society*, 19, 7: 735–51.

Burton, D. (2009) Ways pupils learn, in S. Capel, M. Leask and T. Turner (eds), *Learning to Teach in the Secondary School: A Companion to School Experience*, 5th edn, London: Routledge, pp. 251–66.

Burton, N. (2007) The research process, in P. Zwozdiak-Myers (ed.), *Childhood and Youth Studies,* Exeter: Learning Matters, pp. 146–59.

Burton, N., Brundett, M. and Jones, M. (2008) *Doing Your Education Research Project,* London: Sage.

Capel, S. (2009) Managing your time and stress, in S. Capel, M. Leask and T. Turner (eds), *Learning to Teach in the Secondary School: A Companion to School Experience*, 5th edn, London: RoutledgeFalmer, pp. 36–46.

Capel, S., Breckon, P. and O'Neill, J. (eds) (2006) *A Practical Guide to Teaching Physical Education in the Secondary School,* London: Routledge.

Capel, S. and Gervis, M. (2009) Motivating pupils, in S. Capel, M. Leask and T. Turner (eds), *Learning to Teach in the Secondary School: A Companion to School Experience*, 5th edn, London: Routledge, pp. 124–37.

Capel, S., Heilbronn, R., Leask, M. and Turner, T. (eds) (2004) *Starting to Teach in the Secondary School: A Companion for the Newly Qualified Teacher*, London: RoutledgeFalmer.

Capel, S. and Lawrence, J. (2006) Creating an effective learning environment which promotes 'behaviour for learning', in S. Capel, P. Breckon and J. O'Neill (eds), *A Practical Guide to Teaching Physical Education in the Secondary School*, London: Routledge, pp. 90–9.

Capel, S., Leask, M. and Turner, T. (eds) (2005) *Learning to Teach in the Secondary School: A Companion to School Experience,* 4th edn, London: RoutledgeFalmer.

Capel, S., Leask, M. and Turner, T. (2009) *Learning to Teach in the Secondary School: A Companion to School Experience*, 5th edn, London: Routledge.

Capel, S. and Piotrowski, S. (eds) (2000) *Issues in Physical Education*, London: RoutledgeFalmer.

Carr, G. (1997) *Mechanics of Sport*, Champaign, IL: Human Kinetics.

Carr, W. and Kemmis, S. (1986) *Becoming Critical: Education, Knowledge and Action Research,* Lewes: Falmer Press.

Central Advisory Council for Education (1967) *Children and their Primary Schools: A Report of the Central Advisory Council for Education (England) (The Plowden Report)*, London: Her Majesty's Stationery Office.

Chappell, A. (2006) Safe practice, risk assessment and risk management, in S. Capel, P. Breckon and J. O'Neill (eds), *A Practical Guide to Teaching Physical Education in the Secondary School*, London: RoutledgeFalmer.

Cheffers, J., Amidon, E. and Rogers, K. (1974) *Interaction Analysis: An Application to Nonverbal Activity*, Minnesota: Association for Productive Teaching.

Child, D. (2007) *Psychology and the Teacher*, 6th edn, London: Cassell.

Coates, J. and Vickerman, P. (2008) Let the children have their say: children with special educational needs experiences of physical education – a review, *Support for Learning*, 23, 4: 168–75.

Cohen, L., Manion, L. and Morrison, K. (2004) *A Guide to Teaching Practice*, 5th edn, London: Routledge.

Cohen, L., Manion, L. and Morrison, K. (2007) *Research Methods in Education*, 6th edn, London: RoutledgeFalmer.

Cole, P.G. and Chan L.K.S. (1994) *Teaching Principles and Practice*, 2nd edn, New York: Prentice Hall.

Cole, R. (2008) *Educating Everybody's Children: Diverse Strategies for Diverse Learners*, Alexandria, VA: Association for Supervision and Curriculum Development.

Cooper, P. and McIntyre, D. (1996) *Effective Teaching and Learning: Teachers' and Students' Perspective,* Buckingham: Open University Press.

Crouch, H. (1984) *Netball Coaching Manual*, Kingston-upon-Thames: Croner Publications.

Cox, C.B. and Dyson, R.E. (eds) (1975) *Black Paper 1975 – The Fight for Education*, London: Dent.

Cruickshank, D.R., Beiner, D.L. and Metcalf, K. (1995) *The Act of Teaching*, New York: McGraw-Hill.

Daniels, S. (2008) Physical education, school sport and traveller children, *Physical Education Matters*, 3, 3: 32–7.

Davies, E. (2001) *Beyond Dance,* London: Brechin Books Ltd.

Davis, R.J., Bull, C.R., Roscoe, J.V. and Roscoe, D.A. (2000) *Physical Education and the Study of Sport*, 4th edn, London: Mosby.

Davison, J. (2001) Managing classroom behaviour, in S. Capel, M. Leask and T. Turner (eds), *Learning to Teach in the Secondary School: A Companion to School Experience*, 3rd edn, London: RoutledgeFalmer, pp. 116–27.

DCFS (Department for Children, Schools and Families) (2007) *Children's Plan: Building Brighter Futures*, Annesley: DCFS.

DCFS (Department for Children, Schools and Families) (2008a) *Statistics of Education: Special Educational Needs in England January 2008*, London: HMSO.

DCSF (Department for Children, Schools and Families) (2008b) *Departmental Report 2008*, Norwich: The Stationery Office.

DCSF (Department for Children, Schools and Families) (2008c) *Developing 14–19 Reforms: Next Steps*, Annesley: DCFS.

DCSF (Department for Children, Schools and Families) (2009) http://www.standards.dfes.gov.uk/schemes2/Secondary_PE/ (accessed 1 November 2009).

DePauw, K. and Doll-Tepper, G. (2000) Toward progressive inclusion and acceptance: myth or reality? The inclusion debate and bandwagon discourse, *Adapted Physical Activity Quarterly* 17: 135–43.

Derri, V., Emmanoullidou, K., Vassilladou, O., Kioumourtzoglou, E. and Loza Olave, E. (2007) Academic learning time in physical education (ALT-PE): is it related to fundamental movement skill acquisition and learning?, *International Journal of Sport Science* 3, 3: 12–23.

DES (Department of Education and Science) (1988) *The Education Reform Act*, London: HMSO.

DES (Department of Education and Science) (1990) *Starting with Quality: Report of the Committee of Enquiry into the Quality of Educational Experiences Offered to 3–4 Year Olds*, London: HMSO.

DES/WO (Department of Education and Science and the Welsh Office) (1992) *Physical Education in the National Curriculum*, London, HMSO.

Dewey, J. (1933) *How We Think: A Restatement of the Relation of Reflective Thinking to the Educative Process*, Boston, MA: DC Heath and Company.

DfE (Department for Education) (1995) *Physical Education in the National Curriculum*, London: HMSO.

DfEE (Department for Education and Employment) (1998) *Health and Safety of Pupils on Educational Visits*, London: DfEE.

DfES (Department for Education and Skills) (2002) *Guidance on First Aid for Schools*, London: The Stationary Office. Available online at: http://www.teachernet.gov.uk/_doc/4421/gfas.pdf (accessed 2 November 2009).

DfEE/QCA (Department for Education and Employment/Qualifications and Curriculum Authority) (1999) *The National Curriculum for England. Handbook for Secondary Teachers in England: Key Stages 3 and 4*, London: Stationery Office.

DfES (Department for Education and Skills) (2001a) *The Special Educational Needs and Disability Act,* London, HMSO.

DfES (Department for Education and Skills) (2001b) *The Code of Practice on the Identification and Assessment of Children with Special Educational Needs*, London: HMSO.

DfES (Department for Education and Skills) (2002a) *Key Stage 3 National Strategy. Access and Engagement in Physical Education. Teaching Pupils for whom English is an Additional Language*, London: DfES: 0659/2002.

DfES (Department for Education and Skills) (2002b) *Key Stage 3 National Strategy*, Annesley: DfES.

DfES (Department for Education and Skills) (2003) *Every Child Matters*, Norwich: HMSO. Available online at: http://www.everychildmatters.gov.uk/publications (accessed 15 November 2009).

DfES (Department for Education and Skills) (2004a) *Pedagogy and Practice: Teaching and Learning in the Secondary School, Unit 7 Questioning,* London: DfES. Available online at: http://www.standards.dfes.gov.uk (accessed 2 November 2009).

DfES (Department for Education and Skills) (2004b) *Pedagogy and Practice: Teaching and Learning in the Secondary School, Unit 12 Assessment for learning,* London: DfES. Available online at: http://www.standards.dfes.gov.uk (accessed 2 November 2009).

DfES (Department for Education and Skills) (2004c) *Key Stage 3 National Strategy: ICT across the curriculum, 'ICT in physical education'*, Ref: DfES, 0184-2004 G.

DfES (Department for Education and Skills) (2004d) *High Quality PE and Sport for Young People*, Nottingham: DfES.

DfES (Department for Education and Skills) (2005a) *Secondary National Strategy for School Improvement 2005–06*, Norwich: HMSO.

DfES (Department for Education and Skills) (2005b) *14–19 Education and Skills, Implementation Plan*, London: DfES.

DfES (Department for Education and Skills) (2006) *The Leitch Review: Prosperity for All in the Global Economy – World Class Skills*, London: HMSO.

DfES (Department for Education and Skills) (2007) *Pedagogy and Personalisation*, London: DfES.

Disability Rights Commission (2006) *The Disability Equality Duty*, London: Disability Rights Commission.

Durrant, A. (2009) *An Introduction to Exercise and Sport for People Who Have Autism*, Chelmsford: A. Durrant.

EIS (The Educational Institute of Scotland): http://www.eis.org.uk/.

Elbourn, J. (1999) *How to Develop and Monitor a Safe, Effective and Appropriate Physical Education Programme at Key Stages 3 and 4,* Bristol: Standards for Education.

Elliott, J. (1991) *Action Research for Educational Change,* Milton Keynes: Open University Press.

Elton Report (1989) *Enquiry into Discipline in Schools*, London: Her Majesty's Stationery Office.

Evans, J. and Williams, T. (1989) Moving up and getting out: the classed and gendered career opportunities of physical education teachers, in T.J. Templin and P.G. Schempp (eds), *Socialization into Physical Education: Learning to Teach*, Indianapolis, IN: Benchmark Press, pp. 235–48.

Filer, J. (2007) Bonding through developmental movement play, in E. Marsden and J. Egerton (eds), *Moving with Research*, Clent, Stourbridge: Sunfield Publications, pp. 69–89.

Fitzgerald, H. (2005) Still feeling like a spare piece of luggage? Embodied experiences of (dis)ability, *Physical Education and School Sport, Physical Education and Sport Pedagogy,* 10, 1: 41–59.

Fitzgerald, H., Jobling, A. and Kirk, D. (2003) Physical education and pupil voice: listening to the 'voices' of students with severe learning difficulties through a task-based approach to research and learning in physical education, *Support for Learning*, 18, 3: 23–29.

Flanders, N. (1960) *Interaction Analysis in the Classroom: A Manual for Observers*, Minneapolis, MN: University of Minnesota Press.

Fontana, A. and Frey, J. (2000) *The Interview: From Structured Questions to Negotiated Text*, 2nd edn, Thousands Oaks, CA: Sage.

Free Dictionary (2009) *Safe*, available online at: http://www.thefreedictionary.com/safely (accessed 30 June 2009).

Furlong, J. (2007) Universities and Education, Proceedings of the Universities Council for the Education of the Teacher conference, available online at: http://www.ucet.ac.uk/196 (accessed 24 October 2009).

Gallahue, D. and Donnelly, F.C. (2003) *Developmental Physical Education for All Children*, 4th edn, Champaign, IL: Human Kinetics.

Galton, M. and Croll, P. (1980) *Inside the Primary Classroom*, London: Routledge and Kegan Paul.

Gardner, H. (1993) *Frames of Mind – The Theory of Multiple Intelligences*, 2nd edn, London: Fontana.

Gardner, J. (ed.) (2006) *Assessment and Learning*, London: Sage Publications Ltd.

Garet, S.M., Porter, C.A., Desimone, L., Birman, B.F. and Suk Yoon, K. (2001) What makes professional development effective? Results from a national sample of teachers, *American Educational Research Journal*, 38, 4: 915–45.

Garner, P. (2009) Behaviour for learning: developing a positive approach to classroom management, in S. Capel, M. Leask and T. Turner (eds), *Learning to Teach in the Secondary School: A Companion to School Experience*, 5th edn, London: RoutledgeFalmer, pp. 138–54.

Godefroy, H. and Barrat, S. (1993) *Confident Speaking,* London: Judy Piatkus.

Government Equalities Office (2008) *The Equality Bill*, London: HMSO.

Graham, G. (2008) *Teaching Children in Physical Education: Becoming a Master Teacher*, Champaign, IL: Human Kinetics.

Green, A. and Leask, M. (2009) What do teachers do?, in S. Capel, M. Leask and T. Turner (eds), *Learning to Teach in the Secondary School: A Companion to School Experience*, 5th edn, London: Routledge, pp. 9–21.

Green, K. (2002) Physical education and 'the couch potato society', *European Journal of Physical Education*, 7, 2: 95–107.

Green, K (2004) PE, lifelong participation and 'the couch potato society', *Physical Education and Sport Pedagogy*, 9, 1, May: 73–86.

Griffin, L.L. and Butler, J.I. (2005) *Teaching Games for Understanding: Theory, Research and Practice*, Champaign, IL.: Human Kinetics.

GTCE (General Teaching Council for England) (2007a) Making CPD better: bringing together research about CPD, *Teacher Professional Learning Framework TPLF 07*.

GTCE (General Teaching Council for England) (2007b) A personalised approach to CPD, January 2007, available online at: http://www.gtce.org.uk/network/personal_cpd/personal_cpd_project.pdf.

Guillaume, A.M. and Rudney, G.C. (1993) Student teachers' growth towards independence: an analysis of their changing concerns, *Teaching and Teacher Education*, 9, 1: 65–80.

Hardy, C. and Mawer, M. (eds) (1999) *Learning and Teaching in Physical Education,* London: Falmer Press.

Harris, J. (2000) *Health Related Exercise in the National Curriculum*, Leeds: Human Kinetics.

Harris, J. and Penney, D. (1997) Putting health first: an alternative policy and practice for physical education, *Pedagogy in Practice*, 3, 1: 37–55.

Havnes, A. and McDowell, L. (2007) *Balancing Dilemmas in Assessment and Learning in Contemporary Education*, Abingdon: Routledge.

Hayden-Davis, D. (2005) How does the concept of physical literacy relate to what is and what could be the practice of physical education?, *British Journal of Teaching Physical Education,* 36, 3: 43–8.

Haydn, T. (2009) Assessment, pupil motivation and learning, in S. Capel, M. Leask and T. Turner (eds), *Learning to Teach in the Secondary School: A Companion to School Experience*, 5th edn, London: Routledge, pp. 329–51.

Haydon, G. (2009) Aims of education, in S. Capel, M. Leask and T. Turner (eds), *Learning to Teaching the Secondary School: A Companion to School Experience*, 5th edn, London Routledge, pp. 369–78.

Hayes, S. and Stidder, G. (2003) *Equity and Inclusion in Physical Education*, London: Routledge.

Haywood, K.M. and Getchell, N. (2009) *Life Span Motor Development*, 5th edn, Champaign, IL: Human Kinetics.

Heilbronn, R. (2004) From trainee to newly qualified teacher: your immediate professional needs, in S. Capel, R. Heilbronn, M. Leask and T. Turner (eds), *Starting to Teach in the Secondary School: A Companion for the Newly Qualified Teacher*, 2nd edn, London: Routledge, pp. 3–15.

Hellison, D.R. and Templin, T.J. (1991) *A Reflective Approach to Teaching Physical Education*, Champaign, IL: Human Kinetics.

Her Majesty's Government (HMG) (2005) *Every Child Matters: Change for Children*, London: HMSO.

Hill, C. (2006) *Communicating through Movement*, Clent, Stourbridge: Sunfield Publications.

Hopkins, D. (2002) *A Teacher's Guide to Classroom Research*, 3rd edn, Buckingham: Open University Press.

Hoyle, E. (1974) Professionality, professionalism and control in teaching, *London Education Review*, 3, 2: 13–19.

Hoyle, E. and John, P. (1995) *Professional Knowledge and Professional Practice*, London: Cassell.

HSE (Health and Safety Executive) (1995) *The Reporting of Injuries, Diseases and Dangerous Occurrences Regulations (RIDDOR)*, London: Crown. Available online at: http://www.opsi.gov.uk/SI/si1995/Uksi_19953163_en_1.htm (accessed 4 November 2009).

HSE (Health and Safety Executive) (2005) *Incident-reporting in Schools (Accidents, Diseases and Dangerous Occurrences)*, London: Crown.

HSE (Health and Safety Executive) (2006) *Five Steps to Risk Assessment,* London: Crown.

HSE (Health and Safety Executive) (2007) *Incident at Work*, London: Crown.

HSE (Health and Safety Executive) (2009) *Health and Safety Law: What You Need to Know*, London: Crown.

International Baccalaureate Organisation (IBO) (no date) http://www.ibo.org/ (accessed 13 May 2009).

Joyce, B., Calhoun, E. and Hopkins, D. (2002) *Models of Learning, Tools for Teaching*, 2nd edn, Buckingham: Open University Press.

Joyce, B. and Weil, M. (1996) *Models of Teaching*, 5th edn, Boston, MA: Allyn and Bacon.

Kasser, S.L. and Lytle, R.K. (2005) *Inclusive Physical Activity: A Lifetime of Opportunities*, Champaign, IL: Human Kinetics.

Kelly, L. (1997) Safety in PE, in S. Capel (ed.), *Learning to Teach Physical Education in the Secondary School: A Companion to School Experience,* London: Routledge, pp. 115–29.

Kerry, T. (2004) *Learning Objectives, Task Setting and Differentiation*, Cheltenham: Nelson Thornes.

Khanifar, H., Moghimi, S., Memar, S. and Jandaghi, G. (2008) Ethical considerations of physical education in an Islamic valued education system, online *Journal of Health Ethics*, 1, http://www.usm.edu/ethicsjournal/index.php/ojhe/article/view/82/116.

Kinchin, G., Penney, D. and Clarke, G. (2001) Try sport education?, *British Journal of Teaching Physical Education*, 32, 2: 41–4.

Knowles, M.S., Holton III, E.F. and Swanson, R.A. (2005) *The Adult Learner*, London: Elsevier.

Knudson, D.V. and Morrison, C.S. (2002) *Qualitative Analysis of Human Movement,* 2nd edn, Champaign, IL: Human Kinetics.

Kolb, D.A. (1984) *Experiential Learning: Experience as the Source of Learning and Development*, Englewood Cliffs, NJ: Prentice Hall.

Koshy, V. (2005) *Action Research for Improving Practice – A Practical Guide,* London: Paul Chapman.

Kyriacou, C. (2007) *Essential Teaching Skills*, 3rd edn, Cheltenham: Stanley Thornes.

Kyriacou, C. (2009) *Effective Teaching in Schools*, 3rd edn, Cheltenham: Stanley Thornes.

Lambe, J. and Bones, R. (2006) Student teachers' perceptions about inclusive classroom teaching in Northern Ireland prior to teacher practice experience, *European Journal of Special Needs Education*, 21, 2: 167–86.

Lawrence, D. (1988) *Enhancing Self-esteem in the Classroom*, London: Paul Chapman.

REFERENCES ■ ■ ■ ■

Lawrence, J., Taylor, A. and Capel, S. (2009) Developing further as a teacher, in S. Capel, M. Leask and T. Turner (eds), *Learning to Teach in the Secondary School: A Companion to School Experience*, 5th edn, London: Routledge, pp. 443–52.

Leach, J. and Moon, B. (1999) *Learners and Pedagogy*, London: Paul Chapman.

Leaver, B.L. (1997) *Teaching the Whole Class*, 4th edn, Thousand Oaks, CA: Corwin Press.

Leney, T. (2003) Developing the 14–19 curriculum and qualifications in England – aims and purposes: international and comparative aspects, Discussion paper for Nuffield Review of 14–19 Education and Training.

Macfadyen, T. and Bailey, R. (2002) *Teaching Physical Education*, London: Continuum.

Marland, M. (1993) *The Craft of the Classroom: A Survival Guide to Classroom Management in the Secondary School*, revised edn, Oxford: Heinemann Educational.

Marland, M. (2002) *The Craft of the Classroom*, 3rd edn, London: Heinemann Educational.

Marsden, E. and Egerton, J. (2007) *Moving with Research*, Clent, Stourbridge: Sunfield Publications.

Maude, P. and Whitehead, M. (2006) Observing and Analysing Learners' Movement, CD, afPE.

Mawer, M. (1995) *The Effective Teaching of Physical Education*, London: Longman.

Maynard, T. and Furlong, G.J. (1993) Learning to teach and models of mentoring, in D. McIntyre, H. Hagger and M. Wilkin (eds), *Mentoring: Perspectives on School-based Teacher Education*, London: Kogan Page, pp. 69–85.

McGuire, B., Parker, L. and Cooper, W. (2001) Physical education and language: do actions speak louder than words?, *European Journal of Physical Education*, 6, 2: 101–16.

McIntyre, D. (2005) Bridging the gap between research and practice, *Cambridge Journal of Education*, 35, 3: 357–82.

McKernan, J. (1996) *Curriculum Action Research: A Handbook of Methods and Resources for the Reflective Practitioner*, 2nd edn, London: Kogan Page.

Metzler, M.W. (1989) A review of research on time in sport pedagogy, *Journal of Teaching in Physical Education*, 8, 2: 87–103.

Metzler, M.W. (1990) *Instructional Supervision for Physical Education*, Champaign, IL: Human Kinetics.

Morley, D. and Bailey, R. (2006) *Meeting the Needs of Your Most Able Pupils: Physical Education and Sport* (with CD-ROM), Gifted and Talented Series, London: David Fulton Publishers.

Morley, D., Bailey, R., Tan, J. and Cooke, B. (2005) Inclusive physical education: teachers' views of teaching children with special educational needs and disabilities in physical education, *European Physical Education Review*, 11, 1: 84–107.

Morrison, A. and McIntyre, D. (1973) *Teachers and Teaching*, 2nd edn, Harmondsworth: Penguin.

Mosston, M. and Ashworth, S. (2002) *Teaching Physical Education*, 5th edn, San Francisco, CA: Benjamin Cummings.

Mouratidis, A., Vansteenkiste, M., Lens, W. and Sideris, G. (2008) The motivating role of positive feedback in sport and physical education: evidence for a motivational model, *Journal of Sport and Exercise Psychology*, 30: 240–68.

Muijs, D. and Reynolds, D. (2005) *Effective Teaching: Evidence and Practice*, 2nd edn, London: Paul Chapman (Sage).

Murdoch, E. (1997) The background to, and developments from, the National Curriculum for PE, in S. Capel (ed.), *Learning to Teach Physical Education in the Secondary School: A Companion to School Experience*, London: Routledge, pp. 252–70.

Murdoch, E. (2004) NCPE 2000 – where are we so far?, in S. Capel (ed.), *Learning to Teach Physical Education in the Secondary School: A Companion to School Experience*, 2nd edn, London: Routledge, pp. 280–300.

NASUWT (National Association of Schoolmasters Union of Women Teachers): http://www.teachersunion.org.uk.

National Coaching Foundation (NCF) (1994) *Planning and Practice: Study Pack 6*, Leeds: NCF.

National Union of Teachers (NUT): http://www.teachers.org.uk.

Oeser, O.A (ed.) (1955) *Teacher, Pupil and Task,* New York: Harper and Row.

Office for Disability Issues (2006) *Secretary of State Reports on Disability Equality*, Department for Work and Pensions, London: HMSO.

Ofsted (Office for Standards in Education) (2002a) *Secondary Subject Reports 2000/01: Physical Education*, London: HMSO.

Ofsted (Office for Standards in Education) (2002b) *Good Teaching, Effective Departments. Findings from an HMI Survey of Subject Teaching in Secondary Schools 2000/01* Ref. HMI 337.

Ofsted (Office for Standards in Education) (2003) *Quality and Standards in Secondary Initial Teacher Training*, London: GreenShires Print Group. Available online at: http://www.ofsted.gov.uk/Ofsted-home/Publications-and-research/Browse-all-by/Education/Teachers-and-teacher-training/Routes-into-teaching/Quality-and-standards-in-secondary-initial-teacher-training/(language)/eng-GB (accessed 16 April 2009).

Ofsted (Office for Standards in Education) (2004) *2004 Report: ICT in Schools: The Impact of Government Initiatives*, May 2004, London: HMI 2196 (www.ofsted.gov.uk).

Ofsted (Office for Standards in Education) (2005) *The Secondary National Strategy: An Evaluation of the Fifth Year*. Available online at: http://www.ofsted.gov.uk/Ofsted-home/Publications-and-research/Browse-all-by/Education/Providers/Secondary-schools/The-Secondary-National-Strategy/(language)/eng-GB (accessed 16 April 2009).

Ofsted (Office for Standards in Education) (2008a) *Evaluation of the Primary and Secondary National Strategies 2005–2007*. Available online at: http://www.ofsted.gov.uk/Ofsted-home/Publications-and-research/Browse-all-by/Documents-by-type/Thematic-reports/Evaluation-of-the-Primary-and-Secondary-National-Strategies/(language)/eng-GB (accessed 16 April 2009).

Ofsted (Office for Standards in Education) (2008b) *Assessment for Learning: The Impact of the National Strategy Support*. Available online at: http://www.ofsted.gov.uk/Ofsted-home/Publications-and-research/Browse-all-by/Education/Curriculum/English/Primary/Assessment-for-learning-the-impact-of-National-Strategy-support/(language)/eng-GB (accessed 16 April 2009).

Ofsted (Office for Standards in Education) (2008c) *The Annual Report of HMCI of Education, Children's Services and Skills 2007/08*, London (www.ofsted.gov.uk).

Ofsted (Office for Standards in Education) (2009) *PE in Schools 2005/08: Working Towards 2012 and Beyond*, April, Reference number: 080249 (www.ofsted.gov.uk).

Oppenheim, A. (1992) *Questionnaire Design, Interviews and Attitude Measurement*, London: Cassell.

Parry, J. (1988) Physical education: justification and the National Curriculum, *Physical Education Review*, 11, 2: 106–18.

Parry, P. (2007) *The Interactive Guide to Behaviour Management for Trainee and Newly Qualified Teachers*, Swansea: Inclusive Behaviour Publications.

PEITTE (Physical Education Initial Teacher Training and Education) (2009) Guidance Document for PE ITTE Providers: Supporting Trainees working with Pupils for whom English is an Additional Language, available online at: http://www.peitte.net/ (accessed 2 November 2009).

Penney, D. and Chandler, T. (2000) Physical education: what future(s)?, *Sport, Education and Society*, 5, 1: 71–87.

Penney, D. and Evans, J. (1994) It's just not (and just not) cricket, *British Journal of Physical Education*, 25, 3: 9–12.

Penney, D. and Evans, J. (2000) *Politics, Policy and Practice in Physical Education*, London: Routledge.

Perrott, E. (1982) *Effective Teaching: A Practical Guide to Improving Your Teaching*, London: Longman.

Peters, S. (2004) *Inclusive Education: An EFA Strategy for all Children*, World Bank, www.worldbank.org.

REFERENCES ▨ ▥ ■ ■

Physical Education and School Sport (PESS): http://www.teachernet.gov.uk/teachingandlearning/ subjects/pe/nationalstrategy/Professional_Development/.

Physical literacy, available online at: www.physical-literacy.org.uk.

Piaget, J. (1962) *Judgements and Reasoning in the Child*, London: Routledge and Kegan Paul.

Piotrowski, S. (2000) Physical education health and lifelong participation in physical activity, in S. Capel and S. Piotrowski (eds), *Issues in Physical Education*, London: RoutledgeFalmer, pp. 170–87.

Placek, J. (1983) Conceptions of success in teaching: busy, happy and good?, in T. Templin and J. Olsen (eds), *Teaching Physical Education*, Champaign, IL: Human Kinetics, pp. 46–56.

Pratchett, G. (2000) The use of movement observation to assist the affective development of children with profound and multiple learning difficulties, paper presented at the International Special Education Congress, University of Manchester. July 2000.

QCA (Qualifications and Curriculum Authority) (1999) *The National Curriculum for England*, London: DfEE/QCA.

QCA (Qualifications and Curriculum Authority) (2006) *The Diploma: An Overview of the Qualification*, London: QCA.

QCA (Qualifications and Curriculum Authority) (2007a) *National Curriculum for Physical Education*, London: QCA. Available online at: http://curriculum.qca.org.uk/index.aspx.

QCA (Qualifications and Curriculum Authority) (2007b) *Physical Education: Programme of Study for Key Stage 3*, London: QCA/Crown. Available online at: http://www.qca.org.ukcurriculum (accessed 27 October 2009).

QCA (Qualifications and Curriculum Authority) (2008a) *A Big Picture of the Curriculum*, London: Crown.

QCA (Qualifications and Curriculum Authority) (2008b) *Physical Education Programme of Study,* London: QCA.

QCA (Qualifications and Curriculum Authority) (2009) *Disciplined Curriculum Innovation: Making a Difference to Learners*, London: QCA.

QCA, DELLS and CCEA (Qualifications and Curriculum Authority, Department for Education, Lifelong Learning and Skills and Council for the Curriculum Examinations and Assessment) (2006) *The Qualifications and Credit Framework: An Introduction*, London: QCA.

Raymond, C. (ed.) (1999) *Safety Across the Curriculum*, London: RoutledgeFalmer.

Richardson, V. and Fallona, C. (2001) Classroom management as method and manner, *Journal of Curriculum Studies*, 33, 6: 705–28.

Rink, J.E. (1993) *Teaching Physical Education for Learning*, 2nd edn, St. Louis, MO: Mosby.

Rink, J. and Hall, T. (2008) Research on effective teaching in elementary school physical education, *The Elementary School Journal*, 3: 207–18.

Robertson, J. (1996) *Effective Classroom Control: Understanding Teacher–Student Relationships*, 3rd edn, London: Hodder and Stoughton.

Rogers, C. (1982) *A Social Psychology of Schooling: The Expectancy Process*, London: Routledge and Kegan Paul.

Rogers, C. (2007) Experiencing an inclusive education: parents and their children with special educational needs, *British Journal of Sociology of Education*, 28, 1: 55–68.

Russell, T. and Munby, H. (1992) *Teachers and Teaching: From Classroom to Reflection,* London: Falmer Press.

Schmidt, R.A. and Wrisberg, C.A. (2008) *Motor Learning and Performance: A Situation-based Learning Approach*, 4th edn, Leeds: Human Kinetics.

Schon, D. (1987) *Educating the Reflective Practitioner*, San Francisco, CA: Jossey Bass.

Seltzer, K. and Bentley, T. (1999) *The Creative Age*, London: Demos.

Severs, J. (2003) *Safety and Risk in Primary School Physical Education,* London: Routledge.

Sherborne, V. (2001) *Developmental Movement for Children*, 2nd edn, London: Worth Publishing.

Shulman, L.S. (1987) Knowledge and teaching: foundations of the new reform, *Harvard Educational Review*, 57: 1–22.

Shulman, L.S. (1999) Knowledge and teaching: foundation of the new reform, in J. Leach and B. Moon (eds), *Learners and Pedagogy*, London: Paul Chapman, pp. 61–77.

Siedentop, D. (1991) *Developing Teaching Skills in Physical Education*, 3rd edn, Mountain View, CA: Mayfield Publishing Co.

Siedentop, D. (1994) *Sport Education*, Champaign, IL: Human Kinetics.

Siedentop, D. and Tannehill, D. (2000) *Developing Teaching Skills in Physical Education*, 4th edn, Mountain View, CA: Mayfield Publishing Co.

Siedentop, D., Tousignant, M. and Parker, M. (1982) *Academic Learning Time – Physical Education Coaching Manual*, Columbus, OH: School of Health, Physical Education and Recreation.

Silberman, M. (1996) *Active Learning: 101 Strategies to Teach Any Subject*, Harlow: Allyn & Bacon.

Slavin, R. (2003) *Educational Psychology: Theory to Practice*, 7th edn, Boston, MA: Allyn and Bacon.

Smith, A. and Green, K. (2004) Including pupils with special educational needs in secondary school physical education: a sociological analysis of teachers views, *British Journal of Sociology of Education* 25, 5: 594–607.

Smith, A. and Thomas, N. (2006) Including pupils with special educational needs and disabilities in National Curriculum physical education: a brief review, *European Journal of Special Needs Education*, 21, 1: 69–83.

Spackman, L. (2002) Assessment for learning: the lessons for physical education, *The Bulletin of Physical Education*, 38, 3: 179–95.

Stenhouse, L. (1975) *An Introduction to Curriculum Research and Development,* London: Heinemann Educational.

Stidder, G. (2004) The use of information and communication technology in PE, in S. Capel (ed.) *Learning to Teach Physical Education in the Secondary School: A Companion to School Experience*, 2nd edn, London: Routledge, pp. 219–38.

Stidder, G. and Hayes, S. (2006) A longitudinal survey of PE trainees' experiences on school placements in the south-east of England (2000–2004), *European Physical Education Review*, Autumn, 12, 3: 317–38.

Sutherland, R., Robertson, S. and John, P. (2008) *Improving Classroom Learning with ICT*, Abingdon: Routledge.

Swansea Civil Justice Centre (2002) *Rhian Elizabeth Ashton (Claimant) and Neath Port Talbot County Borough Council (Defendant) Approved Judgment*, Swansea: Swansea Civil Justice Centre.

Taylor, A., Lawrence, J. and Capel, S. (2009) Getting your first post, in S. Capel, M. Leask and T. Turner (eds), *Learning to Teach in the Secondary School: A Companion to School Experience*, 5th edn, London: Routledge, pp. 425–42.

TDA (Training and Development Agency for Schools) (2007) *Professional Standards for Teachers*, London: TDA.

TDA (Training and Development Agency for Schools) Continuing Professional Development, available online at: http://www.tda.gov.uk/teachers/continuingprofessionaldevelopment.

TDA (Training and Development Agency for Schools) Induction, available online at: http://www.tda.gov.uk/induction.

Teachernet (2008) *Health and Safety*, available online at: http://www.teachernet.gov.uk/wholeschool/healthandsafety/ (accessed 30 June 2009).

Tearle, P., Golder, G., Moore, J. and Ogden, K. (2005) The use of ICT in PE in the Exeter Initial Teacher Training Partnership, available online at: http://www.ttrb.ac.uk/attachments/515557e2-a1a6-4e2d-a92d-fc44179625c9.doc.

TES (Times Educational Supplement): http://www.tes.co.uk/.

Thomas, S.M. (1994) Adventure education: risk and safety at school, *Perspectives 50*, Exeter: University of Exeter Press.

REFERENCES ▪ ▪ ▪ ▪

Thorpe, R., Bunker, D. and Almond, L. (eds) (1986) *Rethinking Games Teaching*, Loughborough: University of Loughborough.

Turner-Bisset, R. (1999) The knowledge bases of the expert teacher, *British Educational Research Journal*, 25, 1: 39–55.

UK Legislation (Health and Safety)/UK Parliament Statutes/Health and Safety at Work etc. Act 1974 (1974 c 37), available online at: http://www.hse.gov.uk/legislation/hswa.pdf (accessed 4 November 2009).

Underwood, G.L. (1988) *Teaching and Learning in Physical Education: A Social Psychological Perspective*, London: The Falmer Press.

Vickerman, P. (2002) Perspectives on the training of physical education teachers for the inclusion of children with special educational needs: is there an official line view?, *Bulletin of Physical Education*, 38, 2: 79–98.

Vickerman, P. (2007) *Teaching Physical Education to Children with Special Educational Needs*, London: Routledge.

Vickerman, P. and Coates, J. (2009) Trainee and recently qualified physical education teachers' perspectives on including children with special educational needs, *Physical Education and Sport Pedagogy*, 14, 2: 137–53.

Voice: http://www.voicetheunion.org.uk/.

Vygotsky, L.S. (1962) *Thoughts and Language*, Cambridge, MA: MIT Press.

Waring, M. and Warburton, P. (2000) Working with the community: a necessary evil or a positive change of direction?, in S. Capel and S. Piotrowski (eds), *Issues in Physical Education*, London: Routledge, pp. 159–69.

White, M. (1992) *Self Esteem: Its Meaning and Value in School*, Cambridge: Daniels Publishing.

Whitehead, M.E. (2007) Physical literacy: philosophical considerations in relation to the development of self, universality and propositional knowledge, *Sport Ethics and Philosophy*, 1, 3, December: 281–98.

Whitehead M.E. (ed.) (2010) *Physical Literacy Throughout the Lifecourse*, London: Routledge. Available online at: http://www.observinglearnersmoving.co.uk (accessed 1 September 2009).

Whitehead M.E. and Murdoch, E. (2006) Physical literacy and physical education: conceptual mapping, *Physical Education Matters*, 1 (1): 6–9.

Whitlam, P. (2003) Risk management principles, in J. Severs (ed.), *Safety and Risk in Primary School Physical Education*, London: Routledge, pp. 30–42.

Whitlam, P. (2005) *Case Law in Physical Education and School Sport: A Guide to Good Practice*, Leeds: Coachwise/BAALPE.

Wilson, E. (2009) *School-based Research: A Guide for Education Students*, London: Sage.

Wilson, S. and Cameron, R. (1996) Student teacher perceptions of effective teaching: a developmental perspective, *Journal of Education and Teaching*, 22, 2: 181–95.

Wragg, E. and Brown, G. (2001) *Questioning in the Secondary School*, London: RoutledgeFalmer.

Wright, H. and Sugden, D. (1999) *Physical Education for All: Developing Physical Education in the Curriculum for Pupils with Special Educational Needs*, London: David Fulton.

Youens, B. (2009) External assessment and examinations, in S. Capel, M. Leask and T. Turner (eds), *Learning to Teach in the Secondary School: A Companion to School Experience*, 5th edn, London: Routledge, pp. 352–66.

Young, M. (2003) National qualifications as a global phenomenon: a comparative perspective, *Journal of Education and Work*, 16, 3: 223–37.

Young, R. (1992) *Critical Theory and Classroom Talk*, Clevedon: Multilingual Matters Ltd.

Zwozdiak-Myers, P. (2006) Action research, in S. Capel, P. Breckon and J. O'Neill (eds), *A Practical Guide to Teaching Physical Education in the Secondary School*, London: Routledge, pp. 28–38.

Zwozdiak-Myers, P. and Capel, S. (2009) Communicating with pupils, in S. Capel, M. Leask and T. Turner (eds), *Learning to Teach in the Secondary School: A Companion to School Experience*, 5th edn, London: Routledge, pp. 107–23.

AUTHOR INDEX

SUBJECT INDEX